# Century of the Leisured Masses

# Century of the Leisured Masses

## Entertainment and the Transformation of Twentieth-Century America

DAVID GEORGE SURDAM

Preface by
KEN McCORMICK

OXFORD
UNIVERSITY PRESS

# OXFORD
UNIVERSITY PRESS

Oxford University Press is a department of the University of Oxford.
It furthers the University's objective of excellence in research, scholarship,
and education by publishing worldwide.

Oxford New York

Auckland Cape Town Dar es Salaam Hong Kong Karachi
Kuala Lumpur Madrid Melbourne Mexico City Nairobi
New Delhi Shanghai Taipei Toronto

With offices in

Argentina Austria Brazil Chile Czech Republic France Greece
Guatemala Hungary Italy Japan Poland Portugal Singapore
South Korea Switzerland Thailand Turkey Ukraine Vietnam

Oxford is a registered trade mark of Oxford University Press
in the UK and certain other countries.

Published in the United States of America by
Oxford University Press
198 Madison Avenue, New York, NY 10016

© Oxford University Press 2015

Library of Congress Cataloging-in-Publication Data
Surdam, David G. (David George)
Century of the leisured masses : entertainment and the transformation of
twentieth-century America / David George Surdam ; preface by Ken McCormick.
p. cm.
Includes bibliographical references and index.
ISBN 978–0–19–021156–1 (hardback) — ISBN 978–0–19–021157–8 (paperback)
1. Leisure—United States—History—20th century. 2. Leisure class—History—20th century.
3. Leisure industry—United States—History—20th century. 4. United States—Economic
conditions—20th century. 5. United States—Social conditions—20th century. I. Title.
HD4904.6.S867 2015
306.4'81209730904—dc23
                                     2014024772

1 3 5 7 9 8 6 4 2

Printed in the United States of America on acid-free paper

# CONTENTS

*List of Tables*  vii
*Preface: Veblen and Weber*  ix
    KEN McCORMICK
*Acknowledgments*  xvii

Introduction: Why Leisure?  1

1. Definitions of Leisure  8

2. History and Attitudes Regarding Leisure  17

3. The Economics of Leisure  33

4. Less Work, More Play, and the Rise of Leisure  44

5. The Rise of Expenditures on Leisure Goods and Services  64

6. Patterns in Leisure for the Young and the Old  86

7. The Interaction of Leisure and Public Health  108

8. The Changing Workplace  117

9. The Transformation of the Domestic Economy  130

10. Commercialized Leisure in the Early 1900s  155

11. Mass Entertainment to the Fore  174

12. Improved Infrastructure and Leisure  200

13. Government and Leisure  215

14. Antitrust Issues and the Leisure Industries  223

Epilogue: More Leisure, Better Leisure, Cheaper Leisure  244

*Citations*  249
*Bibliography*  279
*Index*  297

# LIST OF TABLES

1.1  Gross National Product Per Capita, 1900–1970  2
1.2  Per Capita Gross National Product, 1960–2000  3
1.3  Manufacturing Production Workers Output, Earnings, and Hours, 1900–1969  3
4.1  Changing Work Habits of Americans, 1870–1990  46
4.2  Changing Lifestyles and Longevity, 1870–1990  47
5.1  Components of Total Consumption Expenditures, 1909–2008  67
5.2  US Alcohol Consumption, 1900–2000  68
5.3  Visits to National Parks and Other National Sites, 1904–2008  69
5.4  Motor-Vehicle Factory Sales and Miles of Travel, 1904–1969  70
5.5  Number of Bowlers, Golf Courses, and Swimming Pools, 1904–1970  71
5.6  National Economic Indicators, 1945–1961  82
5.7  Real Personal Consumption Expenditures on Recreation, Selected Years  83
7.1  Expectation of Life at Specified Ages, 1900–2003  109
7.2  Death Rates and Causes, 1900–2004  110
8.1  Work-Injury Frequency Rates in Manufacturing, Mining, and Railroads, 1926–1970  121
8.2  Workers Killed or Disabled on the Job, 1970–2000  121
8.3  Employees by Industry, 1900–2000  124
9.1  Birth Rate, Infant Mortality, Maternal Mortality Rate, and Female Life Expectancy, 1900–2000  142
9.2  Household Characteristics, 1940 and 1950  145
11.1  Diffusion of Radio and Television Ownership (First 15 Years)  197

# PREFACE

## VEBLEN AND WEBER

Alfred Marshall wrote that "the two great forming agencies of the world's history have been the religious and the economic."[1] That has certainly been true for the United States. Early colonists were often seeking a place where they could freely practice their religion (though they did not always extend this privilege to people of different religions).[2]

The United States is still widely regarded as one of the most religious of developed countries, and with good reason. A 2006 poll found that 73 percent of Americans believe in some kind of Supreme Being, compared to 35 percent in Great Britain and 27 percent in France.[3]

At the same time, the United States is also regarded as the epicenter of consumerism. Despite astonishing increases in real income over the past century, Americans still seem to have an insatiable appetite for material goods. The relentless pursuit of bigger, better, and more goods is even regarded by some as the fundamental problem underlying most other problems in the US economy.[4]

How can this apparent paradox be reconciled? How can Americans show such reverence for both God and Mammon?

Max Weber offers a partial answer to this question. In *The Protestant Ethic and the Spirit of Capitalism*, Weber argues that intense religious ideals created the conditions for wealth accumulation. Moreover, the behaviors induced by religious fervor became social norms that persisted long after the religious doctrines that promoted them faded.

Weber argues that "people do not wish 'by nature' to earn more and more money. Instead, they wish simply to live, and to live as they have been accustomed."[5] In addition, there is a long history of viewing acquisitiveness as a form of "moral turpitude."[6] So how was it that people were induced to increase production, which at the time could only come from working harder and longer?

The answer, according to Weber, can be found in Martin Luther's idea of a "calling," which "is a product of the Reformation." In contrast to the "egoistic lovelessness" of monastic withdrawal from the world, "this-worldly work in a vocation appears to him [Luther] to be a visible expression of brotherly love."[7] As his thinking evolved, Luther increasingly emphasized "that the fulfillment of one's duties in the world constituted, under all circumstances, the only way to please God."[8]

For the devout, this is strong stuff. Yet Weber argues that Luther was still anchored in economic traditionalism. The spirit of capitalism itself arises only after the emergence of what Weber calls "ascetic Protestantism." This includes Calvinists, Pietists, Methodists, Baptists, Mennonites, and Quakers. Collectively, these groups are often lumped together as "Puritans." The details differ, but what these groups had in common was a belief in some form of predestination. This is stated quite bluntly in the Westminster Confession of 1647: "By the decree of God, for the manifestation of His glory, some men are predestined unto everlasting life, and others foreordained to everlasting death."[9]

The contrast to Roman Catholicism could not be starker. The Ascetic Protestants had done away with the sacraments and other "magical means" to obtain God's grace. It was beyond the power of humans to alter the inscrutable decisions God had made before the foundation of the world.

As there was absolutely nothing one could do to alter one's ultimate fate, it would be natural for the devout to worry about whether they were among the saved. Ascetic Protestantism recommended the demonstration of "brotherly love" in the form of service to others for the greater glory of God. This was primarily to take the form of dedication to one's calling. In Weber's words, "*Work without rest in a vocational calling* was recommended as the best possible means to *acquire* the self-confidence that one belonged among the elect. Work, and work alone, banishes religious doubt and gives certainty of one's status among the saved."[10] The believer could take comfort if (s)he were convinced that (s)he was an agent of God. But this is not as simple as it might appear. One must set aside all personal desires, and work only for the glory of God. Leisure must be banished, because it is time devoted to one's self at the expense of service to God. The Christian life requires "systematic self-control" in "every moment."[11] The "ascetic" in "ascetic Protestantism" should now make sense. As the German mystic Sebastian Franck put it, "now *every* Christian must be a monk for an entire lifetime."[12]

Wasting time became an extremely serious sin. "An unwillingness to work is a sign that one is not among the saved."[13] Pause for a moment and reflect. If you are devout, it would be absolutely unbearable to believe that you are not among the saved. It would be crushing. Consequently, any temptation to neglect one's work had to be resisted. Relentlessly hard work would be necessary for one's own sanity.

But there is more. As one's work is meant to be of service to the community, its value is affected by its usefulness to the community. Working hard to make something nobody wants is a sinful waste of time. Profitability therefore becomes a practical measure of how useful one's efforts are. Thus people are encouraged to pursue profit opportunities when they arise. Baxter, whose *Christian Dictionary* (1673) is said by Weber to be "the most comprehensive compendium of Puritan moral theology,"[14] puts it like this: "If God show [*sic*] you a way in which you *may*, in accordance with His laws, *acquire more profit* than in another way, without wrong to your soul or to any other, and if you refuse this, choosing the less profitable course, *you then cross one of the purposes of your calling. You are refusing to be God's steward*, and to accept His gifts, in order to be able to use them for Him when He requireth it. *You may labour, for God, to become rich*, though not for the flesh and sin."[15]

Working hard at an occupation valued by the community and seeking profit are naturally going to lead to wealth accumulation. But it must only be done for the glory of God. One is never to work to acquire wealth for its own sake. The enjoyment of the fruits of one's labor undermines one's dedication to God. If wealth is sought for its own sake, it is sinful. But wealth acquired in diligent service to God is evidence of God's favor. Weber puts it this way: "Hence wealth is only suspect when it tempts the devout in the direction of lazy restfulness and a sinful enjoyment of life. The striving for riches becomes suspect only if carried out with the end in mind of leading a carefree and merry life once wealth is acquired. If, however, riches are attained within the dutiful performance of one's vocational calling, striving for them is not only morally permitted but expected."[16] Wealth legitimately acquired by hard work is therefore a sign of the elect. As it could not be enjoyed, it was saved. The natural result was the accumulation of still more wealth. Those who sought to please God and so followed the tenets of their religion became rich.

In this fashion, the spirit of capitalism emerged. Wealth was no longer evidence of sin. On the contrary, if it was legitimately acquired, it was a sign that the owner was among the elect. "Now, with Puritanism, every residual of the medieval proverb *deo placere vix potest* [the merchant cannot be pleasing to God] has disappeared."[17]

Theologians of the time were acutely aware of an obvious danger. It might simply be beyond the power of most people to live simply when they possessed significant wealth. At the individual level, it might just be a sign that the individual is not a member of the elect. But the theologians worried about the detrimental effect that extravagant living might have on the community as a whole. John Wesley wrote that

> I fear, wherever riches have increased, the essence of religion has decreased in the same proportion. Therefore I do not see how it is possible, in the nature of things, for any revival of true religion to continue long. For religion must necessarily produce both industry and frugality, and these cannot but produce riches. But as riches increase, so will pride, anger, and love of the world in all its branches. . . . So, although the form of religion remains, the spirit is swiftly vanishing away. Is there no way to prevent this continual decay of pure religion? We ought not to prevent people from being diligent and frugal; we must exhort Christians to gain all they can, and to save all they can; that is, in effect, to grow rich.[18]

Wesley's observation captures the essence of the problem. Devout, religiously motivated behavior generates ever-increasing wealth; increasing wealth makes it ever harder to keep one's focus on God. Wesley therefore advises those who grow rich to give much of their wealth away.

In time, religion evolved and Puritan beliefs began to soften. Wesley himself, while endorsing much of Calvinism, fiercely opposed the doctrine of predestination.[19] But even though religious beliefs changed, the behaviors that Puritanism had required had by that time become social norms.

These norms put down strong roots in the United States. Weber begins Chapter 2 of his book with a long list of quotations from Ben Franklin, including the deathless phrase, "time is money." Franklin exhorts us to work hard, to not waste time, and to be frugal. In other words, he offers us the secret to honestly acquired material success. But in Franklin's hands, appeals to religious duty are entirely absent. His advice is simply to do what wise, responsible people do.

In a nutshell, that is the point of Weber's argument. The Protestant Reformation not only overturned the medieval idea that wealth accumulation was inherently sinful, but it also made wealth a sign of upright behavior. Even after the original religious doctrines changed, the idea that hard work and frugality were the route to success remained.

A corollary pertains directly to this book. Even in the doctrine's secular form, as presented by Franklin, leisure remains somewhat disreputable. Because time is money, one should not waste it. Consequently, the enjoyment of leisure is often tempered with guilt. People certainly take time for leisure, but they also fret about lost time. Although it is impossible to precisely measure the extent to which this is still true, a Google search of the phrase "guilt about wasting time" returned 689,000 hits. The Puritan ethic still haunts us.

John Wesley worried that wealth might lead to extravagant displays. Thorstein Veblen, on the other hand, saw such displays as inevitable. To understand why, we must understand Veblen's ideas about human behavior.

In Veblen's view, the motives for human action come from instinctive proclivities that are the product of human evolution. Because humans live in groups, the survival of the group is important for individual survival. Consequently, both group-regarding and self-regarding instincts developed. Humans use reason to meet the objectives set by our instincts. As Veblen put it, "Men make thought, but the human spirit, that is to say the racial endowment of instinctive proclivities, decides what they take thought of, and how and to what effect."[20]

How the instincts manifest depends on social institutions. Consequently, in different historical eras, the methods by which people seek to achieve their underlying objectives change. One should keep in mind that humans are complex beings, and our instincts can conflict with one another. A bit of introspection should convince the reader that individuals sometimes have conflicting aims.

One important group-regarding instinct is the instinct of workmanship. Veblen defines it as "a taste for effective work, and a distaste for futile effort."[21] People enjoy being productive, and take satisfaction from a job well done. The instinct of workmanship contributes to the survival of the group as well as the individual. It is deeply ingrained, so it is no surprise that people feel guilty about wasting time.

Emulation is another powerful force shaping human behavior. It is necessary for our survival because it is how we learn. Veblen went so far as to say that "with the exception of the instinct of self-preservation, the propensity for emulation is probably the strongest and most alert and persistent of the economic motives proper."[22] Because we want to emulate the "best," we acquire the habit of ranking people from better to worse. In other words, we become status-conscious. In some cases, this is quite useful to the group, as, for example, when we emulate the most efficient workers.

Unfortunately, there is also a sinister side to emulation. That is because human behavior is also affected by self-regarding instincts, such as our desire for self-aggrandizement and our predatory instinct. We want to have high status; from an evolutionary perspective, high status enhances our chance of survival. One way to acquire status is to dominate others. Veblen argues that as soon as technology evolved to the point where an economic surplus emerged, the predatory instinct led to warfare. Captives, often women, were made to work for their captor. In this fashion, productive work came to be associated with low-status slaves.

People emulate those with high status. The best warriors had high status; they also did not work because of the slaves they had taken in battle. In other words, those with high status had leisure time; those with low status did not. Leisure provided evidence of status and consequently became honorable itself.

Warfare, however, was not the only route to status. Shamans, priests, and the like held high status because of their close connection to divine power. They were also able to force others to work for them under threat of divine sanction. Like the elite warriors, the priestly class exhibited the connection between high status and leisure. As Veblen writes, "no employment and no acquisition is morally possible to the self-respecting man at this cultural stage, except such as proceeds on the basis of prowess—force or fraud."[23] Leisure was a sign of status, and productive labor was something to avoid if possible. The only way to avoid useful labor was to force others to work for you. Force (warfare) and fraud (religion) therefore provided the foundation for the leisure class.

Over the centuries, economies and societies have evolved considerably. Productive labor has lost some of the disapprobation associated with it. This may, in part, be due to the Protestant ethic, supported by the instinct of workmanship. It may also be due to its acceptance as a legitimate route to obtaining wealth, which is the modern mark of high status. According to Veblen, blatantly predatory activities are still the "best" way to acquire wealth, but "so long as work is of a visibly pecuniary kind and is sagaciously and visibly directed to the acquisition of wealth, the disrepute intrinsically attaching to it is greatly offset by its meritorious purpose."[24] Nevertheless, there is a clear status hierarchy of employments: "Those which have to do immediately with ownership on a large scale are the most reputable of economic employments proper. Next to these in good repute come those employments that are immediately subservient to ownership and financiering,—such as banking and the law.... Mercantile pursuits are only half-way reputable, unless they involve a large element of ownership and a small element of usefulness.... Manual labour, or even the work of directing mechanical processes, is of course on a precarious footing as regards respectability."[25]

In the distant past, people often lived in small groups, and everyone knew most everyone else. Consequently, one's status was common knowledge. In the modern world, however, most people live in urban areas where we are typically anonymous. As just mentioned, wealth is the modern status symbol. But the question arises as to how a wealthy person can gain the recognition he or she "deserves" in such an anonymous setting. After all, "in order to gain and to hold the esteem of men it is not sufficient merely to possess wealth or power. The wealth or power must be put in evidence, for esteem is awarded only on evidence."[26]

Veblen argues that people display wealth through "conspicuous leisure" and "conspicuous consumption." Conspicuous leisure requires one to provide evidence of "non-productive consumption of time."[27] One way to do so is to wear delicate or cumbersome clothing that makes it obvious that one is not engaged in productive work. One can also be seen recreating in expensive spas, restaurants, clubs, and luxury boxes at sporting events. Of course much of the time one is not in the public eye, so one must also prove that one is not using that time productively. Knowledge of fine wines and cigars, dog breeding, sports, the fine points of etiquette, dead languages, and grammar all serve the purpose.

Conspicuous consumption requires purchases of expensive goods such as big houses, fast cars, jewelry, and costly clothing. It also provides an opportunity to display conspicuous leisure; one must know which goods to buy. In other words, one must spend time learning to become a connoisseur. Buying one Ferrari is better in this sense than buying many Chevrolets.

The behavior of the leisure class sets the standards of what is considered proper behavior. The rest of us simply try to live up to that standard to the extent we are able. As Veblen put it, "The leisure class stands at the head of the social structure in point of reputability; and its manner of life and its standards of worth therefore afford the norm of reputability for the community. The observance of these standards, in some degree of approximation, becomes incumbent upon all classes lower in the scale.... On pain of forfeiting their good name and their self-respect in case of failure, they must conform to the accepted code, at least in appearance."[28]

In practice, people attempt to emulate the class just above them. There is a continual striving to exceed one's peers. It must be stressed that for most people the driving force is simply a wish to "avoid unfavorable notice." In other words, we just want to fit in and not stand out in a negative way. We want, at a minimum, to maintain our status; it is even better if we can augment it. This desire to conform to social expectations is quite powerful. In Veblen's words, "No class of society, not even the most abjectly poor, foregoes all customary conspicuous consumption. The last items of this category of consumption are not given up except under the stress of the direst necessity. Very much of squalor and discomfort will be endured before the last trinket or the last pretence of pecuniary decency is put away."[29] As a consequence, as one's peers acquire more goods and engage in more leisure, one is driven to do the same. Keeping up with the Joneses is a never-ending struggle in a growing economy.

As is well known, Veblen was a relentless critic of the modern business system. The reasons for this are beyond the scope of this essay, but it is important to note that his reasoning has nothing to do with the notion that the system has harmed the poor. Veblen is well aware that the modern economy has benefited the lower classes not only in absolute terms, but also in relative terms:

The modern industrial system is based on the institution of private property under free competition, and it cannot be claimed that these institutions have heretofore worked to the detriment of the material interests of the average member of society ... the system of industrial competition, based on private property, has brought about, or at least co-existed with, the most rapid advance in average wealth and industrial efficiency that the world has ever seen. Especially can it fairly be claimed that the result of the last few decades of our industrial development has been to increase greatly the creature comforts of the average human being. And, decidedly, the result has been an amelioration of the lot of the less favored in a relatively greater degree than that of those economically more fortunate. The claim that the system of competition has proved itself an engine for making the rich richer and the poor poorer has the fascination of epigram; but if its meaning is that the lot of the average, of the masses of humanity in civilised life, is worse today, as measured in the means of livelihood, than it was twenty, or fifty, or a hundred years ago, then it is farcical.[30]

The trend that Veblen observed continued throughout the twentieth century. As a result, both the material standard of living and the amount of leisure time available to average Americans grew. Yet Veblen did not believe that the rising wealth would end the competition for status. No matter how rich one becomes, status depends on how rich one's peers are. In other words, "no general increase of the community's wealth can make any approach to satiating this need, the ground of which is the desire of every one to excel every one else in the accumulation of goods."[31]

The book that follows details the democratization of leisure in the United States. Over the course of the century, the lives of average Americans improved enormously and in ways that had been unimaginable. Professor Surdam describes both the theory and practice of this remarkable phenomenon, unprecedented in human history. Ordinary people at long last have the freedom to allocate a significant amount of time however they please. In Alfred Marshall's prophetic words, "Now at last we are setting ourselves seriously to inquire whether it is necessary that there should be any so-called 'lower classes' at all: that is, whether there need be large numbers of people doomed at birth to hard work in order to provide for others the requisites of a refined and cultured life; while they themselves are prevented by their poverty and toil from having any share or part in that life."[32]

*Ken McCormick, Professor of Economics, University of Northern Iowa*

# ACKNOWLEDGMENTS

I thank Scott Parris and Cathryn Vaulman of Oxford University Press for their enthusiastic and energetic support of this manuscript. I appreciate their efforts on my behalf.

The copy editors, Manikandan Kuppan and Hemalackshmi Niranjan, helped ferret out errors and improved the manuscript's style.

This book had its genesis in discussions with the late Robert W. Fogel, Nobel Prize winner in Economics. He discussed the rise of leisure in the twentieth century in his book on egalitarianism: *The Fourth Great Awakening and the Future of Egalitarianism*. Professor Fogel was a patient, generous advisor on my Ph.D. dissertation examining the economics of the Union Navy's blockade during the American Civil War. My other dissertation committee members, David Galenson and D. Gale Johnson, also proved astute mentors during my years at the University of Chicago.

Participants at the Center for Population Economics at the University of Chicago provided sagacious advice during an early presentation of the book.

The Waterloo Women's Study Club listened to presentations on some of the chapters.

Professor Timothy Fuerst read the manuscript and provided valuable comments. Professor Fuerst made excellent points regarding the macroeconomic aspects of the argument. Professor Lisa Jepsen carefully read the chapter on leisure and the domestic economy. Three anonymous reviewers provided many valuable suggestions for improving the manuscript. One of the reviewers saved me from some errors of omission with regard to some critical articles.

Professor Ken McCormick of the University of Northern Iowa has been a treasured colleague. He graciously agreed to share his knowledge of Thorstein Veblen and Max Weber in the Preface to this book. Ken, an expert on Veblen, is the author of *Veblen in Plain English: A Complete Introduction to Thorstein*

*Veblen's Economics*. He also scrutinized this manuscript; his suggestions greatly improved it.

Professor Ted Karamanski of Loyola University of Chicago recommended the Hays book. Professor Michael Haupert made many fine suggestions and provided encouragement throughout the writing process.

Professor Fred Abraham, Head of the Economics Department, and Farzad Moussavi, Dean of the College of Business Administration of the University of Northern Iowa, provided moral and financial support. The University of Northern Iowa provided me a Professional Development Assignment for Spring 2013, generously affording me a block of time to research and write this book. The College of Business Administration also funded research trips to Chicago.

Student assistants in the Department of Economics, Kayla Gump and Jessy Martin, compiled thousands of note cards. Their efforts saved me quite a bit of time and aggravation. Near the end of the process, student assistant Claire Reinhard cheerfully helped in the checking of endnote numbers and endnotes.

Other students at the University of Northern Iowa—Chandler Fahrner, Susan Butz-Hamilton, Aida Hadzic, and Audrey Grove—provided inspiration. Ms. Butz-Hamilton has a love of studying tourism, as well as a remarkably sunny, optimistic approach to life. Ms. Hadzic was a cheerful, stalwart student in one of my classes. Mr. Fahrner was a positive influence in the classroom and a force on the basketball court. Ms. Grove was a top student in economics and was a delight to work with. The four always ensured that there was a smiling face in class, at the cafeteria, or on the court. Since writing a book is often an isolated activity, their friendliness was invaluable.

The Federal Reserve Bank of Dallas generously granted me permission to reprint two tables (4.1 and 4.2 in this manuscript) from their publication "These Are the Good Old Days!" The University of Nebraska Press also generously granted me permission to reprint one table (5.7 in this manuscript) from *The Postwar Yankees: Baseball's Golden Age Revisited* (Table 4.1).

Sarah Statz Cords did an excellent job compiling the index, as always. This is our seventh effort together.

I dedicate this book to my sister, Sue Surdam-Bean. We spent much leisure time together growing up as children in Pleasant Hill, Oregon.

# Introduction
# Why Leisure?

The rise of leisure in America during the twentieth century has been largely un-heralded. We hear much about the expansion of government spending and the explosion of healthcare expenditures, but few have commented on how the dramatic increase in leisure time and activities has remade our society.

The rise of leisure has been pervasive across the century, whether in terms of expenditures on leisure activities or in the amount of time devoted to leisure. A century ago, iconoclastic economist Thorstein Veblen penned his famous *Theory of the Leisure Class*, a book destined to be much quoted but not always carefully read. The idea that the masses would enjoy large amounts of leisure and expenditures on leisure might have seemed fantastical to Veblen's contemporaries a century ago.

Certainly leisure has been an egalitarian triumph, as one can rub shoulders with the hoi polloi on cruise ships and jetliners, at ballet and opera performances, and at posh spas. Indeed, the truly well-heeled may feel put out, as heretofore exclusive venues have become overrun with the plebian masses.

Why study leisure? Discussions of quality of life are skewed, if increases or occasional decreases in the amount and the quality of leisure are not considered. Gross national product (GNP) only measures goods and services. Gains in leisure also affect the relative quality of life between the poor and rich. The rich continue to have access to higher-quality—or at least more expensive forms of—leisure, but the working classes are likely to have received a greater absolute increase in leisure time and relative increase in consumption than rich Americans during the twentieth century.

## An Overview of the American Economy

By 1900, Americans, as did their peers in Great Britain and parts of Europe, had enjoyed economic growth for most of the previous century. There were, to be

sure, sometimes violent fluctuations in the economy during the nineteenth century, but most native-born Americans enjoyed a higher standard of living in
1900 than had their ancestors in 1800. Life in 1900 would have been very shocking to a Rip Van Winkle asleep since 1800: railroads, telegraphs, huge factories,
and immensely crowded cities.

During the twentieth century, the country's real, per capita GNP skyrocketed
(Tables 1.1 and 1.2).[1] Aside from some recessions and the Great Depression, the
trend was upward. You will note that across your parents' and your lifetimes, the
real GNP per person increased at a hefty 2 percent or greater per annum rate.
Even if the per capita growth rate fell to 1.5 percent per annum, 48 years from
now, per capita GNP would still double.

A quick explanation for the increased per capita GNP is that American workers are far more productive than they were 100 years ago. Average labor productivity, which is loosely correlated to real wages, rose during the twentieth century (Table 1.3).[2] Over the course of the twentieth century, the average worker
produced several times as much as (s)he did in 1900, although productivity
growth seems to have decelerated during the last quarter century, for reasons
that are still being debated. From an international standpoint, the United States
experience is not unique, although relatively few people have experienced such
sustained increases in per capita output.

We need to be careful when considering per capita GNP. Per capita GNP
is only one indicator of living standards. There are important limitations of
GNP.

*Table 1.1*  **Gross National Product Per Capita, 1900–1970[a]**

|      | Using Current Prices | Using 1958 Prices |
| ---- | -------------------- | ----------------- |
| 1970 | $4,808               | $3,555            |
| 1960 | $2,788               | $2,699            |
| 1950 | $1,877               | $2,342            |
| 1945 | $1,515               | $2,538            |
| 1940 | $754                 | $1,720            |
| 1935 | $567                 | $1,331            |
| 1930 | $734                 | $1,490            |
| 1920 | $860                 | $1,315            |
| 1910 | $382                 | $1,299            |
| 1900 | $246                 | $1,011            |

[a] US Department of Commerce, *Historical Statistics of the United States, Part 1*, 224.

*Table 1.2*  **Per Capita Gross National Product, 1960–2000[a]**

|        | Gross National Product | Gross National Product |
|--------|------------------------|------------------------|
|        | Current Dollars        | Chained (2000) Dollars |
| 2000   | $34,907                | $34,907                |
| 1990   | $23,335                | $28,600                |
| 1980   | $12,400                | $22,956                |
| 1970   | $5,095                 | $16,520                |
| 1960   | $2,929                 | $13,938                |

[a] US Department of Commerce, *Statistical Abstract of the United States: 2008*, 437.

*Table 1.3*  **Manufacturing Production Workers Output, Earnings, and Hours, 1900–1969[a]**

|        | Index | All Manufacturing | | |
|--------|-------|-------------------|--|--|
|        | Manufacturing | Average Hourly Earnings | | |
|        | Per Man-Hour[1] | Nominal | Real[2] | Weekly Hours |
| 1969   | 145.7 | $3.19  | $2.52  | 40.6 |
| 1960   | 108.8 | $2.26  | $2.21  | 39.7 |
| 1950   | 81.4  | $1.44  | $1.73  | 40.5 |
| 1940   | 68.7  | $0.66  | $1.36  | 38.1 |
| 1930   | 52.3  | $0.55  | $0.95  | 42.1 |
| 1920   | 32.0  | $0.55  | $0.79  | 47.4 |
| 1910   | 26.6  | $0.19[3] | $0.61[3] | 51.0 |
| 1900   | 22.9  | n.a.   |        |      |

n.a.: not available.

[1] 1958 = 0.

[2] Deflated by Consumer Price Index "All Items," with 1958 = 100.

[3] 1909 figure.

[a] US Department of Commerce, *Historical Statistics of the United States, Part 1*, 162, 169, and 210–211.

Many goods are not sold in the marketplace and do not have explicit prices. When you vacuum your apartment, there is no market transaction, so your actions do not affect GNP. If, instead, you pay someone to come in and vacuum, there would be a market transaction. The amount you paid the person to vacuum your apartment would count in GNP. With the massive switch of women from household production to market production, per capita GNP may overstate the increase in material well-being. Instead of family members singing or telling stories, which does not count in GNP, a family that purchased a phonograph and some discs would suddenly contribute to GNP. Expenditures on leisure activities, therefore, may overstate changes in leisure.

Many goods are sold that are not covered by GNP. An illicit drug deal is a market transaction, but the deal, by its nature, rarely appears in the government's GNP statistics that cover goods and services sold in a legal marketplace. For the purpose of studying leisure, illicit drugs and sex may be considered to count as leisure-time activities and therefore result in an underestimate of expenditures on leisure. On a more benign level, the doctor who visits and diagnoses her neighbor's child for a nominal fee or in exchange for services, and who does not report the transaction in her taxable income, is engaging in the underground economy—economic activities that are not reported to the government record keepers. In some countries, such as the former Soviet Union, the underground economy may have been very significant; in the United States, it is probably non-trivial, but not as significant as in the former Soviet Union. Obviously, we have scant information on the sizes of the illicit and underground economies, although there are ways to make informed guesses—the amount of large denominations, particularly of $100 bills, of American currency in circulation is one clue.[3]

Government-provided services are included in GNP. These services, however, are not transacted in a freely operating market. Therefore, the services do not have an explicit market price. We may not know how much people value national defense, education, safety officials, or visits to national parks.

Government statisticians attempt to adjust GNP for new products and improvements in existing products, but the process is difficult. In 1980, a videocassette recorder (VCR) cost $800 or more; it had nowhere near the recording quality or set of features of a VCR costing $250 in 2000. Yet, each VCR sold in 2000 added less to GNP than in the past. Of course, if we go back to 1960, there were no VCRs. You can make similar arguments for microwaves, cellular phones, desktop computers, arthroscopic surgery, and myriad other goods. The statisticians have difficulty reflecting improvements in the quality of products and services in their GNP figures. Although Americans wring their hands about the current state of public education, in many ways education has improved. No longer are 40 or 50 students jammed into a classroom to learn their letters and figures by rote.[4]

GNP does not incorporate changes in the amount of leisure time taken, which will be a key argument in this book. Americans work fewer hours per year (roughly half as much as in 1870). Many of today's youths will not start full-time, market work until their early to mid-twenties, and many of the males will aspire to retire in their mid-fifties.[5] Today's grandparents may expect 15 years of retirement on average. Americans also work fewer hours at home on chores per year and across their lifetimes (although the lifetime number of hours has not fallen as rapidly, given the greater longevity). We should adjust GNP to reflect the increasing amounts of leisure time taken. Americans could have chosen to work similar, if not more, hours in response to the greater hourly wages resulting from their greater productivity, but for many years they wanted shorter workweeks.

There has also been a shift in the type of work that people do. Extractive industries, such as mining, logging, and fishing, can be both arduous and dangerous. In addition, extractive industries can despoil the scenery. A shift away from these jobs may, for a given level of GNP, indicate better working conditions for American workers.

The distribution of GNP is another important aspect. A rising output level may not mean much, if the poorest segments of society do not share in the general prosperity. In terms of leisure time and spending on leisure goods and services, the gains have been widespread. Across the twentieth century, Americans of all income classes have enjoyed better living standards.

The last statement may seem dubious, given the spate of hand-wringing articles in the 1990s and more recently that bemoan supposedly falling living standards and widening disparities in incomes. A *Wall Street Journal* poll in 1996 revealed that 52 percent of Americans didn't expect their children's generation to enjoy a higher standard of living than they—the parents—did, while 41 percent expected their children to be better off. Surprisingly, perhaps, black Americans were more optimistic: 55 percent thought their children would be better off.[6] Even a glance at consumption from the 1950s and 1970s, compared with the 1990s, reveals this to be silly.

Rising real, per capita incomes strongly suggest improved living standards. What are we buying with our greater incomes? The proportion of our budgets going to food shrank rapidly, leaving us with more discretionary spending on recreation, health, education, and other items. This was to be expected, based on similar experiences in Great Britain and other countries enjoying rising incomes.[7]

Mass entertainment became ubiquitous as the twentieth century waned. Radios and televisions proved immensely popular, and the rate of diffusion of televisions was astounding (from 0.002 percent of households in 1946 to 87 percent in 1960). The contrast of families watching a wide variety of programming in 2000 with settlers on the prairies in 1870 trying to amuse themselves throughout a long winter's night is stark.

Americans often got these amenities earlier than people elsewhere in the world. The other wealthy nations in 1960 badly lagged behind Americans in acquiring hot running water, refrigeration, and automobiles. The prevalence of home-produced clothing may account for the wider ownership of sewing machines in Europe. Having a greater percentages of homes with wood or coal stoves also indicated European delay in affording electric or gas stoves.

# What We Will Examine in This Book

Leisure in America is a multifaceted topic. Even such a basic question as the definition of leisure is complex and dates back to the Greeks. How to measure leisure time and quantify leisure activities, such as spending on recreational or leisure goods and services, will be discussed in the next chapter. The measurement of leisure time will involve a residual approach.

Politicians, clergy, social reformers, and law enforcement officials love to monitor and dictate how people should use their leisure. For some commentators, greater amounts of discretionary time were not necessarily a good thing. The bromide "idle time is the devil's workshop" appears to have been accepted by many. The twentieth century was a continuous parade of outrages, to take one perspective. From an early kiss on the motion picture screen and ragtime music at the beginning of the century to raunchy sex scenes in mainstream movies and gangsta rap in the late twentieth century, some Americans have perceived and lamented a downward trajectory in morals. At the end of the twentieth century, by their reckoning, presumably we should be in a moral morass outstripping the decadent extremes of Babylon or the declining Roman Empire (too bad those civilizations didn't have electronic media).

How did Americans wind up with greater amounts of leisure time? What are the economic principles underlying people's decisions between taking leisure and working? How did economic growth affect these decisions?

A variety of government surveys and sources indicate that the vast majority of Americans enjoyed shorter working hours in 2000 than in 1900. How and why weekly hours and lifetime hours worked fell during the century resulted from several factors. Concurrent with the diminution in working hours, Americans began spending significant proportions of their incomes on leisure activities and services. Spending on recreation, amusement, and pleasure travel rose throughout the century, and new patterns of leisure activities arose.

Americans gained more discretionary hours throughout their lifetimes, in part because of their increasing longevity. Their increased longevity and improved healthiness allowed them to enjoy active forms of leisure for most of their lives.

Even while they are working, though, many Americans enjoy more leisure at work in 2000 than they did in 1900. Working conditions in general have improved. The workplace was a highly disciplined place in 1900, and the rules were, by modern standards, draconian. Working conditions were often dangerous, dreary, and dirty, but these aspects have diminished over the century.

For one group of Americans, the burgeoning leisure society may have seemed chimeric. Women increasingly performed work both at home and in the labor market. Some authors believe that women failed to share in the leisure boom, although they concede that the nature of women's work changed dramatically across the century and entailed much less arduous toil and drudgery. What happened to women's hours of toil versus their hours of leisure?

How people used their leisure hours changed dramatically. The rise of commercialized leisure pleased most Americans, if their spending habits are an accurate reflection. Some observers, though, were lukewarm, if not downright hostile, to commercialized leisure. Commercialized leisure and leisure produced within the home were intertwined with the invention of automobiles and electricity; an improved infrastructure of freeways and airlines also altered leisure patterns. Although the automobile and airlines have drawbacks, they have revolutionized Americans' lifestyles.

Government, whether federal, state, or local, also became a major player in American leisure. Labor laws and government-provided recreational facilities were only the most obvious interventions, but government antitrust, patent, and other laws also affected leisure throughout the twentieth century. Mass entertainment became ubiquitous, but such industries were often dominated by a handful of producers, triggering antitrust concerns.

These factors are the general topics that are covered in this book.

# 1

# Definitions of Leisure

Before I can assert that the twentieth century witnessed an expansion of leisure in America, I need to be precise in defining what is meant by "leisure." The definition is crucial, because it interacts with several other ideas.

If "work" includes both labor-market and household production, then leisure is a general term for non-work, usually enjoyable, activities chosen by the individual. This usage is likely to roughly coincide with most twentieth-century Americans' understanding of leisure, and this book will often use the term in this sense. Leisure is, in economic parlance, assumed to be a "good," in the sense that more leisure is preferred to less leisure. Of course, for the unemployed and for the forcibly retired, more spare time may not be preferred to less spare time, and we might hesitate to label their spare time as leisure. There is another aspect to leisure: people usually choose to increase the time spent in leisure activities as their incomes increase; in economic parlance, leisure is considered a "normal good."

Yet in order to establish that Americans enjoyed more time for leisure and had the ability to spend more on goods and services related to leisure activities, more rigorous definitions are needed. This book will use a residual approach as a definition of "leisure time" for measurement purposes. Economists sometimes measure leisure time in terms of time remaining after labor-market work and basic bodily maintenance (such as sleep, eating, and hygiene). Individuals choose how many hours to work (and to sleep), both on a daily basis and across their lifetime. The hours left over after work in the market and basic bodily maintenance constitute a *supply* of potential leisure hours. This measure of leisure time as the time remaining after subtracting hours for personal bodily maintenance and work for pay from total hours is useful, as there is much available evidence as to workers' labor-market hours. This simple measurement of the supply of potential leisure hours, of course, has drawbacks. Most people would not consider the time spent commuting to work or performing household chores as leisure time. Time devoted to child care may or may not be considered leisure time. Changing diapers and feeding babies would likely fall outside a definition of leisure, while pushing a child on a swing set might be leisure for some people.

We then examine what people do with the time remaining after labor-market work and bodily maintenance. The time remaining interacts with the demand for leisure and the demand for other time-consuming activities; people make choices in allocating time to commuting, household chores, child care, and leisure. We could also consider time spent doing volunteer work.

For example, consider two workers working in adjacent cubicles in a downtown office. When the clock strikes five, they head out the office doors. One worker may live in the neighborhood and has a short walk home, where he or she lives in an apartment and has myriad urban leisure options. The other worker chooses to live in the suburbs in a house with a yard. This worker has a 30-minute commute in each direction, thereby spending an hour on the road. In addition, the second worker may have more household chores, including mowing the lawn and cleaning a larger domicile. The suburban worker's leisure options differ from those of the downtown resident; there are plenty of backyard leisure options, as well as a shopping mall. Both workers decide whether to do household cleaning themselves or to hire these chores out to a cleaning service. The remaining time after household chores and commuting has elements of pleasure and discretion and may be considered closer to the concept of leisure held by most people.

The important thing to note is that, after choosing how many hours to devote to labor-market work and to basic bodily maintenance, individuals *choose* to apportion their remaining time between commuting to work, household chores, child care, and leisure. In terms of measurement, whatever time remains after subtracting hours for the activities described above comprises leisure time. It is useful to realize that in the process of apportioning time between the various endeavors, individuals are simultaneously *choosing* how much time to take as leisure. Their choice could be described as reflecting their *demand* for leisure.

We can make a similar argument for spending on goods and services related to leisure activities ("leisure consumption"). An amateur baseball player, for instance, could choose to use time and materials to make a crude baseball or to whittle a tree branch into a rudimentary bat. The player could opt, instead, to purchase a bat and a ball for use in his or her ball-playing activities. The purchase of the bat and the ball would, of course, appear in the government statistics, while the homemade ball and bat would not. As many people had sufficient discretionary income to afford choosing between making or purchasing their baseball equipment, an observer could presume that a player who chose manufactured equipment preferred spending money on manufactured equipment instead of spending time and effort in making his or her own equipment. The

government compiles statistics on consumption expenditures on leisure or recreational goods and services. There is difficulty, at times, in ascertaining whether
goods and services are or are not for leisure purposes.

The definition and measurement of leisure as a residual of time left after
work, basic bodily maintenance, commuting time, household chores, and some
aspects of child care is not universally held. Certainly there are gray areas in defining leisure. Leisure may be in the eye of the participant. The author enjoys
reading academic press books for both work and leisure, but many people might
not consider such an activity leisure. What have philosophers and other thinkers written regarding leisure?

## Ancient Ideas about Leisure

Although we associate the birth of democracy with the Greeks, sometimes ven-
erated as the "Ancient Greeks," in reality, their society was divided into free men
and slaves (ignoring women for the time being). The famed Greek thinkers reflected upon the nature of man and of leisure. To them—and their view provides
a boundary for a definition of leisure—leisure involved contemplation. I'm certainly no foe of contemplation, but the Greek standard undoubtedly precluded
leisure for the masses. As Sebastian de Grazia points out, "if the many work, a
few have leisure."[1] Along this line of thinking, Plato suggested that "the state provide the necessities for a class of philosophers."[2]

Aristotle considered leisure as freedom from the necessity of labor. Holding an occupation, even being self-employed, was not leisure. Nor should
one confuse amusement and recreation as leisure in Aristotle's framework.
Amusement and recreation are necessarily coupled with labor; one literally
needed to re-create in order to continue working, while "to exert oneself and
work for the sake of amusement seems silly and utterly childish."[3] Although
Aristotle's conception of leisure seems narrow, there were compensating benefits attached to it. "Leisure is a state of being in which activity is performed
for its own sake or as its own end. . . . Happiness can appear only in leisure.
The capacity to use leisure rightly, he [Aristotle] repeats, is the basis of the
free man's whole life."[4]

Ultimately, de Grazia recognizes a paradox. The twentieth century afforded
the masses plenty of free time, but "[a]nybody can have free time. Not every-
body can have leisure. Free time is a realizable idea of democracy. Leisure is not
fully realizable, and hence an ideal. . . . Leisure refers to a state of being, a condi-
tion of man, which few desire and fewer achieve."[5] In a similar vein, Joffre Dumazedier wrote, "I prefer to reserve the word leisure for the time whose content
is oriented towards self-fulfilment [sic] as an ultimate end."[6]

# A Partition of the Daily Hours

The demarcation between leisure and other activities could be vague. Puritans may have considered church attendance and serious reading of the Bible as worthy leisure, while other people attended church out of a sense of obligation. De Grazia's solution was to divide the day into four categories: work, work-related time, free time, and subsistence time.[7] The latter relates to basic bodily maintenance, such as sleep, eating, and hygiene.

The limitations of defining leisure as a residual become clear under de Grazia's "work-related" time: 24 hours a day minus 8 hours for basic bodily maintenance minus hours worked = hours of leisure. Many modern Americans spend an hour or two commuting to and from work; others frequently fly for business. In the latter case especially, one can read, listen to music, surf the Internet, or watch television, but de Grazia points out that you are not completely at liberty to do as you choose. In addition, other leisure-like activities, such as a round of golf or dinner and cocktails with business colleagues or clients, straddle the line between work and leisure.[8]

There is another drawback to using de Grazia's formula, as work is defined as work for pay and not domestic housekeeping or volunteer work. Economists usually examine work in terms of participating in the labor force. Labor involved in household production, while gaining more attention from economists in recent decades, has often received short shrift. Economists, though, recognize the contradiction in this definition of work as only work that is done in exchange for money. This narrow concept of work may neglect much of women's efforts; as historian Susan Currell points out, women's domestic work is undervalued and leads to inequality between men and women: "Rather than a greater equality in the dignity of all labor, as envisioned by some in the thirties, workers who service leisure are very often among the lowest classes economically and socially of all workers."[9]

Patients in hospitals or in jails or prisons may have free time, but they are severely limited in their choices. Other people with a plethora of free time choices may feel compelled to limit their choices to drinking, overeating, drug usage, and risk-taking. One can debate whether their activity is leisure.

During the 1930s, plenty of Americans involuntarily had fewer hours of work. Classifying their idle time as "free time" or "leisure" almost seems to mock their predicament. Their "free time" may be marked by anxiety and a financial inability to partake in many leisure activities.[10] Songwriter Ralph McTell poignantly expressed the pain of unemployment in his song, "Stranger to the Seasons," where the unemployed were out of sync with the seasons.[11]

The association of "free" with "time" is problematic. De Grazia noted, "'Free time' neglects the domination of work that may take over other values that jobs may offer. Leisure is being free of everyday necessity and leisure activities should be taken for their own sake. By this reasoning, leisure is rarely attained in the modern world."[12] For those Americans who are or were involuntarily unemployed, there was an imbalance of sorts between their supply of potential leisure time and the uses of such time for pleasurable leisure. De Grazia believes that concurrent with work's elevation as a good thing was the idea that,"[leisure] was now a matter of time free of work, time off the job. The quest for leisure had been transformed into the drive for free time." His criticism strikes a blow: "Being considered the opposite of work, and work being now calculated by time, leisure too must be figured the same way."[13] With apologies to de Grazia, we will follow this approach and will measure leisure, as best we can.

There is another problem; Max Kaplan asks: How can we quantify time in statistical units comparable to *things*? He believes that the shift to shorter hours was accompanied by an increase in the tempo of work that would not have been sustainable in a 55-hour work week such as existed in 1910. Therefore, shorter hours caused and were as well a result of increased labor productivity. "If . . . our work gives us some creative satisfactions and outlets and our leisure hours are merely boring and unsatisfying, then there is little point to interpreting shorter hours of work as 'good' or as 'progress.'" He also asks whether greater amounts of consumption necessarily imply a better state, especially when much of this consumption has been "the result of the creation of needs by advertising?"[14]

For Kaplan, leisure contains several elements: it is antithetical to work as an economic function; it creates pleasant expectations and recollections; it requires minimal involuntary social-role obligations; it involves a psychological perception of free; it relates to a culture's value; it can be inconsequential or it can be important; and it is often characterized by play. Therefore leisure is rarely a matter of free choice and is often dictated by income, so a clear-cut definition of leisure is difficult.[15]

Closely related to leisure, but distinct, is the idea of play. Johan Huizinga, in his *Homo Ludens*, suggested that "Man the Player" should be considered an important figure in the world's life and activities. Play shares an attribute that some observers attach to leisure: voluntary activity. Huizinga points out, "By this quality of freedom alone, play marks itself off from the course of the natural process." Play is also disinterested: "Not being 'ordinary' life it stands outside of the immediate satisfaction of wants and appetites, indeed it interrupts the appetitive process," it is an interlude.[16]

Huizinga's characterization of play is not too far afield from the Greeks' conception. He agrees with Plato that "God alone is worthy of supreme seriousness, but man is made God's plaything, and that is the best part of him. Therefore every man and woman should live life accordingly, and play the noblest games and be of another mind from what they are at present. . . . Life must be lived as play, playing certain games, making sacrifices, singing and dancing, and then a man will be able to propitiate the gods."[17] Huizinga formally characterizes play as "an activity which proceeds within certain limits of time and space, in a visible order, according to rules freely accepted, and outside the sphere of necessity or material utility."[18]

Making music, while sometimes a chore, comes close to epitomizing Greek and other thinkers' concept of play. Huizinga delineates between music as play and music as not play. He points out that "the term 'playing' is never applied to singing, and to music-making only in certain languages, it seems probable that the connecting link between play and instrumental skill is to be sought in the nimble and orderly movement of the fingers."[19]

For Joseph Pieper, a Catholic philosopher, leisure is liberating, as it allows people to transcend the workaday world and to reach out to "life-giving existential forces" that rejuvenate us for a return to daily work.[20] For Pieper, "[t]he soul of leisure . . . lies in 'celebration.' Celebration is the point at which the three elements of leisure come to a focus: relaxation, effortlessness, and superiority of 'active leisure' to all functions." Leisure is only possible and justifiable as a festival. "*That basis is divine worship* [italics his] . . . man's affirmation of the universe and his experiencing the world in an aspect other than its everyday one."[21]

## Some Gray Areas of Leisure

Since modern Americans spend more hours and years in school than previous generations, the question of whether being in school constitutes leisure or work is an important one. "School" originally meant "leisure," but one wonders whether the schoolchildren of America would characterize the activity thusly.[22] George Lundberg's four criteria that distinguished leisure reveal the ambiguity surrounding the time spent in school. Leisure is characterized by being chosen by the individual, being possibly permanently interesting, being activities that are different from compulsory activities, and being compatible with well-being.[23] While many students may find aspects of school "permanently interesting," some of Lundberg's criteria argue against school as leisure. There are limits on choices for children younger than 16 years old; they are prohibited from working full-time or, at least theoretically, from dropping out of school. It is probable, of course, that schoolchildren perceive being in school as a mixture of work and leisure. Aristotle thought *schole* meant being occupied in "something desirable for its own sake—the hearing of noble music and noble poetry, intercourse with friends chosen for their own worth, and above all the exercise, alone or in company, of the speculative faculty." In a sense, for Aristotle, leisure is connected with learning and creating.[24]

Joseph Pieper builds upon the Aristotelian framework, including the concept of leisure as *skole* or *scola*. He notes, of course, that our conceptions of leisure and school have evolved in the intervening millenniums since Aristotle and his *Metaphysics*: our values regarding work and leisure differ greatly from those of the Greeks, the Romans, and the Middle Ages, "just as we are unable to understand their notion of leisure simply and directly, without an effort of thought."[25] Pieper believes that "leisure appears in its character as an attitude of contemplative 'celebration'. . . . Leisure is possible only on the premise that man consents to his own true nature and abides in concord with the meaning of the universe. Leisure draws its vitality from affirmation."[26]

An economic perspective views being in school as constituting work: students study, and their studying is work that creates human capital. Students may only occasionally be engaging in leisure or consumption when they study. Students can be seen as "self-employed" producers of capital.[27] Part of the opportunity cost of being in school is that of working in a job earning income.

Social commentator Reuel Denney feared that "for many of the young, school turns out to be simply a prison with rather inefficient and wholly unhappy jailers." Some of the young turned toward delinquency for their leisure pastimes. He also noted that, if the young had difficulty cooling their heels in schools and on the streets, the aged had difficulties adjusting to their "disemployment" that "operates more destructively on men than on women."[28] For older Americans facing mandatory retirement, the ensuing free time may lack the necessary elements of leisure.

Some people are on the fringe of the economy—retirees, the unemployed, and unemployables; Harold Wilensky observes that these people "are also those who are most isolated in community and society."[29] His research suggests that men with "orderly careers" tend to have stronger attachments to their communities, as represented by memberships in formal associations, and "greater vitality of primary relations than men whose work histories are disorderly."[30]

## More Modern Definitions

Many commentators developed more nuanced definitions of leisure. Leisure might be divided into two branches: spillover and compensation. Compensation leisure depicts the ways that workers react to stultifying jobs; after work, laborers blow off steam, a sort of cathartic experience. Spillover leisure is an extension of work habits, attitudes, and interests into one's leisure. A carpenter spending her leisure hours building birdhouses is an example of spillover leisure.[31] One can note the obvious difference between this work-based notion of leisure and Aristotle's work-free notion of leisure.

For British workers, according to historian E. P. Thompson, "[b]y the 1830s and 1840s it was commonly observed that the English industrial worker was marked off from his fellow Irish worker, not by a greater capacity for hard work, but by his regularity, his methodical paying-out of energy, and perhaps also by a repression, not of enjoyments, but of the capacity to relax in the old, uninhibited way."[32]

If leisure is associated with "free time," one can ask, "Are people really free?" Chris Rojek provides a thoughtful examination of leisure and suggests that how workers use their leisure confirms their trustworthiness as workers and citizens. He questions the freedom aspect of leisure.[33] He points out that twenty-first-century people facing the transformation of the economy into a service-based economy need, more than ever, to develop interaction skills: "the economic importance of *people knowledge* and *people skills* [italics his] . . . demonstrating sincerity and smiling relations, have considerable economic value in the labour market."[34]

What does it mean for the concept of leisure if these aspects are prevalent, since many definitions of leisure include "voluntary" or "freedom?" Since emotional life is an unrelenting feature of being human, it seems reasonable to propose that the accumulation of emotional intelligence and the practice and refinement of emotional labor can occur at any time and in any place. Rojek asks, "where do freedom or time off reside? Everything we do and every place that we inhabit has emotional learning potential. . . . If we are engaging in labour, even if it is unpaid and pleasurable, we are doing something contrary to leisure as it is conventionally understood."[35]

A related issue deals with accounting for leisure-related spending. Ken Roberts notes that in classifying industries as leisure industries, there are some gray areas. The three main ones, in his estimation, are tourism, out-of-home eating and drinking, and the media. Gambling, tobacco, leisure drugs, and pornography are also among the gray areas of the leisure industry. Automobile traveling and the use of telephone for leisure are often ignored aspects of the leisure industry.[36] The government does not include them in its calculation of expenditures on recreation and leisure.

Roberts emphasizes Chris Rojek's concept of "dark leisure": "Rojek contends that 'edgework' and 'liminality' are features of much leisure behavior. People gain tingle, excitement, by pressing the limits of what they themselves, and society, will tolerate, hence the pleasures of football hooliganism, joy-riding, adultery and dangerous sports. Totally safe, hygienic leisure is relatively boring. Everyone wants to take some risks, though they may also seek—even demand—to be protected from the more serious consequences."[37]

An economist, writing in 1969, struggled to define leisure, having chosen not to use an Aristotelian approach. John Owen's definition of leisure subtracts market employment and household production (which he identifies as house-work, do-it-yourself repairs, commuting time, and time devoted to personal care related to employment) from total hours (allowing hours for sleeping and basic bodily maintenance). He included "certain activities which are essential as well as gratifying, such as sleeping and eating."[38] He avoided defining leisure as free time, since some hours devoted to eating and sleeping were above the amount necessary for survival.

## This Book's Definition of Leisure

Although there is disagreement as to the definition of leisure, I will use the residual approach in measuring leisure time: subtracting hours for personal bodily maintenance, work for pay, commuting time, household chores, and child care from total hours leaves the amount of time available for leisure. It is important to note that individuals make choices with respect to apportioning their time. Chapter 3 describes how people apportion time between labor-market work and non-work activities. Chapter 4 examines the trends in working hours and gives an idea of the changes in the potential supply of leisure hours. I will then discuss the demand side of leisure in terms of how people fill these discretionary hours, including time spent commuting to work, doing domestic chores, and other endeavors. Recent studies of time use allow us to examine in greater detail the trends in the time available for leisure. Chapter 5 shows changes in Americans' spending on goods and services related to leisure.

# History and Attitudes Regarding Leisure

Is leisure desirable? Americans have held ambivalent views toward work and leisure. The desirability of work has fallen and risen over time, often depending on the development of the economy. Americans have recognized that part of Adam and Eve's punishment was that they would have to toil to earn their sustenance, but by the 1920s, Americans could foresee a time when all people would have vastly increased amounts of discretionary, if not completely, free time. Reflecting the ambivalence regarding leisure, Americans have freely criticized the leisure and recreational activities of their fellow Americans. Although the frowned-upon activities may change, such lists of disapproved leisure activities have usually been lengthy ones.

## Ancient Attitudes Regarding Leisure

Jesus Christ implies that work is overrated in the famous passage from Matthew: "They sow not, neither do they reap nor gather into barns; yet your Heavenly Father feedeth them. Are ye not much better than they." A couple of verses later, he adds, "Consider the lilies of the fields, how they grow; they toil not, neither do they spin."[1] Similar to the Greeks, Jesus implied that concentrating upon earning a living and material sustenance distracted man from contemplating God. Greek thinkers equated leisure with contemplation, because contemplation was the aspect of man that was godlike, distinguishing man from animals.[2]

If it seems strict to regard true leisure as contemplation, at least the Greeks and early Christians did not place a premium on work. St. Thomas Aquinas held that "if it was not necessary, there was no obligation to work," while Sir Thomas More's *Utopia* posits a world "where no one works more than six hours a day."[3] St. Thomas Aquinas recognized that man mistrusts that which is effortless and can only enjoy without guilt what he has acquired through effort and trouble.[4]

A more austere concept of the godly life, embodied in monasteries, but emphasized by Luther and later Protestant theologians, resided in the idea that "to work is to serve God." De Grazia pointed out that "[l]abor commanded a new tone. Once, man worked for a livelihood, to be able to live. Now he worked for something beyond his daily bread. He worked because somehow it was the right or moral thing to do."[5]

There were perceived moral and legal brakes on work, though. Work was not supposed to be injurious to his mental or physical health, ruin a man's family, or destroy existing communal loyalties. Labor legislation, therefore, often focused on working conditions, in order to reduce accidents and non-salubrious work environments.[6]

## Puritans and Leisure

Before industrialization, European workers appeared to have a fixed standard of living in mind. Employers hoping to coax more effort and time from workers by offering a higher wage were often frustrated. Workers often simply took the higher wages and worked sufficiently fewer hours to maintain their income and satisfy their level of consumption.[7]

Although settlers in the Chesapeake Bay area predated the Pilgrim and Puritan settlement of Massachusetts, many of the unfortunate Virginia settlers died so rapidly that whatever leisure they enjoyed in their last weeks or months did not greatly affect the course of leisure in America. The Puritans, of course, bequeathed a legacy, albeit one that is commonly misunderstood. H. L. Mencken defined Puritanism as "the haunting fear that someone, somewhere, may be happy."[8]

Historian Perry Miller painted a brighter portrait of a Puritan as "a social person committed to enjoying moderate pleasures in the present [world]."[9] Another historian, Edmund Morgan, also painted a description of Puritans at odds with the stereotype: "in terms one might use for the affable guy next door: 'He liked good food, good drink, and homey comforts . . . he found it a real hardship to drink water when the beer gave out' . . . it is his emphasis on the idea that 'God did not forbid innocent play' that has stayed with generations."[10]

Much of our perceived knowledge of Puritans comes from the writings of that society's literate class, especially of its ministers. These ministers and leaders may have been describing the ideal, but Darrett Rutman asks how closely the reality merged with the ideal. He suspects that an examination of local records, a time-consuming task that few historians have undertaken, might reveal a different reality.[11]

The Puritans believed that "the best recreation combined duty and enjoyment; and both had a serious purpose as well as a social function." A barn or house raising exemplified both aspects: productive purpose and socializing.

Barn and house raisings were a productive party. They thus met the Puritan idea of sober mirth or useful recreation. These gatherings "produced something for the commonweal . . . none was an example of idle behavior whereby leisure or recreation became an end unto itself."[12] The underlying fear was that play "could become so attractive, so compelling, so seductive—so *enchanting* as an alternative ritual—that to allow any aspect of it to separate from the rest of society would inevitably break all the boundaries and break all the rules."[13]

The Puritans enjoyed eating and turned it into a major source of recreation. Eating was a time of social interaction; Puritans enjoyed a relative abundance and variety of foods, unlike most of their European cousins.[14]

Because drinking water was a risky endeavor, colonists turned to heated beverages—tea and coffee—as well as fermented drinks. New Englanders drank alcohol, and within a few decades, people began opening taverns. As with food consumption, Puritans frowned upon excessive consumption of alcohol. Taverns, though, sometimes allowed illegal gaming, such as card playing, and gambling. These activities went against the Puritan notion of approved recreation, as they were not productive. In addition, people might overtly or covertly ask the Lord's assistance in winning, which Puritan leaders viewed as both selfish and as taking the Lord's name in vain. The Puritans were not completely against gambling, though, as they countenanced lotteries. Cotton Mather, however, deplored public lotteries, because it "made the gaming table 'a sacred thing' and elevated it to the level of a pulpit." Another more serious problem with the taverns was the drunkenness, violence, and ill behavior of some patrons.[15]

Puritans disapproved of ball and blood sports, theater, competitive sports, and organ music. They did allow hunting, fishing, and martial competitions because these activities were useful, harmed no one, and "were a natural part of life." Sports, on the other hand, did not refresh the body, inflicted pain or injury, were conducive to gambling, were often played on Sunday, were noisy and disruptive, and had pagan or "Popish" origins. Rather than pass laws against these activities, Puritans relied on "public contempt."[16]

Puritan leaders "rejected the idea of Sunday as a day of leisure and recreation"; rather, celebrating it as a "Day of Joy," Puritans could indulge in two approved recreational activities: reading and listening to sermons. The latter may not strike modern readers as recreation, but Bruce Daniels asserts that sermons not only served as intellectual and spiritual experiences but also as entertainment. The sermon was a form of mass communication, as dominant in Puritan society as any mass communication has ever been in any society. For Puritans, public speaking was a high art form.[17] The Puritans bequeathed a tradition of widespread literacy to America; well into the nineteenth century, Yankee descendants of Puritans were uniquely literate.

To summarize the Puritans' legacy to future Americans, Puritans believed in a stringent moral code, although the morality relaxed throughout the Colonial period. The vague American unease connected with pleasure-seeking is rooted in the Puritan legacy, but the unease also has other antecedents. Other Christian believers also adhere to strict moral codes similar to that of the Puritans. Daniels urges Americans to "stop looking for the ghosts of John Winthrop and Cotton Mather every time we see a prude or fanatic on the American landscape."[18]

## Colonial and Nineteenth-Century Attitudes

Although the English descendants dominated America for generations after the Revolutionary War, the influx of immigrants from Ireland and Germany began to create alternative lifestyles. The English-Americans were scandalized by those fun-loving Germans, who, emigrating in large numbers beginning in the 1840s, believed that the Sabbath should be celebrated with joy—beer and conviviality included. At first, the American establishment was nonplussed by the Germans' habits, but they eventually contrasted the Germans' orderly forms of recreation with other immigrant groups—particularly the Irish—and their allegedly less salubrious recreations.[19] Proper middle- and upper-class Americans undoubtedly shuddered to think what those Irish (Catholic) immigrants were up to during their brief moments of leisure.

Americans enjoyed sporting events. Horse racing was an early favorite in the colonies, along with hunting and fishing. By the early 1800s, entrepreneurs started building summer resorts, but these were, of course, patronized only by the wealthy.[20] There were some surprising professional sports: foot races and skating.

By the early nineteenth century, the general attitude toward leisure had evolved; leisure was "tolerated rather than encouraged."[21] Americans began warming up to recreational activities after the Civil War.

Americans still struggled over whether work, in and of itself, was desirable. If a society accepts the idea that not working is undesirable, then society or the state should protect citizens from being out of work involuntarily; citizens should have a positive right to work.[22] French socialists in the mid-nineteenth century therefore established workhouses to benefit the unemployed; their English counterparts maintained workhouses for the simple idea that not working (unless one was wealthy or of the nobility) was undesirable. In either event, the average poor commoner probably marveled at the subtle difference.

Radical thinkers began to question the dominance of work and the neglect of leisure. French philosopher Francois Fourier tried to construct a community where work would be transformed into play, while Karl Marx called for the abolition of labor "as a necessary precondition for the emancipation of genuinely free and genuinely human self-activity." Marx also thought of "the essence of man as labor," while Sigmund Freud believed that "work and economic necessity are the essence of the reality-principle: but the essence of man lies not in the reality-principle but in repressed unconscious desires . . . he is not in his essence Homo economicus or Homo laborans; no matter how bitter the struggle for bread, man does not live by bread alone."[23]

## Early Twentieth-Century Beliefs

At the dawn of the twentieth century, the American economy was almost unrecognizable from that of 1800, and even the economy of 1860 seemed primitive. Many Americans worked for large-scale employers. Previous labor-management struggles had reduced the workweek to 10 hours or fewer per day for many, or to five and a half days, freeing up Saturday afternoons, for some workers, and people were beginning to contemplate a reduction in the workday from 10 hours (which had been a hard-fought gain) to 8 hours. What the working class would do with their leisure became a pressing question for political, religious, business, and intellectual leaders.

The 1920s brought prosperity to a larger slice of Americans. Whereas spending money on leisure was often a luxury, it was now becoming commonplace, even among the poorer Americans, who could still squeeze a nickel out of a tight budget to attend a nickelodeon. The 1930s, of course, created a different set of issues: Americans with unfilled time, due to unemployment, but little cash to accompany their hours.

As the nineteenth century waned, American Christian and secular thinkers debated whether industrialization would improve living standards and increase leisure time for workers. Some were ambivalent about industrialization because of the vast disparity in income and wealth that it created. While some Christian thinkers hoped that the millennial kingdom would require much less labor and provide much more leisure, by the early twentieth century, Christian fundamentalists envisioned a less delightful future. They condemned the "'congested wealth' of big business—'a whirlpool of mad and maddening excess' . . . and saw union labels on factory goods as 'the mark.'" Fundamentalists, of course, condemned much of the leisure-time activities of early twentieth-century America.[24]

Protestant thinking regarding labor and leisure at the turn of the century was changing. Religious thinkers, as well as rank-and-file Americans, struggled to reconcile their beliefs with the rapidly changing society. Premillennialism expected "imminent catastrophe before 'redemption.'" Herbert Gutman noted

that "the extraordinary psychological strains of early industrialism thus found
expression in the rejection of the secular order and acceptance of a Protestantism of doom, despair, and destruction."[25]

Others expressed hope that blessings would occur not only in heaven but
even on earth through promoting equality and brotherhood among men. Trade
unionists and labor radicals sometimes embraced social Christianity, which differed from the social gospel espoused by middle- and upper-class Americans.
Trade activists and adherents of the social gospel were from different social
groups and were therefore affected differently by industrialization. The early adherents of the social gospel were rarely allied with organized labor, or its collective organizations and protests.[26]

Liberal Protestant clergy began to re-examine the admonitions to work hard.
Puritans may have recognized recreation as healthful and uplifting, but they
frowned upon amusements, especially theater. Amusements allegedly left people
"enervated and drained."[27] As an example of the changing attitudes, William
Channing, dean of American Unitarianism, argued that "man was made to enjoy
as well as to labor, and the state of society should be adapted to this principle of
human nature . . . [God] implanted a strong desire for recreation after labor . . .
made us for smiles more than for tears." Channing encouraged "innocent pleasures" so that people would not seek out less wholesome pleasures.[28]

Congregationalist minister Horace Bushnell saw play as emanating from a
"fund of life that wants to expend itself." Rather than seeing play as an adjunct of
work, valuable solely for its restorative ability, Bushnell thought people worked
so they could play, although he emphasized that he was not derogating work. He
saw play as "where poetry was created, where genius was cultivated, and ultimately where Christian religion resided."[29]

The public began changing its attitudes: amusement was formerly seen as a
product of economic progress, but by 1900, many Americans thought of it as
their natural right.[30] Leisure was now something important, as Lord Lytton
stated: "the civilization of a people is infallibly indicated by the intellectual character of its amusement . . . what a nation does with its leisure is oftentimes just as
significant as how it either maintains itself economically or governs itself."[31]

Industrialization and urbanization changed leisure patterns. The nickel-
odeon/motion picture mass medium scandalized the Anglo-Saxon, Protestant
pillars of society: uncouth immigrants—male and female—sitting in darkened
rooms. Silent movies were highly amenable to immigrant audiences. Even if they
could not read the subtitles, they could usually follow all but the most complicated or abstract plots. The sensation caused by the first kiss on a kinetoscope is
worth recounting: "an osculation so sensational that it caused nation-wide excitement." A reviewer in *The Chap Book* described actors May Irwin and John C.
Rice's kiss: "Neither participant is physically attractive, and the spectacle of their

prolonged pasturing on each other's lips was hard to bear. When only life size it was pronounced beastly. But that was nothing to the present sight. Magnified to Gargantuan proportions and repeated three times over it is absolutely disgusting. . . . Such things call for police interference. . . . The Irwin kiss is no more than a lyric of the Stock yards."[32]

One legacy of American Protestantism was the Sunday blue laws, which remained an issue in many American cities well into the twentieth century. Baseball and football owners fought church groups and saloonkeepers (an odd alliance, if there ever was one) in the late 1800s and well into the twentieth century for the right to play ball on Sundays. Clergy and saloonkeepers worried that action at the ballpark would draw away their respective patrons.[33]

Much of the opprobrium attached to the working class's choice of leisure activities was based, of course, on class and ethnic differences. The upper classes' forms of leisure activities were by definition restricted only to the fortunate few, as Peter Borsay pointed out: "It was no doubt an awareness of this which a character in George Powell's 'Cornish Comedy' had in mind when he posed the question, 'What is a gentleman without his recreations?'" The character's answer, however, makes clear that it was not just the mere practice of leisure, but also the type of recreations enjoyed that was important: "Hawks, hounds, setting-dogs, and cocks, with their appurtenances, are the true marks of a country gentleman." Borsay asked, "What factors determined the character of a gentleman's recreations? Of undoubted importance was the requirement for a substantial expenditure of money and time since this was precisely what the productive orders could not afford." With the rise of a prosperous middle class, the formerly exclusive leisure activities were breached.[34]

As industrialization proceeded, social commentators raised the specter of a work-less society. Machines would free labor, giving everyone more leisure. Americans harbored hopes and fears regarding this new leisure during the Great Depression. If the Machine Age merely displaced workers from jobs, causing them to deteriorate, the Machine Age would mean the end of the present civilization. If the newfound leisure elevated people's use of leisure, then the Machine Age would inaugurate a new era, replete with higher living standards and quality of thought.[35]

One social observer was already alarmed at Americans' use of their free time; Stuart Chase chided white-collar workers for their misuse of their leisure time: "The unimaginative routines of their office work . . . are forcing them in increasing numbers into the cap and bells of Mystic Shriners, Mooses, Rotary Clubs, Kiwanis, the cults of service, Ku Klux Klans—anything which promises color and life, humor and activity."[36]

Another commentator worried that apologists for the factory system failed to realize that basing mankind's comfort on never-ending increases in production was fallacious, as it distracted people from the enjoyment of the superior life and contributed to the diminution of natural resources and man's leisure.[37] Such concerns presaged the rise of conservation in consumption that was in vogue later in the century.

Another strand of criticism revolved around the perceived growing passivity of leisure pursuits. Just before the Great Depression, Chase observed that Americans were becoming "watchers" instead of doers, being content with commercialized leisure served up by profit-seeking businessmen. He coined the term "decreation," meaning "compounding the lost balance through unrewarding forms of play."[38] Chase believed the "most rewarding forms of play . . . are those in which the player participates directly with his own muscles, his own voice, his own rhythm."[39] Implicit in the criticism was a disapproval of leisure forms not favored by the upper classes. George Lundberg made this explicit, appealing to people to employ the "time-tested value scale of the race" and to eschew cheap novels, movie attendance, jazz, and other mass entertainments. He claimed that these forms of leisure were not productive uses of time, and he urged people to move America and, presumably, the white race toward a higher form of civilization.[40]

Jay B. Nash coined a clever term to describe passive leisure: "Spectatoritis," the title of his 1932 book. The Machine Age supplied copious amounts of commodities and leisure time, but for what purpose? Many Americans sat mesmerized by "spectatoritis"—passive amusement—in a mistaken attempt to avoid boredom. Nash used trendy Freudian psychology to diagnose the problem of leisure as an illness rooted in repression and mental illness.[41]

Nash described the rewards of active leisure: "The doer who can throw himself, with a supreme personal enthusiasm into something is the one who can push these strains out of his life. The reward of doing, where there is freedom, is joy." He acknowledged that the leisure must be truly free: leisure foisted on people because of unemployment was not real. Leisure meant a state in which a person was not worrying about basic necessities.[42] He castigated commercial recreation, "much of which might better be called dissipation or wreck-reation" and heaped ire upon the toy manufacturers for manipulating children's playthings that were adult conceived, produced, and selected. The toys deprived children the play of their imagination.[43]

Not all of the commentators were disenchanted with leisure, American style. Along with increased amounts of leisure, industrialization brought forth a wider variety of consumption goods and services. The Greeks might have disdained much of what passed for leisure in modern parlance, but Max Kaplan argued that our material wealth in the Western world affords the masses, "a wider palette on which to paint his chosen fantasies; if he is . . . the reflection and articulation of his arc of culture, then he is embarrassed by the diversity of riches about him."[44]

His thesis was the new leisure, being more than recuperation from work, could allow people the time to contemplate and to create.[45]

Where Alexis de Tocqueville saw a "mass, democratic society; a time of ease, low taste, vulgarization," Kaplan saw a new leisure "that foretells a heaven on earth, that supplants the Christian concept of the devil and the Flesh with the Judaic concept of the good, early life of optimistic outlook and a unity of Spirit and Flesh. It is a leisure permitting of the best and the worst in man."[46]

Kaplan described the irony of high-income businessmen having difficulty adjusting to greater leisure time, while it appeared that workers were better adapting to the change. As with other observers, he believed that "the business-rich are learning how to play from those below."[47]

## Mid-Century Attitudes toward Leisure

The American economy did not lapse into a depression after World War II ended. Americans, instead, now grappled with shortened workweeks, after the war-induced overtime hours of labor, and a growing amount of discretionary income. There were certainly large pockets of poor Americans struggling to make their paychecks cover basic necessities, but the burgeoning middle class now had the time and the money to choose from a wider range of leisure and recreational opportunities. Given the war-torn economies of western Europe, the Soviet Union, devastated Japan, and revolution-torn China, the Americans (and their Canadian neighbors) were unique in achieving a leisured society with plenty of discretionary income.

A cottage industry of pundits commenting on the growing affluence mushroomed during the postwar period. A key question asked was, could Americans cope with affluence and leisure without dissipating? Of course, what the authors meant by "dissipating" depended upon his or her tastes. One person's dissipation was another person's bliss. The Aristotelian concept of leisure as contemplation, available to the select few, and the Veblen concept of conspicuous consumption resurfaced in the discussions of the 1950s. We'll sample social observers' opinions from the postwar period in this section.

To some degree, of course, even many of us who are not professional scolds shake our fingers at leisure miscreants. A conference sponsored by the Jewish Theological Seminary on leisure may have reflected a widespread view: "To waste time is to waste ourselves."[48] The conferees concluded that worship should assume priority for our time.[49]

More secular critics viewed many Americans' choices of leisure activities as wasted time, while others wondered how "free" the time was. Some activities, normally regarded as leisure, could be compulsory in nature—reading, partying, lunching, gambling, going out, and staying home to rebuild the house—before reflecting that modern Americans had less need to toil but without the relief from the belief that only labor was meaningful.[50]

Henry David Thoreau's thoughts resonated with novelist Sloan Wilson: "The order of things should be somewhere reversed; the seventh should be the man's day of toil, wherein to earn his living by the sweat of his brow; and the other six his Sabbath of the affections and the soul, in which to range this widespread garden, and drink in the soft influences and sublime revelations of nature." Wilson, though, did not view our hard-working traditions as unnatural, since America was truly a land where ambitious people could attain wealth, prestige, and status, unlike most of the rest of the world.[51]

Other writers hoped that people freed from production jobs might engage in a "great renaissance" of self-actualization, to attain leisure such as the Greeks advocated but without resting on the backs of slaves. To make this vision a reality, Ernest Havemann realized that people needed to change their habits and their sense of guilt about leisure. He exhorted people to recall the Old Testament wisdom that "there is also a time to laugh and a time to dance."[52] He feared the creation of a "self-appointed elite" who would promulgate a set of approved leisure activities and enforce "its edicts through secret police and brainwashing." Taking a libertarian stance, he urged people to decide for themselves what form of leisure to indulge in—save, of course, for choices that interfered with or injured others. The role for recreation experts would be to show the "rich variety of possible spare-time activities and inventing new ones—and then getting out of the way."[53]

Closely aligned with concerns over Americans' increasing leisure time were fears about Americans' consumption of non-necessities. David Riesman suggested that American society in the 1950s was in the midst of transforming from a "scarcity psychology" to an "abundant psychology." The transformation would lead to the rise of consumer-oriented values and behavior, as typified by the other-directed person.[54]

Some observers criticized aspects of affluence, believing that it generated "modernized poverty." Ivan Illich believed economists failed to recognize that the growing mass of commodities was not creating satisfaction but disutility, which economists could not easily measure.[55]

Some of the criticism of Americans' use of leisure emanated from an animus toward commercialized leisure—a marriage of wasted time with frivolous or harmful consumption of goods and services. Erich Fromm approached the problem of alienation and leisure by asking, if man was alienated from his work and the commodities he buys, how could man use leisure meaningfully? He disliked commercialized leisure, as he thought that industry dictated leisure-time consumption. Nothing in the alienated form of pleasure happened within the person, nor was the person changed.[56] Arthur Pack expressed this view somewhat differently: "leisure must be directed toward other pursuits than the spending of money. Leisure must have nothing to do with money as its primary aim, or it ceases to be leisure."[57]

Karl Oldenberg recognized the falsity of the "jubilee scale," whereby rising productivity resulted in "a parallel rise in consumer welfare." He suggested that the pursuit of consumption would become an endless treadmill, especially consumption that stimulated social ambition and attempted to impress. As consumers reached each new level of consumption, they became accustomed to it and sought another round of novel consumption in order to maintain their status and their need to impress.[58]

One author labeled some people as "pleasure neurotics." Norman Lobsenz identified various psychological maladies that erupted during the weekend and holidays, as people struggled to suppress impulses and feelings that were held in check during working hours. He noted how boredom often filled leisure hours. Those Americans who allowed themselves to indulge in leisure, he wrote, "[take] part in enjoyable activities only furtively or defiantly. Either avenue leads inevitably to a deeper guilt."[59]

Economists wondered whether workers preferred to consume their increased productivity by increasing income and not leisure, although here Juanita Kreps cautioned that if the choice of increased leisure was longer vacation times rather than a reduction in weekly hours, workers might have responded differently. She also pointed out that "[l]eisure in the form of early retirement may have the lowest utility of any form of free time (save unemployment)."[60]

Some observers rebutted critics of American materialism. Jacques Barzun remarked that haute couture was limited to the few in France, "[b]ut go to any village in this country [America] and you will see hardly any difference between the farm girls and the tidy numbers swinging their hips on Fifth Avenue."[61] He continued: "we can perhaps measure our day-to-day civilization by using the two pointers of Waste and Fulfillment. Waste is inevitable. But the accepted purposes which our society fulfills offset or redeem the waste. Our society fulfills more and more purposes, recognizes the desires of more and more different kinds of human beings." He admitted, "[t]his is not without danger—the more abundant the life the greater the danger; but this, if anything, is what must be meant by human liberty—choice . . . your choice of a product, a pastime, or a President alike manifests the variety within the communal life that we call democracy."[62]

Unlike many sociologists and other commentators on leisure, Ken Roberts, a more recent British author, acknowledges the benefits of commercialized leisure. He considers and dismisses several criticisms. He disagrees with those who assert that commerce caters only to the well-to-do. Obviously, there can be no

mass market if vendors cater just to the wealthy. He does not believe that commerce targets the lowest or common denominator, but rather that commerce
generates diversity. He admits that some people believe that the diversity is of a
superficial and trivial nature.[63]

It is useful to note that American leisure and recreation choices were often
shaped by disadvantaged groups. The Anglo-Saxon Protestants often railed
against the activities of blacks, German, Irish, Chinese, eastern and southern Europeans, and other groups. These groups' forms of leisure and recreational activities, though, often permeated American culture.

Economist Thomas Sowell makes a good point when discussing acculturation, as he notes that acculturation has not been a one-way street; quite frequently,
the established Anglo-Saxon Protestant groups have borrowed from the "down-
trodden" racial and ethnic groups. "In reality, the American culture is built on the
food, the language, the attitudes, and the skills from numerous groups." German
immigrants transformed the Sabbath, imbuing it with relaxation and fun. Although the *bier gartens* may have initially scandalized the pillars of society, the
Germans' attitudes toward leisure and recreation quickly permeated American
culture. "American popular music has its roots in the black musical tradition that
produced jazz and the blues. American political machines have been predomi-
nately Irish political machines." American cuisine is an amalgam of hot dogs,
pizzas, spaghetti, tacos, and sushi. "None of these features of American culture is
descended from British settlers. They are a common heritage despite ethnic di-
versities that still exist. Budweiser is drunk in Harlem, Jews eat pizza, and Chinese
restaurants are patronized by customers who are obviously not Chinese."[64]

## More Recent Critiques of Leisure

The economic upheaval of the 1970s, with oil-price gyrations, stagflation, and
ennui, cast the consumerism and leisure activities of the 1950s and 1960s into
doubt. The 1960s witnessed an apparent revolt among some college students, a
backlash against capitalism and the "establishment." Scholars developed new
ideas from which to view leisure and consumption. While some of these critiques were based upon Marxist ideas, others were more favorable toward
capitalism.

The Frankfurt School, a Marxist-based worldview, hoped that as workers
gained free time, they might reflect upon and rebel against capitalism. Workers
organized voluntary groups—not just unions—to provide various services.
They did not, in the main, seriously challenge or overthrow capitalism. They appeared instead to have embraced the goods and services that capitalism offered,
if not capitalism itself.

Herbert Marcuse argued that you may exercise some choices, especially with regard to leisure, but the "treadmill" of paid labor still awaits, and its system of employer control and competitive consumption are still in force. The Frankfurt School appears to have underestimated workers' ability to interact with, rather than merely consume, capitalistic goods and services; workers were able to discriminate between products. Chris Rojek concluded that Marcuse also overstated his argument regarding the masses' slavish acceptance of the system. He noted that the masses are not as oblivious of inequality and exploitation as Marcuse posits.[65]

Marcuse describes desublimation—the temporary breaking free of the chain-mail of constraints—as ultimately *repressive.* "In agreeing to accept a little freedom in leisure, we accept that we must submit to the organized repression of freedom in the rest of life."[66] The popularity of mass entertainment and industries providing leisure-time activities aside, they are simply the crumbs offered by the ruling class to induce a belief among the masses of human progress. The masses, however, appear to be far more conscious of and far more assertive in reacting to inequality and exploitation. People often use the entertainment and leisure options to their own purposes, rather than lapsing into a state of semi-oblivion.[67]

Workers select among the various offerings provided by industry. A variant of the Frankfurt criticism is the "McDonaldization" of the world. McDonalds' genius is that it offers standardized food. If you eat at a McDonalds in Chicago, Illinois, the food should be similar to a McDonalds in Hong Kong. Ken Roberts argues that "[McDonalds, Disney parks, and other successful chains] are so out of the ordinary. . . . They may all exhibit rationalization, but they are still very different from each other . . . consumers have so much choice . . . so many different restaurant chains, holiday packages and so forth."[68] He alludes to another example of this choice: popular music, with its wide variety of genres. Many small producers exist in the recorded music world, filling niches, even in the face of giant conglomerates. He points out that commerce offers more choices and rarely eliminates competition.[69]

Despite Roberts' laudatory response to commercialized leisure, other commentators were more critical. Rojek concedes that Max Kaplan succeeded in raising leisure studies as a serious academic subject, but he believes that Kaplan neglected an individual's experiences and background in thinking about leisure and freedom. What a person did with his or her leisure began drawing serious scholarly scrutiny during the last decades of the twentieth century.[70]

In pursuing postmodernist thinking, Rojek argued, "The old idea that leisure is freely chosen time or time used with the constraints of everyday life . . . was a ladder that enabled us to look at leisure seriously in a social context in which work was deemed to be the central life interest." He warns, "[b]ut it is a ladder that we must now kick away because it produces a false view of leisure as pure voluntarism. . . . In leisure we are not *free*. It is more accurate to propose that in leisure we are differently *positioned*."[71]

How did commercialized leisure become dominant? Some theorists believe that entrepreneurs commercialized folk and amateur leisure forms by co-opting the institutions surrounding these activities. Other theorists think that commercial entrepreneurs usurped technological and cultural innovations and repackaged them for mass consumption.[72] As the twentieth century drew to a close, commercialized leisure providers found a new way to induce patronage. Rojek defines "neat capitalism" as the "knowing, deliberate attempt by entrepreneurs to offer smart solutions to social, cultural and economic questions." He terms it "neat" in reference to the "self-approving manner in which neat capitalism is theorized and practiced." Neat capitalism presents itself as "savvy stateless solutions" to society's problems.[73]

Rojek identifies the "Special Event Management" initiatives as exemplifying "neat capitalism." Entrepreneurs promote events that gather widespread media coverage and that promise to address serious issues, such as AIDS, disaster relief, and feeding the hungry. Participants feel good about themselves, but all too often, after the showy entertainment lineup shuffles off the stage, nothing really has changed. Indeed, feeling they've made a contribution, the participants lose interest in the cause célèbre.[74]

## Dark Leisure as the Underside of Leisure

One of Rojek's chief contributions is his criticism of Leisure Studies' neglect in dealing with "dark leisure." Many people participate in illegal leisure activities ranging from drug use, prostitution, all the way to "entertainment piracy," whereby people illegally download popular songs or movies. Another form of illegal leisure is computer hacking. How does one address prostitution with respect to leisure? Rojek recognizes that a man's hiring a prostitute means leisure, but what does it mean to the prostitute? He cites new studies that suggest prostitutes have varying motivations and experiences.[75] With regard to using illegal drugs, Rojek controverts the standard libertarian argument that the decision is "solely a matter of private conscience . . . it is heavily influenced by peer group pressures and has clear correlations with social and economic factors."[76]

Smoking is another leisure activity drawing fire. Smoking gained rough parity with alcohol consumption as a leisure activity in the West; indeed, many people drink and smoke at the same time (they occasionally gambled at the same time, too). Smoking exemplified conspicuous consumption: "In a nutshell, it made a social and cultural virtue out of waste that was affordable to the non-leisure class. . . . If you were wealthy enough to burn your money away by inhaling to-bacco smoke it provided transparent evidence that you were a person of sub-stance."[77] Today in America, smoking is now associated more with people of slender means.

Smoking may be a victimless crime, but some violent crimes mimic Abraham Maslow's idea of a "peak experience." Rojek pointed out that "peak experience is often the result of breaking the law. Episodes of mugging, violent beatings, theft, sadism, masochism, murder and serial killing produce the same intense joyful excitement and sense of expanding into a wider unity. . . . But they do so by reason of acts which invert the rules of society and stand them on their head."[78]

At the end of the twentieth century, most Americans are far from the Aristo-telian ideal concept of leisure. "Time off" directly contradicts this notion, as it presumes a work-oriented existence. Leisure is, indeed, devoid of any time ele-ment. Leisure as contemplation was attainable by only a very few. Modern no-tions of leisure must recognize positioning in terms of power in all of its forms.[79]

Analyzing leisure requires recognition of the importance of positioning among various sources of power. "Aristotle was wrong to identify true leisure with the world of elite culture. How could he have foreseen the immense redis-tribution of time and wealth achieved in the urban-industrial age? Yet he was right in this positioning of leisure in the scale of human priorities."[80] Rojek con-cludes that a return to elements of the Greek notion of leisure is critical in think-ing about leisure. Leisure is not consumption, since consumption is motivated by capitalist goals of accumulation. Leisure is not "free time" or a distraction from the reality of work. He ends by observing, "Leisure is a school for life. The end of schooling is to maintain and enhance competence, relevance and credi-bility. The successful attainment of this end requires perpetual emotional intelli-gence and emotional labour. Freedom is for the birds."[81]

## The Ambivalence toward Leisure

During the waning decades of the twentieth century, commentators continued to see evidence of Americans' declining work ethic and their misuse of leisure time. Some found that "verbal" commitments to work values were still alive and strong, but researchers noted the diminished willingness to take low-wage jobs, choosiness, and other factors. Jiri Zuzanek wrote, "we have probably entered the stage where traditional ethic of work is giving way to a more personal cost-benefit approach to work."[82]

Few commentators viewed modern leisure activities as an unambiguous ben-efit. Most commentators worried about some facet of leisure, whether its passiv-ity, commercialization, or demoralization. Some social critics assert that the plethora of new goods inspired people to give up leisure for mindless consumption, with some critics claiming that a capitalist conspiracy existed to gull people into buying things they didn't need rather than to satisfy real human needs. Other commentators hoped that culture, learning, and spiritual development might flourish in a world of increased leisure. The Club of Rome worried that economic growth was fouling the planet and exhausting resources. They urged shorter hours of work and an emphasis on leisure that was non-consuming and non-polluting.[83]

Although I will generally view leisure as a good thing and as associated with time away from work—both in the labor market or on domestic chores—clearly there are potential disadvantages to leisure. But in their increased time away from work, people may opt to contemplate or dissipate, as per their preferences, however shaped or misshaped by individual experiences or social conditions and expectations.

# The Economics of Leisure

Economic growth continued throughout the twentieth century. With rising labor productivity and incomes, Americans reconsidered their choices between leisure time and work. The choices between leisure time and work are ones that almost everyone faces. How do people make their decisions pertaining to allocating their time between leisure and work? Because time is a scarce resource, economic analysis is an appropriate tool for addressing this question.

## The Process of Economic Growth

It is important to emphasize how unique the American and western European experiences of centuries of economic growth were. Why have Americans, in particular, produced more and more goods and services per capita?

A simple way to think about production is to recognize that the output of goods and services depends on three factors: labor, capital, and land. The reader might envision a huge funnel into which labor, capital, and land are poured. Production transforms inputs into output; as technology improves, more output can be produced from a *fixed* amount of inputs.

Increasing the number of workers may not improve per capita output, although there is some debate on this point. Some observers believe that having a larger population increases the likelihood that some bright people will devise solutions to society's problems, but many other people subscribe to a variant of Malthusian theory, whereby greater population creates more problems. Nobel Prize–winner Simon Kuznets, an optimist on this issue, suggested that "given sustained levels of living and hence of training and skill per capita, a larger population means more potential contributors to the stock of useful knowledge; and there may well be advantages of scale in the production of useful knowledge equally as important as in the production of simpler economic goods."[1]

Another economist, Julian Simon, wrote: "What business do I have trying to help arrange it that fewer human beings will be born, each one of whom might be a Mozart or a Michelangelo or an Einstein—or simply a joy to his or her family and community, and a person who will enjoy life?" Simon, like Kuznets, argued that "population growth has positive economic effects in the long run, though there are costs in the short run."[2]

Increasing capital per worker should increase per capita output. American workers are blessed with large amounts of capital, thereby raising the workers' ability to produce and their wage rates. You might think, then, that the key to economic growth is to boost the capital stock. If adding an additional unit of capital, though, results in smaller incremental boosts to output, then the gains from sacrificing current consumption for increasing an already large capital stock may not be worthwhile. In other words, once workers are amply endowed with capital, economic growth is unlikely to proceed as rapidly and may even stop.

Capital and labor increased in the United States, and inventors, managers, and entrepreneurs found ways to make inputs more productive, further boosting output. Improved productivity was a prime reason for continued economic growth.[3] Although we often think of improved productivity as being associated with new inventions and discoveries, in many cases, it was the incremental changes and improvements in existing technology, along with better management and organization, that also contributed to the productivity advances. The interaction of more and better capital per worker with technological advances is paramount for workers' earnings. The growth rate of wages is tied to changing productivity of labor, whether generated through more capital per worker or technological advances.

Economist D. Gale Johnson analyzed the Malthusian story. In discussing the rapid increases in output, he identified factors for escaping the Malthusian trap, whereby population growth swamped productivity gains and caused per capita output to fall.[4] First, an agricultural revolution preceded the industrial revolution and the rise of urbanization. Then per capita incomes rose, and urbanization led to increased knowledge and technological advancement, including speedier and wider dissemination of new ideas. Populations increased as death rates fell. Population increase was a ramification of better technology that increased longevity, not of higher fertility rates. Finally, parents made conscious decisions to increase "quality" and not quantity of children.

Certainly, the process appears to have fit the American and British experiences, although not without some detours. Cities initially featured higher death rates, largely due to infectious diseases emanating, in part, from faulty sewer systems and lack of clean water.[5] The high infant mortality rates may have encouraged families to maintain relatively large numbers of children. Over time, however, rising incomes did come into play, raising longevity and reducing the birth rate.

All of the growth theory is very well, but the fact remains that an eighteenth-century person would be shocked by the rapid gains in living standards and longevity. Why did *American* and *British* economic growth occur?

Returning to Johnson's first phase, the vastly improved productivity in agriculture had important reverberations on productivity in general. Nobel Prize–winning economist Robert Fogel and his co-authors, Roderick Floud, Bernard Harris, and Sok Chul Hong, have examined the effects of nutrition on the human body over the past two centuries; they denote this process as the *technophysio theory*. Americans and people in western Europe were among the first to gain from the rapid increase in agricultural productivity. The ramifications of increased caloric intake were dramatic. The human body is much larger than in the past, and people are capable of working longer and more strenuous hours. In essence, improvements in agricultural productivity have had both powerful direct and indirect effects on economic growth. As more people had the necessary calories to undertake physical labor, the labor force grew both in numbers and in individual ability to perform physical work and therefore to contribute to national output. The authors conclude, "Food . . . must be seen not simply as an item of consumption, but as a fuel for future work effort."[6]

Agricultural productivity gains increased caloric intake, although Fogel and his co-authors emphasize that caloric intake must be considered with respect to nutritional status, which balances the intake and claims against nutrients. An individual's nutritional status is affected by physical activity, environment, and exposure to diseases.[7] Reductions in the prevalence and the severity of infectious diseases, improved clothing and shelter, and other factors increased the efficiency of calories consumed. Between 1800 and 2000, the combination of increased dietary energy available for work and the greater human efficiency in converting dietary energy into work output accounted for roughly one-half of British economic growth since 1800.[8] A similar argument holds for the United States.

Historians note the ironic twist that as poor people gained more income, they often switched to foods with lower nutritional values, such as white bread.[9] Americans altered their food consumption from grains toward foodstuffs consisting of fat, oil, and sugar. Rising incomes led people, especially urban residents, to increase their spending on non-grain products, such as meat.[10]

Massive immigration created overcrowding and sometimes overwhelmed the existing water supplies and infrastructure, leading to increased mortality and reduced longevity. Because public health infrastructure had just begun to affect mortality rates during the last decades of the nineteenth century and because inaccurate explanations (such as the miasma theory) persisted for the epidemics that recurred, living in urban areas was risky indeed. Some researchers argue that even though urbanization occurred during a period of rapid economic growth, increased agricultural productivity did not initially keep up with the increase in population; coupled with inadequate sanitation and a misunderstanding of the cause of contagious diseases, people's caloric intake did not sustain adequate nutritional status and delayed the improvement in longevity and mortality until the early twentieth century. Since then, improvements in food production, working conditions, and disease control have boosted longevity.[11]

In general, such economists as Kuznets and Fogel were generally optimistic about population growth. Increased population and concentration into urban areas often created benefits, as innovative minds fed off each other. Many American doctors wanted to be in an urban area, where there were many other physicians. The physicians benefited by being around other physicians. There were other benefits from growing urban populations, including eventually declining death rates among children. Women responded to the greater likelihood that their children would survive by having fewer children. Having fewer children enabled more women to enter the labor market.[12]

The increased productivity and accompanying increases in real wages and living standards raise a critical question: How did Americans allocate the gains in productivity? Did they simply work the same number of hours and consume more from their rising incomes, or did they apportion their gains between consumption, leisure, and workplace amenities? These are questions to be addressed. For instance, a worker facing a 15 percent increase in his or her wage, reflecting greater productivity, could opt to "buy" 5 percent more leisure time and still have 10 percent left to buy more consumption or to buy better working conditions, such as improved safety or climate control.

## The Choice Between Leisure and Work

Economics is a study of how individuals make choices. Economists have created sophisticated models to depict making choices. Economists view individuals in terms of their pursuit of satisfaction or utility. If you consume an apple, presumably you are getting some satisfaction or benefit from consuming it. These satisfactions and benefits can be objective (an apple improves your health) or subjective (an apple is delicious). Many items provide both subjective and objective satisfactions and benefits. Some people characterize economics and its insistence upon maximizing behavior as narcissistic and self-centered, but the theory easily incorporates satisfaction being based partly upon the well-being of loved ones.

In a typical economics course, satisfaction or utility is based upon consumption of commodities and services. These commodities and services raise utility ("goods"), decrease utility ("bads"), or leave utility unaffected ("neutrals").

Leisure is usually, but not always, a "good," while garbage, for instance, is usually a "bad." Economics students study how simple acts of consuming goods, such as apples and bananas, affect a person's satisfaction.

People make decisions regarding apportioning time between leisure and labor every day. A fundamental decision is: How many hours will we work today? Unless they were to the manor born, most people will end up working for pay, whether through self-employment or for an employer. Most people labor, therefore, so they can purchase (or produce) goods and services to consume (consumption). We literally sell our time in order to finance our consumption— time which could alternatively be used for leisure.[13]

Many of us enjoy our jobs, perhaps because of a sense of accomplishment; camaraderie with coworkers or customers affords satisfaction, too. At some point, however, additional work hours or efforts become onerous, and we would prefer less work to more work.[14] The key to this analysis is that the hourly wage (or hourly wage net of taxes) is the opportunity cost of an hour of leisure (forgoing the best alternative use of your time). When the wage increases, the price of leisure time increases.

What factors affect our apportionment of hours between leisure and labor? A crucial factor is one's preference between leisure and consumption, which is an alternative way to think of the labor/leisure trade-off. Some people are willing to relinquish a significant amount of leisure to get even a little more consumption (think of the 1980s icon: Yuppies—young upwardly-mobile or urban professionals working long hours and driving BMWs). Other people have the opposite preference, being willing to trade a significant amount of consumption to get just a little more leisure. American social observer Henry David Thoreau and his treasured, leisurely sauntering about Walden Pond exemplifies the latter case.[15]

The influences of socialization certainly affect individuals' preferences between leisure and labor. "Leisure patterns and sport preferences are often established in early childhood in response to the influence of significant others . . . individual differences dictate tendencies to choose one type of activity or another, the flexibility of human beings makes them enormously responsive to environmental influences."[16]

Returning to the decision of how many hours to work, you may object that you cannot choose your hours of work for a given day; for example, "I work an eight-hour shift on an assembly line." Your objection, while true, does not present an insuperable problem for our analysis. People can augment their regular, eight-hour day by working at part-time jobs.

How do salaried workers fit into this way of thinking? An additional hour of work may improve your chances of getting a pay raise, a promotion, or a bonus. In a sense, there might be an expected increment in your earnings per additional hour worked, thereby creating an opportunity cost of the time devoted to leisure.

Other factors affecting your decision on how many hours to work relate to the current number of hours and the arduousness of the work. The importance of fatigue conditions, which were more prevalent when workers put in more than 50 hours per week in physically demanding jobs, is that "average hourly earnings will underestimate the base or fatigueless wage and will overestimate the price of leisure." If a researcher ignores the presence of fatigue, the estimated hours worked will be overestimated.[17] By this reckoning, changes in fatigue may be a factor in the dramatic decrease in average weekly hours between 1870 and 1910.

Typically, as the wage increases, the price of an hour of leisure is now more expensive, so people substitute away from leisure and toward more hours of work.[18] They work more and earn more income, enabling them to purchase more consumption. When their wage increases, though, since they are selling their time, workers are now better off. When they are better off, they will take more leisure time and work less. Because they earn a higher wage, though, they can take more leisure time and still have more income from which to purchase goods and services, so their consumption increases. When their wage increases, therefore, workers can have it both ways: more leisure (less work) and more con-sumption. A simple example suffices. Suppose you were working 10 hours at $10.00 per hour. When the wage goes up to $11.50, you could work nine hours and have an additional hour of leisure and still have more income: $103.50 versus $100.00. Between the substitution effect due to the change in the price of leisure and the income effect of being better off, workers may choose to increase, decrease, or keep constant their hours of work (and, vice versa, of leisure).

Workers with very low wage rates may be more likely to increase their hours of work in response to an increase in wages. Productive consumption resembles the *technophysio theory* discussed earlier in this chapter. Economies producing a bare subsistence standard of living often require very long hours of work, just for survival. As an economy grows more productive, workers and their families begin to enjoy higher standards of living, which let workers perform with more energy at work, which, in turn, allows them to work longer and to earn more income. The higher income, in turn, creates better health and more energy. Therefore, better physical fitness should lead to higher average hourly earnings.[19] There are limits to this cycle of higher incomes and better health; at some point the benefits dwindle. John Owen believes that Americans attained a sufficiently high agricultural productivity that by the mid-twentieth century, this cycle was not as important as in other countries.[20]

A troubling aspect of our depiction of leisure/labor decisions is that some people may not be very good at making such decisions. Ill-equipped people may suffer from reduced satisfaction from work, as they are shunted to less prestigious or less desirable jobs. Work as a source of satisfaction often increases as the status of the job rises, but this merely exacerbates the disparity between intelligent, industrious people and those with fewer natural attributes. To some degree, however, this fear may not be dire, as satisfying leisure activities and commodities have percolated down the social classes.[21]

Nobel Prize–winner Gary Becker created a framework to expand upon the basic thinking about choosing between leisure time and work. He suggested that satisfaction or utility may be based upon more general variables, such as nutrition, health, status, and so on, rather than simple acts of consumption, such as eating an apple or an orange. Although economists are not psychologists, they could think of using Abraham Maslow's hierarchy of needs: self-actualization, esteem, love/belonging, safety, and physiological. Subsumed within these broad categories are sub-categories; for example, food, water, sex, sleep, breathing, execration, and homeostatis underlie physiological needs.[22]

Becker thinks of the typical household in terms of consumption and production. Household members purchase goods and services as inputs for things that they cannot easily buy in the marketplace. They use these goods and services in order to produce commodities they desire. For instance, you could purchase some flour, butter, eggs, and sugar. You do not directly get satisfaction from these commodities, but using your culinary skills, purchased ingredients, *and time*, you can whip up a tasty pastry, which does provide considerable satisfaction. The market may also allow you to buy the pastry ready-made. You might opt for the ready-made pastry if it takes you a considerable amount of time to bake pastry, if you are an inept baker, or if you earn a relatively high wage.[23]

Becker's model makes explicit the time cost aspect of activities. If you want to play a round of golf, the true cost of golf includes the green fee, amortized cost of equipment, safety cost (you could be struck by an errant ball, golf cart, or bolt of lightning), and time cost. If a round of golf takes three hours and you make $60 per hour, you are forgoing the opportunity to earn $180 instead of playing golf. Many people recognize the out-of-pocket cash cost of golf, but they often don't realize the added cost of time. A retiree may face the same out-of-pocket expenses as a busy executive, but the retiree's time usually has a much lower opportunity cost, if calculated as a forgone wage.[24]

Work hours per day may be affected by commute time, physical effectiveness, and other factors. If you have to get up and prepare for work and then make the commute, you might want to work several hours, rather than a four-hour day, in order to spread the cost of going to work across more hours. The commute and preparation times are, in essence, fixed costs; you incur the same costs of getting ready and going to work, whether you plan to work three, eight, or ten hours.[25] Eight-hour or six-hour shifts may work better, from the employers' perspective, since 24 hours can be split evenly.

Evidence suggests, though, that workers decline an option to work four 10-hour days per week instead of the standard five eight-hour days. Very few workers have chosen such a schedule in either the United States or other nations.[26] Owen cites research arguing that "the standardization [of work hours] that exists may be due in part to a 'taste for standardization' of leisure hours (arising, for example, from a desire to see friends or to watch certain television programs) on the part of the employees themselves."[27]

For many Americans, though, their work days are not fixed in eight-hour increments. Professions such as medicine, law, professoriate, accounting, and engineering entail varying hours. Tax accountants are very busy the first four months of the year, while professors have almost complete discretion over their summer hours. Young medical interns and lawyers seeking to attain partnership put in extremely long hours. These Americans are usually paid on a salaried basis, although employers sometimes award overtime pay or compensatory time. Once professionals gain partnership or tenure, their work hours may not change much, but the nature of their work does. Partners may spend more of their time overseeing fledgling professionals or entertaining clients; tenured faculty may serve on more committees.

Another issue revolves around the question of whether spending on goods and services for recreation is complementary with leisure. If leisure and recreational goods and services are complementary, when a person took more leisure, then his or her demand for recreational goods and services would increase. If the prices of recreational goods and services changed, then the overall price of leisure could be considered to have changed. Since ski equipment and time spent going downhill skiing are used together, they are complements; when the price of ski equipment falls, the demand for downhill skiing will increase.[28]

People also decide how much of their lifetime hours to devote to working. Across a person's lifetime, longevity may affect his or her decision to seek additional education. If expected longevity at age 18 is only 25 years, the calculation of the benefits/costs of further education is different than if it is 50 years.

Economists have described the effect of increased longevity on educational attainment, which, in turn, has spurred increased productivity. Part of the gains in longevity, then, went for more years in school, but these lost years from being in the labor force, presumably, were more than made up for by increased productivity and by increased satisfaction from being educated.[29] Increased longevity made acquiring additional education more attractive, leading to parents investing more in their children and for workers investing in more on-the-job training. This human capital (investment in skills and knowledge) further raised the productivity of workers.[30]

The effect of education on leisure time is ambiguous: improved educational opportunities might offset some of the increased growth in demand for leisure time.[31] Owen attributes the accelerating attainment of education as resulting from greater life expectancy, more subsidies to public schools, and "dynamic propagation mechanism (education of children in one generation leading to educated parents in the next, and thence to a higher level of educational aspiration for their children)."[32]

Two other factors arise. Higher educational attainment may lead to jobs that are more satisfying for non-pecuniary reasons than those offered to workers with lesser educational attainments. If this is true, then the incremental dissatisfaction of work may be lower, leading to workers choosing longer hours of work. The other factor revolves around the question of whether more educated people have an improved ability to enjoy consumption experiences in addition to their higher earning capability, which might lead to greater demand for leisure. "On balance, then, the consideration of these two additional relationships (better working conditions and more appreciative consumption) between education and the demand for leisure would seem to lend further support to the view that there would be a negative relationship between education and the demand for leisure time."[33]

## Changes in the Price of Leisure Time

American workers became more productive during the twentieth century, although the rate of increase appeared to have slowed down in the last two decades. If the labor market was competitive, increased worker productivity should have been reflected by increased real wages. There has been a fairly strong connection between productivity and wages across the twentieth century, although one needs to be careful in viewing this relationship after the 1950s. During the last decades of the century, much of workers' increased compensation came in the form of fringe benefits.

Workers may choose to allocate gains in productivity between both more leisure and greater consumption, so their decisions on how to split the gains will be reflected in their weekly hours. Juanita Kreps provided a numerical example. With per capita GNP being $3,181 in 1965, she considered a productivity growth allowing a possible 80 percent increase in per capita GNP by 1985 to $5,802. She considered an alternative where workers took all of the productivity gains in terms of increased leisure: "the workweek could fall to 22 hours, or the work year could be limited to 27 weeks per year, or retirement age could be lowered to 38 years, or almost half the labor force could be kept in retraining programs, or additional time available for education might well exceed our capacity to absorb such education." Americans instead chose an intermediate position, taking two-thirds in more goods and one-third in more time free of work.[34]

Some economists noted that there was a limit to the leisure/labor trade-off. There could be a limit on consumption due to the scarcity of time, as consumption of goods and services requires time (including time for maintaining and servicing some consumption goods); enjoying a fine glass of claret is not enhanced by speedier consumption.[35]

Becker recognized that consumption takes time, and he incorporated this insight into his model. According to Stefan Linder, Becker's model predicted, "As economic development has continued, attractive alternative ways of using time have emerged. Meditation and speculation have been driven off the market. Whatever the cause, time has thus become de facto an increasingly scarce resource, without the economists having noticed this development."[36] Linder suggested that as the price of leisure rose, people would substitute to more expensive forms of leisure and away from time-intensive forms. He also wondered about the effect upon the cultivation of the spirit. He worried that as incomes rose, consumption of some types of culture would fall. An orchestra, for instance, can hardly be made more efficient in terms of time or inputs needed (you can't really speed up the performances or cut the number of musicians).[37]

One unfortunate result of this behavior is that those people whose well-being depends upon labor-intensive services, such as those in nursing and rehabilitation facilities, will face increasing hardships.[38] For people who are unemployed or underemployed, involuntary free time may be spent in "improving one's chances of a better life in the next world. . . . It has been pointed out that the number of such [religious] holidays is greater in the poor countries than in the rich, and that on the road to riches a country gradually eliminates more and more holidays."[39]

People facing a higher price of leisure may choose to cut down on hours of sleeping or may try to learn while sleeping. Other people may cut back on time devoted to hygiene or eating.[40] While most researchers simply take sleep as fixed, some economists suggest that sleep is actually a choice variable. People may gain pleasure from sleeping. If they get sufficient sleep, people may also improve their productivity at work or on household chores or enhance their enjoyment of leisure activities. Economists Jeff Biddle and Daniel Hamermesh found evidence that people display different patterns in sleep duration (weekends versus weekdays, across their lifetimes, educational attainment, changes in wage rates, children).[41]

## Economic Growth and Rising Standards of Living

Economic growth affords Americans the opportunity to enjoy more leisure time, to work less, and to have greater consumption than Americans in the past.

People weigh the benefits and costs from changing their working hours. Economic analysis suggests that an increase in wage may or may not result in an individual choosing fewer hours of work. Other factors affect a person's decision on how many hours to work.

Will economic growth persist? John Maynard Keynes noted the rapid increases in productivity, including that of agriculture. He predicted 80 years ago that mankind was getting close to solving its economic problem; he was hopeful that a fourfold or more increase in standard of living might occur within his readers' lifetime. He divided needs into absolute ("we feel them whatever the situation of our fellow human beings may be") and relative ("we feel them only if their satisfaction lifts us above, makes us feel superior to, our fellows"). Given his prediction that mankind was solving its economic problem, he anticipated that the absolute needs would be satisfied for all people in the near future, while satisfying the relative needs might prove impossible.[42]

More recently, though, economist Robert Gordon worries that American economic growth has reached a point of diminishing prospects. He cites the retirement of the baby boomers and the exiting of productive working-age men, along with continuing disparities in educational outcomes, as drags upon economic growth.[43]

However the future unfolds, Americans of the twentieth century had a wondrous, if sometimes bumpy, era of economic growth. We next turn to the question of how Americans chose to apportion their hours.

# Less Work, More Play, and the Rise of Leisure

Economists sometimes measure "leisure" in a broad sense. It can be measured as time not spent at market labor and on basic bodily maintenance, so it could include such non-market labor as household chores. An even narrower measurement of leisure time, as used in this book, by measuring uses of time between market work, household work, sleep, household chores, commuting, and leisure, shows dramatically rising amounts of time available for leisure across the twentieth century.

Measuring leisure time is difficult. The Bureau of Labor Statistics keeps track of weekly hours for manufacturing workers. Using the simplest residual method, a reduction in working hours means that manufacturing workers have more hours to devote to other endeavors. Tracking weekly hours for white-collar workers is more difficult.

How did Americans end up with more leisure time and less work? The process resulted from a combination of greater productivity, increased longevity, union activity, legislation, and other factors. Why did the reduction in manufacturing workers' and many white-collar workers' workweek stall after the Great Depression?

## Early Trends in Working Hours

When agriculture predominated in the American economy, people worked from sunrise to sunset and sometimes longer, six days a week. Even in the early manufacturing firms, six-day, 12-hours per day workweeks were common. Such rigorous schedules left little time for contemplation, education, or socialization.

The campaign for shorter hours united workers with disparate interests, whereas campaigning for higher wages sometimes proved divisive. The "Ten-Hour Circular" issued in Boston in 1835 was a pioneering attempt to reduce working hours. Workers pointed out that working 10 hours per day would spread work to more workers and would help raise wages (due to the inherent reduction in the supply of hours of labor). Employers raised concerns of worker dissipation. These basic arguments would echo throughout the nineteenth and twentieth centuries. The shift to manufacturing work was accompanied by hard-won gains for workers in terms of the workday; workers reduced the work-days from 13 to 10 hours by 1860. The workers, instead of gaining roughly one-quarter more in output, chose to increase their leisure time: "Workers gave up that possible increase in their standard of living in return for a significant reduction in the effort, attention, and boredom of their workweek. No similar exchange was made in the twentieth century, which suggests how strongly the nineteenth-century worker valued a shorter workday, even though he enjoyed far fewer goods and services than his twentieth-century counterpart."[1]

After many workers got the 10-hour day, the next goal was for getting Saturday afternoons off. By the early 1900s, although many workers still toiled 50 or more hours per week, workers increasingly fought for an eight-hour day.

Americans worked fewer hours per week, per year, and across their lifetimes (Table 4.1). The workweek shrank rapidly between 1870 and 1950, but the reduction slowed down in the second half of the twentieth century. Workers, though, experienced further reductions in their yearly working hours via two sources. The federal government mandated new holidays during the century, but not all workers gained these days off (many universities hold classes on Veteran's Day, for instance). In addition, employers began offering paid vacation and sick days; both effects whittled down the number of actual hours worked.[2]

With gains in productivity, particularly in the production of food, Americans spent smaller proportions of their increasing budgets on basics such as food, clothing, and housing. With ever-larger proportions of their budgets left over after satisfying basic needs and wants, Americans not only increased but accelerated their spending on healthcare, education, and other categories. The income elasticity of healthcare, education, and leisure were well above one; in other words, for a one percent increase in income, spending on each of these categories of goods and services rose by more than one percent. Consumers accelerated their spending on these goods.

Another portrait of American consumption was the growing consumption of leisure time: Americans used part of their rising wages to purchase leisure. By 1995, leisure dominated consumption expenditures. Americans are living longer, and they are starting work at later ages than in the past. As Table 4.2 indicates, in 1870 few people retired; death usually occurred before a person retired. Of course, much has changed during the period covered by the table. A large proportion of Americans worked on farms in 1870, while by 1990 only a minuscule proportion did so. Many factors contributed to the shifts denoted by the table.

*Table 4.1* **Changing Work Habits of Americans, 1870–1990[a]**

| Year | Workweek (Hours) | Workday (Hours) | Workweek (Days) | Annual Hours Paid |
|------|------|------|------|------|
| 1870 | 61.0 | 10.2 | 6.0 | 3,181 |
| 1890 | 58.4 | 9.7 | 6.0 | 3,045 |
| 1913 | 53.3 | 8.9 | 6.0 | 2,779 |
| 1929 | 48.1 | 8.0 | 6.0 | 2,508 |
| 1938 | 44.0 | 8.0 | 5.5 | 2,294 |
| 1950 | 39.8 | 8.0 | 5.0 | 2,075 |
| 1960 | 38.6 | 7.7 | 5.0 | 2,013 |
| 1973 | 36.9 | 7.4 | 5.0 | 1,924 |
| 1990 | 34.5 | 7.3 | 4.7 | 1,799 |

| Year | Vacation (Days) | Holidays (Days) | Other Absence (Days) | Annual Hours Worked |
|------|------|------|------|------|
| 1870 | 0.0 | 3.0 | 8.0 | 3,069 |
| 1890 | 0.0 | 3.0 | 8.0 | 2,938 |
| 1913 | 5.0 | 3.5 | 8.0 | 2,632 |
| 1929 | 5.5 | 4.0 | 8.0 | 2,368 |
| 1938 | 6.0 | 4.5 | 8.0 | 2,146 |
| 1950 | 6.5 | 6.0 | 9.0 | 1,903 |
| 1960 | 7.0 | 7.0 | 9.0 | 1,836 |
| 1973 | 8.0 | 7.5 | 9.0 | 1,743 |
| 1990 | 10.5 | 12.0 | 10.0 | 1,562 |

[a] Federal Reserve Bank of Dallas, "These Are the Good Old Days," 4–5.

With longer lives, the provision of Social Security, and a greater ability to accumulate sufficient assets, Americans began enjoying lengthening retirement years.[3]

## Union Efforts to Reduce Weekly Hours

Labor unions played a role in attaining a shorter workweek for the working class. Historian Benjamin Hunnicutt attempts to explain why the efforts to reduce the workweek stopped after the Great Depression. He describes how organized labor used the desire of American workers for shorter hours to enroll members

*Table 4.2* **Changing Lifestyles and Longevity, 1870–1990[a]**

| Lifetime Activities | 1870 | 1950 | 1973 | 1990 |
|---|---|---|---|---|
| Age starting work (avg.) | 13.0 | 17.6 | 18.5 | 19.1 |
| Life expectancy (years) | 43.5 | 67.2 | 70.6 | 75.0 |
| Retirement age (avg.) | death | 68.5 | 64.0 | 63.6 |
| Years on job | 30.5 | 49.6 | 45.5 | 44.5 |
| Retirement (years) | 0.0 | 0.0 | 6.6 | 11.4 |
| Annual hours worked | 3,069 | 1,903 | 1,743 | 1,562 |
| Annual hours home work | 1,825 | 1,544 | 1,391 | 1,278 |
| **Lifetime Hours** | | | | |
| Working at job | 93,604 | 94,389 | 79,307 | 69,509 |
| Working at home | 61,594 | 81,474 | 67,151 | 59,800 |
| Waking leisure | 99,016 | 216,854 | 266,129 | 308,368 |

[a] Federal Reserve Bank of Dallas, "These Are the Good Old Days," 5.

and to enlist support. Non-union workers also pushed for shorter workweeks. The push for shorter hours also spurred "important constitutional issues in the early twentieth century, leading to the writing of some of the most progressive legal opinion of that time."[4] Many people approved of the reform because they thought the increased free time would benefit workers, both by improving work performance and increasing production. These reformers saw free time as helping to address social concerns surrounding health, citizenship, morality, family, and religious issues.[5]

Economists and historians came to different conclusions as to why workers' weekly hours declined and then stagnated. "Economists see increased wages as a central reason that work hours have declined, whereas historians see the reverse."[6]

The economists cited reasons such as "the reduction of fatigue, the availability of consumer credit, advertising and better marketing, patterns of family work

and work at home, the 'price of recreation,' easier work, and stability of employment." Some historians were reluctant to agree with the economists or to devise
new explanations, because they hesitated to accept economists' assumptions
that workers understood they had a choice between leisure and work and that
they were able to act on such a choice. Instead, historians see "workers' desire for
shorter hours as a means to an end, as part of a calculated economic strategy
rather than one element in a 'rational' choice in the marketplace. From this point
of view, what the workers 'knew' was not shorter hours *or* higher wages but
shorter hours *for* higher wages." Historians believed that workers wanted both
(who doesn't?). They emphasized legislation, employer decisions, and labor
demand, even more than did the economists. The historians did not accept the
possibility that workers had the freedom and bargaining ability to set their hours,
instead believing that employers or market forces dictated the working
conditions.[7]

The American Federation of Labor reiterated its demand for shorter hours at
its 1926 convention, continuing a decades-long effort. The union thought that
reducing hours of work would restore assembly-line workers' vitality and health;
as time passed, their argument emphasized salutary effects on psychological
health, as well as intangible benefits.[8]

The campaign for shorter hours was connected to fears about growing consumption. Many worried about industrialists exploiting the workers by getting
labor to toil unnecessarily long hours to produce and to purchase things they did
not need or really want. Some commentators believed that workers had to be
persuaded or duped into buying these products.[9]

There was another aspect to workers' agitation for shorter weekly hours.
During the late nineteenth and early twentieth centuries, "insistence upon the
shorter work day is to be accounted for by the general feelings among the workers that shortening the work period both increased wages and contributed
toward a solution of the problem of unemployment."[10]

Spreading work among workers was not a new idea. The Ten Hours Bill and
later legislation aimed at reducing working hours were not necessarily passed
primarily to afford workers more leisure time. Indeed, many employers and government leaders, among others, worried that more free time would be deleterious to workers. Instead, labor leaders often viewed the legislation as a way of
spreading work around for more workers.[11] The battles for legislation regulating
women's and children's work hours saw similar arguments.

Religious groups agitated for shorter workweeks. Jewish leaders hoped that
the five-and-a-half days workweek would restore, at least partially, the Sabbath.
They were at odds with Christian leaders pushing for "Blue Laws" outlawing various activities on Sundays. In the end, religious leaders united to push for the
five-day workweek.[12]

In the struggle for an eight-hour day during the early decades of the twentieth century, some workers immediately sought second jobs, but this practice subsided as workers adjusted to their additional free time, often filling the time with commercial amusements. The turn toward commercialized leisure worried both union leaders and recreation professionals.[13]

Recreation leaders disliked commercial amusements because they allegedly stifled individualism and creativity, induced passivity, neglected natural needs, obscured real culture, and led to immorality. In the recreation leaders' view, the purpose of recreation was to liberate the individual; public recreation facilities would provide access to a community's culture and would allow workers to retain their individuality. Hobbies and public recreation could have allowed adults to express themselves and improve their physical well-being and health.[14] James Truslow Adams bemoaned how producers turned out copious amounts of goods that required consumers' willingness to purchase: "the owners above setting ever higher standards of living and the operatives below pressing steadily past them in an orgy of material well-being."[15]

Business leaders initially opposed the five-day workweek; many of them claimed that increased leisure time for workers meant increased dissipation. Some, such as John E. Edgerton, president of the National Association of Manufacturers, professed concern for workers but thought, "the emphasis should be put on work—more work and better work, instead of upon leisure—more leisure and worse leisure."[16] Eventually, though, some businessmen recognized opportunity in the push for shorter hours, as the recreation market faced greater demand.

Modern readers may be surprised to hear that the Senate and a House committee passed a bill in 1933 mandating a 30-hour workweek for businesses engaged in interstate and foreign commerce. Alabama senator Hugo Black introduced legislation for a 30-hour week, which passed by a 53–30 vote. The bill covered workers in a variety of mining and manufacturing industries that engaged in interstate or foreign commerce. An amendment by Arkansas senator Joseph Robinson to set the workweek at 36 hours with no more than eight hours in any one day failed, when 35 Democrats failed to support it. Robinson claimed that President Franklin Roosevelt favored the amendment.[17] Roosevelt, prodded by business leaders who disliked the mandated aspect of the bill, killed the bill before it reached the House floor for a final vote; Roosevelt later regretted his actions.[18]

Benjamin Hunnicut employed regression and correlation analysis to identify the factors leading to the shorter workweek. He found that unemployment failed to account for much of the drop. He noted that increases in the real wage were slowest in the quarter-century before World War I, yet the workweek continued to fall sharply during those years, calling into question the argument that wage increases fostered shorter hours before 1914. He found that the immigrant's original country was an explanatory variable, as immigrants from Italy, Poland, and Russia tended to choose shorter hours and more leisure time.[19]

## Uses of Leisure Time during the 1930s

Concurrent with the push for shorter working hours, people sought information on what workers did with their leisure time. During the Great Depression, the National Recreation Association surveyed 5,000 people. The Association cited the statement of the National Commission on the Enrichment of Adult Life: "What the American people do in their spare time henceforth will largely determine the character of our civilization."[20]

These 5,000 people were 16 years and older, with a preponderance of females. The respondents lived along the Atlantic Coast, with half living in Newark and Boston. The study, published in 1934, showed that the 10 most popular leisure activities were reading newspapers and magazines, listening to radio, attending movies, visiting or entertaining others, reading books, auto riding for pleasure, swimming, writing letters, and conversation. During the early years of the Great Depression, many people altered their leisure activities toward more home-centered and less costly activities. Many people professed a desire to partake in more outdoor activities, but most of these activities involved spending money. The survey indicated a divergence between what people wanted to do and what they actually did, usually because of cost.[21]

The survey revealed that people with shorter but more dependable hours of work used their leisure time "increasingly in a wider range of varied activities than are people of any other employment status." Since many Americans experienced drops in their incomes, it is no surprise that the survey revealed drops in activities that involved money costs, such as motion picture attendance and swimming. The shortfall in leisure activities was not greatly offset by public provision of recreational activities.[22] In addition to cost as a factor for lessened leisure activities, other factors cited by survey respondents included "no proper clothes," "inadequate facilities in neighborhood," "no money for carfares," and "too discouraged or worried because of loss of job or lack of income to concentrate on anything." An additional factor was "the fear of harming their only clothes," which revealed the parlous state of many Americans. With regard to outdoor activities, as Americans moved from larger to smaller living spaces, there were fewer opportunities for gardening or for working around the house.[23]

## Economists' Explanations for Reduced Hours

Economists debated the causes and consequences of the shortening of the workweek. John R. Commons believed that organized labor viewed reduced work hours
as leading to higher wages and less technological unemployment through spreading work across more workers. Commons and other early twentieth-century labor
economists recognized that workers were motivated by more than just economic
issues; they wanted more leisure time to spend with their families and communities, so they could enjoy cultural, religious, and traditional activities.[24] John Maynard Keynes worried about what workers would do with their leisure time and
prosperity: "for the first time since his creation man will be faced with his real, his
permanent problem—how to use his freedom from pressing economic cares, how
to occupy the leisure, which science and compound interest have won for him, to
live wisely and agreeably and well."[25]

As discussed in Chapter 3, rising wages spurred two effects. Workers were
better off with higher wages, so they took more time for leisure (an income
effect). The higher wages, however, raised the price of leisure time, so workers
substituted toward work and consumption and away from leisure time (the substitution effect).[26] The interaction of the two effects determined whether workers chose to work more or to work less. One could argue that the significant drop
in weekly hours between 1870 and 1935 was the result of the income effect
dominating, while the post-Depression stagnation in weekly hours meant that
the two effects largely offset each other.[27]

What about leisure's effect on consumption? Economists worried about
overproduction and underconsumption. Veblen suggested that underconsumption would be kept in abeyance by "the emulative propensity of man." Hazel
Kyrk argued that economic inequality and innovation would keep spurring consumption. The introduction of new luxuries, initially consumed by the wealthy,
would spur workers to earn enough to attain the luxuries: "luxuries for the well-
off that eventually turned into 'necessities' for workers."[28]

## An Era of Stable Working Hours

Employed American adults experienced little net gain in their leisure time in the
three decades after World War II. Hours worked per week for "men not in
school" rose slightly between 1948 and 1969, which were both years of relatively full employment. Employed women had about six hours less free time per
week than employed men. Employed women were engaged in unpaid work-like
activities—including commuting time and household chores—in addition to
the hours in paid employment. Married women who shifted from full-time

housewife to employed wife possibly experienced a net increase in their overall hours employed at paid labor and domestic chores, even though they could pur-chase many time-saving devices and products.[29]

The eight-hour day hasn't changed much since the 1930s, although for many workers, the day is punctuated by coffee and lunch breaks. Why the downward trend in working hours per day for those who worked stabilized is in an interesting question. In the case of the assembly line, having three eight-hour shifts makes sense. As discussed earlier, for many people, eight hours may be an optimal trade-off. There are fixed costs of sorts in going to work at all on any given day: preparing a sack lunch, putting on dress clothes (tying ties), doing one's hair, commuting, and taking the children to day care. Therefore, people may decide that, if they are going to incur these costs of going to work, they might as well spread the fixed costs over a significant block of time. Some workers, however—transit workers, for instance—may work eight hours per day but via split, four-hour shifts in order to handle commuters' peak travel times.

The desire for increased consumption may have explained part of the work-ers' decisions to maintain relatively stable weekly hours during the second half of the twentieth century, but there is a concurrent explanation. Owen observed that after World War II, the real hourly wage increased rapidly, but so did the cost of childrearing. To maintain the "quality" of one's children, workers maintained their work level. Because of the low birthrates during the 1930s, many families appeared to have tried to catch up in terms of the number of children in their families after the war. With rising incomes after the war, parents also felt suffi-ciently confident to invest more in their children, including more education. In-creased schooling raised the average cost of rearing a child. Between the "baby boom" and the increase in education, the escalating cost of raising a child di-verted resources from other forms of consumption and from savings in many households during the postwar period. These factors made reducing working hours less attractive.[30]

During the immediate postwar years, workers emphasized greater consump-tion relative to more leisure time. John Owen suggests that workers did so be-cause, in addition to demographic changes, there was pent-up demand for con-sumer goods, so "workers tried to catch up on purchases of clothing, household appliances, and other consumer durable goods. There was very little demand for a further reduction in worktimes."[31]

After World War II, scholars were still calling for government regulation of leisure and the compulsory teaching of leisure skills. Certainly, economists con-tinued to paint rosy pictures of the future, when Americans would have, accord-ing to one estimate, 660 billion more hours of leisure in 2000 than they enjoyed in 1950; other researchers thought 660 billion more was absurdly low. One researcher predicted during the 1960s that eventually "2% of our population, working in factory and on farm, will be able to produce all the goods and food that the other 98% can possibly consume, that this day will arrive no later than 25 years from now . . . jobs would disappear so rapidly that the government would have to begin paying citizens *not* to work."[32]

While admitting that many Americans still felt harried, Ernest Havemann pointed out that many used their leisure by taking second jobs and that the wealthiest took less leisure than other Americans: "the housewife never had it so good, thanks to all her appliances and her packaged foods, and that if she feels pressed for time it is only because she has undertaken so many new activities that her grandmother never considered, like serving as den mother and keeping minutes for the PTA (Parents-Teachers Association)."[33] An anthropologist observed, "One trouble with us Americans is that we carry our work habits over into our leisure hours." Other Americans felt harried, perhaps, because they spent their leisure time trying to be productive, whether by improving their mind or practicing a sport or dance.[34]

Even if the average number of weekly hours fell, Sabastian de Grazia suggests that this did not necessarily result in more leisure. He noted that some researchers proceeded from assuming that productivity increased to determining what income workers could have earned, if their work hours had remained constant. These researchers then calculated that American workers divided productivity gains between higher incomes and free time, with two-thirds going to earning more pay and one-third to more free time. De Grazia disputed these researchers' basic premise that the workweek had fallen as much as was claimed; therefore he also rejected their belief that workers accepted part of their increased productivity in terms of increased free time.[35]

De Grazia deconstructed the typical observation that the workweek had fallen considerably from 1850 to 1960, by roughly 31 hours a week. In addition, American workers received vacation, holiday, and sick leave time, dating from the 1920s; he did acknowledge that earlier retirement and greater longevity provided more free or leisure time. He begins by granting that the work hours, indeed, have fallen. He then demonstrates that the modern reckoning on increased leisure time is illusory; he suspects that some of the reduced time was consumed by longer commute times, as workers opted to live farther from the workplace (suburbanization). He lists moonlighting, women working, driving children to school activities, running errands, home improvement, and other factors as chipping away the increased free time the Machine Age had promised to grant; he, in fact, attributes some of male workers' decreased hours at the workplace to increased hours worked by females. Once at home, male workers devoted some of their free time to assisting their working wives in maintaining the household. The intensity of labor also affected the thesis that accounting for leisure requires simply looking at the hours not at work. De Grazia claims that assembly-line workers found work so draining that they needed more hours each evening to recuperate than had workers of the 1850s, who operated at a slower pace.[36]

An article in *Business Week* buttressed de Grazia's argument, as by 1953, such do-it-yourself tasks as maintaining the family lawn and gardening created a boom for power equipment such as lawn mowers and garden tractors. Some buyers cited the high price of domestic labor, but others admitted that prestige was a factor in purchasing such equipment.[37]

These issues aside, Americans participated in many leisure activities. One survey found that American adults' participation rates in many recreational activities varied little between gender and age groups, although males reported more frequent participation than did females. Participation rates fell as the age of the respondents increased. The survey also found that Caucasians had higher levels of participation, while African-Americans had the lowest rates. Higher incomes were associated with increased participation in golf, tennis, snorkeling, and hiking, among other activities, while hunting, off-road motor vehicle driving, fishing, and outdoor swimming in natural waters were not affected by income.[38] Another researcher suggested that Americans in the 25–44-year-old category had increased free time between 1965 and 1975, but that people in the 45–64-year-old group had mixed changes in free time, with men having less and women having more. Another study showed that American adults felt "more pressed for time" in 1985 than in 1965.[39]

Although weekly hours of leisure may have stagnated, some researchers failed to account for the greater prevalence of paid vacations, paid holidays, and paid travel time, and thereby tended to understate the decline in hours of work and the increase in hourly earnings.[40] Juanita Kreps allocated the increase in nonworking hours between reduction in the workweek, years of retirement, holidays and vacation time, and sick leave. She estimated a total average annual increase in non-working time of 1,655 hours.[41]

## The Debate about Working Hours, Circa 1990

Juliet Schor's *The Overworked American: The Unexpected Decline of Leisure* received considerable publicity two decades ago. Several prominent labor economists have refuted her findings. Her book remains interesting, because some commentators still claim that Americans are working longer hours and because it reveals how some evidence paints an inaccurate picture of Americans' working hours. Her basic conclusion was that after labor's gains in reduced hours per week by the 1930s, the later twentieth century witnessed a slow, creeping increase in yearly hours. "When surveyed, Americans report that they have only sixteen and a half hours of leisure a week, after the obligations of job and household are taken care of. Working hours are already longer than they were forty years ago." According to her research, the increase in the hours worked was greater for women than for men, roughly three times greater.[42]

Schor acknowledged that her findings conflicted with those of economists Gary Burtless and John P. Robinson, both of whom found reduced working hours per week and increased leisure, but she advised readers to be skeptical of their claims. Schor believed that capitalists faced incentives to force workers into "long hour jobs" and not hire new workers in order to save on fringe benefits. She believed that workers often had little discretion over their time, although they could choose to moonlight, switch jobs, or retire. She used a simple and effective approach to delineating leisure time. She added the hours of paid employment to the hours of household labor to derive "total working hours." The residual hours comprised leisure time.[43]

John Robinson and Geoffrey Godbey have studied how Americans used their time, starting with a study examining time use in 1965. Their preferred method of quantifying time usage was the time diary, a method that differed from that used by Schor. They were well placed to refute or to confirm Schor's findings, given their long-term analysis of time use. As Robinson and Godbey put it in their introduction, "we were told by the editor [of the *New York Times Book Review*] that we had to 'draw blood.'"[44]

Their data suggested that Schor was wrong; Americans were working fewer hours than a few decades earlier. There was no evidence to suggest that women were particularly hard-hit by these changes in work hours. They also challenged the belief that men's housework hours were trivial and were not increasing.[45] They addressed other questionable beliefs throughout their book. With respect to how Americans used their free time, they questioned whether Americans had turned away from religion, reading, participating in the arts, organizational and volunteer activities, and other issues. They also examined whether video and computer games were crowding out other activities. Their key conclusion, though, was this: "we argue that Americans have more free time than they did 30 years ago and that free time is likely to increase even more in the future."[46]

Robinson and Godbey divided time into four categories: paid work (contracted time), household/family care (committed time), personal time, and free time. They used the term "contracted time" to "connect it to the contractual work arrangements implicit in the schedules that workers made with their employers. This included paid work done at home, as well as work breaks and other nonwork activities at the place of work." Commuting time was considered separately, with a fifth category—travel, "which can be seen either as a separate maintenance activity connecting the four other types of time or as a necessary ad-junct to each time."[47]

Typical surveys pertaining to time use have flaws. Robinson and Godbey suggest that people are unable to accurately compile daily and weekly estimates of several activities. Quite frequently, the estimated hours for the specified activities added up to significantly more than the 168 hours in a week; college students' estimates, for instance, added up to 250 hours per week. The two researchers conclude, "the estimate approach has a built-in bias toward overreporting." They provide evidence that the overreporting has increased between 1965 and 1985, with women more likely to overestimate their workweeks, especially those working over 35 hours a week.[48]

They found that among the economically active population, the work hours of employed women fell between 1965 and 1985, but that the percentage of women in the labor force increased. "The fact that the working women who report working fewer hours decreases the total number of work hours put in by women by almost 20 percent in large part accounts for the increased free time we find." For men, they found a decline from "about 47 hours in 1965 to 43 hours in 1975 to under 40 hours in 1985. This is important because . . . these men are putting more time into housework—although hardly enough to offset their 7-hour decline in paid work."[49]

The two researchers note that Americans often treated time as money, going back as far as Benjamin Franklin, if not before. But what money value should be placed on time? Hourly wage? Take-home hourly wage? They describe how most of the predictions (e.g., that women's housework is valued more if the woman doing it has a higher working wage-rate) that use market wages as the price of an hour of leisure do not bear empirical scrutiny. Another conundrum was identified: "The greater the demand, the scarcer the supply, the longer the line. So we wait in line to hear people perform, in traffic to reach favorite beaches and in offices to consult prestigious lawyers."[50]

From an initial balance between work time and leisure time, the increased productivity meant that work time became more valuable, destroying the balance between work and leisure. People tried to increase the productivity or yield of leisure time by speeding up participation in activities and by using material goods with their leisure activities. This resulted in shifting from intrinsically slower-paced leisure activities that could not be combined with material goods toward those activities that could be speeded up or easily combined with material goods. These factors may have accounted for the general perceived scarcity of time.[51]

Many Americans at the end of the twentieth century apparently continued to feel harried. One way to cope with a perceived reduction in leisure time was to practice what Robinson and Godbey termed "time deepening":

Time-deepening assumes that, under pressure of expanded interest and compulsion, people are capable of higher rates of "doing." Rather than thinking of human behavior in "either-or" terms—that is, a person does either one activity or another—some people develop the ability to do both Activity A and Activity B. Time-deepening can occur in at least four ways: (1) Attempting to speed up a given activity.... (2) Substituting a leisure activity that can be done more quickly for one that takes longer.... (3) Doing more than one activity at once.... (4) Undertaking a leisure activity with more precise regard to time.[52]

People buying bottled orange juice instead of frozen concentrated juice demonstrated this phenomenon: people did not want to use time thawing and mixing the frozen concentrate. Robinson and Godbey supplied their own examples of time-deepening, including a suggestion that pornography or prostitutes are speedier routes to sexual satisfaction. They pointed out that few men have the time for a mistress. "Speed and brevity are more widely admired, whether in serving food, in the length of magazine articles [think of *People* or *Time*], or in conversation." For some Americans, time-deepening may have boomeranged, as a substantial proportion of Americans blamed leisure activities for making them feel rushed.[53]

Similar to "time-deepening," Americans seem intent on using their leisure time more intensively during the 1990s than in previous years. Rather than sunbathing on the beach, they seek "intense activity and personal mobility ... active vacations." In polls, two-thirds of Americans want to see more than one specific destination or attraction and want to be involved in activities and sightseeing, rather than relaxing and resting. Americans indulged in sports tourism (traveling to see sports events) and ecotourism (a sustainable form of natural resource–based tourism that focuses primarily on experiencing and learning about nature). Outdoor activities, such as boating, bird watching, hiking, backpacking, downhill skiing, and primitive area camping, grew by at least 50 percent between 1982–1983 and 1994–1995. Some outdoor activities, though, fell—hunting, horseback riding, sailing, and fishing.[54]

Demographic factors affect free time. For women, the trend toward smaller families in the last decades of the twentieth century probably meant more free time or at least an offset to the decline in free time related to entering the paid labor force. There was a 50 percent decline in women in the traditional full-time housewife role, from 30 percent in 1970 to 15 percent in 1990. A lower proportion of men were in the triple role of father, spouse, and worker, leading to more free time. A key fact, though, was that the "biggest increases are found for the percentages working but having *neither* [italics theirs] marital nor parental responsibilities—from 10 percent of women and 11 percent of men in the 1970s to 16 percent and 21 percent most recently." In terms of groups, older men and older women reduced their hours, while younger women increased their hours in employed labor. College-educated, higher-income, and self-employed people tended to work more hours, too.[55]

So why did Schor come up with different conclusions? Robinson and Godbey suggest that Schor did not use their 1965 time-diary data or their 1985 data. She averaged government data on work hours and workweeks that showed increased hours of work, but these data did not reveal such increases under earlier analysis. She also based her findings on a 1988 Harris Poll finding that claimed hours of work had increased. Another researcher, Richard Hamilton, concluded that "[t]he Harris workweek 'finding' [used by Schor] appears to reflect changes in the methods used rather than any real change. The same conclusion appears justified with respect to his finding about leisure time." Hamilton thought that there were no major changes in work or leisure between 1973 and 1985 and certainly no significant increase in work.[56]

In addition to debates about the trend in leisure time, other observers, such as Jeremy Rifkin, author of *The End of Work*, worried that leisure time and opportunities were not evenly spread among the population: "A fair and equitable distribution of the productivity gains would require a shortening of the workweek around the world and a concerted effort by central governments to provide alternative employment in the third sector—the social economy—for those whose labor is no longer required in the marketplace."[57] In Rifkin's thinking, the third sector reflecting the "social economy" is important. He notes that French social scientists derived the idea of "social economy" during the 1980s to make explicit the difference between the third sector and the market-exchange economy. French economist Thierry Jeantet says, "the social economy is best understood in terms of results that add considerably to what traditional economics does not know how to or want to measure."[58]

Rifkin described how many workers in the past earned just enough for subsistence and a few amenities; the workers' reticence to increase their hours of work vexed many business owners. The capitalist-owners wanted workers to provide more labor and to buy more of their products. Some owners tried a different approach. W. K. Kellogg, of cereal manufacturing fame, organized his plants so that workers had a six-hour instead of an eight-hour shift while taking home the same amount of wages. By doing so, Kellogg spread the work among more workers, while enjoying greater productivity from his workers.[59]

Spreading available work across more workers was one of Rifkin's main policy suggestions, but he also urged that a value-added tax be placed on entertainment and recreation industries and a tax deduction for each hour of volunteer time. The tax deduction would create a "shadow wage:" an implicit wage per hour of volunteer time.[60] For instance, someone making $20 per hour, who is in the 35 percent federal tax bracket, would see a reduction in her income tax of $7 for each hour spent volunteering.

## Recent Findings on Trends in Leisure Hours

More recent researchers have provided greater detail in parsing uses of time. They separated time devoted to market labor, household production, commuting, and child care, and sleep to examine changes in leisure time. Economists Mark Aguiar and Erik Hurst examined leisure hours for Americans between the ages of 21 and 65, who were neither students nor retirees. They defined "core market work" as including time spent on jobs and overtime, including time spent on work at home. They defined "total work" as including core work plus time commuting to work and other work-related ancillary activities.[61]

The two economists found that average hours of core market work remained constant for non-retired, working-age adults between 1965 and 2003. The constant average was the result of men working fewer hours, while women worked more hours. With regard to total work hours (market and non-market), though, both men and women enjoyed a decrease of roughly eight hours between 1965 and 2003.[62]

Aguiar and Hurst also divided hours spent on household production. "Core nonmarket work" included meal preparation and cleanup, doing laundry, and other chores. Another category was time spent "obtaining goods and services." The third major category, hours devoted to child care, revealed an ambiguity. Many parents reported that certain aspects of child care, including playing with or reading to children, as highly pleasurable (presumably changing diapers would not rank so highly). Adults generally preferred many child care activities to "core nonmarket work."[63]

Aguair and Hurst examined trends under four different definitions of leisure. Under these definitions, both men and women enjoyed more leisure across the time period examined. "Interestingly, the decline in total work hours (the sum of total market work and total nonmarket work) was nearly identical for both men and women." They estimated that this decline was 8.3 hours per week for men versus 7.9 hours per week for women. Men achieved their savings in total work by cutting back on market work (although partially offset by increased non-market work), while women incurred more market work hours and fewer hours spent in home production.[64] Men and women had increasing amounts of leisure time between 1965 and 1993; between 1993 and 2003, women's hours declined. Aguiar and Hurst attributed this to increased time spent in child care. Since child care was considered one of the more enjoyable activities, the researchers placed no judgment on whether this trend was preferable or not.[65]

One major change was that less educated men and women enjoyed "much greater increases in leisure compared to their more educated counter-parts." Indeed, college-educated men had very little increase in leisure hours.[66]

Another recent study painted a less optimistic portrait of the state of leisure in America across the twentieth century. Valerie Ramey and Neville Francis examined hours worked per member of the working age population (a per capita measure). They found that while "hours per member of the working-age population [ages 14 and up] have declined by between five and six hours per week," this decline was concentrated in the 14–24 and 55+ age brackets. They found that the decrease for the younger group was offset by longer hours in school. With respect to hours spent in home production, they estimated that women reduced their weekly hours spent in this endeavor, but that men increased their hours in household production by a similar amount.[67] For adults of ages 25–54, "leisure for this group is about the same now as it was in the early 1900s." What increase there was in lifetime leisure hours was due to increased longevity; this increase, though, was dramatic: almost 50 percent. Across their lifetimes, a person born in 2000 was likely to have an average of four more hours of leisure per week than a person born in 1890.[68]

Aguiar and Hurst attributed some of the differences between the studies to fact that Ramey and Francis were examining allocation of time per capita; given the changing proportion of children in the population, Ramey and Francis's estimates would be more pessimistic with respect to gains in leisure. Ramey and Francis suggest that differences in the two sets of researchers' findings may revolve around classifying child care, using a different data source, and counting meals at work as "work."[69]

## Vacation and Holiday Policies

Employers and employees negotiated different paths to shorter hours. The initial impetus was for shorter and fewer work days, with the growing rigidity of an eight-hour workday, but employers and employees began to investigate the benefits of paid vacations.[70] John Owen suggests that reducing hours toward eight hours per day generally raised productivity, as workers remained fresh. Further reductions from eight hours, though, often had minimal effects in raising productivity; by introducing paid vacations and holidays, employers and employees might tap into another method for raising productivity. Owen admits that demonstrating whether any such positive effect exists, or determining its magnitude, was difficult.[71]

Vacations contributed to the increase in leisure time. A hundred years ago, most American workers received no vacation time and had no expectation of receiving such. Some business owners and managers began to experiment with paid vacations. They hoped to rejuvenate their labor force (both physically and mentally), improve morale, reward loyal and continuous service, and reduce turnover. Some companies hoped to foster goodwill not only with their workers but in their larger communities via their "enlightened policies." White-collar workers often got paid vacations well before the laborers. Some employers experimented with rewarding continuous employment with vacation time or with more vacation time. Not all employers were convinced of vacation time's value; they worried about worker dissipation and demoralization. Some employers noted that workers on vacations sometimes sought temporary jobs, so there would be little rejuvenation occurring. According to a *New York Times* article, some employers penalized workers for tardiness and absences by reducing or withholding their paid vacation. Throughout the 1920s, the debate occupied newspapers, scholarly journals, and trade periodicals.[72]

Owners of manufacturing plants grappled with how to implement vacations. Having a few workers absent could create problems on assembly lines. One solution was to shut down the entire plant. Many factories had regular shut-down periods, whether due to routine maintenance, slack times, or to integrate new machinery, whereby all production workers were temporarily laid off (without pay). For them, instituting a paid vacation plan that coincided with their shut-down periods made more sense than allowing workers discretion in choosing their time off.[73]

Would a vacation prove restorative, or would workers fall prey to idleness and dissipation? For the upper class, extended vacations elicited both envy and condemnation. Before the Civil War, wealthy Southerners presented a specter of idle wealth; many Northerners were critical and contemptuous of these slave aristocrats, fearing that they "threatened the republic, while a population of hardworking, useful men ensured its success."[74] Southerners recognized the value of hard work, even though the wealthier ones left the really onerous work to their slaves, but they felt that Northerners were too preoccupied with work and too acquisitive. Some Southerners engaged in the conceit that they used their free time to pursue higher callings.[75]

The resort experience began to be affordable by middle-class Americans in the second half of the 1800s. Railroads offered cheap, reliable transportation to resorts, many of which the railroad owners themselves built. Railroads contributed to the expansion and the democratization of vacationing.[76]

The trick was inducing middle-class Americans to venture to the resorts; many of these white-collar workers were somewhat hesitant to engage in idleness that spanned several days. In some cases, professional associations and organizations provided a boost for resorts by scheduling meetings. Religious groups saw an opportunity to assuage the ambivalence regarding idleness by

opening camps. The religious camps had stringent rules and regulations and offered healthy, wholesome activities. Unions opened up Unity Houses, where
their members could hear lectures and gain knowledge of interest to their work
situation. Union leaders may also have hoped to exert control over their members' leisure time. Eventually, as more Americans acquired vacation time and
had rising incomes, resorts became less of a haven for the well-to-do. When
African-Americans, immigrants, and blue-collar workers finally began participating in vacations, the institution truly became a mass phenomenon.[77]

One way to assuage whatever guilty feelings people had about vacation or other
spare time was to fill that time with uplifting and self-improving activities. With
regard to tourism, many Americans sought to fill their tours with perpetual motion,
seeing as many historical and natural sites as possible. According to sociologist
Dean MacCannell, tours sought to "create the impression in the sightseer of having
firsthand experience with society's serious side," which he dubbed "alienated leisure . . . a perversion of the aim of leisure: they are a return to the workplace."[78]

Historian Cindy Aron characterizes such tours as "an attempt to make vacationing less frivolous, to relate leisure to work."[79] The popularity of World Fairs in America demonstrates Aron's point. The Chicago World Fair was a showcase not only for
America but for white, middle- and upper-class Americans, a chance to demonstrate what they had built and to celebrate American institutions, all in one location.
The fair, though, also provided some low-brow culture and entertainment.[80]

Organized labor was lukewarm about pursuing vacation time. Most unions
wanted a shorter workweek, not only for the salubrious effects on workers but to
ameliorate the unemployment problem. The fact that unions were in industries
plagued by seasonal and cyclical unemployment may have accounted for the
unions' indifference toward vacations.[81]

By the end of the twentieth century, paid vacations and sick leave were the norm
for full-time American workers (Table 4.1). Some commentators, though, bemoaned American vacation and sick leave policies in comparison with those of
Europe. They lauded Europeans for their generous vacation and sick leave policies.

De Grazia observes that under both Protestantism and the secular French
Revolution, the frequency of holidays to observe saints fell off markedly.[82] The
observance of new holidays, such as Thanksgiving, Memorial Day, Veteran's Day,
and Martin Luther King Day, became widespread, but American workers may
not have as many holidays as workers did in previous eras.

## The Gains in Leisure Hours

American workers enjoyed a much shorter workweek by the 1930s compared
with 1900, although the trend toward shorter workweeks slowed thereafter.

On the other hand, workers started receiving at least a week of paid vacation and a few more holidays.[83] They also began receiving paid sick leave. Workers tended to enter the workforce later and to leave it earlier, reducing the lifetime number of hours worked. Trends in commuting time, household production, and child care still left more hours available for leisure by century's end.

What did Americans do with their increased leisure time? Did they achieve the Aristotelian ideal of spending time in contemplation? Did they indulge in higher callings? Did they fulfill the fears of many social commentators by engaging in dissipation? We turn to the ways Americans spent their time and money on leisure activities.

# 5

# The Rise of Expenditures on Leisure Goods and Services

By the end of the twentieth century, leisure activities had permeated all levels of American society. Workers had more time available for leisure activities. Rising incomes afforded Americans more discretionary income. On what did they spend their increased discretionary incomes? Although many wonderful leisure activities entailed only a time cost and no out-of-pocket expenditures, Americans were willing to spend money to augment time spent in leisure activities. Entrepreneurs offered more attractive goods and services with which to fill leisure time; these goods and services may have increased the demand for leisure time. Aside, perhaps, from luxury yachts and private performances for the wealthy, by 1960 Americans with average and even below-average incomes enjoyed an array of leisure choices that in variety and quality rivaled most of what the Rockfellers and Vanderbilts of 1900 enjoyed. Indeed, wealthy Americans often pioneered the use of new leisure goods and services, usually paying high prices for a relatively low-quality product. As producers responded to the demand for a new good or service, they often became more efficient and created innovations to the good or service. Eventually they produced cheaper, higher-quality goods and services for the masses.

Attitudes toward consumption evolved. Protestant thinkers urged people to work and to save. The combination of long hours and savings often resulted in wealth. The next question was what to do with the wealth. Protestant leaders believed that owning copious amounts of goods could distract people from their calling and their work. Luxury goods and idleness were temptations that all too few people could resist.[1] Since Protestants understood the bromide "you can't take it with you," they urged their fellows to view themselves as stewards of what-ever worldly wealth came their way, who would be held accountable for what they did with the wealth entrusted them, making it "at least hazardous to spend any of it for a purpose which does not serve the glory of God but only one's own enjoyment."[2]

# Rising Levels of Income and Leisure Spending

We've seen that by the late 1920s, most Americans had more leisure time than in 1900. A key question arose: Were leisure time and leisure commodities complements (used together) or substitutes (used in lieu of one another)? If recreational goods were used together with leisure time, then decreased inequality in leisure expenditures would imply that the inequality in leisure time diminished, too. Some recreational goods and services, though, may have been used to compensate for a lack of leisure time. A trip to the nickelodeon provided quick amusement for workers hard-pressed for any time to relax. In later years, technologies such as portable radios, Walkmans, and iPods could enable people with limited leisure time to gain some amusement or relaxation while engaged in work-related tasks.[3]

Economist Dora Costa tracked spending on leisure and recreational goods and services. She concluded that as people's incomes rose to high enough levels, their spending on leisure consumption continued to increase, albeit at a slower rate. The net result was that spending on recreation rose as a percent of consumption from 1888 to 1991.[4]

She cautions that the government figures on recreational expenditures include reading for non-entertainment purposes but do not include amounts spent on vacations and travel, alcohol, tobacco, and restaurant meals. The definition of leisure spending, then, affects the income elasticities (whether the proportional change in leisure spending matched, exceeded, or was smaller than a proportional change in income), but the general pattern seems to hold. She concludes that "income no longer limits recreational activities as sharply as it did in the past. By lowering the price of entertainment, technological change has made recreation affordable to all and has improved the standard of living of those in the lower deciles of the income distribution. The increase in public recreational facilities has had the same effect. . . . Leisure is now less of a luxury."[5]

Why did the income elasticity of demand for recreational goods fall during the twentieth century? Rising incomes may be an explanation. For a consumer at subsistence level, spending $10 per movie might be a luxury in the sense that as the consumer's income rises by, say, 5 percent, the consumer might increase his or her spending on attending movies by more than 5 percent. As the consumer's income rises significantly, he or she may continue to attend more movies, but the rate of increase may fall. At high enough levels of income, a consumer might start cutting back on movie attendance and start attending live theater. Finally, if the income elasticities of demand for recreation fell sharply for poorer Americans, it could indicate rising relative living standards for the poor compared with richer Americans.[6]

## Leisure Activities for the Masses

An article in *Business Week* in 1953 stated, "Leisure has been democratized," before adding, "you used to read a good deal about the leisure class, but something seems to have happened to it. One thing . . . is that too many people joined it and the point went out of it." The author estimated that "as much as 15% of total consumer expenditures is spent for leisure." With the two-day weekend, workers could travel more easily to leisure and recreation sites, as well as indulge in group amusements. Restaurants began selling take-out meals, while retailers stayed open for evening hours as consumers eschewed Saturday shopping. The article concluded, "If we were willing to accept the standard of living of 1870, most of us could presumably get by with a five-hour week."[7] Of course, few Americans would have been content with 1870 standard of living.

Consumption of recreational goods and services tell a similar story of improving living standards. As a proportion of consumption expenditures, "recreation" expenditures jumped from 3 to 9.4 percent between 1909 and 2000 (Table 5.1); this proportion, though, paled against the rise in medical expenditures. There were spurts in the proportion between 1909 and 1929 and between 1969 and 2000.[8]

The "personal consumption expenditures, by type of product" data reflect the changing nature of recreation. For most of the twentieth century, the sub-categories for "recreation" included "radio and television sets, records, and musical instruments," "toys and sport supplies, nondurable," "wheel goods, durable toys, sport equipment," and "books, maps, magazines, newspapers, sheet music." The current categories include "video and audio equipment," "information processing equipment," "services related to video and audio goods and computers," and "pets, pet products, and related services." In addition to the new recreational products and services, existing recreational products and services have improved. Incorporating improvements in the quality of products and services into expenditure data or indexes is a difficult process. One ramification of the failure to incorporate the improvements in motion pictures was that the admissions charge part of an estimated recreation price index was biased upward.[9]

The government figures for spending on recreation do not encompass all leisure spending. If one considers consumption of alcohol and tobacco as leisure spending, then the overall proportion spent on leisure pursuits may have been stagnant across the twentieth century. Decreases in spending on alcohol and tobacco almost exactly offset the percentage of increase in spending on recreation. Americans curtailed their imbibing of alcoholic beverages until 1940—due to Prohibition and to the effects of the Great Depression—before a resurgence over the second half of the century, except for wine (Table 5.2). They also, however, slaked their thirst by buying more non-alcoholic beverages.

*Table 5.1* **Components of Total Consumption Expenditures, 1909–2008 (in Percent)[a]**

| Year | Basics | Alcohol | Tobacco | Recreation | Medical |
|------|--------|---------|---------|------------|---------|
| 1909 | 57.8 | 6.2 | 2.2 | 3.0 | 2.7 |
| 1919 | 57.8 | 3.3 | 2.4 | 3.6 | 3.3 |
| 1925 | 54.1 | 2.4 | 2.1 | 4.0 | 3.4 |
| 1929 | 50.7 | 2.5 | 2.1 | 4.7 | 3.6 |
| 1933 | 52.9 | 1.5 | 2.7 | 4.8 | 4.3 |
| 1939 | 49.8 | 5.1 | 2.6 | 5.2 | 4.3 |
| 1944 | 54.9 | 6.3 | 2.4 | 5.0 | 4.3 |
| 1946 | 52.2 | 5.8 | 2.3 | 6.0 | 4.3 |
| 1949 | 49.4 | 4.4 | 2.3 | 5.7 | 4.6 |
| 1954 | 48.6 | 3.8 | 2.1 | 5.5 | 5.1 |
| 1959 | 46.3 | 3.3 | 2.1 | 5.6 | 5.8 |
| 1964 | 44.9 | 3.1 | 2.0 | 6.1 | 6.4 |
| 1969 | 42.8 | 2.8 | 1.7 | 6.4 | 7.4 |
| 2000 | 25.9 | 1.1 | 1.0 | 9.4 | 16.2 |
| 2008 | 25.4 | 1.1 | 0.8 | 9.2 | 18.5 |

Basics: Food, including non-alcoholic beverages; clothing; housing (rent and imputed rent). Does not include household operation.

[a] US Department of Commerce, *Historical Statistics of the United States, Part 1*, 316–320; US Department of Commerce, *Statistical Abstract of the United States: 2011*, 442.

The US government tracks spending on recreation by consumers only. These figures underestimate the true spending on leisure.[10] Various government agencies at national, state, and lower levels spend sums on parks and other recreation endeavors. Spending on other commodities and services, too, may be indirect spending on leisure. Americans use their automobiles not only to commute to work but also for leisure purposes, whether taking a trip or driving to the local bowling alley. Undoubtedly, a significant proportion of consumer expenditures on automobiles and personal trucks, including the vehicles themselves, maintenance, and gasoline, are for leisure purposes. Dining in restaurants provides another example: How much of such dining is for leisure purposes versus simple bodily maintenance?

The government does track visits to National Parks and other publicly provided recreational sites. Table 5.3 shows the dramatic increase in visits to various national sites.

*Table 5.2*  **US Alcohol Consumption (Gallons per Capita), 1900–2000[a]**

| Year | Type of Alcohol | | |
|------|--------|-------|------|
|      | *Spirits* | *Beer* | *Wine* |
| 1900 | 1.27 | 16.01 | 0.40 |
| 1911 | 1.46 | 20.69 | 0.67 |
| 1917 | 1.62 | 18.17 | 0.41 |
| 1920 | 0.22 | 2.61 | 0.12 |
| 1930 | 0.08 | n.a. | 0.03 |
| 1935 | 0.70 | 10.45 | 0.30 |
| 1940 | 1.02 | 12.58 | 0.66 |
| 1945 | 1.22 | 18.86 | 0.73 |
| 1950 | 1.02 | 17.41 | 0.93 |
| 1980 | 2.0 | 24.3 | 2.1 |
| 1990 | 1.5 | 23.9 | 2.0 |
| 2000 | 1.3 | 21.7 | 2.0 |

n.a.: not available.

[a] US Treasury Department, Bureau of Statistics, *Statistical Abstract, 1900*, 340; US Treasury Department, *Statistical Abstract, 1901*, 775; US Department of Commerce, *Statistical Abstract*, 2002, 130.

Although Table 5.4 does not differentiate between driving to leisure sites versus driving to work or for errands, the tripling in miles driven lends indirect support to the contention that Americans incurred increased transportation expenses in traveling to tourist attractions (and we haven't even mentioned bus, train, and airplane travel for leisure purposes). Americans also spent time and money on participatory athletic activities, as witnessed by the postwar increases in the number of bowlers, golf courses, and swimming pools, to name just a few (Table 5.5).

In his estimation of spending on leisure and recreation during the 1930s, Jesse Steiner identified some gray areas. Should candy, chewing gum, tobacco, liquor, prostitution, and gambling be included in accounting for expenditures on recreation and leisure? How much of the total expenditures on automobiles should be considered leisure and recreational? With these caveats in mind, he estimated the annual cost of recreation as $10 billion per year just before the Great Depression. Almost two-thirds of the estimated expenditure was due to vacation travel and the use of automobiles and motor boats for pleasure. He noted that commercial amusement lagged far behind expenditures for travel. Steiner compared his estimate with that of Stuart Chase. Chase included candy, chewing gum, non-alcoholic beverages, food consumed at banquets and entertainments, tobacco, liquor, prostitution,

*Table 5.3* **Visits to National Parks and Other National Sites, 1904–2008 (in Thousands)[a]**

| Year | Visits All Sites | Visits National Parks |
|------|------------------|-----------------------|
| 1904 | 121 | 121 |
| 1920 | 1,058 | 920 |
| 1929 | 3,248 | 2,757 |
| 1933 | 3,482 | 2,867 |
| 1939 | 15,531 | 6,854 |
| 1944 | 8,340 | 2,646 |
| 1946 | 21,752 | 8,991 |
| 1949 | 31,736 | 12,968 |
| 1954 | 54,210 | 17,969 |
| 1959 | 68,901 | 22,392 |
| 1964 | 111,386 | 34,047 |
| 1969 | 163,990 | 42,519 |
| 1990 | 258,700 | 57,700 |
| 2000 | 285,900 | 66,100 |
| 2008 | 274,900 | 61,200 |

All Sites: National parks, national monuments, national historical and military areas, and national parkways (1904–1969); includes other national sites (1990–2008).

[a] US Department of Commerce. *Historical Statistics of the United States, Part 1*, 396 (1904–1969); *Statistical Abstract of the United States: 2011*, 771.

and gambling in his estimate of $21 billion; Steiner related that adjusting Chase's estimate to match his definition left $11.8 billion.[11]

While it would be too much to claim that all roads lead to leisure, the expenditures on leisure were intimately tied to new technologies, with electricity, the automobile, television, and the Internet being some of the more dramatic examples, as will be examined.

## An Overview of Expenditures on Leisure

As a family's income rose, its purchases of basic commodities usually decelerated. A Department of Commerce survey for 1929–1940 showed that home appliances, cars, jewelry, and recreation spending were more sensitive to changes in income than other items in the family budget.[12]

*Table 5.4* **Motor-Vehicle Factory Sales and Miles of Travel, 1904–1969[a]**

| Year | Passenger Cars | | Passenger Vehicles |
|------|----------------|-------------|--------------------|
|      | Factory Sales  | Urban Miles | Rural Miles        |
| 1904 | 22.1    | n/a     | n/a     |
| 1920 | 1,905.5 | n/a     | n/a     |
| 1929 | 4,455.1 | n/a     | n/a     |
| 1933 | 1,560.5 | n/a     | n/a     |
| 1939 | 2,888.5 | 122,805 | 115,378 |
| 1944 | 0.6     | 93,679  | 77,264  |
| 1946 | 2,148.6 | 148,497 | 136,153 |
| 1949 | 5,119.4 | 175,686 | 171,044 |
| 1954 | 5,558.8 | 210,671 | 246,733 |
| 1959 | 5,591.2 | 279,931 | 297,393 |
| 1964 | 7,751.8 | 342,755 | 339,474 |
| 1969 | 8,223.7 | 468,275 | 395,620 |

*Note:* Factory sales in thousands; miles in million vehicle-miles.

[a] US Department of Commerce, *Historical Statistics of the United States, Part 2*, 716 (1904–69). *Statistical Abstract of the United States: 2011* does not appear to have similar data.

A study done by the University of Pennsylvania's Wharton School of Business indicated a different pattern: "as family income goes up the proportion of recreational spending does not go up. . . . Further, expenditures for TV, radio, and musical instruments, among the largest items within recreational spending, are also highly sensitive [to changes in income]." There were large differences, though, across regions. Poor families in the suburban West tended to spend the largest proportion of their income, 9 percent, on recreation, while families in small Southern cities spent only 2 percent. This finding may be reflective of the differences in the availability of commercial entertainment in the semi-rural South and the urban West. These expenditure studies, however, did not account for travel and vacation.[13]

Max Kaplan noted the paradox of the wealthy American businessman, who must "learn to play when he retires." He points out that Veblen's greatest difficulty was that he wrote when the class divisions in America were becoming fuzzier.[14] Mirroring Veblen, Kaplan points out that *conspicuous consumption* is motivated by the esteem of having something the have-nots do not, and that the poor try to emulate the rich. "Here, perhaps, is the core of Veblen's sharp irony, for, unlike Marx, he offers no solution."[15]

*Table 5.5* **Number of Bowlers, Golf Courses, and Swimming Pools, 1904–1970[a]**

| Year | Number of Bowlers | Number of Golf Courses | Number of Swimming Pools |
|------|-------------------|------------------------|--------------------------|
| 1904 | 2 | n/a | n/a |
| 1920 | 27 | n/a | 359 |
| 1929 | 147 | 299 | 1,010 |
| 1933 | 148 | 370 | 1,148 |
| 1939 | 535 | 358 | 1,181 |
| 1944 | 910 | 409 | 1,447 |
| 1946 | 1,060 | 340 | 1,449 |
| 1950 | 1,937 | 454 | 1,616 |
| 1955 | 2,514 | 478 | 2,233 |
| 1960 | 5,374 | 585 | 2,846 |
| 1965 | 7,617 | 1,005 | 4,745 |
| 1970 | 7,623 | 518 | 2,555 |

*Note*: Number of bowlers in thousands.

Series H 849–861 shows municipal and county park and recreation areas. Most of the facilities declined in 1970 from peaks in 1969. No explanation given.

[a] US Department of Commerce, *Historical Statistics of the United States, Part 1*, 398–400; US Department of Commerce, *Statistical Abstract: 2008*, 753.

Kaplan stood Veblen's conspicuous consumption on its head: "Veblen's major thesis falls on the simple fact that this country has grown so wealthy, and that the wealth is less marked in the accumulation of money with which to buy things than in the accumulation of things that conceal monetary inequality. . . . This provides everyone with the opportunity of buying against his own tomorrow, and, as often as not, not tomorrow as it will be but as it *should be* or as it is *hoped that it will be*." Another source of the blurring of economic class in America was the mass media, which by definition depended on a large audience and on the creation of widely known stars.[16]

The number of hours required to earn a subsistence standard of living fell rapidly across the twentieth century. Americans could have chosen to sharply reduce their hours worked below the levels of the 1930s, but they did not. They chose ever increasing amounts of consumption and, after the 1930s, a modest reduction in hours worked per week. There have been many critics of Americans' decision to increase consumption in lieu of greater amounts of leisure time. The critics usually disliked expenditures on mass consumption, but they often downplayed the growing variety and improved quality of available goods.[17]

Critics distrusted American consumers' ability to choose wisely. "Consumer republicans [a form of ideal Jeffersonian independence] argued that the marketplace undermined that independence by keeping them ignorant of goods. Consumerists argued that people lacked technical knowledge or necessary experience in the wide variety of goods required in 'getting and spending' a living, at nearly any income level."[18] Robert S. Lynd wrote, "the vast majority of American consumers were 'illiterate,' lacking in basic knowledge about goods and unable to assess their qualities."[19]

Commerce and religion combined to create an American style of consumption, according to Jackson Lears. American Puritanism could not stem the trend toward earthly pleasures rather than heavenly pleasures. "Religion and commerce combined to redefine abundance in psychic rather than physical terms." He continues by describing how some consumers purchased the most fashionable goods they could, even if it meant scrimping on basic commodities, such as food and shelter.[20]

Americans spent their money on a wide range of alternative leisure outlets. By 1957, Americans spent far more money on music than on all spectator sports, and that they did not eschew classical music, such as Beethoven's Ninth Symphony.[21] Americans liked to vacation abroad; in 1956, Americans spent more on travel abroad than for coffee or for petroleum, the country's leading imports. Although many observers disdained Americans' choices of leisure, it is important to recognize that "these activities include a broad range of mental or emotional activity, from complete boredom, disinterest, and insensibility to complete and exciting creativity, inner struggle, and participation in the affairs of the world."[22]

Lears did acknowledge the prevalence of television watching, citing Nielsen research that revealed Americans watched television for more hours than they engaged in productive economic activities. Television was the leisure colossus, and John Houseman's observation that television was more than just the latest gadget—it synthesized radio, the printing press, and the motion pictures, with greater convenience—was astute. Americans were buying more books, but the rate of increase paled beside that of television; at least they were also attending evening classes in large numbers.[23]

## Early Consumer Expenditure Surveys

During the postbellum years, Americans noted the urbanization and industrialization taking place. A large working class developed in the cities, as immigrants poured into the country and rural Americans moved to urban areas. Many business, political, and social leaders wondered how the urban working class was faring, and states led the way in conducting consumer surveys. These surveys provide much of what we know quantitatively about consumer expenditures.

Daniel Horowitz's *The Morality of Spending* provides a fascinating look at consumer expenditure surveys, with respect to both the surveyors and the surveyed. Surveys of consumer expenditures were subject to bias. He referred to Daniel Bell's observation that by mid-century, Americans were less concerned about work and achievement and more concerned about obtaining hedonistic pleasure.[24]

Horowitz began by examining how surveyors involved in the early consumption expenditure research both quantified and criticized their subjects' expenditure patterns. One common belief was that the working class demonstrated a lack of self-control, as witnessed by alcohol consumption and other cultural behavior at odds with the prevailing Protestant beliefs. The surveyors generally belonged to a group believing in the virtues of "hard work, plain living, and the belief in the uplifting power of Culture." He granted that the conservative moralism gradually revised its attitudes toward workers and immigrants, but that they maintained an attitude of superiority toward these groups. As the twentieth century and mass commercialized consumption became pervasive, a new set of moralists, again typically white Protestants, began to laud immigrants' folk traditions because such traditions might have helped resist the tide of commercialized consumption. Old-line conservatives and new moralists differed, but both groups deplored the rise of mass culture and the attendant perceived lack of self-control that were turning the nation toward materialism. Both groups "believed that pleasures purchased in the marketplace were compensation for personal and cultural failures."[25]

The survey personnel gradually lessened their criticism of workers' expenditure choices, although such judgments still recurred. The surveyors misunderstood and mistrusted the communal and expressive aspects of the workers' lives, especially in conjunction with saloons, amusement parks, and movies. "The middle-class authors hoped that immigrants and workers would turn to 'higher' things as their incomes increased."[26]

The government, too, weighed in on what were necessary and what were unnecessary expenditures. Congress enacted excise taxes, especially during the World Wars. The government placed excise taxes on many luxuries, both to fill the Treasury and to curb extravagance and useless expenditures. The popularity of the motion picture industry made it a prime candidate, and a 10 percent tax was levied. Admissions to baseball games were similarly taxed. For card-playing Americans, the tax went from two cents to seven cents per deck of cards. Other providers of entertainment and recreation faced higher taxes under the title "Special Taxes."[27] The legislators taxed liquor and tobacco. Horowitz described the legislators' choices of luxury commodities and services to tax as a "curious mélange," ranging from liquor to street fairs, from museums to yachts.[28]

The perception that the workers were spendthrifts was not supported by consumer expenditure surveys. An 1875 survey revealed little evidence of working-class extravagance in spending. The conservative, defensive patterns of spending by the working class indicated that workers had not become fully integrated into mass consumption. Even those families well into the middle-class range of $2,500 or more cautiously spent money for excursions, vacations, vehicles, and domestic servants.[29]

Some surveyors criticized their subjects for *excessive savings*, driven by a fear of poverty in old age. Martha Bruere chided the middle-class educators, whose budgets she studied. Did she chide them for riotous living? Borrowing for cars and appliances? No, she chided them for what she deemed their excessive savings (roughly 12 percent of income) and unwillingness to bear children, thereby having "stolen from the community the children [they] might have had."[30]

As late as the Progressive era, surveyors remained dubious about workers' leisure that involved expressive and communal activities, although they were "somewhat equivocal about giving full recognition to forms of recreation—pageants, plays, celebrations—where no money changed hands." Horowitz cites the surveyors' attitudes to their insensitivity toward the workers' cultures. The surveyors associated the attractiveness of the saloons, dance halls, and other commercialized leisure venues with overwork in tedious jobs. These commercial venues, of course, diverted workers from more wholesome and beneficial forms of leisure.[31]

Although many of the surveyors were censorious regarding working-class and immigrant workers' expenditure patterns, some were sympathetic to their subjects. Robert Chapin and Margaret F. Byington recognized that immigrants' choices of leisure reflected their cultural background and were not just forms of dissipation.[32] Louise M. Bosworth conceded that young single women spent some of their earnings on clothing, but they did so "in order to be able to obtain and keep a good job." While expressing some criticism of the women's expenditures, Bosworth came to believe that the women "were neither selfish nor extravagant. By giving money to her family after she had spent 'a reasonable amount' on herself, she devoted 'a much larger sum to the welfare of others.'"[33]

Economist Simon Patten sympathized with immigrants' patterns of leisure, but he wanted to sustain Puritanical beliefs while undergirding them with scientific backing—in other words, a "reconciliation of the Protestant ethic with an economic growth based on increasing consumer demands." He hoped economic prosperity would induce people to spend their money on education, culture, and philanthropy, once their basic needs were met.[34]

## Leisure Expenditures after World War I

After World War I, American families began loosening up their expenditures. Surveys indicated that half of the families took a vacation; perhaps more worrisome for conservatives, the typical American family contributed a paltry amount of its expenditures to church and to charity, although this amount was not too different than in the past. Movies dominated recreation expenditures, with even poorer households devoting the bulk of their recreation spending on the medium. Just one family in five owned an automobile, but Jessica B. Peixotto, a researcher studying family budgets of typographers, observed that some families rationalized buying an automobile by scrimping on diet and housing, and by making small economies throughout their budgets, including other forms of amusements.[35]

Attitudes toward spending were changing from the traditional Puritan stress on abstinence and living within one's means to a new gospel that consumption spending kept the economy humming and was becoming a duty of citizenship. According to Robert Lynd, Americans disavowed the old custom of balancing one's budget to fit one's income to a new custom of raising one's income to match one's expenditures.[36] He identified a psychological basis for the emphasis on consumption, citing the selling of commodities to substitute for real solutions for insecurity and the tensions of living in modern society. Merchandisers were alert to provide panaceas. With easier transportation and communication, he conceded that the "factor of geographical isolation and the accidental effects of the size of the city in which one lives" were receding.[37]

There was a significant increase in spending on leisure goods and services by the 1920s, but the Great Depression slowed this trend. The Depression, however, did not completely reverse consumer expenditures on recreation.

The Great Depression revealed that Americans loved their leisure. Leisure spending continued to increase during the decade, spurred partly by declining food prices that freed up more of (declining) budgets for spending on non-essential items. Currell repeated contemporary sociologists' fears that "the Depression was potentially an uncontrolled spending bonanza."[38]

Robert Lynd surveyed consumption expenditures for the President's Research Committee on Social Trends in 1933. He highlighted the commodities that were formerly limited to the wealthy—radio and travel—"as a result, the past decade has witnessed increasingly the manufacture of luxury and quality goods in any necessary adulteration to reach low incomes."[39] Americans used installment buying more than ever, with automobiles, furniture, radios, and electrical household goods heading the list of items purchased on credit. He noted that installment credit and small loan credits encouraged consumers to purchase relatively expensive items or to fritter away money on several smaller items. Another trend was a change in perspective regarding children, who now were seen in terms of economic outlays rather than potential economic assets (as labor).[40] The resulting change in perspective meant that, in the face of rising standards of living, the distribution of family income was shifted toward all of the members of the family, rather than being concentrated on the parents, typically the father.[41]

Among the more traditional forms of leisure, reading remained popular with Americans. By the 1930s, advances in printing photos had led to the publication of *Life* and other photo magazines. *Life* proved remarkably popular upon its introduction. Adults also read pulp fiction magazines. *Literary Digest* stated that there were more than 200 of them selling 8 million copies a month. These magazines cost a dime or fifteen cents. Publishers of pulps were quick to respond to public acceptance or rejection of titles.[42]

Magazines distributed through grocery chains and supermarkets were one source of competition for the major magazine distributors.[43] These food-store magazines were useful for consumers, store owners, advertisers, and magazine publishers. The magazine publishers found a cheap distributing network for its magazines. The advertisers liked the cheap distribution and the targeted audience—housewives doing grocery shopping. Stores appreciated the goodwill the magazines brought. The customers got a bargain-priced magazine aimed at them.[44]

Americans also enjoyed outdoor activities. Steiner cited the popularity of hunting, fishing, and camping, although he made an erroneous prediction that hunting and fishing would disappear as popular sports and would be limited to exclusive clubs able to purchase rights to forests, lakes, and rivers, unless conservation were enacted.[45]

With the prosperity of the 1920s, Americans purchased large numbers of motorboats, although the numbers of sailboats, rowboats, and canoes declined. Steiner observed that the motorboat phenomenon was another example of the trend toward recreations involving significant expenditures. He indicated that the boom in new boats outstripped the number of docking and mooring accommodations. At the upper end, yachting clubs sprang up throughout the country. Golf spread to the middle class, as golf courses multiplied eightfold between 1916 and 1930. Expenditures on golf equipment comprised over a third of the total value of sporting and athletic goods manufactured in 1929. Golf's popularity occurred despite the necessary outlays for equipment and greens fees: "no other single sport approaches golf in the amount of money annually invested in equipment."[46] Helping to boost and sustain Americans' enjoyment of outdoor activities, the daylight savings movement provided an extra hour of daylight for urban workers. Apparently the measure was not as popular outside the cities.[47]

Farmers were not participating in the commercialized leisure boom. Although their incomes in terms of commodities were respectable in most cases, their cash incomes were often relatively low, leaving little for recreational expenditures. Farmers devoted an average of 1.4 percent of their "cost of living" to recreation, but Steiner hoped that as farmers became more integrated into the cash economy this proportion would increase. In addition, farmers suffered from isolation and bad roads.[48]

Another interesting aspect of consumer expenditures during the 1920s and 1930s involved the move into smaller apartments and houses. Lynd cited a study of New York City and the surrounding area showing that the number of rooms fell from 4.19 in 1913 to 3.34 in 1928. The interesting question was whether the move toward electrical appliances reduced the need for space or whether the cost of the appliances (or incomes) forced people to live in smaller spaces. He later mentioned the trend of purchasing canned and prepared foods in relation to the small dwellings and kitchens; he thought these increased the amount of leisure available to women. With incomes shrinking after 1929, many housewives began to switch back to less fully processed forms of food, to which they added their labor—home canning exemplified the trend. Another explanation was that the decline of servants contributed to the trend toward smaller apartments.[49]

During the early years of the Great Depression, a few articles appeared that detailed Americans' spending on leisure and recreation. One study estimated that "America's annual bill for recreation just before the depression set in was, conservatively, $10,165,857,000." The study noted that much of the expenditure reflected "a new popular interest in recreation that has revolutionized the habits of the people and created an unprecedented willingness to spend money freely for sports and amusements."[50] A *Business Week* article observed that in 1929, American spending on leisure was "about as much as it costs to operate the federal government." The article suggested that even the published amount was too low, since the expenditures did not include consumption of alcoholic beverages or domestic travel. It did confirm the dominance of commercialized recreation and of the passive form of most leisure activities.[51]

Julius Weinberger's "Economic Aspects of Recreation" was one of the most cited works covering expenditures on recreation during the Great Depression. He estimated that Americans spent 8.12 percent of national income on leisure-time pursuits. The year 1935 was a moderate year for such expenditures, as expenditures on leisure-time activities were 50 percent higher in 1929 (he did not adjust for the deflation in prices between 1929 and 1935). Automobile touring exhibited stability, while purchases of radio equipment had dropped significantly from 1929 (although this may have been partly because of saturation of the market). He noted that leisure activities requiring frequent, small expenditures (periodicals and motion picture theater admissions) tended to be more stable than purchases of leisure durable goods.[52]

Weinberger divided his estimates of consumer spending into recreation products, recreational services, and vacation travel. Since government spending on recreation was not done by consumers, his estimates did not include them. The first category took about half the expenditures, while the other two categories equally split the remainder.[53]

Spending for leisure products such as books, periodicals, toys, and games received a relative boost during the Great Depression, as consumers shifted from spending on durable recreational goods toward the non-durable goods. Weinberger noted that consumer spending on recreation tended to mirror changes in incomes, although he predicted that spending on recreation would exceed 10 percent of national income during the 1940s.[54]

Weinberger identified two major characteristics of recreational tendencies: Much of the expenditures were for goods and services only recently available—automobiles, motion pictures, and radio broadcasting—and most of the spending was for *passive* recreation. He thought the trend toward passive recreation arose from three sources: the growth of cities that made outdoor activities less convenient, the availability of commercialized recreation, and the increasing proportion of older people.[55]

Looking at the early years of the twentieth century, Weinberger's figures show that total expenditures for recreation products grew "irregularly" until 1929 and then fell off, although they rebounded in 1935. He noted that the economic downturn in 1921 also led to a diminution of these expenditures. His tables did not include all possible types of spending on recreational pursuits, because "of the impossibility of securing even approximate estimates of their annual volume. Chief among these are the materials employed in the pursuit of the many different kinds of hobbies, such as stamp collecting, gardening, knitting and crocheting." With regard to alcoholic beverages, for obvious reasons, he had scant reliable data for the years of prohibition; with prohibition's repeal in 1933, he had some data for 1935.[56]

One form of recreation and leisure stood out: travel for pleasure, primarily by automobile. Americans had traveled considerably in the previous century; however, much of that travel was by railroad. The automobile proved a formidable competitor to travel by rail, which fell by one-third between 1919 and 1935. Although people scrimped to maintain their standard of living during the 1930s, auto touring remained popular: "Americans spent almost as much on gas, oil, and other vacation car operating expenses in 1933 as in 1929, $1,102 million and $1,040 million, respectively." The expenditures on auto travel were greater than any form of amusement and doubled expenditures on motion pictures. Automobile travel was subsumed within vacation travel; vacation travel comprised more than half the total expenditures for recreation since 1931.[57]

George Lundberg and his colleagues found similar patterns of leisure as had Weinberger, but they cited demographic factors, such as the large proportion of children in the population, although the number of children per family declined—by one-third. He believed that the 20 percent of the population who were housewives had enjoyed a reduction in drudgery because of changing technology.[58]

At the beginning of the twentieth century, historians noted that during the Victorian period, there was a shift, "particularly among the middle class, from public to private sphere, community-oriented to home-based leisure."[59] Unlike the Victorian- or Edwardian-era homes, Lundberg's contemporaries chose to spend much of their leisure time outside the family home. When asked where they spent their "best time," only small minorities listed home. In the case of Americans with limited budgets, though, many remained home because they did not feel that their clothes were good enough to be seen in public.[60]

Lundberg's study identified increased commuting times as cutting into leisure time. He advised government subsidization of railroads and other public forms of transportation, but he admitted that the railroads were lukewarm to the subsidization possibility.[61]

## Purchases of Consumer Durables

Concurrent with spending on recreation and amusements, Americans were altering their spending patterns in another manner. Martha Olney studied patterns of consumer purchases of durable goods during the 1920s. She found that households substituted durable goods for savings, although there was a smaller substitution for perishable goods. She designated the 1920s as a period of a "consumer durables revolution," denoting a shift in the demand for consumer durables and not merely a change in relative prices. Although noting that the relative price for durable goods fell in general during the 1920s, the real change was in how consumers saved. Instead of putting money away, they purchased durable goods that provided a stream of services for several years.[62] Automobiles, household appliances, and what she termed "the entertainment complex"—radios, pianos, and other musical instruments—showed growth, while furniture, house furnishings, china, and tableware fell. Purchases of consumer durables shifted from furniture, china and tableware, and jewelry and watches before the twentieth century to automobiles and other durable goods in the 1920s.[63]

Households resorted to credit in purchasing durable goods. Outstanding debt per household tripled between 1900 and 1918 and doubled during the 1920s, but when the debt was deflated by a price index for major durable goods (signifying the amount of durables per dollar of credit), "the amount of goods bought with credit increased enormously."[64] Much of the debt was incurred to purchase automobiles, with five times as much debt outstanding in 1929 as in 1922 for this good. As the prices of automobiles fell during the 1920s, the number of cars purchased on credit was greater than the proportional change in outstanding loans. Edwin Seligman estimated that more than three-quarters of radios, pianos, phonographs, and household appliances were purchased on credit, with furniture having only a slightly lower rate. According to his estimate, only one-quarter of jewelry was purchased with credit. Automobiles, radios, and phonographs, for instance, represented 25 percent of annual disposable income.[65]

Olney is cautious in assessing advertising's role in the consumer durables revolution. She highlights advertising's role in promoting new products—advertisements alerted consumers to the availability, purpose, and desirability of new products. If firms had to rely on publicity and word of mouth, it would have taken longer for the public to have gained knowledge of a product's existence. She concludes, "Businesses certainly did not depend only on advertising but made it just one component of their overall marketing efforts."[66]

One possible explanation for the surge in spending on consumer durables was that the surge allowed for substituting machines for servants. Olney describes how the answer depends upon the relative prices of maids' labor, durable goods, and one's own time. She alludes to another possibility: Did changes in demand lead to more debt-financed purchases of appliances and thereby push married women into the labor force, so the family could more readily meet its new financial obligations?[67] Harry Oshima also noted that because of mass production, "prices of consumer goods, especially durables, purchased by lower-income groups fell substantially more than those purchased by upper-income groups (for example, Ford cars versus Cadillacs)."[68]

Robert and Helen Lynd took a dim view of the growing use of installment credit to purchase new appliances and cars. They viewed installment buying as "a repressive agent tending to standardize widening sectors of the habits of the business class."[69] The Lynds bemoaned "the homogeneous and vacuous lives of the middle class ... [where] consumers were victims who accepted commercial goods and experiences, on the terms on which the economic system and advertisements offered them . . . [but] people rarely derived genuine pleasure from modern kinds of consumption."[70]

Advertisers and their associated social scientists were eager to find ways to manipulate consumers. Walter Dill Scott, a psychologist and author of *Influencing Men in Business*, identified appeals to prestige as effective, "the eagerness with which we attempt to secure merchandise used by the 'swell and swagger' is absurd, but it makes possible for the advertiser to secure more responses than might otherwise be possible."[71] Others opted to emphasize beauty, acquisition, self-adornment, and play in creating effective mass distribution of products. Ads demonstrated the path around the ills of modern industrial life. The ads scrupulously avoided depicting the reality of, say, factory life.[72]

In selling fashion, wealth was likely a dominating factor. Therefore, the styles should, among other attributes, prove that the wearer did not labor for his or her sustenance.[73] Stuart Ewen added, "What Thorstein Veblen had theorized as the conspicuous consumption habits of the leisure class were now propagated as a democratic ideal within mass advertising. In order to sell the commodity culture, it was necessary to confront people with a vision of that culture from which the class masses of dissatisfaction had been removed."[74]

## Postwar Leisure Consumption

Leisure patterns changed dramatically after World War II. In the immediate aftermath of the armistice, the pent-up demand for leisure burst, leading to temporary booms for the motion picture and professional sports industries. Spending on recreation jumped in 1946, but in real terms—adjusted for changes in the general price level—the jump was not quite so dramatic (Table 5.6). The motion picture industry enjoyed a boom in 1946, but the industry's long-run trend was dismal. Major league baseball, too, enjoyed a prosperous period between 1946 and 1949 before experiencing a downturn and decade-long stagnation.

While pundits believe that television punctured these booms, a more nuanced explanation involves the demographic phenomenon dubbed "the baby boom." Television lagged the baby boom. The returning veterans married and started families, with a marked uptick in births during 1946 that persisted for a generation. Americans began switching from what we shall label "public leisure" in favor of "private leisure." Spending on toys, radios, televisions, and other leisure activities usually done in the privacy of one's home assumed greater importance in overall spending on recreation (Table 5.7). The joys of staying home with the family or the expense of leaving home for the evening might have induced parents to stop going out to ball games and movies.[75]

Distinguished historian David M. Potter asked how America's economic abundance affected its character. For him, "[t]his factor is the unusual plenty of available goods or other usable wealth which has prevailed in America—what I shall call 'economic abundance.'" He argues that "unique circumstances, conditions, and experience are apt to produce unique traits and attitudes among the people as a whole."[76]

Potter demonstrated America's abundance by citing figures on daily caloric intake. In 1949, Americans far outstripped the rest of the world in their average daily caloric intake: 3,186 versus less than 2,700 for all other people. A later generation might not view this fact as so beneficial, but, for most of European settlement of what became the United States, observers had noted the richness and variability of the American diet.[77]

*Table 5.6* **National Economic Indicators, 1945–1961ª**

| | ($000,000,000s) | | (000,000s of nominal $) | | | |
|---|---|---|---|---|---|---|
| | GNP | REAL GNP | CPI | Sp. Rec. | Movies | Sports |
| 1945 | 211.9 | 355.2 | 53.9 | 6,139 | 1,450 | 116 |
| 1946 | 208.5 | 312.6 | 58.5 | 8,539 | 1,692 | 200 |
| 1947 | 231.3 | 309.9 | 66.9 | 9,249 | 1,594 | 222 |
| 1948 | 257.6 | 323.7 | 72.1 | 9,692 | 1,506 | 232 |
| 1949 | 256.5 | 324.1 | 71.4 | 10,010 | 1,451 | 239 |
| 1950 | 284.8 | 355.3 | 72.1 | 11,147 | 1,376 | 222 |
| 1951 | 328.4 | 383.4 | 77.8 | 11,564 | 1,310 | 220 |
| 1952 | 345.5 | 395.1 | 79.5 | 12,102 | 1,246 | 220 |
| 1953 | 364.6 | 412.8 | 80.1 | 12,720 | 1,187 | 221 |
| 1954 | 364.8 | 407.0 | 80.5 | 13,077 | 1,228 | 224 |
| 1955 | 398.0 | 438.0 | 80.2 | 14,078 | 1,326 | 230 |
| 1956 | 419.2 | 446.1 | 81.4 | 14,979 | 1,394 | 237 |
| 1957 | 441.1 | 452.5 | 84.3 | 15,333 | 1,126 | 242 |
| 1958 | 447.3 | 447.3 | 86.6 | 15,817 | 992 | 249 |
| 1959 | 483.7 | 475.9 | 87.3 | 17,381 | 958 | 269 |
| 1960 | 503.7 | 487.7 | 88.7 | 18,295 | 951 | 290 |
| 1961 | 520.1 | 497.2 | 89.6 | 19,506 | 921 | 306 |

*Note*: Gross National Product; Real Gross National Product (Implicit Price index 1958 = 100); Sp. Rec. (Spending on Recreation); Movies; Sports (Spectator).

ª US Department of Commerce, *Historical Statistics of the United States, Part 1*, GNP/Real GNP on 224; CPI on 210; Sp. Rec. on 401, Movies, and Spectator Sports, 401.

Abundance changed the American family. Potter noted that American children by the mid-1950s no longer had as much reason to fear that their parents would die early. Potter observed that the parent-child relationship had also changed, since fathers had more hours of leisure to interact with his children. Mothers, too, had divested themselves of many of the arduous household chores due to mechanical inventions and, instead, shared more of their time with their smaller numbers of children.[78]

Potter observed, "The politics of our democracy was a politics of abundance rather than a politics of individualism, a politics of increasing our wealth quickly rather than of dividing it precisely."[79] Americans demonstrated their economic abundance around the world: "every American who was overseas between 1941 and 1945 was in

*Table 5.7* **Real Personal Consumption Expenditures on Recreation (Selected Years)**[a]

| Year | Toys | Radio/TV | Movies | Sports | Private | Total | %Private |
|------|------|----------|--------|--------|---------|-------|----------|
| 1945 | 1,034 | 469 | 1,574 | 126 | 3,525 | 6,663 | 52.9 |
| 1946 | 1,633 | 1,231 | 1,692 | 200 | 4,968 | 8,539 | 58.2 |
| 1947 | 1,628 | 1,345 | 1,394 | 194 | 4,911 | 8,088 | 60.7 |
| 1950 | 1,836 | 2,194 | 1,116 | 180 | 6,161 | 9,044 | 68.1 |
| 1953 | 2,033 | 2,207 | 867 | 161 | 6,542 | 9,290 | 70.4 |
| 1960 | 2,983 | 2,779 | 627 | 191 | 8,491 | 12,066 | 70.4 |

Explanations

All amounts in $000,000s.

Toys: Non-durable toys and sport supplies and wheel goods, durable toys, sport equipment, boats, and pleasure aircraft.

Radio/TV: Radio and television receivers, records, and musical instruments, and radio and television repair.

Movies: Motion picture theaters.

Sports: Spectator sports.

Private: Toys + radio/TV + books and maps + magazines, newspapers, and sheet music + flowers, seeds, and potted plants.

[a] Reprinted from Table 4.1 of Surdam, *Postwar Yankees*, 332; US Department of Commerce, *Historical Statistics of the United States, Part 1*, 401. Deflated by Consumer Price Index (All Items, 1800–1970), with 1946 = 100, in US Department of Commerce, *Historical Statistics of the United States, Part 1*, 210.

some respects a revolutionary agent of social change." What was it, Isabel Lundberg, asks, that the native populations everywhere wanted from the American military personnel? It was their material goods, including white bread. Potter notes, "Very few Americans, picking and choosing among the piles of white bread in a super-market, have ever appreciated the social standing of white bread elsewhere in the world. . . . To afford it signifies that one enjoys all the comforts of life."[80]

*Life* magazine detailed the booming leisure market at the end of 1959. Reporter Robert Coughlan surveyed a range of industries and suggested that the leisure business was an important new economic force. He surmised that alcohol consumption could be considered a leisure industry, citing the $10 billion taken in by that industry. He expressed surprise that Florida's deep-sea fishing was "nearly as big as its citrus fruit and cattle industries combined" and that the "amount spent on dogs is equal to all the salaries and fees paid for legal services." The pleasure-boating business was growing rapidly, with Americans owning 8 million of them. Coughlan connected the boom in boats with government efforts to create lakes, in order to control flooding and to provide electric power. For other water recreation, swimming pools were sprouting throughout suburbia, partly because banks and homeowners real-ized that pools boosted the property value. Bowling had reinvented itself, thanks in part to the installation of automatic pin-setting machines that elimi-nated the pin boy (whom Coughlan characterized as "undependable, usually surly"). One industry, golf, seemed to have stagnated, at least in terms of the number of courses. He cited the do-it-yourself and gardening pursuits as pos-sibly dubious forms of leisure, suggesting that many practitioners wished they had paid professionals to take their place.[81]

John Owen conducted a thorough analysis of leisure and recreational spend-ing for 1900–1961. Using regression analysis, he detected that as the relative price of recreation fell, the demand for leisure increased. This finding supported the argument that leisure time and recreation were complements in consump-tion (used together, rather than in lieu of).[82] With respect to Gary Becker's idea of viewing leisure time and leisure goods and services as inputs, Owen noted that "a maximum of 10 percent of leisure activity input was market recreation (a minimum of 90 percent was time). Moreover, this maximum can only be ac-cepted by ignoring the value of time of non-employee members of the family."[83]

By the 1960s, a counterculture critique of commercial abundance developed. Norman O. Brown's Life Against Death examined commercialized society and ex-plored alternatives to the pursuit of prosperity: "There is something in the human psyche which commits man to nonenjoyment, to work."[84] Jackson Lears dis-cussed Ivan Illich's Toward a History of Needs and Christopher Lasch's The Culture of Narcissism—the descendants of Veblen, Vance Packard, and John Kenneth Galbraith. Lears concludes, "Accurate as these critiques were, they tended to con-fuse high consumption with hedonism; to overlook the suspicion of play at the core of the managerial ethos; and to omit any discussion of the aesthetic and sen-suous pleasures that might have existed in a genuine 'culture of abundance.'"[85]

## More Recent Patterns of Leisure

Americans continued to participate in many types of outdoor recreation throughout the twentieth century. More than three-quarters of Americans par-ticipated in outdoor recreations regularly, with significant increases in spending between 1976 and 1981.[86]

Tourism is now the globe's largest industry. Ken Roberts believes that al-though information technology will improve our ability to engage in virtual tourism and other industries devoted to filling leisure time, tourism is unlikely to diminish. "The experience of actually being there cannot be bettered or closely stimulated by guide books, TV holiday programmes or the internet." Tourism is not completely commercialized, but it comes in for much criticism, ranging from damage to the environment to fabricated experiences. Roberts points out that the combination of vacation or holiday time, reliable transportation, and affordability allowed consumers to exercise their preference for tourism.[87]

Although spending on sports does not match that of spending on tourism, Roberts mentions a special facet of sports: "sport probably has a larger presence in our lives on account of its wide and deep cultural resonance. . . . People may idolize film and pop stars, but they do not feel that the stars belong to them, and are representing them in quite the same way as top sports players." Sports so pervades both British and American cultures that the secondary sports-related markets, such as apparel and gambling, thrive on it.[88]

Part of the reason Americans spent so much on leisure and recreation was often because of declining prices relative to wages. Modern Americans did not have to work as long to buy basic commodities. Such things as a gallon of milk, loaf of bread, three-minute long distance call, electricity, computing power, convenience food, and airline travel required much less work time to acquire than in the past.[89] This drop in labor-time required to purchase such commodities reflected workers' growing productivity.

Americans continued to spend increasing amounts on recreational pursuits, even in the face of higher gas prices and a sluggish economy during the 1970s. The number of visits to national parks doubled from that of a decade previously, while sales of recreational vehicles increased by 25 percent. They continued to eat out and to enjoy motion pictures. The long-run trend in overseas travel continued during the twentieth century.[90]

By 1993, Americans spent $341 billion on recreation and entertainment, or 9.43 percent of all "non-medical consumer spending." The comparable figure in 1979 was 7.71 percent. Personal consumption expenditures for recreation rose from $281 billion in 1990 to $431 billion in 1996. Spending on entertainment and recreation weathered the 1991 recession without difficulty, and some observers attributed the healthy spending on the growing numbers of households headed by 34–54-year-olds. Americans were spending increased amounts of money, in particular, on gambling experiences, amusement parks, and new technologies. One gambling casino investor chortled, "People just love the excitement of betting."[91]

## More Leisure, More Spending on Leisure

Americans devoted greater proportions of the consumption expenditures to leisure-related goods and services throughout the twentieth century. There was some ambiguity, due to the definitions of expenditures on leisure, although the general upward trend was unmistakable. Americans used some of their savings in spending on food and other basics to enjoy leisure goods and services.

# 6

# Patterns in Leisure for the Young and the Old

Some groups of people may take a somewhat ambivalent view of their leisure time. If leisure is associated with freedom, what happens when leisure time is not freely chosen but is, instead, thrust upon people due to retirement or unemployment? What about youth sequestered in the school system for over a decade? Do they view school as leisure, work, or a mix?

The economists' depiction of workers allocating their time between leisure and work needs to be adjusted for people who cannot convert time into income: the unemployed and the involuntarily retired. Additional units of leisure might yield smaller incremental gains to a person's satisfaction (denoted as diminishing marginal utility), just as with increased units of consumption. If so, the distribution of leisure time across a person's lifetime might not be optimal (too much leisure time during retirement years and too little during peak earnings years), and people might prefer a mechanism to smooth the path of leisure hours across the lifetime. With respect to consumption, by saving and dissaving, people already attempt to smooth the consumption of goods and services across their lifetime. People rarely can smooth their leisure time in a similar fashion. Then there are some people who have such high rates of time preference—in other words, they are impatient for immediate consumption or leisure—that they will not save. In such cases, the government might mandate forced savings.[1]

Of course, people in their forties and fifties may be working long hours, reaping high incomes but with relatively small amounts of leisure time. This phenomenon raises the question of whether longer vacation periods during an individual's working years would be more beneficial than earlier retirement.[2]

# Changing Demographics

Certainly changes in American demographics have led to altering the patterns of leisure time and spending on recreation. One of the biggest demographic events of the twentieth century was the baby boom of 1946–1964. *Business Week* published a table showing that there were many more married people over the age of 14 in 1951 than in 1940, much more than could be explained by population increase alone. The periodical concluded, "That's good news. Marriages keep the market coming."[3] The baby boom and lengthening life spans enlarged two groups of consumers who were not in the labor force: children and retirees. *Business Week* observed, "That puts an extra strain on the middle group ... the population growth will be a factor in preventing any long-term economic debacle. People create the market, and in time the added population will soak up almost any amount of new productive capacity." Already those growing legions of children were sparking a boom in children's and infants' wear, toys, and baby food producers.[4]

# Not Their Grandparents' Retirement

Much of the gains in leisure time related to the growing prevalence of retirement. Retirement is an ever-changing concept. Few Americans enjoyed retirement before 1900; death usually rudely terminated any such hopes. Many older people, if they did retire, were relegated to living with adult children. In New England, though, the youngest son and the parents signed a contract: in return for the title to the family farm, the son had to provide a detailed list of goods and services for his parents.[5] By the 1950s, many more Americans survived to age 65, and retirement was becoming an accepted and anticipated state.

As the oldest baby boomers reached the age of 65 in 2011, retirement is likely to evolve some more. With septuagenarians such as the Rolling Stones still playing to sold-out concerts attended by their "tweener" and baby boomer generations of fans, retirement is no longer a time of quiet acquiescence to decrepitude and contemplation.[6]

The mean age of men and women awarded retirement benefits fell more than five years from 68.7 since 1950, although the trend decelerated during the later years of the twentieth century thanks to Social Security rules that established age 62 as the earliest to receive any benefits. Concurrent with the declining ages for being awarded benefits, American male labor force participation decreased steadily after 1950; the pattern for women was more complicated. There was a drawback to the falling retirement ages and reduced labor force participation rate: "[it] tends to raise the economic dependency burden placed by the elderly on younger cohorts still in the labor force. This, in turn, tends to make increases in per capita income harder to achieve, even as the costs of income transfers to the elderly rise." Many countries around the world facing aging populations and growing debt burdens may see their economies stagnate in years to come.[7]

The earliest retirees may have been involuntarily forced out of their jobs. An article in *Business Week* in 1953 reflected some of the downside of burgeoning leisure. Many of the retirees surveyed in 1953 said they did not retire of their own accord, and they felt they had too much leisure.[8]

The old-style retirement meant a few, declining years devoted to contemplation of the afterlife and sedentary activities.[9] Older men and women often lived in their children's homes or with friends, thereby surrendering independence and authority. Only a few American males enjoyed even a brief retirement. During the twentieth century, though, retirement evolved as growing numbers of men began retiring at younger ages. They retired with the anticipation of enjoying their leisure time and engaging in stimulating, if not strenuous, activities, including travel and golf. Rising incomes and greater anticipated income in retirement, thanks to pensions and Social Security, may have contributed to the trend toward earlier retirement, and the expectation of enjoyable leisure time eventually pulled rather than pushed older Americans into retirement.[10]

Although some observers believed that increasing rates of retirement were due to chronic disorders, economist Dora Costa disagrees and asserts that "[r]etirement rates increased despite, not because of, improving health." She continues by suggesting that relying upon 65 as the start of "old age" is inappropriate, especially for purposes of Social Security.[11]

Unemployment had mixed effects on the retirement decision. For men over 65, becoming unemployed became less of a factor in determining when to retire as the century progressed. For younger men, a lengthy spell of unemployment became more likely to trigger retirement in the latter part than at the beginning of the twentieth century. The obvious explanation was that men in the late twentieth century were more likely to have the financial means to retire than men in 1900.[12]

In the past, about one-third of retired males re-entered the labor force, usually because they found they could not afford to retire. Although the re-entry rate was slightly lower in 1990, the reason given by many of the re-entrants was boredom, not financial need; many of the re-entrants were highly educated.[13]

When incomes were low, older Americans no longer capable of working often faced unattractive alternatives. Living with relatives was disruptive; adult children frequently had to choose between allocating scarce dollars between their own children and their aging parents. Economists Brian Gratton and Carole Haber believe that Social Security's political popularity was due to "the New Deal offer[ing] an attractive alternative, a public intergenerational exchange. By giving the elderly a guaranteed income in old age, Social Security released kin from the familial system and its acrimonious disputes, placed the exchange in the state, and put off intergenerational dispute to a distant future."[14]

Older Americans appreciated the opportunity to remain in their own homes, and Eleanor Roosevelt used this preference to persuade people to support Social Security.[15] Demographic changes also altered retirees' options. Because of smaller families and reductions in marriage rates in late-twentieth-century America, many retirees do not have adult children with whom to co-reside. The situation will be worse in China, as parents of the "one-child" generation reach old age. By definition, they will have only one child, at best, to look after them.

The effect of Social Security and old age pensions on the retirement decision is a key question. Union Army pensions provided an experiment of sorts; veterans were given additional financial resources, and they were much more likely to remain independent than males who were not receiving such pensions. In addition to income effects, older Americans may find independent living more attractive in modern times than in 1900, especially with the growth of retirement communities replete with amenities. Finally, older Americans are now more likely to retire simply because they seek leisure time.[16]

What were the effects of leisure time on retirees? Sociologist L. C. Michelon noted that retirement had different effects on individuals, with some duplicating the frenetic pace of their work lives by "doing anything to use up time"; for others, it "is the beginning of a long, terminal hibernation characterized by lonely and maddening inactivity. Between these extremes is the rare individual who can look ahead to the golden years, make the needed changes in values, and substitute new, vital activities for the meaning of work." He concluded, "the satisfying and creative uses of leisure in retirement conduce to a way of life that brings tangible results and opens new horizons for people whose potential talents were never really known"; he also noted that women seemed to adjust better to leisure in retirement than men.[17]

Some observers claimed that the Americans who enjoyed leisure in retirement, no surprise, were those with the educational attainment and wealth to take advantage of their opportunities. Ernest Havemann worried about the recent high school dropouts and people of low intelligence—how would they earn sufficient income to maintain themselves and to enjoy their leisure hours? He alluded to the possibility that the schools could teach "a philosophy appropriate to our new age of easy abundance . . . [but] who will teach the teachers?" before concluding, "[i]t may take a long time, the more pessimistic thinkers believe, before the Age of Leisure provides any real spiritual comfort and happiness for the great bulk of people."[18]

Investigators found that people who were healthy and exercised were more likely to cope well with old age.[19] Fortunately, modern Americans are not just living longer but are remaining in good health longer, often due, in part, to regular exercising.

Many older Americans, though, have difficulty adjusting to retirement. These Americans made work their top priority throughout their adult years, so that they have difficulty adjusting to new priorities. Surveys indicate that many older Americans would prefer to continue working, even if they don't need to financially.[20]

Some researchers postulated that old age was characterized by a loss of control and effectiveness. Leisure is usually seen as predicated upon having control and freedom; although older people gradually lost control and freedom over other aspects of their lives, they might retain some control over their leisure pursuits and therefore gain some life satisfaction. Some studies found that environments with plenty of leisure opportunities increase retirees' participation in leisure, and that retirees with low rates of participation might actually be latent participants, if placed within an environment with more leisure options.[21]

Retirees often filled their time with travel. Older travelers (defined as 55 or older) differed from other travelers. The older people traveled farther and stayed longer than other age groups. For the retired older people, the duration of travel is not surprising. Balazs splits older people into two market segments: the "well to do" traveler and the "elderly" traveler. The former is younger (50–64 years old) and represents a potentially more lucrative segment to the travel industry. Many of these travelers have significant income or wealth from which to fund luxury travel accommodations at peak times. The elderly travelers tended to be over 65 years old, traveled more often, and preferred group travel.[22]

Clearly, leisure in retirement is affected by one's economic and health statuses. By century's end, though, more Americans over 60 years of age were in better shape both financially and health wise.

## Youth and Leisure

During the twentieth century, Americans' years of schooling increased dramatically. With child labor laws enacted in the first years of the century and the wider provision of public schools, a growing proportion of American youth did not enter the labor market for full-time work until their late teens or even their mid-twenties. High school graduation rates and college enrollment soared. Schooling, though, occupied an ambiguous position with regard to leisure and to work.

According to the 1900 Census, 1.75 million children, aged 10–15, were gainful workers. Most of these children, of course, were not in school on a regular basis. Within a few decades, very few children of similar ages were in the non-farm labor force. Concurrent with the eradication of child labor, high school graduation rates rose from less than 14 percent in 1900 to 83 percent in 1999. During the same period, college graduation rates rose from 3 to 25 percent. These educated Americans proved quite productive, and their greater productivity was reflected in their higher wage rates relative to workers with less education.[23]

In terms of kindergarten, elementary, and secondary schools, enrollment rose from 78.3 percent of children, aged 5–17, in 1900 to 97.8 percent in 1970. The gap in enrollment rates between whites and blacks narrowed considerably over those 70 years. The number of college degrees granted soared from 29,375 in 1900 to over a million by 1970. Of course, the G.I. Bill in the aftermath of World War II dramatically hiked the number of degrees, from a wartime low of 141,582 to 496,874 in 1950. While the numbers fell during the 1950s before rebounding, by 1962 the number of degrees awarded exceeded that of 1950 and has trended upward ever since.[24]

What did children do, when they were not engaged in school or work? Douglas Kleiber and William Rickards examined leisure among school-age children. They clarified some semantics: "Leisure in the first sense is **perceived opportunity**. It is **free** [bold in original] time without necessarily dictating a purely expressive or personal behavioral orientation. But it does seem reasonable to contrast it with the 'work' of school attendance, largely because it is compulsory and is generally regarded as a mean of social control." They link modern children's leisure with Aristotelian views of leisure as "self-development, self-expansion and self-actualization."[25]

Whether youth participated in leisure activities within the family has changed over time. During the Victorian era, home was where the family spent most of its leisure time together: playing games or musical instruments, reading, and viewing the world through a stereoscope.[26] Other home entertainment activities ranged from games to scripted theatricals, tableaux (recreation of a famous scene from history or literature), and group pageants.

Melanie Dawson argues that "the context that helps explain these trends is the changing narrative of belonging to a middling social tier."[27] She notes that the working classes' entertainment choices did not directly reflect their everyday lives; they engaged in communal activities. Therefore, the work-based games of the mid-1800s were unlikely to have been borrowed from working-class origins: "The very act of placing manual work on display was, in part, proof of readers' and participants' distance from it, for leisurely displays make light of what were for actual workers the grinding, inescapable hardships of life. In this sense, playing at work situated participants in play as significantly distanced from the bodily labors of the working classes."[28]

Progressive-era reformers turned their attention to the lack of wholesome recreational and leisure activities for working-class Americans and their children. Many working-class families were housed in crowded tenements with little space for children to play. Playing on the street had its dangers, especially with runaway horses and errant drivers; there were also certainly unsavory temptations lurking about the streets. Some reformers believed that private or public provision of playgrounds and other recreational facilities might divert children from deleterious forms of play toward wholesome, regulated play. The National Recreation Association (NRA) promoted recreational facilities during the first decades of the 1900s.[29]

The Young Men's Christian Association (YMCA) had existed for decades. The organization espoused Muscular Christianity and had branches throughout America. The YMCA had professional leadership and social services. Prior to 1900, some private groups funded playgrounds in the largest cities in the country, but these efforts could not fulfill the need.[30]

Not all youth patronized wholesome YMCA-sponsored activities. During World War II, commentators worried about the way adolescents used their spare time. The juvenile delinquent began assuming his or her shape in the minds of Americans. James Gilbert, in his A Cycle of Outrage, views the debate regarding mass culture and its effects on children as an example of an episodic notion. "Since the control of youth is, even in the best of times, problematic, and since the cultural history of the United States is filled with dramatic changes in the content and form of popular culture, the seduction of the innocent by culture is a primary example of an episodic notion."[31]

The youth culture, while celebrated (or reviled) during the 1950s, began during the generations before the baby boom (the oldest boomer would have been a mere 14 years old in 1960). American youth had carved out a uniqueness well before the 1950s. Paula Fass describes the upheaval caused by and reflected by the young during the 1920s, especially the young people who attended college. Their mores shocked older Americans and inspired a "culture war" between generations. Of course, one should not draw this divide too broadly, as the college-bound youth were a minority of all youth. In any event, fashionable youths of the 1920s drew considerable interest and ire. Their choices of music and dance scandalized their elders.

Jazz music raised many concerns, much as rock 'n' roll would 30 years later. Fass writes, "traditionalists looked at youthful pastimes like jazz and dancing and saw rude passion, Negro lewdness, sensuous movement." The Ladies Home Journal, a bastion of traditionalism, believed that the crusade against "Unspeakable Jazz" was "of as great importance to-day to the moral well-being of the United States as the prohibition crusade was in the worst days of the saloon."[32] Similarly hysterical language could be found in many publications.

Certainly many movies and books depicted the youth as leading decadent lives during the "Roaring Twenties." With widespread disregard for the law, as exemplified by adults flouting the Prohibition laws, youths may have felt disillusioned with society. The cynicism surrounding America's involvement in the recent war also contributed to widespread ennui and cynicism. Fass argues that the young people's actions during the 1920s were misunderstood. To her, the brouhaha over jazz concealed the process of youths "redefin[ing] what was proper according to their own tastes . . . it was a way of assimilating to their own uses one of the truly new artistic forms of twentieth-century America."[33] A dance, with its wilder dancing styles, was both respectable and a form of socializing. The dance allowed young men and women to meet and to experiment with the opposite sex.

Many Americans, especially those who did not set foot on any college campuses, would have agreed with Christian Gauss, who wrote, "With the general obscuring of the college's original purpose and function, it has unfortunately become a kind of glorified playground. It has become the paradise of the young."[34] For Fass, the college atmosphere was largely freed from adult supervision, but it was one that required peer groups who dictated moral codes and responsible behavior for the young; however, to many older adults, the youthful mores appeared irresponsible.[35]

College students became trendsetters for fashion and behavior. Much of their trendsetting revolved around fads. Fass saw fads as a modern concept. "Even the term is modern—describing a sudden explosion of interest in some commodity that becomes widespread and rabidly popular but then quickly disappears to be replaced by another fashion or interest equally ephemeral." For youth, fads served to mark association among their age cohort and to demonstrate their loyalty to their peers. "Fads were one effective way in which the needs of the young were being channeled into the historical conditions of a changing society."[36]

The 1920s supposedly represented a sexual revolution of sorts, but Fass interprets the situation differently. Youths of the 1920s formulated new rituals for interaction between men and women. Dating was a new institution, an aberration from the usual group socializing without couples. Dating implied a pairing, although one less formal than courting, which implied future marriage.[37]

The diminished adult supervision of children percolated from college students down to their younger siblings. Even in high school, urban youth often spent their evenings outside the house—think of the fictional character Andy Hardy, played by Mickey Rooney, asking for keys to the family car. Rural adolescents tended to remain home more evenings than their urban cousins. In addition, families were getting smaller, especially among the middle and upper-middle classes. Parents devoted more time and affection to their smaller number of children.[38]

According to a Playground Association study conducted in 19 cities in the 1920s, most of the boys' leisure time was spent away from home, on the streets, in alleys, parks, schoolyards, and playgrounds. About half the boys described their activities as "doing nothing or hanging around." Ellen Wartella and Sharon Mazzarella wrote, "Child savers were concerned that such ill-spent leisure would lead to moral degeneration, particularly in the absence of control by family, church, and school."[39] During the 1930s, a larger proportion of children attended school into their later teen years, giving them time to spend with peers and a chance to establish their own culture. In schools, teenagers spent much of their days in "a world dominated by peers . . . the mass media, by targeting the teenage market for cultural products, helped to create a separate teen culture."[40]

Wartella and Mazzarella drew two conclusions from their studies of children's use of leisure. Young people since the 1920s have "developed increasingly autonomous, peer-oriented, and commercialized leisure-time pursuits that have repeatedly been criticized by their parents." They pointed out that public anxiety over children tended to focus on children at younger and younger ages, from the college students of the 1920s to the teenagers of the 1940s and 1950s, down to elementary students in the 1980s. Although each mass medium sparked debate about its adverse effect upon children, television had "a more profound effect on children's leisure time than earlier mass media."[41]

Intellectuals did not share the majority's enthusiasm for mass culture, but they were largely reduced to gnashing their teeth and writing editorials. In the 1950s many people worried whether mass culture, especially advertising, comic books, films, and, later, rock 'n' roll, "had misshaped a generation of American boys and girls." Americans believed that the generation born just before and during the Great Depression was particularly prone to juvenile delinquency. Certainly, there were plausible reasons to think so. During World War II, with fathers and some mothers serving in the military and many mothers working outside the household, many children had reduced parental supervision. Many children, too, sought employment. Because authorities worried about potential upswings in juvenile delinquency, they may have created a self-fulfilling prophecy, as they spent time looking for such outbreaks of delinquency.[42]

Gilbert claims that for many Americans during the postwar era, "youth culture was synonymous with delinquency, or at least they suspected that this might be the case." The increased share of mass culture directed toward youth raised fears that middle-class sway over public culture was waning (to say nothing of upper-class sway). Adults viewed teenage culture as one infested with criminal and lower-class values: "To say the least, this was a familiar, although curious, conclusion. Mass culture was charged with spreading lower-class values, suggesting an incongruous alliance between some of the most powerful corporations in America and some of the nation's least articulate or important citizens."[43]

That mainstay of 1950s youth culture—rock 'n' roll—was partially the result of larger economic forces. Even before rock 'n' roll, social critic David Riesman blasted the pop music industry, which he believed could "mold popular taste and eliminate free choice by consumers." He admitted, though, that the major producers were unable to control swings in consumer tastes, which meant that music executives had to react quickly to the changing tastes. Since many of these new popular genres originated with groups on the social fringe, the incumbent firms in the industry were at a disadvantage relative to the new producers in discovering new artists. Riesman interviewed a number of young people regarding their musical tastes. He found that peer pressure shaped stated preferences: "The fear is to be caught liking what the others have decided not to like." He recognized that even the aficionados of hot-jazz, while overtly rebelling against conformity, may have simply exchanged one, majority-imposed, conformity with another form of conformity among the self-styled non-conformists.[44]

The government's intervention in the mass entertainment industries of radio and television was crucial to understanding the rise of rock 'n' roll. The government stymied the spread of FM radio stations and halted the licensing of television stations. The latter edict meant that television would be in the hands of networks, and these networks had already dominated radio. In contrast to the huge capital investments required for television and, to a lesser degree, radio, entrepreneurs launching record companies could do so with relatively little capital. The executives of radio and television networks were preoccupied with their companies' larger interests, and they largely ignored their record divisions. Independent radio stations innovated to combat the network stations. Owners of small record labels and independent radio stations investigated new musical styles, such as country and western, rhythm and blues, and hillbilly, and new ways to deliver music to listeners. In addition, more retailers were itching to enter the record market and to break the big labels' chain of stores. Music historians Steve Chapple and Reebee Garofalo also suggest that the drab state of popular music—they use Frank Sinatra, Frankie Laine, and Johnny Ray as exemplars—also made listeners, especially young listeners, susceptible to a new, exciting musical form.[45]

Rock 'n' roll would be tied to the new technology of the 45 rpm record. The smaller disc was less fragile than the old 78 rpm and the new 33.3 rpm records, which meant it could be easily shipped at lower costs. It was also perfectly suited for pop singles and could be printed and disseminated quickly, allowing the original company recording a song to get it on the market before cover versions appeared.[46]

The independent labels—Sun and Chess—catapulted Elvis Presley and Chuck Berry to fame. Their successes were not flukes, as by 1957, independents were producing twice as many rock 'n' roll hits as the major labels; the independents were beginning to dominate the entire pop singles charts.[47]

If rock 'n' roll was reviled commercialized music, there were plenty of other products competing for young Americans dollars. A social critic noted, "These days, merchants eye teenagers the way stockmen eye cattle."[48] Other observers were not so pessimistic or condescending. Steven Miles believes that young people and canny marketers fed off each other, in what Miles calls a "mutually exploitative" relationship: the idea that "young people actively engage with the mass media and to a degree forge it in their own image is a sound one, but is only ever partially realized." Young people's choices were liberated from their parents' culture, but they were constrained to the ones offered by the mass media: "it provides them with the canvass, but the only oils they can use to paint that canvass are consumerist ones."[49]

Teenagers' purchasing power exploded after World War II due to the general prosperity and to their willingness to work after school. An article in *Life* magazine listed the teenagers' collective material goods: 10 million phonographs, one million TV sets, 13 million cameras. The article estimated that teenagers and their parents would spend $10 billion on teens, more than the total sales of General Motors. The article pointed out that the number of teenagers jumped from 18 million to 28 million during the decade.[50]

Gilbert Seldes quickly grasped teenagers' burgeoning purchasing power and large companies' ignorance of this fact. He, himself, was still a teenager when he decided to do impromptu market research. He parlayed his savvy and information into becoming a sought-after consultant to marketing firms. In order to obtain information, he hired a large number of teenagers to query and to quantify their friends' purchasing habits. From this mass of information, he identified candy, soft drinks, comic books, and gum as foremost among the items that teenagers purchased. Marketers quickly responded to Seldes's findings, issuing various publications for use in schools. Some critics viewed these publications as, at best, self-serving and, at worst, manipulative. Teenagers not only purchased commodities with their own money, they often influenced family purchases of durable goods and clothing.[51]

Psychiatrist Robert M. Lindner worried about youth in the 1950s: "youth today has abandoned solitude in favor of pack-running, of predatory assembly, of great collectivities that bury, if they do not destroy, individuality. . . . In the crowd, herd or gang, it is a mass mind that operates a mind without subtlety, without compassion, uncivilized."[52]

In a glimpse of the future, Seldes reported that teenagers loved to talk on the telephone—proving, perhaps, that today's youths' obsession with cell phones, texting, and so on are merely reflections of their grandparents' predilections; teenagers spent an hour per day on the telephone. Girls spent more time on average than boys. The telephone, of course, kept young people in touch with their friends and facilitated their social life.[53]

As the century passed the midway point, the leisure patterns of much younger Americans—children—caused hand-wringing galore. Wartella and Mazzarella argue that "television in late twentieth-century America has thrust children into the adult world at an earlier and earlier age . . . autonomous youth cultures developed around leisure activities, and . . . the mass media became the social catalysts promoting, sustaining, and commercializing the leisure of each succeeding youth culture."[54]

## The Comic Books' Menace to Society

Before television, though, there was another menace. If ever there was a commercialized product aimed at children that operated in a "wild West" style, it was the comic book industry. This industry is worth examining in detail, as it mirrored previous crusades against comic strips, dime novels, and penny dreadfuls, and it presaged rock 'n' roll, rap, and other controversial youth cultural trends. The industry's response to criticism about its product is also instructive; in economic terms, self-censorship resulted in the concentration of the industry into the hands of fewer producers.

A few publishers dominated sales of comic books, but there was potential for new entrants to thrive. The industry was nimble enough to adapt to new genres. Genres came and went; witness the quick ousting of super heroes in favor of crime comics between 1946 and 1947, with 30 new titles in 1948 alone. By the time the real-life crusaders started protesting and investigating, crime comics' wave may have already ebbed, to be replaced by romance comics. Hard on the heels of romance comics were horror comics; by 1952, about one-third of the hundreds of comic titles were horror-oriented.

The monthly circulation of comics had jumped from 3 million in 1939 to over 40 million in 1946, with Superman-DC comics and Fawcett Comics leading in circulation in 1946. Of this circulation, a handful of publishers produced 25 million, while a larger number of independents had a combined circulation of 15 million per month. Many firms folded up quickly.[55]

Who read comic books? Adult readership comprised a large proportion of readers, especially in smaller towns (where children's readership tended to be high, too). The adults reading comics did not all live in households with children, as one-fifth of the households without children had adult readers of comic books.[56]

Children read the advertising in comic books and were swayed by it. A survey showed that one-third of the students asked their parents to buy something based on an advertisement, and a slightly higher percentage of parents said they had purchased something their child saw in an advertisement. Most of these products pertained to consumables, such as candy bars, cold cereals, and bottled soft drinks. The advertisers were aware of the effectiveness of their advertisements.

While politicians and social critics worried about comics' effects on children's behavior, they might have worried more about marketing executives "branding" children (to use modern parlance). A Nehi Corporation (Royal Crown Cola) official stated: "To grow in sales steadily, we must plant our brand names in the youth mind. Surveys revealed that comic books were the best medium to do this."[57]

The comic book industry, though, suffered a major decline by the mid-1950s. By the mid-1950s, the ranks thinned considerably, as the number of titles published plunged from 650 to 250. The story becomes, "What killed (or maimed) the comics industry?" The traditional story is that Congressional ogres, aided and abetted by prudes, imposed censorship and ousted such creative geniuses as William C. Gaines from the industry. But several researchers have sketched a more nuanced storyline.

Newspapers had featured comic strips for decades. Comic strips, like dime novels, had attracted criticism for their rude, crude, slapstick humor, often aimed at immigrant groups. An anonymous article in the *Ladies Home Journal* was typical:

> [Comic strips are] cheap and demoralizing, there is not even an occasional flash of humor. The whole vulgar mess is the work of a shabby crowd of vulgarians whose only claim to 'fun' lies in crude exaggeration ... these pictures and jokes actually teach our children irreverence and lawlessness by ridiculing home discipline, by making cheap fun of age, dignity, good breeding and all the pieties and amenities which make the family the most sacred and important of human institutions.... We parents must face this appalling influence.[58]

Educators and activists bemoaned comic strips, but very little was done. Comic strips were simply too popular. Comic books started appearing in significant quantities during the 1930s. Early criticism centered on comic books' diversionary power. Literary critic Sterling North characterized comics as "badly drawn, badly written and badly printed—a strain on young eyes and young nervous systems ... [that] spoil a child's natural sense of color, their hypodermic injection of sex and murder make the child impatient with better, though quieter stories."[59] Reuel Denney did not share the hysteria surrounding comic books' effects on children. He suggested that "social groups ... want to control their children's reading without being aware that children's reactions to reading are determined more by their sense of fictional forms than they are by contents."[60]

A Senate committee investigating comic books made the connection between comic books and juvenile delinquency explicit. The testimony was often based on hearsay, anecdotal charges that juvenile delinquency was rising, in part, due to comic books. J. Edgar Hoover, head of the Federal Bureau of Investigation, though, expressed doubt "that an appreciable decrease in juvenile delinquency would result if crime comic books of all types were not readily available to children."[61]

Crime comics drew the ire of many adults. *Crime Does Not Pay* was an exemplar of the new crime comics genre, with "Crime" emblazoned in large block letters. One historian characterizes the rest of the cover as "a tempest of excess." The comic initially sold 200,000 copies but gradually climbed to one million by 1947. Since purchasers of comics frequently shared them with several friends, the comic's publisher, Charles Biro, bragged in a banner across the top of each issue: "More than 5,000,000 Readers Monthly."[62]

After the Congressional uproar over comic books and facing changing tastes by comic book readers, *Crime Does Not Pay* ended its run as a tired, irrelevant comic. In a futile act, the comic even featured a New York City Police Department Women's Bureau officer, Mary Sullivan, on the cover with her endorsement: "I approve of their magazine as a good moral influence on our youth. I recommend it to parents as a powerful lesson for good behavior." One could hardly imagine a worse fate for a comic book. Other crime comics tried such lame stunts as inscribing, "Not Intended for Children" and "For Adults Only," on their covers. The crime genre no longer paid.[63]

The comic industry was not without irony. Max Gaines introduced *Picture Stories from the Bible*, gaining approval from various religious groups. This comic competed with *Classics Illustrated* (formerly *Classics Comics*).[64] Needless to say, proponents who believed that comics might be of educational use were in the minority, although two children's librarians suggested in *Library Journal* that comics satisfied a child's desire for "excitement, adventure and hero worship." They derided children's books as "written down to childish levels, and strive to be correct, innocuous, and entertaining at the same time."[65]

By the 1940s, comics were becoming sensationalized in order to attract readers. Sidonie Gruenberg argues that "it is the very qualities for which the comics have been condemned by critics that give them force and make them socially significant. For it is these qualities that enabled them to catch the attention and hold the interest of the children." Gruenberg was one of the hopeful minority, who stressed the potential educational value of comics, even lauding Max Gaines and *Picture Stories from the Bible*; Gaines's son, William, would not fare so well. Gruenberg recognized that comics "have become almost universally intelligible. As a medium of expression they are coming to be at least as free as the press and, for purely economic reasons, much more so than the cinema and the radio." Josette Frank, staff adviser to the Children's Book committee of the Child Study Association of America, also believed that some comics had redeeming value, although she deplored the "portrayal of horror or torture" or comics that "exploit the female form or picture amorous embraces." During the Senate hearing of 1954, Senator Estes Kefauver accused Frank of being an adviser for Fawcett Publications, in an attempt to undercut her credibility.[66]

In an editorial to the *Journal of Educational Sociology*, Harvey Zorbaugh stated that a recent national poll found three-quarters of adults surveyed viewed "comic books a[s] 'good, clean fun.'" Then again, Zorbaugh also stated, "Comic characters are among the widely known influential personalities of the day. . . . Their impact on our culture is seen at every hand. They have influenced our diet and health habits [Popeye and spinach] . . . and set a fashion in boys' clothes [Buster Brown].'"[67]

David Hajdu believes that while comic books were "uninhibited, shameless, frequently garish and crude, often shocking, and sometimes excessive, these crime, horror, and romance comics provided young people of the early postwar years with a means of defying and escaping the mainstream culture of the time, while providing the guardians of that culture an enormous, taunting, close-range target." He later wrote, "Comics were capital in the social economy of childhood, void among adults."[68]

A civil libertarian described the hysteria over comic books: "The anti-comic book crusade spread through the country with the speed of a virulent contagion. . . . In a number of places, incensed groups seized all the comic books they could lay hands on, piled them high on a bonfire, and burned them amidst elaborate ceremonies."[69]

A key factor spurring the postwar scrutiny of comic books was concern over juvenile delinquency.[70] Amy Nyberg believes that comic books stood in for the sins of mass media. The comic books made for a convenient target, since they were aimed at children, even though many adults read them; they were immensely popular; and they were the least regulated of the mass media.[71]

All the anti-comic book crowd needed was a link between juvenile delinquency and comic books. Fredric Wertham was to supply this link. Nyberg pointed out that Wertham aimed his *Seduction of the Innocent* toward a general audience, so he did not establish his theoretical argument as fully as he might have, a tactic that earned him scorn from many critics. Wertham was convinced that the solution to stemming violent behavior lay not with treating the individual but in reforming the society that shaped those individuals. He advocated using "social psychiatry" to treat the social environment of patients, "arguing that juvenile delinquency reflected the social values of society and that comic books were not a mirror of a child's mind but 'a mirror of the child's environment.'" James Gilbert believes that Wertham "deliberately and effectively used comic books as a way to draw attention to his broader agenda of social reform."[72]

Gilbert suggests that the comic book industry gradually absorbed the lessons Hollywood had learned in previous censorship battles. Hollywood established a production code, ostensibly to clean up its product. Individual theaters, though, were unable to placate local citizens' groups, because they had no discretion over film content due to block booking (whereby theater owners had to take a group of films, instead of choosing individual films for their theaters). The major studios preferred this method of centralized censorship, because "to allow censorship on a local level would have necessitated a curtailment of industry power. This, in turn, would make an uniform production code far more difficult to enforce."[73]

By the 1950s, though, the major studios' monopoly power was reduced, and block booking was prohibited. Gilbert points out the irony of the situation: local theaters' ability to pick and choose individual films meant that the family film fell out of favor. The theaters and producers realized that "the audience was increasingly segmented as the industry recognized the especially lucrative youth and teenage market." He concludes, "the movie industry tried to have it both ways: it claimed to be helping in the national fight against delinquency, while it exploited public interest in, and even fear of, juvenile culture."[74]

The comic book industry sought to forestall unfavorable publicity and legislation by establishing the Association of Comic Magazine Publishers (ACMP) and a code, which was based on Fawcett Publication's in-house code. Although the code focused on the topic of the hour—crime—it also contained provisions on sex, obscenity, and treatment of racial and religious groups, including edicts such as: "Ridicule of or attack on any religious or racial group is never permissible" and the remarkably vague, "No drawing should show a female indecently or unduly exposed, and in no event more nude than in a bathing suit commonly worn in the United States of America." The code proved to be ineffectual.[75]

Estes Kefauver was a senator from Tennessee who harbored presidential aspirations. He served on highly publicized committees investigating organized crime and professional sports. He also chaired a Senate committee investing crime in a different medium: comic books. The committee found little definitive evidence linking comic books and juvenile delinquency. The legislators expressed no opinion nor recommended any action regarding comic books for the time being. Kefauver would try again.[76]

Comic book aficionados blame Wertham for the ensuing comic book upheaval. Martin Barker takes a sympathetic view of Wertham, but the psychiatrist's actions were questionable.[77] Wertham claimed a survey found "that seventy-five per cent of parents are against comic books. (The other twenty-five per cent are either indifferent or misled by propaganda and 'research')." He did not cite any sources for the 75 percent figure. He added that his own and his colleagues' studies showed that comic books systematically poisoned the "well of childhood spontaneity. Many children themselves feel guilty about reading them. The worst sector of comic books is increasing and the best, if there is a best, is getting smaller. The comic-book publishers seduce the children and mislead the parents." He also claimed that comic books displaced good children's books. Nyberg took a less sympathetic view of Wertham than did Barker. She detailed how Wertham manipulated public opinion with biased anecdotal evidence.[78]

William C. Gaines's testimony was dramatic, amusing, and disastrous, both to himself and to many in the comic book industry. I say "many" and not "all" because some publishers gained from the eventual demise of their competitors, such as Gaines. Many in the comic book industry undoubtedly agreed that making Gaines a scapegoat for the industry's ills was good public relations.[79] Certainly the Senate committee was pleased by the ouster of Gaines; legislators gained a cheap victory at the expense of many artists and production workers in the industry, many of whom would never work in the comic industry again.

The second hearings in 1954 may have been intended to coerce the comic book industry to clean up the contents of its publications by creating negative public opinion. The industry leaders realized Senator Kefauver's gambit and formulated a revised, tougher code, although some publishers wanted to use a First Amendment argument in litigation. The leading publishers "agreed that horror comics would have to be sacrificed in order to demonstrate the industry was serious about its pledge to clean up comics. The words horror and terror were banned from comic book titles, and scenes dealing with the walking dead, vampires, ghouls, cannibalism, and werewolves were prohibited."[80] One can only imagine how aghast the comic book crusaders would be, if they saw the new millennium's fascination with *The Walking Dead*, *Buffy the Vampire Slayer*, and their ilk. Then again, there were academic conferences held to deconstruct *Buffy the Vampire Slayer*.

For many of the largest comic book publishers, this capitulation and subsequent self-policing afforded them the opportunity to rid the industry of upstart independents, who had often resorted to more lurid, sensational stories. William C. Gaines had suggested such an industry association to police content, but he became one of the casualties: "And it was always an ironic thing to me that I was the guy who started the damn association and they turned around and the first thing they did was ban the words weird, horror and terror from any comic magazine . . . those were my three big words."[81]

The new code proved fatal to many publishers, although there were other reasons for a retrenchment in the comic book industry. Nyberg takes issue with the received tale of persecuted genius William Gaines and many others being hounded out of the industry by a Puritanical code. The new code helped industry leaders concentrate the comic book industry into the hands of fewer, larger, more respectable publishers. Nyberg reported that when Gaines tried to steer the committee toward the monopolistic practices of the Comics Magazine Association of America, Kefauver wasn't interested.[82]

Nyberg takes a skeptical view of the hearings' outcome. She writes, "The association's public relations firm also believed the new code had accomplished what the industry had set out to do. The code allowed the critics to believe that they had won the battle. At the same time, the code prohibited only the most extreme forms of violence."[83]

David Hajdu, too, suggests a multi-causal explanation for comics' decline in the mid-1950s. One factor was the disruption in the distribution of comics. When industry leaders American News Group and Union News consented to alter their distribution practices, many comic publishers had to find new distributors. Another factor was the self-imposed censorship; the comic industry so diluted its content that the bleached comics were no match for television and motion pictures. "All the dark craziness that made comics so interesting and so successful [was] stripped away," said Harry Harrison, artist and writer, "They were so juvenile that *Howdy Doody* was more interesting. Television didn't kill the comics. [It] didn't have to. The job was already done."[84]

The comics industry's self-imposed censor, Comics Magazine Association of America, proved to be more rigorous than the supplanted ACMP comics' code or even the motion picture industry's code. The code imbued publishers with the idea that "comics should reflect dominant American values."[85] Some comic publishers did not subscribe to the code, not because they could not comply, but because they disagreed with it.[86]

## Toys and Playthings

Another industry catering to children drew fire from commentators. *Business Week* reported that leisure accounted for $341 billion of disposable spending in 1994, of which playthings were the largest component at $65 billion. Gambling ($28 billion), cable television ($19 billion), and amusement parks ($14 billion) were gaining on TVs/VCRs and printed publications. Stephen Kline describes the relationship between toys and mass marketing, conveyed largely through television. He observes that how children play reflects the social environment and is a part of the socialization process. He further notes, "toys are also the first possessions to be called 'mine,' the first things children can learn to influence on their own, and the first objects children begin to purchase and collect."[87]

Helen Schwartzman, too, sees an importance in children's play: "Children at play learn how to be sensitive to the effects of context and the importance of relationships; they develop the capacity to adopt an 'as if' set towards objects, actions, persons, and situations. . . . These abilities are certainly all of great consequence to the individual and to society."[88] Brian Sutton-Smith suggests that in the consumer society, toys are not just playthings, but prototype consumer goods, because they are also the "possessions with which children can learn the materialistic culture habits of late-twentieth-century, American civilization."[89]

Toy manufacturers exploited the deregulation of American television in 1982. They were now free to advertise "licensed character toys." The sale of playthings increased fourfold between 1977 and 1998. Adults encouraged or corrupted children's imaginations with symbolic media offered by the entertainment market, whether through video games, dolls, or role-player equipment. The licensed toys accounted for three-quarters of toy sales, while toy makers "transformed themselves from manufacturers of playthings into orchestrators of marketing plans."[90]

Kline attributes the rising spending on playthings to the insinuation of commercial television into family life, with its repeated showings of products aimed at children; with the growth of the children's television audience, merchandisers could profitably market products to target or create children's preferences for toys. Toy merchandisers had become the biggest spenders for children's advertising; they also developed and produced their own children's television programming, which were essentially 30-minute advertisements. By 1988, children between the ages of 9 and 15 received $4.75 billion in allowances, causing marketers to tread the thin line between responsible and exploitive advertising to children.[91]

## The New Bachelor of the 1950s

For the first half of the twentieth century, middle-class American males adhered to the old tradition that a man should strive to be productive. Although there were glimmers of an alternative, consumption-based lifestyle, the 1950s witnessed a flowering of male identity based upon consumption. Bill Osgerby uses the term "lifestyle," coined by French theorist Pierre Bourdieu, to denote "patterns of taste and consumption used by social groups to distinguish themselves as distinct and coherent class formations." This concept built upon Max Weber's argument that social stratification was not merely based on economic relation, "but also on the degree of 'status' attached to the patterns of living and cultural preferences of different social groups." The new lifestyle for affluent, young American men during the 1950s emphasized fun and the "art of living," a concentration upon "personal gratification and individuality and established through the consumption of distinctive cultural goods and signifiers."[92]

Osgerby theorizes that in the rapidly changing world of the 1950s, younger middle class men sought and generated new identities based upon consumer desire and consumption, especially those of hedonism, heterosexual gratification, and fun. In the end, however, these changes merely shook but did not overturn basic societal power relationships.[93]

The 1950s "playboy" had antecedents. Osgerby describes the changing demographics of America's large cities at the turn of the century. The growing number of single young men created a "bachelor subculture." The phenomenon was not associated with lower economic prospects, as immigrant and working-class native males were more likely to marry than middle-class white native males. Howard Chudacoff pinpointed the "myriad leisure-time diversions" that developed in the late nineteenth century, "many of which tempted and filled the everyday lives and leisure time of young, independent men and women" and that created a "new heterosocial culture, one that brought together young, unattached men and women in social and sometimes sexual relationships that minimized personal commitment."[94]

The magazine *Playboy* may have exemplified this male hedonistic culture, but, despite Hugh Hefner's unwillingness to admit it, *Playboy* had its precursor: *Esquire* magazine. This publication began in the depths of the Great Depression, 1933, and aimed at upmarket male consumers. The magazine was an instant hit, and its stress on being a "peerless arbiter of good taste" set it apart. While the magazine differed from traditional Protestant-male mores, its masculine consumerism "sought to adapt rather than overturn the existing social order."[95]

The ethos of this more hedonistic, consumerist lifestyle coincided with improving living standards after World War II. The ethos, however, clashed with a growing domesticity for men. Throughout the 1950s, men faced social pressures to marry, raise a family, and settle down. To be a breadwinner was the goal, and men who willfully departed from this role might face social opprobrium. Aside from the hedonistic lifestyle pushed by *Esquire* and *Playboy*, there were undoubtedly many American males who simply did not want to conform to the social norms. Perhaps some decided that suburbia and family life made for a banal existence.[96]

By the end of the 1950s, *Life* magazine devoted most of its December 28, 1959, issue to leisure. The magazine's editorial admitted that the growing amount of leisure time was not an unalloyed benefit. The issue included an article by Sloan Wilson, author of *The Man in the Gray Flannel Suit*, who criticized the "confusing eulogies of leisure, which, without the most careful definition, seem to be calls for sloppy self-indulgence."[97] These exceptions aside, most of the issue was optimistic and laudatory about the trend, in which the postwar leisure spending boom accounted for 8 percent of America's GNP.

Automobile manufacturers picked upon on this new lifestyle phenomenon. The manufacturers designed automobiles to fulfill leisure and status needs simultaneously. Ford's "Mustang" proved tremendously popular in the mid-1960s. Ford sold the sports car not as a means of transportation, of course, but as a lifestyle statement.[98]

As some American youths drifted into the counterculture during the 1960s and 1970s, many viewed them as rebels against the established order. In

Osgerby's view, "rather than representing the antithesis of the consumer society, the counterculture can itself be seen as a developmental phase in the evolution of the new, consumption-oriented petite bourgeoisie." He sees the counterculture as helping the new middle class in their fumbling toward "'hip' individuality and sensuous indulgence through hedonistic and 'youthful' patterns of consumption."[99] Thomas Frank observes, "rather than representing the nemesis of advanced capitalism, 'the counterculture may be more accurately understood as a stage in the development of the values of the American middle class, a colorful installment in the twentieth century drama of consumer subjectivity.'"[100]

## Black Americans' Leisure

Black Americans' leisure patterns remain largely unplumbed by scholars, but presumably what attention white reformers paid the issue was disapproving. Richard Butsch asserts that reformers had "limited success . . . either in co-opting space for their own leisure or controlling the recreations of the working class," despite repeated efforts. Even the supposedly benevolent efforts of the parks movement could be viewed as oppressive: "the parks movement . . . [was] supervision designed to police working-class uses of the streets and to put workers' children under state control."[101] These observations could be applied to the growing African-American populations in Northern cities.

During World War II, some African-American and Mexican-American youths sported showy clothes labeled "Zoot suits." The roomy trousers and suitable accessories made not only a fashion statement, but an inherently political statement. Historian Luis Alvarez sees Zoot suiters' "preference for items and pastimes that many considered extravagant and leisurely flouted popular constraints on consumption in favor of contributing to the war effort." Not all Americans understood or countenanced Zoot suiters, and whites attacked Zoot suiters in several cities. Alvarez believes, quite plausibly, that Zoot suiters were not obstructing the war effort. "What they did with the clothes, watch chains, and hats they bought, and how they used those commodities to stylize their bodies, both expressed their own aesthetic autonomy and revealed their unique perspective on wartime consumption. Moreover, zoot consumption quite possibly revealed nonwhite youth's willingness to be a part of wartime society, as long as their identity and dignity were respected."[102]

## Changing Patterns of Leisure

American's senior citizens and youngsters have been at the forefront of changing leisure patterns. Older Americans enjoyed longer and more active retirements than ever before. Retirement became an anticipated rather than dreaded event. Younger Americans, though prone to fads, became trend-setters, although their antics often disturbed their elders. Young males spearheaded the rise of a more hedonistic lifestyle.

America is greying rapidly, now that the baby boomers are reaching 65. Almost 50 years ago, Nobel Prize–winner Paul Samuelson extolled the Social Security program for being a Ponzi scheme: "The beauty of social insurance is that it is *actuarially* [italics his] unsound." Unlike Mr. Ponzi, the government's scheme could theoretically go on forever, if its two underlying pillars persisted: "the national product is growing at compound interest and can be expected to do so for as far ahead as the eye cannot see. Always there are more youths than old folks in a growing population." He concluded, "A growing nation is the greatest Ponzi game ever contrived. And that is a fact, not a paradox."[103] Unfortunately for Professor Samuelson's prediction, birth rates fell and productivity gains proved more elusive throughout much of the final decades of the twentieth century.

Although Social Security may be an inadequate and unsatisfactory way to finance retirement, the real question is whether Americans of working age can support both a large cohort of aging baby boomers and a cohort of young people. If the answer is negative, the future of pleasurable leisure during retirement may become bleak.

# The Interaction of Leisure and Public Health

Of course, income, consumption, and wealth are not the only variables determining the "quality of life." Key components in the rise of leisure time, goods, and services have been improvements in health and longevity and the growing resistance to chronic and debilitating diseases. Most Americans can now anticipate several years of active living while in retirement—a block of leisure time known to only a few adults throughout history. Americans are living much longer than their predecessors, with some of the most rapid increases in longevity occurring between 1850 and 1950 (Table 7.1). Most of the increase occurred before the health profession's efficacy increased dramatically after the 1930s. The debate as to the causes of the increased longevity revolves around apportioning the credit to better sanitation, better living standards, and medical advances.

## The Turnover in Causes of Death

The bromide "don't drink the water," amended with "don't breathe the air," would have been an appropriate warning for Americans living in cities at the dawn of the twentieth century.[1] Water- and airborne diseases were the leading causes of death in 1900 (Table 7.2). Pneumonia, tuberculosis, and diarrhea/enteritis were the three leading causes of death as a percentage of all death in 1900, with heart disease and stroke rounding out the top five. In 1997, heart disease, cancer, stroke, and chronic lung disease comprised the top four, with the first two being by far the most predominant causes of death. Children under the age of five years were over 30 percent of the victims in 1900, while that figure fell to 1.4 percent in 1997. The Centers for Disease Control stated, "Disease control resulted from improvements in sanitation and hygiene, the discovery of antibiotics, and the implementation of universal childhood vaccination programs. . . . Local, state,

*Table 7.1* **Expectation of Life at Specified Ages, 1900–2003**[a]

| | At Birth | | At Age 20 | | At Age 60 | |
|---|---|---|---|---|---|---|
| | *Male* | *Female* | *Male* | *Female* | *Male* | *Female* |
| 2003 | 74.7 | 80.0 | 55.8 | 60.8 | 20.4 | 23.7 |
| 1989–1991 | 71.8 | 78.8 | 53.3 | 59.9 | 18.5 | 22.9 |
| 1979–1981 | 70.1 | 77.6 | 51.9 | 59.0 | 17.5 | 22.3 |
| 1970 | 68.0 | 75.6 | 50.3 | 57.4 | 16.2 | 21.0 |
| 1960 | 67.4 | 74.1 | 50.1 | 56.2 | 15.9 | 19.7 |
| 1949–1951 | 66.3 | 72.0 | 49.5 | 54.6 | 15.8 | 18.6 |
| 1939–1941 | 62.8 | 67.3 | 47.8 | 51.4 | 15.1 | 17.0 |
| 1929–1931 | 59.1 | 62.7 | 46.0 | 48.5 | 14.7 | 16.1 |
| 1919–1921 | 56.3 | 58.5 | 45.6 | 46.5 | 15.3 | 15.9 |
| 1909–1911 | 50.2 | 53.6 | 42.7 | 44.0 | 14.0 | 14.9 |
| 1900–1902 | 48.2 | 51.1 | 42.2 | 43.8 | 14.4 | 15.2 |

[a] US Department of Commerce, Bureau of the Census, *Historical Statistics of the United States, Part 1*, 56; US Department of Commerce, Bureau of the Census. *Statistical Abstract of the United States: 2008*, 74.

and federal efforts to improve sanitation and hygiene reinforced the concept of collective 'public health' action."[2]

Improved longevity was recognized by the 1930s. Leo Wolman and Gustav Peck, writing in *Recent Social Trends in the United States* during the early years of the Great Depression, highlighted improved health across income classes in America. This improvement was reflected in the diminishing mortality rates from pulmonary tuberculosis, which they characterized as an economic disease, and in infant mortality, which was tied to family income. They credited public health policies and improved medical facilities for these gains.[3]

The movement of labor from rural to urban areas required advances in public health—advances dependent to a large degree upon the formulation and dissemination of the germ theory of air- and waterborne illnesses. This is not to deny that the miasmatic theory had its public health triumphs. Effective public health measures, including sewage treatment and clean water, combined with better nutrition to significantly eradicate water- and airborne diseases. Improved nutrition from advances in agricultural productivity helped combat these diseases by providing greater resistance. Since people must eventually die, the reduction in the scourges of the past has been partially counterbalanced by rising incidences of cancer.

*Table 7.2* **Death Rates and Causes (Per 100,000), 1900–2004[a]**

|      | *1900* | *1910* | *1920* | *1930* | *1940* | *1950* | *1960* | *1970* | *2004* |
|------|--------|--------|--------|--------|--------|--------|--------|--------|--------|
| DR:  | 17.2   | 14.7   | 13.0   | 11.3   | 10.8   | 9.6    | 9.5    | 9.5    | 8.2    |
| Tu:  | 194.4  | 153.8  | 113.1  | 71.1   | 45.9   | 22.5   | 6.1    | 2.6    | n.a.   |
| Sy:  | 12.0   | 13.5   | 16.5   | 15.7   | 14.4   | 5.0    | 1.6    | 0.2    | n.a.   |
| Ty:  | 31.3   | 22.5   | 7.6    | 4.8    | 1.1    | 0.1    | 0.0    | 0.0    | n.a.   |
| SF:  | 9.6    | 11.4   | 4.6    | 1.9    | 0.5    | 0.2    | 0.1    | 0.0    | n.a.   |
| Di:  | 40.3   | 21.1   | 15.3   | 4.9    | 1.1    | 0.3    | 0.0    | 0.0    | n.a.   |
| WC:  | 12.2   | 11.6   | 12.5   | 4.8    | 2.2    | 0.7    | 0.1    | 0.0    | n.a.   |
| Me:  | 13.3   | 12.4   | 8.8    | 3.2    | 0.5    | 0.3    | 0.2    | 0.0    | n.a.   |
| MN:  | 64.0   | 76.2   | 83.4   | 97.4   | 120.3  | 139.8  | 149.2  | 162.8  | 188.6  |
| Db:  | 11.0   | 15.3   | 16.1   | 19.1   | 26.6   | 16.2   | 16.7   | 18.9   | 24.9   |
| MC:  | 345.2  | 371.9  | 364.9  | 414.4  | 485.7  | 510.8  | 521.8  | 496.0  | 222.2  |
| In:  | 202.2  | 155.9  | 207.3  | 102.5  | 70.3   | 31.3   | 37.3   | 30.9   | 20.3   |
| Ga:  | 142.7  | 115.4  | 53.7   | 26.0   | 10.3   | 5.1    | 4.4    | 0.6    | n.a.   |
| Ci:  | 12.5   | 13.3   | 7.1    | 7.2    | 8.6    | 9.2    | 11.3   | 15.5   | n.a.   |
| MV:  | n.a.[1] | 1.8   | 10.3   | 26.7   | 26.2   | 23.1   | 21.3   | 26.9   | 15.3   |
| AF:  | n.a.[2] | 15.4  | 11.8   | 14.7   | 17.2   | 13.8   | 10.6   | 8.3    | n.a.   |
| OA:  | 72.3   | 67.0   | 47.9   | 38.4   | 29.8   | 23.7   | 20.4   | 21.2   | 22.8[3] |
| Su:  | 10.2   | 15.8   | 10.2   | 15.6   | 14.4   | 11.4   | 10.6   | 11.6   | n.a.   |

0.0: Less than 0.05.

[1] 1910 and 1920, excludes automobile collisions with trains and streetcars, and motorcycle accidents.

[2] 1900–1920, includes legal executions; 1900–1908, food poisoning; and 1900–1905, motor vehicle accidents.

[3] Total accidents: Motor vehicle accidents.

DR: Death rate per 1,000.

Tu: Tuberculosis, all forms.

Sy: Syphilis and its sequelae.

Ty: Typhoic and typhoid fever.

SF: Scarlet fever and streptococcal sore throat.

Di: Diphtheria.

WC: Whooping cough.

Me: Measles.

MN: Malignant neoplasms.

Db: Diabetes mellitus.

MC: Major cardiovascular-renal diseases.

In: Influenza and pneumonia.

Ga: Gastritis, duodenitis, enteritis, and colitis.

*Table 7.2* (**continued**)

Ci: Cirrhosis of liver.
MV: Motor vehicle accidents.
AF: Accidental falls.
OA: all other accidents.
Su: Suicide.

[a] US Department of Commerce, *Historical Statistics of the United States, Part 1*, 58–59; US Department of Commerce, *Statistical Abstract of the United States: 2008*, 87.

The germ theory sparked renewed fears of immigrants. People began to fear "street cars, paper money, and library books . . . thought to be threatening carriers of deadly microbes. But nothing caused more alarm than unwashed immigrants in neighboring slums."[4]

Unclean water and contaminated milk took a heavy toll in lives, especially among infants and young children. The germ theory was crucial in recognizing the source of infant diarrhea and dehydration. Even if children survived contaminated liquids, their poor diets and exposure often rendered them unfit for military duty years later. Military officials in 1917–1918 were aghast that over 30 percent of potential recruits were physically unfit. To combat this wastage, philanthropists and taxpayers began funding clean milk supplies.[5]

Public health officials also began encouraging the provision of prenatal care for expectant mothers. The campaign worked so well that the vast majority of babies born in 1956 were delivered in hospitals, a reversal of 1935, when a majority were delivered outside hospitals.[6]

At the individual level, Americans began taking steps to improve their health. Some clergy began encouraging physical exercise. Recognizing that white-collar Americans had less opportunity to keep their bodies fit through hard physical exertion, these clerics argued that Americans needed strong bodies. They advocated what came to be known as "Muscular Christianity," to be accomplished through athletics and play.[7]

## Longer Lives, Healthier Lives

Not only have Americans increased their longevity for the past 350 years, they've succeeded in creating a more egalitarian longevity. Comedian Sophie Tucker once said, "I've been rich and I've been poor. Believe me, honey, rich is better."[8] For much of history, rich people have lived substantially longer than poor people. One of the great achievements of the agricultural and industrial revolutions in the Western world has been the diminution in the gap in longevity between the poor and the rich. In 1875 there was a gap of 17 years between the average life expectancy of the British elite and that of the population as a whole. There is still a social gap in life expectancy among the British, but today the advantage of the richest classes over the poorest classes is about a year.[9]

Unfortunately, the trend toward equalization in life expectancy between rich and poor has been reversed somewhat for the past few decades. In America, some groups of poor people, such as black males living in Harlem, had death rates that reputedly approached those of third-world countries. In Britain, while the rich are living longer than ever, some of the poor were experiencing rising death rates. Life expectancy for some of the poor may have been worse than it was in the early 1950s. Although one might not be as surprised to find widening health gaps between rich and poor in the United States, with its apparently widening income gaps, the British situation is a puzzle. British citizens have access to the National Health Service, a universal healthcare service. Although real incomes for poorer Britons may have fallen somewhat, no one seriously believes that they fell so significantly as to directly cause dramatic increases in the death rate. Poor Britons still enjoy a standard of living that would be envied by the majority of people throughout the world. It therefore appears that the absolute level of poverty is not the main culprit for the worsening health of poor Britons. An intriguing possibility is that relative levels of income contribute to overall health. As an article in the *Economist* points out, "Status and stress are among non-monetary factors that appear to be significant."[10] The direction of causality is difficult to ascertain: Does stress cause lower income, or does lower income cause stress?

Although differences in longevity between races has narrowed, African-Americans still experience worse health outcomes on average, including greater susceptibility to chronic conditions, shorter stature, and, ironically, higher body mass indexes (BMI), implying a different sort of malnutrition: over-nutrition. The BMI is calculated as "the ratio of weight in kilograms to height in meters squared." The increasing incidence of obesity, with its nasty side effects, may retard further increases in longevity.[11]

There have been dramatic changes in life-cycle patterns in America. During Colonial times, Americans married at roughly the same age as they did in 1950, which was relatively young compared to other eras. There ends the similarity between our Colonial ancestors and our grandparents. The Colonial Americans, if they survived to majority, had a good chance of reaching current-day middle age, while our grandparents lived, on average, to 77. The Colonials continued to produce children up to their late thirties, while the modern American typically stops before the age of 30. Given the Colonial Americans' early deaths, few of them suffered from empty nest syndrome. Modern American parents have decades of living after their children have left home, although there is a trend toward children moving back in with their parents.[12]

The earliest English settlers of Virginia and Massachusetts struggled greatly, but within a hundred years, their living standards were approaching those of England and France, then the leading European economies. By the end of the second century of English colonization, American diets were the envy of the Western world. In addition, the natural rate of population growth in the United States was quite rapid.

Meat consumption has long been a proxy for living standards. In 1880, Michael Mulhall wrote, in his *Progress of the World*, that a country's prosperity was reflected by the prevalence of meat in its citizens' diet. In 1756, "an astonished traveler wrote of the United States, 'Even in the humblest or poorest houses no meals are served without a meat course.' European migrants were delighted to discover that in the United States, 'every day is like Christmas day for meat.'" Although producing meat instead of vegetables and grains required more land and resources, Americans opted for meat over potatoes and bread. Americans are not unique in their preferences. Lebergott points out that, "people worldwide eat meat . . . when they . . . have enough food or enough wealth . . . eating cereals and tubers only when they must. And a leading English Marxist has found it reasonable 'to take meat consumption as a criterion of standard of living' of the working class. For centuries, cheap meat constituted one of America's attractions.'"[13]

At the end of the eighteen century, England and France still had difficulty providing enough calories to sustain their populations. A significant proportion of the population barely had enough calories for a career in beggary. They could sit on the street and beg, but they were incapable of moderate or heavy labor.[14] Indeed, one of the more recent tools in measuring well-being—examining height and weight data—is illuminating. If you look at suits of armor in a museum, most of the suits would comfortably fit the author (5'6", 155 lbs.). Many people were stunted (short stature) and wasted (underweight) due to a lack of calories. They were more vulnerable to the infectious diseases swirling about them. People today are much bigger and more resistant to infectious diseases.

Many American cities had polluted air and water. Pittsburgh and the other heavy manufacturing and extracting centers were dirty places. The meat packers of Chicago discarded their waste in a pool of water that almost became jellified with filth and noxious gases. Since horses were an important form of transportation, the city streets were clogged with horse manure, to say nothing of dead horses. On hot days, the manure would be pulverized into dust. In Chicago, supposedly it was against the law to eat outdoors, because of the sanitation problem. On rainy days, the many unpaved streets became muddy, filthy places to walk. Women, with their long skirts, were accused of tracking filth and disease into their homes. In an era before the germ theory became accepted, many public health measures were ineffectual.

Unless you were a hermit, you had to be wary of being around other people. Infectious diseases were implacable killers for much of American and world history. In 1900, out of a city of over 100,000, perhaps 800 people per year would have died from various infectious diseases (Table 7.2). In addition, infant mortality rates were much higher in 1900. Indeed, if infant mortality rates from the 1800s had continued to the present, perhaps one-fifth to one-third of you reading this book would not be alive. There was also no guarantee that, even if you survived infancy, you would make it to majority. By century's end, it was very rare for modern Americans to die between the ages of one and 18, and these deaths are often the result of accidents, suicides, or homicides.

Such diseases as polio were not only crippling but terrifying. Parents feared their children would contract the disease. "No one was exempt from becoming a victim of the fear generated by the disease. Even in relatively homogenous and well educated communities neighbor turned on neighbor."[15] Public health efforts in promoting vaccinations have resulted in the vast majority of children being immunized against several heretofore deadly diseases and have contributed to the reduced mortality among children. Vaccination proved highly successful in eradicating smallpox and polio.[16]

As noted, because a much higher proportion of infants survive to adulthood, the American age distribution has been tilting toward older ages, which, of course, entails a different set of issues, such as degenerative diseases. Cancer and heart disease have vaulted to the top of the mortality rankings.

The increased death rates from cancer and cardiovascular/renal conditions reflect the diminution of infectious diseases. Is that a sign of deteriorating living standards? In a sense, since you have to die from something, rising death rates from cancer and cardiovascular conditions are signs that people live long enough to incur these conditions. Some observers call these conditions "rich man's diseases," as many poor people succumb to other causes long before incurring cancer and heart disease.

The AIDS situation has caused an increase in the death rates from infectious diseases since 1980. However, notice that the death rate of 11 per 100,000 pales before the death rates from influenza and pneumonia in 1900, which is not to belittle the AIDS situation, but to demonstrate how much progress we've made in treating and containing diseases.

## Public Health Measures

Americans and their British cousins began investing in public health during the last years of the nineteenth century. Robert Fogel and his co-authors discussed the process between investment and payoffs: "Failure to take account of these extremely long lags between investments and payoffs leads to puzzling paradoxes." They cited the 1930s, when male heights increased and life expectancy rose by four years, despite the economic upheaval and diminished incomes. They attributed this to the "huge social investments, by both government and private enterprise, made between 1870 and 1930, whose payoffs were not counted as part of national income during the 1920s and 1930s even though they produced a large stream of benefits during these decades." These investments in biomedical research, clean water and milk supplies, slum clearance, swamp draining, and effective quarantines provided long-lasting benefits.[17]

The diminution in infectious diseases had another consequence. Because infections require energy to sustain the immune system's response, people living in food-deficient situations are susceptible to protein energy malnutrition. Malnutrition, meanwhile, can raise the risk of infections, especially among children, as nutritional deficiencies can affect cognitive performance, the immune system, the susceptibility to diarrhea, pneumonia, measles, and malaria, and therefore raise child mortality rates in developing countries.[18]

As Americans' longevity increases, the possibility that people simply have additional years of coping with degenerative diseases or chronic debilities might cast doubt on the benefits of increased longevity. Fogel and Dora Costa have extensively studied the health of older Americans; they scoured a unique database: Union Army veteran pensions. The veterans of the winning side in the Civil War received pensions; initially, the pensions were based on disability stemming from the war, but the program eventually evolved into an old age pension. Recipients were required to undergo annual physicals, and physicians forwarded the data to Washington, D.C. Fogel, Costa, and their associates were able to construct a database that covers hundreds of thousands of men across many years of their lives. "The health of the elderly relative to their counterparts today remained poor for several decades after 1910." Union veterans, for instance, were far more likely to be blind than similarly aged men later in the twentieth century.[19]

Union Army veterans at older ages were much more likely to suffer from chronic disorders than modern American males. "The exposure to chronic malnutrition and infectious environments explains why people in the past had poor health over their lifetimes and died earlier. Reduced exposure to infectious environments has led to a significant decline in the age-specific prevalence of chronic diseases during the twentieth century."[20] Elsewhere, Fogel and his co-authors state, "Across the whole age range, healthy life expectancy has risen along with life expectancy, while the incidence of disability has fallen and estimated disability-free life expectancy has risen."[21]

## Economic Benefits of Increased Longevity

Longevity, even in crowded urban areas, began to improve by the early 1900s. With longer life expectancies, investment in human capital became more attractive. Americans, particularly in the Northeast, had high rates of literacy, but relatively few had high school or college degrees. As Americans invested in human capital, they became even more productive, leading to a beneficial cycle of growth unparalleled in human history. Americans used their increased longevity both to earn higher incomes but also to take more leisure, especially in the long block of time during retirement. Not only did they take retirement, they had greater financial resources and better health from which to enjoy their years away from employment.

Americans of the twenty-first century face a new form of malnutrition: too many calories and too many "bad" calories. Combined with less-active jobs, obesity rates are rising. Will the rise in obesity end Americans' increasing life expectancies?

# 8

# The Changing Workplace

Americans are not just living longer. They may work as many hours per week as their predecessors did in the 1930s, but the nature of their work has changed considerably.

By the early twentieth century, American workers had grudgingly acquiesced to time-labor discipline. Historian E. P. Thompson describes how British workers were transformed from unruly, ill-disciplined laborers to orderly, disciplined workers during the eighteenth and nineteenth centuries. The conversion was, in the main, similar to the struggle in the United States between pioneering factory owners and their workers. Thompson emphasized the importance of time pieces, although employers and employees fought over time. He related two anecdotes. In the first, the owner of the Crowley Iron Works was outraged that "sundry clerks have been so unjust as to reckon by clocks going the fastest and the bell ringing before the hour for their going from business, and clocks going too slow and the bell ringing after the hour for their coming to business, and those two black traitors Fowell and Skellerne have knowingly allowed the same." His solution was to lock up the clock, with only the clock-keeper having access.[1]

Time worked both ways, in a sense, as in the second anecdote, a Dundee factory boy reminisced: "in reality there were no regular hours; masters and managers did with us as they liked. The clocks at the factories were often put forward in the morning and back at night, and instead of being instruments for the measurement of time, they were used as cloaks for cheating and oppression."[2]

## Economic Aspects of Changing Work Conditions

Since workers weigh the satisfaction or dissatisfaction from an additional hour of leisure versus the sum of the additional satisfaction (dissatisfaction) from an hour of work and the added satisfaction from an hour's wage, improvement in working conditions should increase the satisfaction (diminish the dissatisfaction) of additional hours of work. Such a result implies that a worker would choose to work longer.[3]

With regard to coffee breaks and paid lunch breaks, Owen compares these with the earlier traditions among craftsmen of slowing the work pace or indulging in lackadaisical Monday efforts. These "general slowing down of the work pace, are ways of taking it easy that may compete with the shorter work day in providing more leisure time."[4] He thought the overall effect on hours worked would be ambiguous, due to competing income and substitution effects; workers were better off with coffee breaks but faced a negative substitution effect (assuming that wages are rising).

## The Changing Nature of Work

Jobs have generally become less onerous, as technology has improved. An ever-dwindling proportion of Americans are employed in physically demanding, dangerous, repetitive jobs, especially those in the extractive industries. Perhaps there is irony involved in that at a time when our economy is adept at providing sufficient calories for arduous labor, we no longer require such levels of calories. Indeed, many Americans seek out arduous activities for their leisure pursuits; some of these people use such activities to balance their enjoyment of caloric intake with health, a form of bodily maintenance.

The change to a service economy has other benefits: typically, the jobs are safer and the diminution of heavy industry reduces pollution. Pittsburgh is no longer synonymous with smog. Many of the jobs of the past were, by our standards, incredibly dangerous. Why did people voluntarily accept such risks? Did they value their lives less than we value ours? An economist would ask, what were their alternatives? A similar question arises regarding child labor. Did the parents with low incomes in 1900 care for their children less than modern parents care for theirs, or did they face an unenviable set of choices?

Other jobs reflected the low standards of living. During the 1800s, a number of people were listed as "rag-pickers." These were people who wandered around picking up loose pieces of cloth scraps (among other discarded items), including discarded clothing. Cloth was at such a premium that some people could make a rudimentary living collecting such debris. In contemporary America, though, we have people collecting discarded cans and bottles.

Most modern Americans now work in a climate-controlled, filtered-air environment, with many enjoying levels of comfort and privacy undreamed of in the workplaces of the past. Certainly the Internet has injected an element of leisure into the workplace. Few bosses would issue a long list of workplace rules such as those that bedeviled shop girls and factory workers a century ago.

Chris Rojek points out the growing ambiguity between work and leisure: "Leisure and play became the new means of culturally savvy self-expression.

It was no longer necessary to insist on strong divisions between the worlds of work and leisure. The meaning of each merged into the other, so that work could be a kind of play and leisure a kind of work."[5]

## Job Conditions, Pre-1900

Working conditions in industrializing America left much to be desired, especially from a twenty-first-century perspective. Charles Dickens's novels painted memorable portraits of the sheer misery associated with burgeoning industrialization. The jobs were dangerous drudgery. One should not forget, however, that rural working conditions were not a paradise. Much farm work was arduous and tedious and frequently forced farmers to retire due to debility; of course, farmers were not the only workers facing such physical breakdown from job-related tasks. Theodore Dreiser's description of Sister Carrie's first day working at the shoe-making factory captured the body- and soul-numbing conditions. Charlie Chaplin's *Modern Times* satirized modern, but soon-to-become relatively obsolete, factory work, but an even earlier thinker, economist Adam Smith, recognized the changing nature of work.[6] While working on a factory assembly line may not have been as demeaning or taxing as being a galley slave in the ancient world, workers strove for better conditions.

Job conditions did not always improve; George Lundberg believed that jobs in the past were "formerly often fraught with variety and high adventure and therefore had its own recreational aspects," while current manufacturing jobs had "little possibility of dramatic developments or variety in the operation of a punching machine. The former type of work might leave one tired, but not taut; restful sleep was its remedy. The latter type results in a craving for explosive stimulation as a relief."[7]

Lundberg's disclaimer aside, modern-day Americans would find working in a factory during the late nineteenth century a dismal experience. Many bosses were petty tyrants, who deemed worker discipline as crucial in maintaining productivity: no laughing, singing, talking, eating, or, in the case of shop girls, sitting down. The list of rules in a corset factory was representative. In addition to the previously mentioned strictures against eating, talking, and singing, workers who were more than five minutes late were fined. Workers an hour or more late were refused admittance (with, presumably, corresponding loss of pay). The forewoman required an excuse ticket for workers to leave the room.[8] Employees were not allowed to drink alcoholic beverages, either at work or off work, and they were sometimes required to attend public worship on the Sabbath.

Marshall Field pioneered the department store in the United States. Salesclerks at Marshall Field faced a mixture of rules. They were required to look respectful, to be circumspect when discussing customers or company business, and not to sass customers. An element of paternalism existed, as female sales-clerks were allowed to go home before dark. Field's executive Harry Selfridge apparently instilled an esprit de corps among his workers, as they took pride in working for the store.[9] Other salesclerks faced somewhat harsher edicts, such as not being allowed to sit down during their shift or being charged for any short-age in the cash register till.

Crowley, of the Crowley Iron Works mentioned above, "found it necessary to design an entire civil and penal code, running to more than 100,000 words, to govern and regulate his refractory labour-force." He felt compelled to do so, no doubt, because, "I having [sic] by sundry people working by the day with the connivance of the clerks been horribly cheated and paid for much more time than in good conscience I ought and such hath been the baseness & treachery of sundry clerks that they have concealed the sloath & negligence of those paid by the day."[10]

Aside from the authoritarian regime, workers were frequently crowded into stuffy, noisy, smelly offices or factories. Of course, in most cases, supervi-sors and owners also did not work in luxurious, air-conditioned offices. Workplace safety was primitive by modern standards. Over time, workers ne-gotiated with employers for safer and more comfortable workplace environ-ments, sometimes trading part of their productivity gain for such amenities in lieu of higher wages.

Many skilled workers set their own pace. Although they might be at work six days a week, not all workdays were created equal. Herbert Gutman describes some coopers: "Coopers felt new machinery 'hard and insensate,' not a blessing but an evil that 'took a great deal of joy out of life' because machine-made barrels undercut a subculture of work and leisure." Workers responded by lounging about on Saturdays, among other resistance to work discipline.[11]

In addition to long, dreary workweeks, workers faced dangers. What sort of risks did workers face? Today people bemoan sweatshops around the world. During the period of industrialization, many observers disliked factory work, viewing it as deleterious to workers. You may recall the "Disney-fied" version of Mary Poppins. The chimney sweep played by Dick Van Dyke seemed a roman-tic, if scruffy, character. In reality, a chimney sweep led a harsh, probably brief, life. The boys tended to be small and malnourished; the work was arduous, dirty, and devastating to their health. The fine dust adversely affected many of the sweeps' lungs. Of course, mid-nineteenth-century London could not afford to provide all of its workers with pleasant working conditions.

Work was also highly dangerous in many industries (Tables 8.1 and 8.2). A Carnegie plant in Pittsburgh had injury rates among its recent immigrants at nearly 25 percent per year.[12]

*Table 8.1* **Work-Injury Frequency Rates in Manufacturing, Mining,
and Railroads (per Million Man-Hours Worked), 1926–1970[a]**

| Year | Manufacturing | All Mining | Coal Mining | Class I Railroads |
|---|---|---|---|---|
| 1970 | 15.2 | 28.9 | 42.6 | 11.5 |
| 1960 | 12.0 | 29.8 | 43.4 | 7.3 |
| 1950 | 14.7 | 46.3 | 53.3 | 14.2 |
| 1940 | 15.3 | 65.2 | 70.4 | 11.5 |
| 1931 | 18.9 | 79.9 | 89.9 | n.a. |
| 1926 | 24.2 | n.a. | n.a. | n.a. |

[a] US Department of Commerce, *Historical Statistics of the United States, Part 1*, 182.

*Table 8.2* **Workers Killed or Disabled on the Job (per 100,000 Workers),
1970–2000[a]**

| | Death Rate | | Millions of Disabling Injuries[1] |
|---|---|---|---|
| | Manufacturing | Non-Manufacturing | |
| 2000 | 3 | 4 | 3.9 |
| 1990 | 5 | 9 | 3.9 |
| 1980 | 8 | 15 | 2.2 |
| 1970 | 9 | 21 | 2.2 |

[1] Disabling injury defined as one that results in death, some degree of physical impairment, or renders the person unable to perform regular activities for a full day beyond the day of the injury. Due to change in methodology, data beginning 1990 not comparable with prior years.

[a] US Department of Commerce, *Statistical Abstract of the United States: 2008*, 420.

During the construction of the Central Pacific Railroad over the Sierra Nevada mountains in California, laborers were lowered over cliffs in baskets to place and detonate dynamite. "The pick of the Irish drilling crews were lowered in great wicker baskets from the high ledges and there suspended in mid-air while the tarriers drilled like devils, then tamped their powder into the holes, lighted the fuses, and yelled for the boys above to haul them up before the blasts let go. Lives depended both on the ropes and on quick response and sometimes the ropes broke, again the windlass was slow. And then there was sure to be another wake." On the Central Pacific, the death rate was artificially increased by the habit of some workers of exploding the blasts while the Chinese were still working in the cuttings beneath.[13]

The Panama Canal, an American engineering marvel, was a veritable death march, with one worker in five dying each month at times. The railway's doctor, J. A. Totten, found it difficult to properly dispose of the bodies, but he hit upon the idea of selling unclaimed bodies wholesale to medical schools and thereby making the railway hospital self-sustaining.[14]

If construction work was dangerous, operating railroads was hazardous, too. Prior to automatic couplers, a trainman would have to stand between two cars to insert a pin to link the cars. The trainman stood to lose fingers or to be crushed between the cars. Prior to airbrakes, brakemen had to run along the top of the moving cars and manually apply the brakes. Exploding boilers on steamboats and locomotives were other hazards. According to the *Historical Statistics of the United States*, 2,550 railroad workers died on the job in 1900; an additional 5,300 passengers and other people died in connection with railroads.[15] The whaling industry, too, was a highly hazardous undertaking.

Even within many older Americans' lifetimes, there were some terribly risky jobs. Coal mining during World War II featured death rates that were comparable with combat troops. With the growing demand for coal, mine owners pushed workers harder in order to meet production goals: "As of May 1943, the armed forces had sustained a total of 27,000 casualties, while in the same period, 35,000 miners were injured—2,000 fatally."[16]

According to the *Statistical Abstract for the United States* (1999), there were between 5,000 and 6,300 fatal work injuries in 1997. The rate of deaths per 100,000 workers has fallen dramatically since 1960, to about one-fifth the 1960 rate. Transportation deaths, including highway accidents, aircraft, water vehicle, and railroad accidents, accounted for over 40 percent of the fatalities. Assaults and violent acts comprised roughly 20 percent of the fatalities, with homicides accounting for four-fifths of these deaths. The matter-of-factly labeled "contacts with objects and equipment" accounted for 17 percent; falls for 12 percent; exposure to harmful substances or environments 9 percent; and fires/explosions for 3 percent.[17]

Extractive industries, such as oil, mining, logging, and agriculture, headed the list of dangerous occupations in late twentieth-century America. Coal mining had a fatality rate of 36 per 100,000 workers in 1994; white-collar workers in finance, insurance, and real estate had a rate of one per 100,000 workers. In addition, some industries had high non-fatal injury and illness rates. Meat-packing plants are still nasty places to work; Upton Sinclair's *The Jungle* exposed the dangers and nastiness of the industry a hundred years ago. More recent rates of non-fatal injuries and illnesses at meat-packing plants led all occupations with 32.1 per 100 workers per year. Many of the other contenders are in heavy manufacturing.[18]

Heavy manufacturing may enable workers with less education to earn fairly high wages, but they impose health and pollution costs among the workers and the environment. In the conversion of the economy from a manufacturing base to a service base, the loss of such jobs is not an unmitigated one.

Even if the occupational death rates were falling, many workers still developed occupational diseases. Public health reformers and other citizens began recognizing the debilitating effects of many industrial jobs around the turn of the century. Reformers such as John B. Andrews and Alice Hamilton investigated phosphorous and lead poisoning. Other investigators sought to protect women and children from dangerous machinery and unhealthy working conditions; the government created the US Public Health Service in 1910 and the Division of Industrial Hygiene and Sanitation in 1914 in response to these situations. Some industrialists took responsibility for their workers and provided company doctors. State legislatures began enacting workers compensation laws during the second decade of the century; these laws charged experience-based premiums, creating an incentive for employers to improve safety.[19]

The mix of jobs changed considerably across the century. In 1900, many of the most common jobs involved hard physical labor or subservience (servants). Table 8.3 shows the decline of the mining, transportation, and manufacturing industries in terms of employment. Between 1900 and 1970, the number of "private household workers" fell by almost one-fourth, even though the labor force expanded by 2.75 times; the number of farm laborers and foremen was just one-fifth the number in 1900. The number of laborers in 1970, except farm and mines, barely increased over the 70 years. The "30 best jobs" were increasing rapidly, while the "30 worst jobs" were decreasing steadily between 1970 and 2000.[20]

The shift of workers between occupations reflected a change in the American economy. In the past, a man's earnings often depended upon having a strong back; today, a person's earnings is more dependent upon having a strong mind crammed with knowledge and training. Wealth is no longer primarily measured in terms of land and physical capital; modern Americans now carry much of their (human) capital in their heads (which is why one should wear a helmet when riding bicycles or motorcycles).

## The Changing Workplace in the Early 1900s

The work force transformed between 1910 and 1930. Agricultural employment fell, while mining employment was stable. Manufacturing and mechanical

*Table 8.3*  **Employees by Industry, 1900–2000ª**

| | Min | CCo | Manf | Tra | Trde | FIRE | Serv | Adm | Agr |
|---|---|---|---|---|---|---|---|---|---|
| | *Percent of Total "Employment by Industry"* | | | | | | | | |
| 2000 | 0.4 | 7.0 | 14.7 | 7.2 | 20.6 | 6.5 | 36.8 | 4.4 | 2.4 |
| 1990 | 0.6 | 6.5 | 18.0 | 6.9 | 20.7 | 6.8 | 33.1 | 4.7 | 2.7 |
| 1980 | 1.0 | 6.3 | 22.1 | 6.6 | 20.3 | 6.0 | 29.0 | 5.4 | 3.4 |

| | Min | CCo | Manf | Tra | Trde | FIRE | Serv | Gov |
|---|---|---|---|---|---|---|---|---|
| | *Percent of Total "Employees on Nonagricultural Payrolls"* | | | | | | | |
| 1970 | 0.9 | 4.7 | 27.4 | 6.4 | 21.1 | 5.2 | 16.5 | 17.8 |
| 1960 | 1.3 | 5.3 | 31.0 | 7.4 | 21.0 | 4.9 | 13.7 | 15.4 |
| 1950 | 2.0 | 5.2 | 33.7 | 8.9 | 20.8 | 4.2 | 11.9 | 13.3 |
| 1940 | 2.9 | 4.0 | 33.9 | 9.4 | 20.8 | 4.6 | 11.4 | 13.0 |
| 1930 | 3.4 | 4.7 | 32.5 | 12.5 | 19.7 | 5.0 | 11.5 | 10.7 |
| 1920 | 4.3 | 3.1 | 39.0 | 15.7 | 14.6 | 3.3 | 11.3 | 8.6 |
| 1910 | 4.9 | 6.2 | 36.1 | 15.5 | 16.5 | 2.2 | 11.1 | 7.5 |
| 1900 | 4.2 | 7.6 | 36.0 | 15.0 | 16.5 | 2.0 | 11.5 | 7.2 |

Industries:

Min: Mining

CCo: Contract Construction

Manf: Manufacturing

Tra: Transportation

Trde: Trade

FIRE: Finance, Insurance, & Real Estate

Serv: Service

Adm: Administrative (government), "workers involved in uniquely governmental activities, e.g., judicial and legislative"

Agr: Agriculture

Gov: Government, Federal, State, and Local

All figures are percent of total "Employees on Nonagricultural Payrolls," 1900–1970; percent of total "Employment by Industry," 1980–2000. Agriculture not included in 1900–1970 figures. The two panels are not strictly comparable. May not sum to 100 due to rounding.

ª US Department of Commerce, *Statistical Abstract: 2002*, 385; US Department of Commerce, *Historical Statistical of the United States, Part 1*, 137.

pursuits and transportation employment rose by over a third each, but these increases were dwarfed by increases in trade and the combined professional services.[21]

If skilled workers lamented their replacement by machinery, worse was to come during the late 1800s. Factories began installing assembly lines and pushed specialization to its extreme, with workers performing a single, low-skill task. The assembly required a higher degree of regimentation, and management sought ways to discipline workers.

The assembly line required large amounts of capital. Owners and management naturally wanted to run the machinery efficiently, but workers resisted efforts to harness them to the machinery's most efficient rate. Frederick Winslow Taylor diagnosed the culprit in the failure of capitalists to speed up production: "essentially one of 'soldiering'—that is, of workers habitually choosing to produce at less than their maximum possible rate . . . through a careful study of individual jobs and judicious selection of incentives or bonus pay, employers could structure the workplace so that soldiering would be eliminated." Previous attempts at using piece rates foundered on the under-utilization of the capitalist's machinery; workers chose their own pace, which often fell below that of the machine's capacity. However, relatively few large employers ever implemented Taylorism into their factories.[22]

International Harvester Corporation attempted to use scientific management and welfare capitalism. It issued a brochure to its Polish common laborers, hoping to educate them in English: "I hear the whistle. I must hurry. I hear the five minute whistle. It is time to go into the shop. . . . The whistle blows at five minutes of starting time."[23]

Employers sought various tactics to bolster productivity. Some Americans valued music for its potential utility in improving society, but some employers recognized that music might be useful. Some progressive industrialists hoped that music at work would invigorate and rejuvenate workers. They encouraged workers to form musical ensembles, both to refresh and to express themselves. Some employers found music helped raise output and efficiency, while reducing absenteeism, especially on Monday mornings. F. H. McConnell chronicles British manufacturers' attempts to use music on the factory floor. He states that the purpose wasn't so much to speed up the work effort but to "mitigate the deadening effect of monotonous tasks." One young female worker explained: "Music acts like a tonic when you feel yourself getting tired."[24]

During World War II, the British government studied ways to improve or to maintain worker productivity. As with earlier attempts by industrialists, the government found that "the woman soldering connections became tired not only from physical exertion but because of boredom. Music distracted the workers from their tasks without taking their eyes off the job." These efforts reflect the long tradition of work songs used by slaves, chain labor, textile workers, and other manual laborers.[25]

Muzak was invented to help soothe people in factories and to boost productivity of workers doing repetitive tasks (rather than to annoy shoppers or occupants of elevators). In other situations, the British Broadcasting Corporation broadcast music designed to "invigorate workers on the factory floor."[26]

Climate control boosted productivity and improved worker comfort. While many manufacturing processes required specific temperature/humidity combinations for successful production, other processes simply generated heat and humidity as a matter of course. Climate control was lacking in many factories and offices. Offices often closed when the weather became too hot and humid. As owners and managers began to discover that increased worker comfort, with regard to climate, improved output, they began to install air conditioning. Gail Cooper notes that air conditioning's acceptance in offices "was no doubt helped by the fact that management and office workers often shared the same general work space." As modern office buildings often had sealed windows, climate control became necessary.[27]

## Postwar Trends in the Workplace

*Business Week* highlighted the leisure market in 1953. The periodical noticed that leisure was even encroaching on the workplace, with firms granting two coffee breaks per day for their employees—thereby boosting sales of coffee and snacks.[28] Contrast that with earlier factory rules prohibiting eating and drinking even non-alcoholic beverages on the job.

From having no paid vacation time in 1900, the vast majority of American workers had gained two weeks or more of such by century's end. The number of paid holidays rose from three or four to over seven by the end of the century. American workers also received several days of paid sick leave or personal time. A growing majority of workers, even in smaller business establishments, received paid rest and cleanup periods. A small minority of workers enjoyed paid lunch breaks.[29]

The 1950s witnessed the rise of that white-collar institution: the three-martini lunch. Walter Kerr deconstructed this much ridiculed and maligned practice. Business people gathered together to break bread, drink martinis, and conduct deals, and the first two items were charged to expense accounts. Kerr suggests that "[t]hese meetings represent, of course, the twentieth-century dream of the longish, relaxed lunch period," while acknowledging that to other observers, the lunch "is a rationalized break from the sales charts and a chance to down a few drinks that will keep the rest of the afternoon from becoming too strenuous." He did not share the latter view, since he had observed business people continuing to work at their desk instead of seeking other lunch companions, when such lunches were canceled.[30]

Another trend at the workplace was employees engaging in leisure-type activities, such as reading newspapers, talking with friends, and so on. Conservative supervisors attributed this new work phenomenon to a deteriorating work ethic, but young bosses accepted such behavior. Ernest Havemann wondered whether "we will avoid exacerbating our consciences by pretending to work 35, although such subterfuges as time off for shopping and hairdos will actually cut the week to 30 hours or fewer."[31] The ubiquitous Internet afforded workers newfound diversions from work. A quick Google search of "personal internet use" called up numerous articles on the subject. Workers can now access pornography, make stock trades, buy stuff on Amazon.com, and engage in other activities while ostensibly at work.[32] Workers apparently created rationales justifying their behavior, including overwork, insufficient incentives, insufficient challenges, dissatisfaction, and boredom. In the crowning indignity for employers, almost half of the workers surveyed spent work time looking for new jobs.[33]

Richard Edwards established that worker/management relations evolved over time, as management implemented different controls, starting with entrepreneurial control (the owner was the direct supervisor), hierarchical control, technical control, bureaucratic control, and structural control. Hierarchical control involved foremen, who closely supervised workers. The foremen had power to punish and fire workers, usually without a grievance process. Workers naturally resisted this form of control. Technical control was driven by the machinery and technology: "in the new power-driven mills all machines operated together, and the operative had neither any cause nor any right to move about the mill. Instead, the workers became nearly as much locked in place as the machinery." The assembly line substituted the "technical for human direction and pacing of work [which] simultaneously revolutionized the relation between foreman and workers."[34]

With the failure of these previous schools of thought regarding control of workers, employers tried to draw lessons for use in the future. Edwards concludes that the agenda for structural control needed to arise from a legitimate overall structure dealing with the work itself and defined precisely, based on management's control of special knowledge, with positive rewards for work, and restriction of supervisors' capriciousness. Bureaucratic control, which resulted from the formal structure of a firm, arose after World War II. Edwards describes it as a "elaborate system of bribes, and like all successful bribes, they are attractive."[35] "[The bribes] are also corrupting. They push workers to pursue their self-interests in a narrow way as individuals, and they stifle the impulse to struggle collectively for those same self-interests. All this elaboration of job titles, rules, procedures, rights, and responsibilities is, of course, neither accidental nor be-nevolent . . . it is simply a better way to do business."[36]

According to Edwards, "[w]elfare capitalism failed because it did not deal with the fundamental issue of power within the firm." It was, instead, a publi-cized attempt to bribe workers into acquiescing to employers' authoritarian and paternalistic agendas, which the employees repudiated. He added that, out of the wreckage of welfare capitalism, "only those programs that directly contrib-uted to productivity, such as physical exams and industrial safety measures, tended to be retained."[37] Edwards believed that the strikes at Pullman and U.S. Steel arose from the interaction between work organization and collective worker resistance.[38]

Even now, with computers ubiquitous in the workplace, Edwards sees them as tools for controlling labor. Computer feedback systems afford employers an ability to monitor employees that was undreamed of in the past. Gone are the foremen, replaced by the microcomputers directing and controlling processes. A recent article in the *Atlantic* describes how "Big Data" (a 2012 buzzword, possi-bly obsolete by the time this book is published) is "transforming hiring, firing, and your chances of getting ahead."[39]

Belying Edwards's ominous description of the computerized work environ-ment, companies in Silicon Valley scramble to attract and to retain highly edu-cated technicians and creative people. In addition to salaries, these companies have created a different work environment. Some of the workplaces in Silicon Valley feature such leisure amenities as volleyball courts and a large, fire-engine red slide. From a 1900 perspective, these workers would appear to be pampered beyond belief. Megan Garber refers to the keen competition among employers as a "perks arms race." The employers realize that satisfying workers helps to retain and motivate them. She notes, though, that "[w]hile the workforce at large chases the hazy idea of 'work-life balance,' Facebook and fellow firms emphasize the blur between the two. It's not 'work' and 'everything else,' these offices pro-pose; work *is* everything else."[40] Whether Silicon Valley is pioneering the not-so-brave future remains to be seen. American workers, though, have clearly trans-formed the workplace from a draconian, authoritarian place into a more pleasant environment.

Although technology, especially the Internet and e-mail, makes it feasible to work from home, it also means that work may be spread over more hours. Some Americans lament the fact that they are always accessible to their employers: the technology has changed from telegraph to telephone to pager, and on through the latest electronic gadget. Some employers recognize this intrusion and are trying to compensate. With the switch toward creative and intellectual work in-stead of tending an assembly line, some employers are beginning to lessen their hierarchical organization in order to foster creativity and collaboration.[41]

# The Fun New World of Work

The history of American labor is rife with violence and tragedy. Bloody strikes recurred, while industrial accidents scarred memories of generations of Americans. Many jobs were tedious, dangerous, and dirty. Supervisors held sway over workers.

By the end of the twentieth century, most Americans worked in clean, climate-controlled environments; they enjoyed coffee and lunch breaks. Although dangerous jobs persisted, relatively few Americans worked under such conditions. Petty bosses undoubtedly still roam the corridors of offices and shops, but their pettiness is, for the most part, corralled within fairly narrow bounds. The ubiquity of desktop computers and laptops afforded American workers individual choice in music as well as opportunities to amuse themselves and to inject leisure activities into their workdays, although these machines also extended the boss's reach.

# The Transformation of the Domestic Economy

Women may have been one group that did not enjoy greater amounts of leisure during the twentieth century. Their combined hours worked at employment or at home were seemingly immune to change. Regardless of whether their overall hours of work fell, one characteristic is certain: domestic work became much less arduous.

Women's roles have changed considerably during the twentieth century. Over the course of her lifetime, a woman could assume roles ranging from daughter, to single woman, to married woman, to mother, to married woman in retirement, to widow, and, often, divorced woman. Her workload shifted with her change in status.

Much of what follows in this chapter focuses on women's roles in household production, usually as a wife and mother. There will be some discussion about single women, especially younger single women.

## Economic Aspects of Women's Labor Choices

In the earlier discussion of an individual's choice between leisure time and work, we disregarded situations in which an individual is part of a family unit. Economists have examined a family unit in which the father was the main source of income. Women provided secondary incomes. A woman's choice regarding working for pay depended in part upon the man's income.

As before, when an individual's wage rate goes up, the individual faces two opposing effects. As the wage increases, the implicit price of taking an hour off increases; a worker would tend to substitute away from leisure time and toward work. As the wage increases, the worker is better off and would increase the amount of leisure time (and reduce work). The two effects mean that whether a worker chooses to work more or less is an empirical question.

If a worker is part of a family in which the father is the primary income earner, the analysis changes. When the father's income goes up, all family members are better off (assuming there is some sharing of income among family members). The standard 1950s textbook question asked whether wives of higher-earning husbands were as likely to be in the labor force or to work as many hours; the answer to both questions would be no.[1]

Economist Elyce Rotella elaborated on this basic story: What if a woman's wage increased? "Increased family income will have its accustomed negative effect on market work by increasing the demand for leisure and home production . . . there will be two substitution effects because an increase in the market wage increases the price of leisure time and raises the value of market work relative to home work. Both will tend to increase the amount of time devoted to market work as wages rise." Jacob Mincer found that the positive effect of a woman's increased wage more than offset the negative effect on leisure time of an increase in the family income, so that women's labor force participation did increase. Studies demonstrated that the overall effect of an increase in women's wages was toward women's increased workforce participation. Rotella did find a dichotomy between married women and single women with regard to the family-income model described above. She found the model worked best for married women in 1930 and single women in 1890.[2]

Women's wages have increased across the twentieth century. As a recent *Time* magazine cover pointed out, women "are rapidly overtaking men as America's breadwinners."[3] An economics textbook today might discuss the family's leisure/work decisions in more gender-neutral terms, since it can no longer be assumed that a male is the breadwinner. Everything described in the previous paragraph, then, would be reworded in gender-neutral language.

## A Brief History of Women's Labor

Women's roles in the American economy have evolved through the centuries. While girls and women usually resided in households headed by men for most of American history, widows and, occasionally, divorced women might head a household. In the early 1800s, young single women began working in factories. They often lived apart from their families, and their leisure-time activities spurred worries about their morals. During the twentieth century, the growing number of single women and divorced women in the labor force changed the roles of women, as well as their workloads, whether in the market economy or with regard to household production. Although much of this chapter examines the plight of women's hours and efforts in household production, a growing number of women juggled labor-market work with household production, including child care.

American women were the main source of home manufactured goods as recently as the late nineteenth century. The frontier woman was a tough, resourceful person. One observer wrote of his encounter with such a woman: "She is a very civil woman and shews nothing of ruggedness or Immodesty in her carriage, yett she will carry a gunn in the woods and kill deer, turkeys, etc., shoot down wild cattle, catch and tye hogs, knock down beeves with an ax and perform the most manfull Exercises as well as most men in those parts."[4] This woman may have been more "manfull" than most frontier women, but this was no denigration. These women shared the same dangers as men: hostile indigenous tribes and rogue whites, wild animals, and exposure to the elements. Since few colonial Americans had either access to or the money to buy many manufactured goods from England or the local towns, economic historian Edith Abbott was not making much of an exaggeration when she claimed of the Colonial period: "It would not be far wrong to say . . . agriculture was in the hands of men, and manufacturing, for the most, in the hands of women."[5]

As America became urbanized, many of the traditional and highly varied tasks of women rapidly disappeared from their hands, being taken over by bakeries, pharmacies, groceries, laundries, and clothing manufacturers. Even women's responsibility for children diminished, as the size of the family shrank. Between 1800 and 1900 women cut their fertility by 50 percent. A measure of the shrinkage in the activities of at least the middle-class urban wife and mother was provided by the increasing availability of domestic servants, which peaked in the 1870s at one servant for each 6.6 families.[6]

The new development in women's participation in the economy after 1900 reflected changes within the economy as a whole. Just as women had supplied the demand for cheap, ready labor in the early days of manufacturing, as the American economy became more diverse, larger in scale, and more bureaucratic, women filled many of the new jobs in the rapidly expanding white-collar sector of the economy. The white-collar sector had scant need for sheer physical strength, so women were not at such a disadvantage. However, it took decades for women to assume a significant proportion of office jobs. In 1870 women had constituted very few of all office workers; by 1930 that proportion was 52 percent.[7] Domestic service was still the occupation employing the most women well into the twentieth century.

The professions also expanded during these years, allowing women new opportunities to diversify their jobs in these areas. Whereas in 1870 more than 90 percent of women in professions were teachers, this proportion fell as women entered other professions in greater numbers. Starting from a low base, the number of women college teachers, lawyers, and judges increased by 500 percent or more between 1910 and 1930, but the number of female physicians fell in that time period.[8]

The Progressive era featured legislation directly affecting women in the labor force. Protective labor laws and mothers' pensions sought to keep single women with children at home while discouraging single women without children from being seduced by the prospect of earning money or falling into sin. Proponents of such legislation worried about the ill effects of unregulated working conditions on women's childbearing ability and the disruption of the sex-segregation of jobs. In addition, they feared that young, white, native-born, middle-class girls might be diverted from proper marriage if they held a job, or might even fall into vice and despair. The mothers' pension movement worried about the deleterious effects of women's employment on their children and also about women competing with men for scarce jobs.[9]

In the wake of the Supreme Court's 1908 ruling in *Muller v. Oregon*, legalizing the 10-hour day, state legislators quickly enacted many laws governing women's working hours and conditions, ranging from limits on the weights women could lift to requiring seats for female workers in department stores. Frances Perkins provided figures showing that women and children suffered higher rates of occupation injuries and death, when she argued that women and children needed protective legislation. These gender-specific laws, though, served to segregate women and to create an aura that women were less capable than men.[10] Economist Claudia Goldin points out that prominent liberals and feminists remained divided about protective legislation well into the 1960s, when "prominent liberals opposed the Equal Rights Amendment on the ground that it would jeopardize protective legislation."[11]

Lest we think that men alone held what many modern Americans would consider regressive attitudes regarding women in the labor market, let's examine some past commentators. At the end of the nineteenth century, Helen Campbell, a professional economist and undisputed friend of working women, stated that "the employment of married women is fruitful of evil," and she went on to cite official government objections to the employment of mothers outside the home.[12] In 1936, a Gallup poll found that 75 percent of women disapproved of married women working.[13]

The rapid increase of women in white-collar and professional jobs should not obscure the continued concentration of women in a relatively small range of occupations. By 1940, women were represented in at least 250 occupations, but almost 90 percent of all working women had been counted in no more than 10 percent of those occupations in 1910. Also worth noting is the fact that although the number of working women had been steadily rising throughout the period, in 1940 women still constituted slightly less than 25 percent of the total labor force.[14]

Despite these gains, married women often faced institutionalized barriers to jobs. Employers, relying on different likelihoods of remaining in the labor force, might have hesitated to hire single women, given the greater likelihood such a worker would exit the labor force upon marriage. In some cases, though, where there was little increase in productivity after an initial period but a rising pay scale based on tenure with a company, employers had an incentive to get rid of veteran female employees. A bar against retaining married women helped employers release relatively highly paid women, whose wage exceeded their productivity. Some British firms used substantial dowries to encourage women to marry and to leave the labor force. Married women may have been discouraged, too, by the long hours required of most jobs early in the twentieth century; the rise of part-time jobs may have provided the flexibility that married women wanted and needed in order to balance household and paid-work duties. The 1950s witnessed the elimination of the marriage bar; this resulted from changing attitudes about older women workers and a relative dearth of young females (and males) due to the low birth rates of the Depression and war years.[15]

World War II abruptly disrupted the labor force. With the drafting of millions of young males into the military, women were needed to replace men in production jobs. The federal government campaigned to enlist women in the labor force, including married women with children. As a result, women filled all kinds of jobs, from many of which they had been previously excluded or for which no training had been available to them. A Women's Bureau study at the close of World War II stated that fully two-thirds of women who had worked in eating and drinking establishments had transferred to war industries for the better pay and conditions. As early as 1942, more than 600 laundries had to shut down because the women who usually worked in them had moved to better jobs and no other labor was available to take their places. Thousands of black women, for the first time in their lives, were released from their customary dependence on domestic service jobs. During the four years of war, the female labor force reached 20 million, an increase of 57 percent over the 1940 figure, with a shift toward older, married women.[16]

If women with children worked, what did they do with their children? Many women were wary of government-sponsored or run day-care centers. A public opinion poll in 1943 found that 56 percent of the women queried said they would not send their children to such day-care centers, even if they were free. Women already holding jobs stated that they preferred relatives or friends, rather than public facilities, to care for their children; and these attitudes toward child-care centers persisted.[17]

Shortly after the end of World War II, millions of women left the labor force voluntarily or were laid off, but millions of other women entered the labor force, leaving a net loss of half a million. The novel and significant point was that the increase in the number of working women that the war had instigated did not subside with the advent of peace; even before the war ended, polls showed that many women were loath to relinquish their jobs to returning veterans. Women aged 45–54 began to participate in the labor force as never before. By 1960, women aged 45–54 had higher rates of labor force participation than younger women aged 20–24, traditionally the age group most likely to participate in the labor force.[18]

Women were not just flooding the labor market. In the recent past, women have expanded their toeholds in many formerly male-only bastions. Economists Francine Blau and Lawrence Kahn wrote of the 1970s: "although many of the broad outlines of these occupational differences between men and women remain, the disparities have been much reduced. Women are now less concentrated in administrative support and service occupations, with 41 percent holding such jobs in 1999 compared to 15 percent of men. Women now hold 45 percent of managerial jobs [which may mean longer hours]." They noted that women were now employed in formerly male occupational bastions and that women were much less represented in traditionally female occupations; for instance, in 1960 about half the female college graduates went into teaching, but this percentage fell to below 10 percent by 1990.[19]

Why did women surge into the labor market throughout the twentieth century? Lower fertility and accessibility of divorce are candidates as explanations. Another possible story is that women have to work, in order for American middle-class families to survive financially. Economist Stanley Lebergott presents data that imply a subtler story. The rise of mechanical gadgets promised to substitute capital for labor in running a household, thereby freeing up time. Initially, wives depended upon their husband's earnings to acquire these labor-saving devices. What to do with the increased discretionary time? Another concurrent desire might have been to use some of the wives' increased leisure to buy leisure for husbands; in other words, couples preferred to spend more leisure time together.[20]

## Women's Leisure as the Twentieth Century Dawned

Married women during the late nineteenth century had few formal leisure opportunities. The New York Factory Investigation Commission describes how women spent spare moments sitting on tenement steps or leaning from window sills to converse, visiting friends and family, and taking walks. Men reserved the right to skim off some money from their pay for personal use, including transportation fares, lunch money, and recreation items. Some men, of course, took out money for alcohol and tobacco. Given the stringency of family budgets, the working man's personal discretionary income may have proved a source of contention. There remained very little money in the budget for leisure spending on wives and children.[21]

Working women experienced a wider variety of jobs as the twentieth century dawned. Instead of serving as domestics or sweatshop labor, educated women could aspire to jobs in offices or department stores. These jobs required respectable attire. Although nineteenth-century jobs for women had highly variable hours, increased unionization and legislation designed to protect women, but also to protect male workers from competition from women, reduced hours to a more regular six-day, nine-hours per day workweek. The regularity of working hours provided working women with new opportunities for leisure. The onerous, oppressive work environments may have spurred men and women to seek out a good time during their leisure time. "Earning a living, an economic necessity for most young working-class women, was also a cultural experience organizing and defining their leisure activities."[22]

There wasn't much point for a young woman to remain in her room in a boarding house, which was usually shared with other young women. The boarding house's matron needed to ensure a respectable reputation, so young women were constrained regarding with whom they could associate and when. Their rooms were typically drab and cold and did not invite lazing about.[23]

Where did young New York working women go for leisure and entertainment? Dancing halls were a popular destination. Young women could temporarily escape "the maintenance of respectability, daughterly submission" while enjoying and adjusting to "the attractions of autonomy and romance . . . and the glittering appeal of urban nightlife. . . . Promenading the streets and going places with the crowd, young working-class women 'put on style.' Dress was a particularly potent way to display and play with notions of respectability, allure, independence, and status and to assert a distinctive identity and presence."[24] There were hundreds of dancing halls in New York City; for novices, there were plenty of dancing academies. To women and men working in drab surroundings during the day, the dancing halls with their glittering lights, pulsating music, and excitement proved enchanting. One popular dancing style was "tough dancing," a dance that permitted physical contact and, according to outraged critics, simulated the sex act.[25]

For leisure entrepreneurs, handling the "woman question" required finesse. During the nineteenth century, impresarios P. T. Barnum and Moses Kimball attracted women to their museums. Theater owners cleaned up their venues by eradicating prostitutes. These advances aside, many entertainment venues remained male dominated and posed risks for women entering therein.

Parallel to the entertainment venue owners' efforts, women were becoming more active in club and church work, as well as politics, agitating for reform. These activities created the "'New Woman,' which signaled greater personal autonomy and social participation, placing new categories of behavior under the rubric of female respectability." Working-class women patronized commercial picnic grounds, beer gardens, and dance halls. Women were part of the growing commercialization of leisure that transformed recreation into a commodity and created a heterosocial culture of mixed-sex amusements.[26]

The genius of the Coney Island amusement park operators was their stress on family entertainment and a suppression of male culture. The operators eradicated sleazy con games, fake sideshows, and other unsavory aspects. They aspired to middle-class respectability in order to draw from a wider clientele. To create such an atmosphere, the operators enclosed their parks and funneled entrants through a single entryway.[27]

During the early twentieth century, motion pictures and vaudeville theaters became places where women could enjoy entertainment. The early nickelodeons proved popular with working-class and other women. For a nickel they could relax, entertain their children, and socialize with other women. Matinees were especially popular with women. Motion picture theater owners wanted to encourage movies as a family event in order to gain respectability. These owners and other purveyors of commercialized leisure co-opted the idea of women as shoppers and participants in urban life by easing women's introduction to commercial entertainment. Owners of vaudeville theaters located their venues near major shopping districts: "Like the department store, the quintessential urban space for women in the late nineteenth century, these vaudeville houses were palaces of consumption, amusement, and service." Historian Kathy Peiss points out that the leisure industry did not want to create a homosocial women's culture; instead, they encouraged men and women to view leisure as a mixed-sex activity, promoting heterosocial and heterosexual pleasure and retaining the ethos of familism but in a commercial and consumption-oriented context.[28]

The early silent movies "projected stylized images of women and men that expressed the heterosocial world of commercial recreation and urban life . . . helping to legitimize a heterosocial culture."[29] The New York nickelodeon and theater owners understood women's attraction to movies, and they encouraged female patrons. The owners, though, were ambivalent about their working-class audience, as many aspired to attract middle-class audiences. Women found the movies "convenient places for meeting men, courting, and enjoying an inexpensive evening's entertainment. . . . The theater's darkness and the vocal familiarity of the audience encouraged opportunities for intimacy and 'spooning.'"[30]

The motion picture industry quickly realized that glamour, sensations, and romance were key selling points of motion pictures. They eventually jettisoned their hesitation to identify popular actors and began publishing fan magazines. Other groups, though, were not as enthusiastic about motion pictures, or at least those shown in nickelodeons. Some Protestant clergy and their congregations fought to impose Sunday closing laws on nickelodeons.[31]

The reformers fought a rear-guard action against these burgeoning leisure activities for young women. Reformers "perceived working women as unwilling female victims and as enthusiastic members of the promiscuous lower orders . . . women enjoyed a social life in public halls and the street where, the YWCA observed, 'young girls . . . in this unconventional out-of-door life are so apt to grow noisy and bold.'" Reformers hoped to induce young women toward well-regulated leisure in order to elevate them to respectable behavior. Peiss, though, noted that the reformers, many of them women, observed recreation from a female perspective shaped by the experience of a clearly demarcated "women's sphere" during the nineteenth century. Nor were women the only subjects for reformers' efforts. "The problem of working women's recreation became simply one element in the comprehensive effort to reconstruct community life and save the family." Reformers recognized the need for recreation as a way of renewing workers for their tedious and strenuous working hours.[32]

Regardless of the reformers' efforts, women's leisure had changed significantly from "education, uplift, and sisterly bonds" to "social freedom, freer sexuality, and mixed-sex fun." Even reformers sympathetic to the changing opportunities offered working-class women "understood some of the liabilities of the modern culture for women, its potential for exploitation, as well as its alluring freedoms and pleasure."[33]

## A Woman's Work Is Never Done?

My mother, who was not prone to complaining, used to sing the ditty, "Man may work from sun to sun; But woman's work is never done." The couplet may resonate with modern American women.

Whether women gained leisure time has been debated for decades. George Lundberg and his associates conducted a time-use survey of 2,460 subjects, covering 4,460 days during the 1930s. They found that women in the labor force averaged 40 hours per week between employment and domestic chores, although they cautioned that many activities overlapped. Despite their time diaries, many women, especially those in the suburbs who had higher incomes, reported having "no leisure at all." But Lundberg and his associates associated this phenomenon to obligatory social activities that did not feel like leisure.[34]

Stanley Lebergott painted a more optimistic portrait of American women's plight during the twentieth century by asking, "How much did this 'outward movement of duties previously performed in the home' cut housewives' work?" He believes that women spent many fewer hours in household and family duties per week, more than enough to offset their increasing number of labor-market work hours. Because the massive increase in labor force participation occurred after 1950, the additional income from working wives explains the extreme rise in consumption after that date. Lebergott's estimates are widely quoted by economists, but Valerie Ramey disputes them. While she admits that women's hours spent on household production have fallen, the hours have not fallen as steeply as Lebergott suggests. Apparently he misinterpreted an earlier study. The hours spent in meal preparation was by all members of the household and not just the woman. Lebergott found a decrease of 42 hours in women's weekly hours on household production between 1900 and 1966, while Ramey found a decrease of only six hours for the same period.[35]

By the 1980s, the debate livened. John Robinson and Geoffrey Godbey's survey of Americans' use of time found a downward trend in the average weekly hours of housework by women. Their 1985 data suggested an average of 19 hours per week; men performed 10 hours per week. They noted that another survey, the 1987 National Survey of Families and Households (NSFH), estimated 31 hours per week for women and 16 for men; Thomas Juster and Frank Stafford came up with 19 hours for women and 8 hours for men in their 1981 survey. Robinson and Godbey note that the NSFH survey diverged the most from their findings for frequent activities, such as cooking and cleaning.[36]

A new trend arose in the 1980s. Working women often delegated preparing dinner to their children. According to a Yankelovich survey, almost one-quarter of children aged 6–15 cooked their own dinners (usually prepared, microwavable foods). Half of the teenage girls reported purchasing groceries for the family on a weekly basis; Graham did not report whether teenage boys purchased groceries for the family.[37]

As Lebergott put it, "consumerism" appeared when housewives began to buy goods they had once produced. Women switched from being manufacturers, as described earlier, to being buyers of manufactured goods, especially of prepared foods.[38] "Twentieth-century advances in U.S. household operations were not achieved by central planning any more than by capitalist altruism. They came as housewife after housewife quietly diverted part of rising family incomes to new products." Women substituted toward prepared food and using more kitchen appliances, initially using their husband's income. "The percentage of wives in the labor force, 6 percent in 1900, was only 13 percent by 1929. By 1990, husbands still provided 80 percent of family income. Hence they paid most food-factory profits and wages. Perhaps they did so graciously, perhaps not. If husbands empathized with their wives, they increased their own utility. In any event, housewives changed the world of entrepreneurs, and of workers—-to their mutual advantage."[39] They were able to keep their homes cleaner with less effort.

## Expectations on Homemakers

Part of the reason that women may not have experienced greater amounts of leisure time was that those women who managed their households full- or part-time found themselves on a perpetual spiral of rising expectations.

Suellen Hoy describes Americans' changing attitudes toward dirt in *Chasing Dirt*. Europeans remarked on how dirty Americans were before the Civil War. Part of the Americans' dirtiness no doubt resulted from living on farms and in crude homesteads, often with dirt floors. Attempts to maintain cleanliness were stymied by the extraordinary effort required to wash clothes and to keep a tidy household. Women often did laundry one day per week instead of less frequently, when dirt would harden upon the fibers, making it even more difficult to clean. As Hoy puts it, "[Women] may have been rewarded with clean laundry, but their efforts also produced 'wrenched shoulders, arms, wrists, and scalded hands.'" Farm women especially faced a daunting task cleaning their families' clothing; Hoy describes how these women were vociferous in wanting indoor plumbing and electrical washing machines, in order to lessen the sheer drudgery in their lives.[40] The lack of indoor running water also made keeping oneself clean inconvenient.

Middle- and upper-class women faced opprobrium if they failed to maintain a tidy home. Nineteenth-century social critics debated whether dirt and filth implied a moral failing or poverty. Certainly the latter implication seems apparent enough—many poor Americans lacked indoor sanitation and well-constructed houses until well into the twentieth century. The immigrants crowding American slums, though, seemingly lent credence to a moral failing—American elites blamed ignorance and moral weakness for the immigrants' failure to meet American standards of cleanliness, never mind the fact that Americans had only recently elevated their own standards of cleanliness (nothing like the zealousness of the newly washed). Sanitary reformers, though, had a point, regardless of moral failure or poverty: cleaning or eliminating the most noisome areas of the cities promised benefits for all.[41]

Not all women were passive about urban filth. In one case, women activists forced an owner to remove his pile of manure; the women claimed the manure invaded their households, exposing their families to health risks and necessitating more cleaning. In order to help Americans, especially those in large cities, keep clean, city authorities began constructing municipal water supplies and sewers. These large-scale public works took decades to complete, but the idea that all homes should have indoor running water became established.[42]

Sanitary reformers concentrated on cleanliness, but they were less willing to embrace the germ theory. Americans had reason to question the germ theory's validity, as it "was difficult to understand and even more difficult to prove." The American medical journals were notably silent on the germ theory between 1876 and 1881; lay readers in America, though, were kept informed about germ theory via *Popular Science Monthly* and other publications.[43] After 1881, the American medical establishment suddenly embraced the germ theory. Joel Mokyr and Rebecca Stein provide an economic analysis of the importance of the germ theory and its effects on households. Proponents of the germ theory had to persuade women that protecting their families depended upon keeping a clean house. Mokyr and Stein argue that the Fogel thesis of higher incomes being tied to lower mortality was inadequate and lacked consideration of the "increase in the demand for health-enhancing goods due to changes in consumer information." In a later paper, Mokyr argues that the understanding that "household work and certain health-enhancing goods could help prevent infectious disease was, without doubt, a major factor in the sharp decline in mortality after 1870."[44]

Cleanliness, of course, could help prevent disease, even if the public health authorities did not completely understand or accept the germ theory. By removing garbage, improving drainage, and providing sewage removal, as well as providing an improved water supply, the reformers, whether they embraced miasmatic or dirt theories of disease, were improving community health. In addition, they alleviated the need to impose quarantines; because quarantines disrupted the economy, business leaders had a motive to favor the miasmatic theory that dispensed with quarantines. Many infectious diseases were waning even before "the full effects of the bacteriological discoveries made themselves felt."[45]

Children benefited greatly by the improved environment promoted by public health reformers and authorities. Infant death rates plummeted during the decades straddling 1900 (Table 9.1).[46]

New products helped in the struggle against dirt. Air-conditioning manufacturers touted air conditioning's ability in helping keep outdoor dirt and dust out of homes. Housewives no longer needed to open windows to air out their homes. One observer noted that white cotton sheets, rugs, and draperies fared much better in air-conditioned houses.[47]

Some mundane items, such as screens for windows and doors, helped housewives resolve the dilemma of keeping the flies out while retaining suffocating heat, or vice versa. The author's mother regaled him with stories of being paid a penny for each hundred flies she killed back in 1920s North Dakota. Obviously, keeping flies and other pests out of homes reduced the possibility of disease transmission.

If homes were unclean, so were bodies. Public health officials also urged Americans to maintain personal hygiene, especially through washing their hands. Women assumed responsibility for their families' hygiene. Of course, keeping oneself clean depended greatly on having access to indoor running water. The diffusion of indoor running water lessened the drudgery of and the time needed to fill bathtubs and washbowls. By the 1950s, running water had induced Americans to take multiple baths per week (inaugurating the nightly bath ritual with small children; even here, parents attempted to turn bathing into recreation, as witness the ubiquitous yellow rubber ducky) and to spend millions of dollars on products that made them smell better. Hoy writes, "Nearly a

*Table 9.1*  **Birth Rate, Infant Mortality, Maternal Mortality Rate, and Female**
             **Life Expectancy (per 1,000 Population and Live Births), 1900–2000[a]**

|      | Birth Rate | Infant Mortality Rate | Maternal Mortality Rate | Female Life Expectancy |
|------|------------|-----------------------|-------------------------|------------------------|
| 1900 | 32.2       | n.a.[1]               | n.a.[1]                 | 48.3                   |
| 1910 | 30.1       | 99.9[2]               | 6.08[2]                 | 51.8                   |
| 1920 | 27.7       | 85.8                  | 7.99                    | 54.6                   |
| 1930 | 21.3       | 64.6                  | 6.73                    | 61.6                   |
| 1940 | 19.4       | 47.0                  | 3.76                    | 65.2                   |
| 1945 | 20.4       | 38.3                  | 2.07                    | 67.9                   |
| 1950 | 24.1       | 29.2                  | 0.83                    | 71.1                   |
| 1955 | 25.0       | 26.4                  | 0.47                    | 72.8                   |
| 1960 | 23.7       | 26.0                  | 0.37                    | 73.1                   |
| 1970 | 18.4       | 20.0                  | 0.22                    | 74.8                   |
| 1980 | 15.9       | 12.6                  | n.a.                    | 77.4                   |
| 1990 | 16.7       | 9.2                   | n.a.                    | 78.8                   |
| 2000 | 14.4       | 6.9                   | n.a.                    | 79.7                   |

[1] Not available.

[2] Earliest figure is 1915.

[a] US Department of Commerce, Bureau of the Census, *Historical Statistics of the United States, Part 1*, 49, 55, and 57; US Department of Commerce, Bureau of the Census. *Statistical Abstract of the United States: 2008*, 64, 74, and 82.

century after their dirt chasing began in earnest, Americans were known world-wide for their cleanliness—sophisticated plumbing, luxurious bathrooms, daily habits of bathing or showering, soft toilet tissue, shiny teeth and hair, and spotless clothes."[48]

According to Jackson Lears, "A preoccupation with cleanliness often carrying racial overtones, had been a central theme in bourgeois culture for at least half a century. It intensified as technological advances made soap and water more widely available. Personal hygiene became a crucial piece in the puzzle that upwardly mobile strivers were constantly trying to assemble. As early as the 1850s, clean hands joined white skin, white bread, and white sugar as emblems of refinement." Advertisers played on consumers' fear of germs to the extent that "[b]y 1930, advertising people were beginning to glimpse the possibility of total victory. [John B.] Watson excitedly told the J. Walter Thompson staff about S.T. 37 mouthwash: 'If one could be taught to rinse the mouth in the morning after breakfast, after lunch, and at night, one would have, ALMOST ALWAYS [caps in original], a sterile mouth!' The medicalization of the discourse of the body meant that hospital standards of cleanliness were being applied to previously unregulated areas."[49]

The bulk of Americans' efforts to eradicate dirt from their lives fell upon women. A spotless home became desirable not only for health reasons but also as a source of pride.[50] Maintaining a clean house and clean clothes, of course, meant keeping up with rising standards as new cleaning products and appliances became available.

In the 1980s, working professional women began to refuse basing their self-worth on a spic and span house and on cleaning their house themselves. Mary Powers, associate director of the Good Housekeeping Institute, stated: "There's a whole new generation of women out there who wouldn't be caught dead on their hands and knees scrubbing a floor." Those women with the financial resources to afford weekly housekeeping paid for just enough hourly labor to keep things "from getting worse," according to a woman employed as a five-hour maid. Even the daughter of Heloise, the homemaker advisor, admitted that she was not meticulous about keeping her house clean. Buttressing these impressionistic anecdotes, sales of cleaning products had fallen for a decade since the mid-1970s, although a particular toilet bowl cleaner that promised to eliminate the need for scrubbing flourished. Other products, including self-defrosting refrigerators, would prove popular. Husbands did not appear to ameliorate things, as they were accused of claiming "the most pleasant of the household chores, such as cooking and babysitting, rather than the mopping and toilet scrubbing."[51]

## Domestic Chores Become Less Arduous

Have you ever looked closely at photos of pioneers? Many are just a few years older than most college students, but they look much, much older. Part of this is because, given the lengthy exposure times for photographs, people couldn't hold a smile (it could have also been because people had bad teeth in the olden days and remained closed mouthed), making them look stern and often haggard. However, they may look old at least partly because of the sheer physical demands on both men and women.

Mundane aspects of living for women, such as domestic chores, became less burdensome and less physically wearying during the twentieth century. At the turn of the century, American women could be perceived as beasts of burden. Whether or not they worked more hours than their modern-day sisters, those hours they did work were physically brutal. Unless a woman was fortunate enough to have sufficient income to hire domestic help, she was confronted with a variety of tasks requiring muscle. She often had to carry wood, coal, and water.

Although carrying water from a stream to a campsite may seem romantically rustic, carrying water for daily cooking, cleaning, and laundry quickly loses its charm. Before electric-powered refrigerators, when the ice man cometh, he left a dripping floor. Disposing of melted ice, too, was a chore, as even modern Americans discover when defrosting their freezer compartments. Of course, if a woman disdained or could not afford an ice box or electric refrigerator, she had to go grocery shopping every day to obtain fresh food. If gas or kerosene was used to illuminate the house, they stained the upholstery and curtains (Table 9.2). Cleaning these items was a strenuous task.

Gone are the butter churns and the hand-wrung laundry machine. Lebergott aptly and sardonically observes, "the housewife with a good strong back and shoulders could get several hours of healthy exercise each week washing clothes." Americans were fortunate in that they no longer washed their clothes in a nearby stream, but women still had to carry water from a well or a common faucet in a tenement. After boiling the water, a housewife could hand crank a mechanical washer (capacity four shirts). The fun was not over: "Once the wash was done, the housewife could wring the clothes out by hand or lift them straight up, heavy with water, and put them through a separate wringer. Handy turnbuckles could be loosened or screwed tight. Some women, however, felt that 'the ordinary tub wringer [required] about as much work to hold the tub as to turn the wringer.' They therefore spent an extra $1 on a better wringer."[52] It wasn't until 1960 that almost three-quarters of American households had an electric washing machine, and one has to believe that the dissemination of such machines was a godsend.

Cooking often entailed not only food preparation, but slaving over a hot stove and an oven. Meals and meal cleanup absorbed a quarter of a woman's weekly hours. The number of hours spent preparing meals fell sharply, as the advent of prepared foods and electricity cut the drudgery and the time required to prepare meals. Modern nutritionists and food scolds excoriate modern diets, but it is likely that Americans have rarely eaten better than they do today, even including fast food. With the year-round plethora of vegetables and fruits at the local grocery store, Americans enjoy a variety and quality of food that would have boggled the minds of even the most visionary nutritionist of 1900. Unless a 1900 woman went to the butcher for fresh cuts of meat, she might have relied on packed meat. The accounts of packed meat from the mid-1800s stagger the mind: 50 pounds of salt were required to preserve 200 pounds of beef or pork.[53]

American women of the twenty-first century may grouse, but many of their time-consuming errands revolve around traveling in a vehicle equipped with amenities that would leave their ancestors slack jawed: interior climate control, nearly flawless musical reproduction (or television/video screens for the youngsters in the backseats), well-cushioned and contoured seats, privacy, and no unpleasant or foul odors from a horse or loud noise and cinders from a train.

*Table 9.2* **Household Characteristics (Percentage of Reporting Units), 1940 and 1950**[a]

|  | 1940 | 1950 |
|---|---|---|
| Running water | 69.9 | 89.8[1] |
| No water supply within 50 feet | 5.1 | n.a. |
| Flush toilet in structure | 64.7 | 75.5 |
| Outside toilet or privy | 32.2 | 22.4 |
| No toilet or privy | 2.8 | 2.1 |
| Bathtub or shower | 60.9 | 73.2 |
| No bathing equipment | 39.1 | 26.8 |
| Electric lighting | 78.7 | 94.0 |
| Kerosene or gasoline | 20.2 | n.a. |
| Mechanical refrigerator | 44.1 | 80.2 |
| Ice | 27.1 | 10.6 |
| Other or none | 27.4 | 9.3 |
| Cooking fuel: coal or wood | 35.1 | 7.8 |
| Cooking fuel: gas | 48.8 | 59.6[2] |
| Cooking fuel: electricity | 5.4 | 15.0 |
| Heating fuel: coal | 54.7 | 34.4 |
| Heating fuel: wood | 22.8 | 17.1 |
| Heating fuel: gas | 11.3 | 29.7 |
| Radio | 82.8 | 95.7 |
| Television | 0.0 | 12.0 |

[1] Reporting with kitchen sink.
[2] Utility and bottled gas.
n.a.: not available.
[a] US Department of Commerce, *Sixteenth Census of the United States: 1940, Housing, Vol. II, General Characteristics, Part 1*, 20–23, 36, 38, 40, and 42; US Department of Commerce, *Seventeenth Census of the United States, Census of Housing: 1950, Vol. I, General Characteristics, Part I*, United States Summary, I-9.

Besides the labor-saving appliances, American women faced less dirt. Women's housework was made easier by the introduction of screens for windows and doors; paved streets eliminating mud; substitution of gas and electricity for coal and wood for cooking and heating; public health and private expenditures to eradicate insect and vermin; and, of course, household appliances. Smaller families contributed, too: fewer dirty diapers, fewer grubby hands, and less physical

child care. Larger houses and apartments after World War II, though, may have
offset some of this savings in time and effort.

Lebergott may have been too optimistic about the extent of the reduction in
women's toil, as other researchers believe that for women not employed in the
market, total hours worked appear stable. One of the conundrums facing labor
economists is the fact that total hours worked for full-time housewives appeared
to have remained relatively fixed for over five decades—this despite the widespread introduction of washing machines, dryers, microwaves, vacuums, refrigerators, electric ovens and stoves, and other appliances. How did this happen?[54]

Appliances offered ambiguous relief for women. Susan Strasser argues,
"Indeed, according to at least one study, the device [garbage disposal] saved
labor for men by shifting garbage tasks to women. In ninety-nine Boston families
studied during the late 1960s, wives took substantially more responsibility for
garbage in the households that owned disposers."[55] This was not, however, the
version of household life being sold with the disposer. The *House and Garden*
advertisement that In-Sink-Erator reprinted for the plumbing trade showed a
smiling husband holding a disposer behind his back. "'Darling . . . you're much
too nice to be a garbage collector,' the caption read. 'K.P. is O.K. for GI's, but not
my loving wife.'"[56] Strasser notes, "This adman's vision of a housewife's fantasy
bore little relation to negotiations about consumption expenditures, nor to the
division of labor in many households. In fact, many women did not take out the
garbage, but delegated the task to husbands, who could now demonstrate their
love by saving themselves a trip to the trash can [similar to a man giving his wife
a fishing rod for her birthday]." Hoy, though, suggests that garbage disposers
were popular with women.[57]

Spending for household appliances in the 1920s did not appear to have reduced,
much less eliminated, women's sense of fatigue and worry. Ruth Lindquist raised
the question, "Should we attribute a part of the fatigue to greater dissatisfaction and
less willingness to accept the routine of housework which may seem drudgery to
many modern women in an age which is more largely pleasure-seeking and leisure-
demanding than earlier years have been?"[58]

Ruth Schwartz Cowan's *More Work for Mother* is a standard in the field of
studies of women's work efforts and lives. Cowan's basic thesis is that the stream
of appliances and technology created in the wake of industrialization did not
reduce the hours that women worked, although it reduced physical exertion and
risks: "As industrialization took some forms of productive work out of our
homes, it left other forms of work behind. That work, which we now call 'housework,' has been transformed in the preceding hundred years . . . this is the process that I have chosen to call the 'industrialization of the home.'" Economist Joel
Mokyr points out, though, that the reduced physical exertion and risks may have
contributed to the stability in women's household production hours. Making a

task less arduous reduces the effort or cost of doing it and may expand the time devoted to the activity.[59]

Cowan stresses that the transformation in women's household duties must be seen in a context of changing technological systems. The advent of electricity led to the possibility of electric washers, dryers, stoves, ovens, and vacuum cleaners. Millions of Americans made decisions pertaining to purchasing new appliances, but their choices were constrained by outside influences: "Householders did their share in determining that their homes would be transformed . . . but so did politicians, landlords, industrialists, and managers of utilities."[60]

Cowan identifies several changes in technological systems, demonstrating in each case how new appliances proved labor saving—not for mothers but for husbands and, sometimes, children. Men no longer had to carry water from a well, a stream, or a pump; they no longer had to chop and carry wood or coal. Her observations, of course, depend upon whether these chores were originally performed by men or by women; as we've seen, Lebergott believes that women performed these tasks. Indoor plumbing meant that women no longer had to heat water on a stove and then carry it to the laundry. While the tasks were undoubtedly rendered less onerous, the demands for mothers' services rose, as mentioned previously. Cowan claims that labor-saving devices merely reorganized the housewife's work but did not reduce her hours of housework.[61]

In terms of cooking, she argues that mill-ground flour did not save time for women, because they were "spending considerably more time working with that flour than her grandmother had." The stove may have "augured more work for mother," because now she could produce more elaborate meals. She also had to clean the stove (presumably they had to clean the fireplace, before stoves were common).[62]

Manufactured cloth meant more sewing and more clothing to wash. Cowan points out that many fabrics were not washable, but that the great gain of using cotton cloth was its ability to be washed repeatedly. Thus, again and again, labor-saving devices proved, at best, to lessen the physical toil, but not the actual hours of work for women. The net result, though, was that industrialization "probably had, overall, improved their standard of living—but they still had a great deal of hard work to do. . . . American women living toward the end of the twentieth century probably ate a more varied diet, suffered less from the cold, enjoyed more space and more luxuries in their homes, and kept their bodies and their clothes cleaner than their mothers and grandmothers who had lived earlier." So far, so good, but many of the improvements resulted in the lessening of adult males' and children's chores, not women's.[63]

Cowan suggests that understanding why housework did not disappear requires knowing the history of transportation.[64] Changes in the transportation system were a key piece in understanding why women's hours of labor have not changed much across generations of Americans. Unlike most aspects of industrialization where households purchased products, in the case of transportation, "housewives have moved from being the receivers of purchased goods to being the transporters of them." A declining number of readers may recall the milkman, as a vestige of various deliverymen. Many products were brought directly to the home; coal delivery men brought coal to the coal chute. In urban areas, many other commodities could be obtained by a short walk. Rural housewives benefited from large mail-order firms, such as Sears and Montgomery Ward. Now they could order a plethora of commodities and have them delivered, often by rural free-delivery mail.[65]

The automobile also differed from other industrialized products; rather than freeing men from labor, the automobile consumed women's time, as the housewife drove the car to pick up products and to chauffer children and husbands (to commuter stations). Cowan admits that the question of why automobile driving was not dominated by men is a bit of a mystery; she suggests that the automobile manufacturers encouraged women to be interested in automobiles and that the introduction of automobiles was concurrent with the "new girl." In addition, as housewives assumed the chores of delivering goods and chauffeuring family members, many retailers began to adopt "self-service" in their stores while curtailing delivery services.[66]

Many household chores became less time consuming, but Cowan demonstrates that most households chose to dispense with servants and outside help. She describes how many housewives would hire laundresses to help with the laundry. With new electrical washers and dryers, the housewife fired the laundress and did the laundry herself.[67]

According to Cowan, the twentieth-century changes in household technology had two major effects: they continued the process of separating women's work from that of men and children, and they increased the productivity of housewives. Compared to her 1890 grandmother, a 1930 or 1950 housewife could, in the same number of hours of labor, produce more varied and elaborate meals, cleaner clothes, cleaner floors, cleaner toilets, healthier children, ad nauseam: "modern technology enabled the American housewife of 1950 to produce singlehandedly what her counterpart of 1850 needed a staff of three or four to produce: a middle-class standard of health and cleanliness." What remained, though, were the hours of labor, as women's increasing productivity was offset by increased time driving the automobile while taking care of errands.[68]

Another way to think about this is that if a woman earned wages for performing all of these services, her rising productivity would have resulted in a similar increase in her wages. Recognizing this goes to the heart of Cowan's belief that many people do not perceive households as producing anything particularly important. If housewives received an explicit payment, then their productivity and output would be realized by the even dimmest observer. Cowan concludes, "modern labor-saving devices eliminated drudgery, not labor."[69] Her observation is important, but one should not minimize the great gain to women from the elimination of drudgery. Few of us would want to undertake the strenuous effort required to perform the work of a 1900 housewife.

Two other researchers were more optimistic about the state of women's leisure hours. John Owen argues that as real wages rose for women, it became more attractive for women to take jobs, often part-time, and to purchase prepared household goods and appliances that lessened their hours of housework. He does not believe that, on net, this resulted in fewer net hours of leisure for women, surmising that as men earned higher wages and took more leisure time, so did women.[70]

The *United States Time Use Survey*, conducted in 1965 and 1969, studied women's time spent at housework. The survey entailed having women keep a diary of activities at 15-minute intervals for a full day. Joann Vanek thought that several factors created the potential for reduced work for women: smaller families, urban instead of farm living, and fewer boarders. Vanek examined the findings and compared them to previous surveys from the 1920s. She found that women spent a stable number of hours per week doing housework. Rural and urban women reported similar hours, although Vanek cautions that women living on farms also did what was defined as farm work in addition to housework. She also identified the advantages that urban women had in having nearby markets and commercial services.[71] Non-employed women spent an average of 55 hours per week doing housework, while employed women spent 26 hours.

The nature of housework had changed over time. Time spent shopping and doing managerial chores increased, as did the time devoted to child care, food preparation, and cleaning up after meals. Vanek noted that time spent in tasks associated with consumption, such as shopping, household management, and travel to shopping areas increased. In the 1960s, "[c]ontemporary women spend about one full working day per week on the road and in stores compared with less than two hours per week for women in the 1920s."[72]

Vanek suggested that non-employed women may have had larger families and younger children or less household assistance. She examined the argument that women in the labor force could use their earnings to purchase appliances and household help. In both cases, the survey data provided little support for these theses. She also conjectured that modern technology streamlined household chores and allowed women to maintain a higher-quality household than in the past. Vanek thought that non-employed women found that their services were not regarded as equal to the wage earner's efforts; in an attempt to raise the value of their housework in the eyes of family members, non-employed women "schedule work so that it is visible to others as well as to themselves . . . [and] feel pressure to spend long hours at it."[73]

Valerie Ramey discusses the conundrum of improved household technology being associated with only modest drops in women's weekly hours spent on household production. One possible counterweight was the economies of scale; in other words, as the number of members in the household increased, the weekly hours needed to maintain the household would not increase proportionally. For instance, vacuuming a domicile would take the same amount of time whether there were one or four members in the household (setting aside whether more occupants would require more frequent vacuuming). If this was true, then the shrinking households of the twentieth century would mean that weekly household hours would not decline proportionally with the decrease in household members. Another possible explanation was that in the later decades of the twentieth century, American houses were getting larger. The Levittown tract houses were initially 800 square feet; by 1990 the average size of a new house was greater than 2,000 square feet. These larger houses probably required more time to maintain a given level of cleanliness.[74]

Lebergott points out that a literary staple—the male boarder—disappeared during the twentieth century. Many urban immigrant families had boarders and lodgers. These extra members of the household required added toil by the housewife—more cleaning and another mouth to feed. Whatever the boarder or lodger paid was not, of course, a net gain, but the extra income undoubtedly helped many families survive. Farm families often housed extra people during harvest and planting seasons. With rising incomes, fewer American families were willing to sacrifice privacy by taking in boarders. The disappearance of boarding and lodging combined with smaller families to alleviate crowding in American homes. The number of persons per room fell from 1.13 in 1910 to 0.62 in 1970.[75]

## Alternatives Not Taken

What were the alternatives to the labor-saving devices purchased by so many American families? Susan Benson believes that families purchasing such appliances as electric washing machines had to resort to "dire scrimping" on other household expenditures, or that a car meant cutting back on leisure spending. The working class had to consider their purchases carefully, as "the impulse for consumer gratification constantly warred with the need for self-denial, all in a context in which the satisfaction of basic needs was by no means guaranteed."[76] Benson's observation suggests that perhaps the needs were not so basic.

Some feminists in the past urged commercialization of cooking and cleaning. Such businesses might have exploited the economies of scale inherent in large-scale laundries and cooking establishments. Commercial laundries have existed for as long as home laundry appliances. Married couples chose to invest in a washer and dryer in lieu of patronizing commercial laundries. Although some observers lamented this choice, there were good reasons for couples to have done so. An article in *Business Week*, circa 1952, pointed out the seeming anomaly in household purchases of washing machines. The machine was idle for most of the time, so it was underutilized. "All this idle machinery is an impossible economic waste." The author then resolves the conundrum by observing that while the capital is idle, it saves labor in the sense of being there when needed—no need to load up the car and drive to a laundromat.[77]

In addition to the convenience, people may have also preferred doing laundry themselves instead of having it done by a third party. Some Americans were squeamish about sending their laundry out to be handled by strangers, especially in light of the germ theory. Manufacturers of laundry machines had an incentive to play up this fear, as it meant selling more equipment to householders.[78]

Another potential alternative was socialized domestic work that would exploit the gains from economies of scale and specialization. "Material feminism" involved groups establishing day-care centers, public kitchens, and community dining clubs. Some scholars posit that businesses disliked such schemes, preferring to sell individual households a full accoutrement of appliances, but other observers believe that husbands preferred individualized attention from their spouse or that couples opted to "preserve family life and family autonomy."[79] Certainly the communal aspects of "material feminism" seem radical, although the Amana Colonies in Iowa and a few other communal communities experimented with these concepts.

Cowan suggests two other factors to consider. The first is that there were alternatives to the industrialization of the household. The second is to ask why housewives acceded to putting in the same hours for an ever-improved household. Cowan observes that between 1870 and 1920, many people moved into boarding houses where meals and household chores were provided. Some social critics bemoaned this process, especially for its alleged deleterious effects on women. "If she makes anything out of her life at all, she is obliged to do it through outside activities." This was the key to understanding why some people, such as Charlotte Perkins Gilman, approved of boarding houses. Gilman thought that applying industrialization and mass production to its logical conclusion seemed a way to uplift people. Living in a boarding house or a communal situation would allow for economies of scale and specialization: mass-produced meals cooked for the community and laundry done for the community or home-delivered meals and laundry services. These were alternative ways to free up women for other endeavors. Although it made sense to Gilman, the vast majority of Americans rejected such innovations.[80]

Cowan believes that "[t]echnological systems that might have truly eliminated the labor of housewives could have been built, but such systems would have eliminated the home as well—a result that most Americans were consistently and insistently unwilling to accept."[81] She concludes that the gender division of labor was so deeply entrenched that late twentieth-century Americans had yet to remake it.[82] She believes that women freely chose to spend the hours doing housework, given the higher standards of living they were able to produce for their families; they could take satisfaction in what "they did there had enormous value. . . . Small wonder then that these women . . . accepted the yoke of women's work in the home and viewed the modern tools with which they did it as liberating, rather than oppressive, agents."[83]

Cowan disagreed with the argument that women used some of the time saved by labor-saving appliances to enter the paid labor force in order to help purchase durable goods such as appliances and also to free up leisure time for their husbands. She asserts that there is no empirical evidence for it, even though the theory is plausible. She notes that housewives started entering the labor market years before modern household technologies were commonplace, and the housewives most likely to enter the labor market were those who likely had the fewest labor-saving devices. "Indeed, in the early postwar years, some married women were entering the labor force precisely in order to acquire those attributes of affluence."[84] Economists Jeremy Greenwood, Ananth Seshadri, and Mehmet Yorukoglu argue that "without the labour-saving household capital ushered in by the Second Industrial Revolution it would not have been feasible for women to spend more time outside the home."[85]

Juanita Kreps wrote that the evidence implied that the higher the husband's income, the less likely the wife would work in the market, but also that highly educated women "are likely to work for pay, whether or not they are married. The fact that these women earn higher salaries, this advantage being reinforced by the greater appeal of jobs that are available to college-educated women, more than offsets the fact that in general these women are married to higher-income men."[86]

More troubling, though, was why women did not take *any* of the savings in drudgery and exertion in the form of leisure, as claimed by several scholars; why would they consume all of their gains in attaining higher standards? Then again, perhaps Robinson and Godbey, Lebergott, and Owens were correct: women's hours of labor did fall.

Labor market factors may have induced women to continue to labor in the household and job for the same amount of hours in the past. First, the implicit price of women's labor in doing household chores was relatively low. The labor market, for various reasons, typically offered lower per-hour compensation for women than for men. If women could have earned more in the labor market, then the implicit cost of them doing household chores would have increased and presumably, by economic reasoning, they would have done less household work.[87]

## What to Do with Their Leisure Time?

If women had gained more time for leisure throughout the twentieth century, there was no shortage of commentators waiting to suggest on what they should devote their newfound leisure time. Commentary on women's use of leisure took a sinister turn, when recreation leaders and eugenics advocates found common ground during the 1920s and 1930s. The white, middle- and upper-class women who indulged in leisure activities instead of marrying and bearing children were putting American civilization [that is, white Protestant civilization] at risk. Combined with fears of more effete white males sequestered in their offices, women's voluntary barrenness was just short of race suicide. Weaver Pangburn stated the burning question, "shall we have large families among the groups most fitted to have them?" Eugenicists and recreation experts both advocated wholesome, family leisure that would ensure healthiness and fecundity.[88]

Suggested methods for promoting fecundity among these white women were for them to use their leisure to "streamline themselves into perfect mates and commodities for the newly leisured male. Available as leisure commodities, elite white women were expected to provide scientifically managed homes and bodies for the replication of genetically perfect humans. . . . A woman's leisure, then, could be used to rebuild oneself into the kind of mate who would be desirable to a higher grade of male, one who could support a family alone, so that her need to work was greatly diminished. Leisure, in this way, becomes a form of female 'work,' a manufacturing of oneself in order to produce further leisure."[89]

Social commentators also worried about another aspect: women's spending patterns. During the Great Depression, women's spending power decreased, but observers believed that women were easily duped into "wasteful materialistic purchasing" proffered by modern invention or that they would "spend their reduced incomes in increasingly bizarre and improper ways. Gambling, smoking, or drinking in bars, women were not treated like the heroic Forgotten Man but as selfish mothers who should be spending in a way that was beneficial for her family. These sentiments fueled the presumption that social welfare should serve to curb the jazz age-style spending of out-of-control female consumers before America fell victim to a matriarchy of irrational shoppers." Christine Frederick, though, argued that while women controlled the vast majority of family spending money, they acted prudently. She urged women to use scientific management, of which she was an expert, although she acknowledged and respected feminine "instinct" in making purchases.[90]

## Woman's Work Is Never Done, But It Is Now Easier

The debate regarding the course of women's combined market and non-market work has continued in recent years. Researchers confirmed that there was a significant drop in the time spent in home production by women between 1965 and 1975. Valerie Ramey suggests that "the fact that the biggest declines [in hours spent] were in cooking, cleanup, and clothing care leads one to wonder whether the diffusion of 'TV dinners,' dishwashers, and polyester in the late 1960s and early 1970s had more impact on time spent in home production than the diffusion of washing machines and vacuums."[91]

*Newsweek* reported in 2002 the results of a University of Michigan time-use study. Although women still did the bulk of the housework, men were catching up. The report mentioned that male assistance with household had increased up to 1985 and then stalled. The key finding was that people were not emphasizing a clean house as much as in the past. Instead of a couple performing 52 hours of household chores per week in 1965, by the end of the century a couple performed less than 40 hours per week. The authors termed this "vanishing housework." With the economic boom during the 1990s, women reduced time spent on housework and replaced some of the hours with labor market work.[92]

Women may or may not have enjoyed the same increase in leisure time that men did, but their workload was lighter than in the past. Machines reduced the sheer physical toil involved in conveying water and fuel to the household. The substitution of capital for labor in cleaning clothes saved much hard labor. If women used their savings in time formerly spent keeping house and clothes cleaned on ferrying children to and watching them participate in activities and going shopping, I suspect most would agree that such a trade-off was desirable and beneficial for themselves and for their families. Once the children leave the house and the spouse retires, then perhaps the possibility of equal hours of leisure becomes realistic.

# Commercialized Leisure in the Early 1900s

We have seen that consumer expenditures on leisure goods and services maintained a steady rise throughout the twentieth century. There are several economic aspects worth considering with respect to the rising expenditures on leisure. Although many commentators have lamented the domination of commercialized leisure, businesses supplying such goods and services offered an unprecedented range of choices.

## The Transformation of Leisure Activities

This chapter and the following chapter detail the rise of industries providing commercialized ways to spend leisure time, which we denote as leisure industries. These industries have transformed the way Americans use their leisure. Many of these industries, if not particularly large in revenue compared with manufacturing industries, loom large in the public's consciousness. In this chapter, we will look at the rise of commercialized leisure, including amusement parks, saloons, and theaters. These leisure activities were joined by mass entertainment industries, which we will focus on in the next chapter.

At the beginning of the twentieth century, most Americans had to produce their own leisure activities, including hunting, fishing, music making, dances, games, and other endeavors. Many of these leisure activities are still popular in the twenty-first century. Theater, saloons, penny arcades, and a few other commercial leisure offerings were well established by 1900, but the twentieth century multiplied the leisure offerings. Not only did Americans enjoy more options, but, in many cases, they also enjoyed higher-quality options. Instead of listening to a local singer, Americans could choose to listen to top opera singers on records, cassettes, and compact discs. Rather than simply read about the greatest baseball players, sports fans could see them on television. Television and the motion picture allowed Americans to watch Laurence Olivier perform "Hamlet," instead of hoping that he might come to a theater near them.

In Chapter 14, we will examine how many leisure industries—such as recorded music, motion pictures, professional sports, radio, and television— became heavily concentrated and often became vertically or horizontally integrated. Monopoly power is often associated with higher prices and less innovation, but many leisure industries, although concentrated, had sufficient competition to spur producers to constantly improve their products and to introduce new ones, while often reducing prices.

Many of the leisure industries competed for consumers' dollars, but in many cases they complemented each other. The radio industry did not displace the phonograph industry but eventually became a vehicle for promoting sales of recordings. The industries, in other words, sometimes interacted to mutual advantage.

## Complaints about Industries Providing Leisure Goods and Services

Social critics have lambasted mass entertainment and commercialized leisure goods and services; these observers believe that much, if not most, mass entertainment makes consumers passive. However, we shall see that consumer sovereignty reigned, as companies scrambled to meet consumer preferences. Although producers offered a limited choice of products, consumers still exercised discretion in choosing among these products.

One of the commentators' main complaints about commercialized leisure was that wealthier Americans could afford more and better forms of such leisure than could poor Americans. Wealthy Americans, however, subsidized the masses by being the pioneering consumers of products, usually paying much higher prices for an initially lower-quality service or good; as products became desirable, profit-seeking business owners used mass production to cut costs, giving the masses access to these products. Competition between producers spurred innovation, leading to higher quality products.[1]

Mass media in the twentieth century often required less sacrifice to obtain as the years passed. Richard Butsch points out that the nickel admission to the nickelodeon was about one-fortieth of a day's pay for a laborer. As economic prosperity continued in the 1920s, many neighborhood theaters charged a dime for admittance; the rate of increase in this ticket price, though, often lagged that of the laborer's wages. He compares the price of a television and the years of entertainment it provided with other visual mediums such as theater to further demonstrate the falling prices of some forms of mass entertainment.[2]

Contrary to many social critics' claims, Americans have proven adept at using leisure goods and services in unanticipated ways. The Internet quickly transformed from a platform for academics to share ideas and papers to a multimedia one. The early pioneers of the Internet may not have anticipated the rise of pornography or the explosion of social media on the Internet.

Consumers often mixed leisure goods and services. Recorded music proved complementary with dancing, reading, contemplation, and so forth; recorded music could also perk up workers bored with repetitive tasks or working in offices.

Consumers craved convenience and portability. With regard to recorded music, miniaturization made portability possible (Walkmans, iPods); consumers gained more control of what and when they consumed music, for instance. Convenience and portability marked motion pictures and televisions. By the end of the twentieth century, Americans could watch their favorite television shows and motion pictures on highly portable laptop computers and DVD players.

Although some social commentators blamed the motion pictures for being susceptible to manipulation by the ruling groups, Stephen Jones points out, "[i]f the leisure industry was to give consumers what they wanted, it could hardly ignore working-class tastes, even if bourgeois ideology was weakened as a result . . . cultural production was not necessarily commensurable with the ideological needs of capitalism."[3] The cultural elites hated motion pictures; however, it was not obvious that these groups dictated film content or the development of the industry. Recent Jewish immigrants dominated several of the major motion picture studios. Mass communication drew people across the social spectrum to share their leisure time, although this development sometimes led to mass, standardized, and passive forms of leisure.[4]

Residents of large cities led the growing demand for recreation. Incomes may have been higher in cities than in smaller towns and rural areas and, of course, the concentration of people helped create sufficient numbers of interested aficionados to sustain leisure activities, such as watching professional baseball clubs. Workers in manufacturing began seeing reduced working hours, freeing up time for leisure pursuits. Commentators noted that, with the growth of commercialized leisure, "a significant aspect of modern recreation is the trend away from the more simple pleasures to activities that require considerable outlay for facilities and equipment for play."[5] This trend was possible only because incomes were rising sufficiently rapidly to permit more discretionary spending.

## Amusement Parks and Wholesome Leisure

Amusement parks had disreputable antecedents. Bartholomew Fair in London during the mid-nineteenth century attracted unruly mobs, as described by Ben

Jonson; in 1855 authorities closed the fair, founded in the twelfth century, due to the disorder. World fairs helped uplift the public's perceptions of fairs; the world fairs' emphasis on education and uplift, even if such displays were often barely concealed propaganda, attracted millions of attendees.

By the early 1900s, amusement park operators had learned some lessons, including the importance of attracting middle-class patrons. One way to do so was to keep out the riffraff; operators enclosed their parks and monitored and enforced correct behavior. The amusement park industry declined after the early 1920s, as wider ownership of cars made other forms of travel and recreation available; indeed, widespread ownership of cars proved a handicap for many urban amusement parks, as they lacked sufficient parking.[6]

Walt Disney helped rejuvenate the amusement park industry; he refined George Tilyou's recipe when building Disneyland. Similar to Tilyou's Coney Island amusement park, Disney wanted to create a space where unpleasant events and unpleasant people could not intrude. Disneyland, after an initially slow start, quickly asserted itself as the most successful amusement park in America, with almost 4 million visitors during the first year. The Disney formula allowed "visitors to walk right into and experience the historical environments and fantasy worlds they passively watch on the television screens in their living rooms."[7] Disney was able to parlay a successful television show, along with his amusement park, to immense popularity, in part because the television show was a vehicle for publicizing the amusement park, and vice versa. Disneyland and its successor parks have never been seriously threatened by economic changes. Although baby boom children initially helped fill Disneyland, the pleasant memories ensured that baby boomers would return again and again as adults to the original park in Anaheim, California, and its sister parks.[8]

Other entrepreneurs began imitating Disneyland's basic characteristics: cleanliness, safety, pleasant people, and courteous employees. Millicent Hall summarizes the modern amusement park industry: "Everything in the theme park—even the minor events and the employees—is controlled, yet the total package creates the illusion of spontaneity" to which James Adams adds, "Each attraction is designed much like an assembly line, with long, regimented waiting lines leading to fixed cars or boats, which carry guests on an undeviating path through the event in a set period of time."[9] Although some large corporations developed chains of amusement parks, Walt Disney World Resort remains the most popular tourist attraction in the world, and the various Disney parks combined often earned more than half of the industry's revenues. The amusement park industry later combined with a larger phenomenon—the growth of tourism as an industry.[10]

By 2000, amusement and theme parks generated more than $8 billion in estimated revenues. Although the amusement park industry lagged spectator sports, gambling casinos, and golf courses and country clubs in revenues, the industry still generated more than 6 percent of revenues on arts, entertainment, and recreation services.[11]

## Alcohol, Saloons, and Cabarets

If one considers consuming alcoholic beverages to be a form of leisure, saloons, taverns, and cabarets loom large in the leisure industry. Although expenditures on alcoholic beverages were not included in the Department of Commerce's calculations of expenditures on recreational activities, the drinking establishments did a brisk business.

Sizable pools of single men congregated in large cities that were manufacturing centers or smaller towns based on extractive industries. These men were a social problem, as David Courtwright pointed out: "Men who congregate with other men tend to be more sensitive about status and reputation. Even if they are not intoxicated with drink or enraged by insult, they instinctively test one another, probing for signs of weakness. Declining peer challenges can lead to ostracism; accepting them often leads to fighting."[12] Fortunately for America during the postwar era, the proportion of single men dropped precipitously. The median age of first marriage for men declined from 25.1 in 1910 to 22.6 in 1955, which meant that the proportion of married men under 25 rose from one in every five to one in every two.[13] Young men were, in a sense, domesticated.

Prior to the 1900s, though, the problem for single men was finding leisure opportunities. Working-class single men often did not or could not patronize higher-class forms of leisure. Many found leisure in the local saloon. Saloons not only provided camaraderie but also a myriad of social amenities, ranging from the prosaic, such as providing toilet facilities, to extending loans and being a meeting place for political or economic organizing. The saloons also served as a source of sustenance, not only of the liquid type. The "free lunch" was a vehicle whereby brewers could subsidize saloons and attract larger crowds of drinkers. By buying a beer for a nickel, the patron received a free lunch that historian Jon Kingsdale considered equivalent to or better than a ten-cent lunch in a restaurant. To ensure that men drank, the "free lunch" was typically of a salty nature. Cities differed in their responses to the free lunch. Saloons were required by law to supply free lunches in Boston, while such were prohibited in Atlanta. The requirement of a free lunch in Boston saloons may have been a way to force out saloons that were not sponsored by a brewery. Beer appeared to displace distilled liquor over the second half of the nineteenth century. By 1911–1915, adult per capita consumption of beer was 29.53 gallons, almost 11 times as much as in 1850.[14]

Although many reformers painted a picture of drinking establishments as rife with violence and dissipation, Ken Roberts claims that in more recent years, "[c]ommerce has civilized drinking, and what was formerly the Western way of drinking is currently spreading in Eastern Europe. Commerce wants people . . . to drink, and to do so regularly, which is only likely if drinking can be made harmless and therefore socially acceptable. The owners . . . do not want customers to become drunk and disorderly, or too ill to continue to work and sustain their leisure spending."[15]

Many people wanted to mix drinking and dancing. The taxi-dance halls employed young women, who danced with men who paid per dance, often in both money and drinks. As the reader can guess, the taxi-dance halls raised fears among some sociologists and moralists: "Any recreational institution so contradictory to traditional American standards as the taxi-dance hall could not arise in the cities of the United States without calling forth opposition to it. . . . The fact that taxi-dancers were required to dance with all-comers, that the establishment was closed to women patrons, and that proprietors did not favor women supervisors furnished grounds for these suspicions [of immorality and prostitution]." Paul Cressey noted that the taxi-dance halls did not originate out of a desire to circumvent conventions but in response to neighborhoods with large proportions of single men: "The taxi-dance hall may thus be viewed as a natural outgrowth of certain urban conditions rather than as a moral violation."[16]

For those who liked to drink in more sophisticated venues, cabarets provided such environments. The cabaret evolved from restaurants and other forms of activities. A cabaret served food and drinks while providing music and other entertainment. Delmonico's was a pioneering restaurant catering to wealthy New Yorkers by the mid-nineteenth century. It met a need by providing a place for wealthy men and women to dine out and socialize. Other restaurants and public hotels gradually became places for upper-class women to seek social company and entertainment, including dancing with hired professional dancers.[17]

Whether or not cabarets originated in Europe, in America they provided exotic experiences, with a bohemian style. Cabarets played a role in making jazz dancing acceptable.[18] In this way, perhaps, cabarets were another outlet for people to rebel ever so slightly against the established mores; come morning, they could revert back to their usual behavior.

Cabarets also provided an opportunity for people to flaunt their economic success by allowing them to spend money impulsively. People came to the cabarets to make an impression, and the way to make an impression was to spend lavishly. Women enjoyed the entertainment and the chance to see fashionable clothes. The all-girl revues featured young women in a multitude of expensive outfits. Ziegfeld girls changed their costumes repeatedly during their shows.[19] Gilbert Seldes believes that businessmen found in cabarets "everything against which he is working; leisure and laziness and incontinence; carelessness of time and money; what seems to be an impertinent indifference to getting on."[20]

Saloons receded into importance and were displaced by taverns and bars, but the concept of having a place to relax and drink never died out. In the immediate postwar period, bars and taverns received a technological boost: television. Bars and taverns did not embrace radio the same way they did television. Bar owners were important early buyers of televisions, especially in the larger cities in the Northeast. It is possible that because New York City was the center of television during the first few years of the new medium, the bar/television phenomenon was exaggerated there. People crammed into bars to watch sporting events; some bartenders worried that the patrons spent more time gawking than they did drinking. The television also allegedly reduced conversation, which had been a staple of barroom activity.[21]

Tavern owners experimented with how to charge for television; some raised the price of drinks, while others imposed drink minimums. One tavern owner reserved the front row of seats for scotch drinkers, while the back row was for beer drinkers. It wasn't long, though, before complaints arose. Patrons sometimes argued over which show to watch (not that there were too many choices in the early days, except in New York City and a few of the larger cities). Some of the patrons simply wanted to watch television and were not copious imbibers. The "large screen" sets measured 25 by 19—inches, that is, although some purchased projection devices.[22]

Televisions and taverns raised concerns among clergy and benevolent groups. Some church groups and the Salvation Army in New York's Bowery tried to raise funds to purchase televisions "so that men who are determined not to drink will not be lured into barrooms by television."[23]

Given the popularity of taverns with televisions, producers of rival forms of leisure hoped that government tax authorities would try to reduce the profitability of this threat by levying amusement taxes or by forcing taverns with televisions to pay for licenses as places of amusement. The owners of sports teams debated whether the telecasts of games in the tavern were siphoning fans from the ball park, or whether they were creating new fans. Since major league baseball's attendance decline did not become apparent until 1949 or 1950, the early taverns with television probably did not seem much of a threat. One tavern owner, Al Schlossberg, in Chicago told reporters, "I figure maybe dese guys is goin to hockey games or fights, an' I say, why not bring hockey or fights here, so guys can see sports and drink atta same time. So I buy dese gadgets. Slump in business stopped."[24]

## Music for Millions

Recorded popular music was one of the great mass entertainment industries of the twentieth century. Americans loved music. Some religious denominations made music an integral part of their worship service. For home leisure, singing was a common leisure activity. The twentieth century witnessed an explosion in the availability of music. Social commentator Jacques Barzun rhapsodized about the phonograph: "This mechanical civilization of ours has performed a miracle . . . it has, by mechanical means, brought back to life the whole repertory of Western music. . . . [Today] neglected or lesser composers come into their own and keep their place. In short the whole literature of one of the arts has sprung into being—it is like the Renaissance rediscovering the ancient classics and holding them fast by means of the printing press. It marks an epoch in Western intellectual history."[25]

Composers and song writers worked with music publishing houses to disseminate new songs. Musical theater and vaudeville were two mechanisms for introducing new songs. Composers and song writers had to persuade performers to use their compositions.

To reproduce favorite songs, Americans purchased pianos. Families did not purchase pianos solely for their musical capacity but also to make a statement about themselves and to gain prestige: "the piano not only became symbolic of the virtues attributed to music, but also of home and family life, respectability, and woman's particular place and duty."[26]

Men wanted their wives and daughters to be cultured, and a piano was a vehicle for inculcating culture. As historian Timothy Day observes, "most [men] would not wish to learn the instrument themselves." He suggests that the mechanical (player) piano was suitably matched for men. Men could now demonstrate their masculinity by sitting and discussing the instrument's technical aspects. Later inventions, such as the phonograph and radio, also held this virtue for men.[27]

The American piano manufacturing industry was quite diffuse. Many piano manufacturers bought parts from a myriad of producers; the manufacturer then assembled the pianos. The process resembled that of the early automobile manufacturing industry before mass production. Owners proved resistant to the idea of merging or creating holding companies in order to concentrate power in the industry. While there were hundreds of manufactures, a handful achieved national prominence, and eventually the industry's output became concentrated in the hands of 25 corporations and holding companies. These holding companies and mergers, however, did not result in domination by any one firm or handful of firms.[28]

Although the owners of piano manufacturing companies were relatively staid in their approach to monopolization, they quickly embraced publicity and advertising. A company would often sign a well-known pianist to play its pianos during a concert tour, which was usually underwritten by the company. Some firms eventually became prominent in the minds of the buying public, but even if they did not, their expenditures on concert tours enabled many Americans to see concert pianists.[29]

Many modern Americans may associate player pianos with machines in pizza or ice cream parlors. The early twentieth-century player piano technology, however, was highly sophisticated. Once manufacturers agreed upon industry standards (65- or 88-note machines), the interchangeability between rolls and machines proved popular. Another popular facet of player pianos was the ease of play; Aeolian marketed its Pianola by boasting about its simplicity. Some manufacturers boasted that their technique of recording "was capable of transcribing onto the piano roll not only all the artist's movement of keys and pedals, but the exact measurements of hammer velocity at the moment of impact with the strings as well." The performers themselves apparently believed in this quality of reproduction, as "every concert artist of any prominence made rolls for Welte, Duo-Art, or Ampico, and attested to the faithfulness of their reproduction." Readers may attribute these comments to advertising and publicity efforts; however, Craig Roell points out, "[u]ntil the advent of the high-fidelity phonograph and magnetic tape recorder, there existed no more advanced technology for recording piano music than the reproducing piano. Those fortunate enough today to hear a restored instrument perform ... will be shocked by the ghostly realism."[30]

Piano manufacturers took a different approach to advertising player pianos than they did with regular pianos. The companies emphasized the concept of "repeated experience." Just as a Kodak camera from the 1890s allowed people to share visual memories, the player piano allowed people to enjoy a piece repeatedly. To the modern mind, inured to almost ubiquitous recording, understanding how novel to our ancestors was the idea of being able to listen to, say, your daughter's piano recital again after the actual performance is difficult; for people in 1900, the experience must have been "priceless," as the modern advertisement intones.[31]

Pianos showed up in motion picture theaters. Theater owners sometimes credited good music for influencing patrons' decisions on which films to attend. The grand theaters in large cities often employed an organ, but many theaters used a piano to "add life to love scenes, anxiety to chase scenes, or zest to transitions. From 1905 to 1925, nearly every manufacturer of coin-operated player pianos also made 'photoplayers,' instruments designed especially for movie houses."[32]

Composers aimed their talents at supplying America's pianists with popular music. Ragtime, although excoriated by some, proved remarkably popular, both as sheet music and for player pianos.[33] Composers initially allowed manufacturers of perforated rolls for player pianos and discs for phonographs to record and distribute their music without payment of royalties.

Initially, the composers held no copyright on their work, if produced for a reproduction medium. The composers and their publishers felt that the reproductions spurred sales of sheet music. After several years without copyright protection for composers, President Theodore Roosevelt and many others felt the composers should have copyright laws to the reproductions, which seems equitable.

Unfortunately, a bill to grant composers such rights played into the hands of an aspiring monopolist. A piano manufacturer, Aeolian, which produced player pianos, was planning to team up with the Music Publishers' Association to monopolize the industry. Congress investigated the industry and discovered Aeolian's monopoly bid. If Congress passed a rule protecting the composers, or if the courts issued a similar ruling, then the publishers would grant Aeolian exclusive rights to reproduce their sheet music on perforated rolls for 35 years. Aeolian also approached music retailers and negotiated the right to raise the prices of their perforated rolls to compensate the manufacturer for royalty payments, while forbidding retailers from cutting their price. Aeolian, therefore, was trying to vertically integrate from the input (sheet music) through the retailer. The kicker was, according to Roell, "[n]one of these secret contracts would go into effect, however, until the Supreme Court or Congress changed the copyright law." Since this potential setup was likely to be extremely lucrative for Aeolian, the company spent large sums to persuade the public and legislators to approve a copyright law.[34]

The Supreme Court ruled in *White-Smith Company v. The Apollo Company* (1907) that the perforated rolls were part of the player piano and therefore were not copies. With the court's denial of copyright protection for composers, Aeolian poured more money into a campaign to get Congress to pass such a law. After the usual parrying, Congress passed a Copyright Act of 1909, which granted composers copyright but not exclusivity. A composer could prohibit mechanical reproduction of his work; if he permitted any company to reproduce his work mechanically, then all makers could reproduce the work upon payment of royalties of two cents per roll or disc sold. The Copyright Act defeated Aeolian's attempt to monopolize the music industry.[35]

By the mid-1920s, commercialized radio was growing rapidly and provided keen competition for Americans' leisure time. Some piano companies chose to use the new medium to publicize and to sell their pianos, while a few piano manufacturers produced radios. Radio advertising proved a useful way to gain the public's attendance. The 1920s, though, were not a particularly prosperous decade for the piano manufacturing industry.

Although radio may have dampened the demand for pianos, many urban Americans found themselves with smaller living spaces, making a grand piano inconvenient. Piano manufacturers responded by introducing baby grand pianos, which enabled some manufacturers to survive the decade. Even advertising could not resuscitate the piano market during the 1920s, despite the general prosperity.[36]

Thomas Edison invented the phonograph. He intended to rent the phonograph to businesses for the purpose of dictation; he did not immediately grasp its potential for recording music. He let his invention lie unused for several years. As with most inventions, Edison's initial effort was primitive and was not intended for recording music. During the interim, Emile Berliner developed a gramophone, while Alexander Graham Bell invented the graphophone. These inventors and their business backers fought over patent infringement.

Edison and the other inventors also misperceived the phonographs' purpose in the home. They envisioned the machine as a supplement to home music making, a way for families to record a performance by their daughter or son, instead of a medium for pre-recorded discs and cylinders; they did not recognize its potential as a leisure good.[37]

Jesse Lippincott sought to combine these patents and inventions into the North America Phonograph Company, and he set up exclusive sales areas.[38] The cartel failed, since businesses proved unenthusiastic about renting or buying these machines for dictation. The cylinders and discs could record only a limited range of sounds; they were inconvenient to operate; and they required constant changing of cylinders and discs. Had Beethoven's Ninth Symphony been recorded, it would have required several discs just for the final movement and would have sounded terrible to modern audiophiles.

Although the North America Phonograph Company was failing, one bright spot emerged. An entrepreneur in San Francisco installed a machine requiring a nickel to operate. The consumer heard a brief song for his or her nickel. The nickel-in-the-slot machine was contemporaneous with nickelodeon motion picture devices.[39]

Americans found the novelty of hearing recorded sound worth their nickels, and businesses purchased machines for their arcades. In order to keep these nickel-in-the-slot machines profitable or to sell machines to consumers, producers had to have product to play. There were three drawbacks to commercial recording. The quality was limited, as the recording technology was unable to capture much of the tonal spectrum. The wax cylinders and discs had limited playing time, initially around two minutes. Finally, the recording process itself boggles the modern mind. Picture a singer or a small group of musicians surrounded by, say, 10 phonographic recording machines. The singer performs her aria, and 10 cylinders are inscribed. She then repeats her performance for the next 10 cylinders. The ability to supply recordings clearly lagged the growing demand for cylinders.[40] At first, no one could devise a way to create a master disc from which to press large quantities of a recording.

Professional musicians were wary of recording, as they feared the recordings would provide competition for their live performances. They also feared that the reproduction would not do justice to their talents. Enrico Caruso and his famed tenor voice proved well matched for the recording technology of the time. He recorded several arias that proved popular. He became rich by recording, but, more important, his success encouraged other musicians to record.[41]

Because the gramophones were mechanically simpler, they could be priced by the National Gramophone Company at 15 dollars, as opposed to Edison's and Columbia's models at a minimum of 40 dollars. The latter two firms attempted to denigrate the gramophones, but the new machine proved a durable competitor. Edison and his rivals realized that they needed to lower the price of their equipment, if they hoped to make the phonograph affordable for a mass market; by the end of the 1800s, Edison's company was able to market a spring-motor model at 25 dollars. This price was still more than a week's earnings for most working-class men.[42]

After the flat-disc was introduced to the market by the French firm Pathe, Edison's cylinder declined in relative popularity. Whether or not discs had superior sound quality relative to cylinders, they possessed decisive advantages: they were easier to handle and were less bulky. The disc players were also easier to operate.[43] When Edison began making disc phonographs, he appealed to an upper-end market. His consoles sold for $200 to $800 and were intended for "people of cultured and elegant tastes." Along with this marketing niche, Edison chose to personally interfere with the musical genres issued by the company; in the end, his tastes and vision proved mismatched with those of most Americans.[44]

The Big Three producers—Edison, Victor, and Columbia—peacefully coexisted during the 1910s after forming a patent pool, with occasional attempts to fix prices and to adjudicate patent disputes. Andre Millard characterizes the companies as vertically integrated firms devoted to producing a large output at a relatively low cost per unit. Each had a national network of dealers. The Big Three did face inroads by smaller entrants. The Big Three's original patents were expiring, and the 1910s were years of relative prosperity; both factors encouraged new entrants. Large department stores, among other retailers, began eroding the Big Three's retailing of phonograph discs. These larger vendors offered cheap records that cut into the Big Three's sales. In addition, by the 1920s, industry observers started to suggest that the market was saturated.[45]

Although the Big Three maintained a tacit truce, each firm recognized that it was still competing with the other two firms and numerous smaller companies. Each company sought to improve its product, and innovations continued to be offered to consumers. Some of the improved sound technology proved a difficult sale. The flared horns, so endemic of old-fashioned phonographs, were unattractive, and phonograph executive Eldridge Johnson and his engineers worked to redesign the equipment to be acceptable as furniture.[46]

Buying a phonograph was just the first step. The machine required discs. Dance music proved popular, and Americans purchased recordings of their favorite dance tunes. Since the Big Three tied up most of the mainstream, top-flight talent, smaller, independent firms had to resort to recording new types of music, such as jazz. Jazz and rural music were musical niches largely neglected by the Big Three. With farmers enjoying prosperity before and during World War I, an expanding market for music preferred by rural audiences existed. By the 1930s and 1940s, motion pictures introduced many popular songs, leading to movie studios owning or aligning with music publishing firms.[47]

The discs were not cheap, either. Discs featuring top-name performers commanded as much as $5, while discs with lower-tiered artists cost $1.50. Although this does not seem like much to today's consumer, $5 in 1905 was more than many workmen's daily wages. Since the disc had such a limited playing time, replete with scratches and surface noise, Americans of a century ago were paying much more for a lower quality product.[48] From their vantage point, of course, Americans of 1905, if they had the money, apparently thought the price worthwhile.

The phonograph industry evolved rapidly. Electricity altered recording and listening practices. The recording process advanced rapidly with the advent of electrical recording using microphones and amplifiers. Soon the recording studio was a place where perfection was possible and eventually mandatory. Companies learned how to make master discs, thereby avoiding the repetitive recording practices of the early years. Better fidelity and better materials improved the discs' durability and sound quality. In the 1940s and 1950s, high fidelity and then stereophonic recordings became available. Columbia and RCA also introduced new discs after World War II: 45 rpm and 33 rpm. Columbia's 33 rpm discs proved well matched for classical music, while RCA's 45 rpm discs fit well with the nascent rock 'n' roll music wave of the 1950s. The initial clash of speeds, though, was a hindrance, as phonographs were not always equipped to handle both speeds. Magnetic tape in the late 1950s improved sound quality, while cassette tapes proved more convenient and more portable than phonographs. Eight-track tapes had a brief period of popularity, but such tapes and cassettes were replaced by compact discs.[49]

Sony Corporation eventually reduced the size, increased the quality, and reduced the price of stereo phonographs. The new stereo phonograph systems completed the process of taking a product designed for the wealthy and converting it into an item of mass consumption with ease of use and portability. The Sony Walkman cassette player proved highly popular with its convenience and portability during the 1980s.[50] Along the way, though, some technology failed to capture the public's fancy, such as quadrophonic discs and the minidisc.

During the postwar years, the major record labels tended to stick with established genres, such as classical and big band music. The independent labels made inroads by recording country and western, rhythm and blues, and rock 'n' roll. These smaller labels' success made them desirable to the bigger companies, and a series of acquisitions eliminated many of the independents.[51]

Radio had initially reduced the demand for phonographs. The first half of the Great Depression proved devastating to the remnants of the phonograph industry. By 1932, total sales of records were just 6 million, about one-seventeenth the number sold in 1927. Gelatt attributes the decline of the record industry to radio, because the record manufacturers were unable to quickly capture the new sounds heard on the radio. Other factors included RCA's indifference to the record industry and the continued high prices for records and equipment. Gelatt also argues that the country had grown tired of "canned music," as represented by the record industry.[52]

The phonograph and record industries rebounded in the second half of the Great Depression, due in part to the repeal of prohibition that made going out to clubs and bars more popular. These establishments began installing jukeboxes. The jukebox, basically a return to the coin-in-the-slot concept of the industry's early years, arose from obsolescence. Teenagers flocked to venues featuring now-updated jukeboxes. By the end of the 1930s, there were 225,000 jukeboxes requiring 13 million discs a year. The jukebox inspired teenagers to purchase discs of songs they heard on the jukebox.[53]

Along with the advances in technology after World War II, there was a boom in the number of companies publishing long-play recordings, from 11 to 200. Although most of these companies quickly faded, a few, such as Chess and Atlantic, had a marked effect on music.[54] Chess and Atlantic turned to the music of African-Americans—blues, be-bop, and gospel, among other genres; Atlantic survived into the 1960s, when Warner Brothers bought it.[55] The record industry resembled a lottery, with hundreds of firms hoping to find an Elvis Presley; many of the major producers overproduced in order not to fall behind. Although the industry remained concentrated in the hands of RCA Victor, Decca, Columbia, and Capitol—with a combined market share of over three-quarters—these firms rested uneasily, as they scrambled to remain relevant in the industry.[56]

Rock 'n' roll burst onto the American consciousness during the mid-1950s. Teenagers purchased the records, usually 45 rpms, in astonishing quantities. What adults perceived to be a fad became an enduring phenomenon. The advent of television had knocked out most of radio's dramatic and comedic shows, so surviving radio stations turned to canned music to fill their programming; rock 'n' roll proved a popular filler, coinciding with the "Top Forty" format. Some pundits, such as

Robert Frank, predicted that only the most popular musicians would be commercially viable, creating disproportionate rewards for the top and a drastic reduction for the second best, but the music industry was and remains characterized by a mind-numbing variety. Indeed, the technology allowed performers whose fans numbered in the hundreds to a few thousand to successfully issue recordings.[57]

The music industry evolved again in the 1980s. With cable television beginning to saturate the nation, television's demand for programming leaped upward. One genre that proved popular was the music video. In a sense, motion pictures and television programming aimed at teenagers in the 1950s and 1960s proved to be precursors to using rock 'n' roll in motion picture or television programming. With the debut of Music Television (MTV), many musicians found they could promote their music via well-produced videos. Some performers even parlayed their musical talent into television or movie stardom. The new medium for rock 'n' roll further eroded independent labels' ability to compete with the largest companies, as the independents lacked the resources to produce slick videos. Independent labels again found themselves the target of a wave of takeovers. "The independents came and went as each new wave of popular music at first sustained them and then ebbed and left them prey to the major companies. Technological innovation had largely worked against them, because it was normally initiated by the majors, with their links to the manufacturing side of the business, and it raised the stakes of doing business in the world of recorded sound."[58]

The glory of phonographs and later sound reproduction technology, then, was allowing a consumer to listen when and how often he or she wanted both during leisure time and even at work or while commuting. Consumers also gained a selection of music for listening, although in the early years this selection was limited by technical constraints, as certain types of voices or instruments did not record well. The phonograph expanded the market for each performer. If you could not see Caruso, because you lived in a remote town, you could purchase some of his recordings. A century after Edison's invention of the phonograph, recorded music was a $3 billion industry, with over half a billion long-play records, 45 rpm singles, cassette tapes, and DVDs sold per year.[59]

## Theater and Vaudeville

Before motion pictures, people found entertainment in live theater and vaudeville. These entertainment venues were well established as leisure-time activities before the twentieth century. Although theater continues to this day, vaudeville was disappearing rapidly by the 1920s. Vaudeville's legacy continued on radio, movie screens, and television, though, as the Marx Brothers and other vaudevillians performed for the three younger mediums through most of the twentieth century.

Both vaudeville and the theater struggled to gain respectability. Vaudeville evolved from earlier concert saloons. Theater operators, such as B. F. Keith, began trying to attract women and children; in order to do so, they had to prohibit various male gaucheries. They also built ornate theaters and employed uniformed ushers, "strictly supervised to cater to patrons as though they were servants."[60]

Theater possessed many similarities to motion pictures. The star system was a primary commonality, and, in some cases, stars switched back and forth between the two mediums. Theater patrons demanded to see stars, and those who were popular with audiences could command larger salaries; theater producers began to pay stars so much money that the production lost money, so the producers tried to cut back on other costs.[61]

Prior to the twentieth century, most theaters were composed of stock companies, a group of actors and stagehands that produced various plays. Cities of any size usually had at least one stock company. This form of theater began to evolve into a concentrated production process, whereby stars and their accompanying troupe began to tour the country. The combination troupe originated in New York City and gradually displaced stock companies, as patrons wanted to see the highly polished productions.[62]

In both vaudeville and theater, as the industries matured, a certain concentration ensued. Middlemen between the theaters and performers appeared. Theaters and vaudeville formed chains or circuits; acts would tour the circuit according to an arranged schedule. By the turn of the century, the Theatrical Syndicate monopolized the booking of theater combination productions (a theater combination production was one that included the star actors and a troupe of lesser actors and stage workers), while Keith and Albee did the same with vaudeville. The Syndicate booked productions exclusively in their own theaters while refusing to perform in any other houses if the productions played elsewhere: these tactics froze out other booking agents while forcing production groups to sign with the Syndicate. Because Klaw and Erlanger, key players in the Syndicate, owned many theaters, their ability to book productions into a circuit of "one-night stands" (theaters in cities between major cities but on rail lines) forced producers to sign with them or to become economically infeasible. Within a few years, the Syndicate controlled over 500 playhouses. By doing so, their productions competed with independent productions; guess whose productions received preferential booking![63]

Klaw and Erlanger dominated the theater industry in the early years of the century, but the Shubert brothers and David Belasco took them to court, where a New York City grand jury indicted Klaw and Erlanger for conspiracy in restraint of trade. Judge Otto A. Rosalsky dismissed the indictment, partly because he believed that theatrical amusements were not "articles of trade and commerce" and therefore were not subject under the antitrust laws. The Shuberts would later use this judicial reasoning in their own antitrust case.[64] The audience may have, however, gained from the concentration of booking; they were assured a standardized product that reliably appeared at the theater.

The stock market crash hit the two leading theater groups, Shubert and the Erlanger companies. Shubert emerged from the debacle and became the lone player, owning many Broadway theaters and controlling the United Booking Office. They used minimum guarantees and stop-limit clauses (if total receipt fell below a threshold for two consecutive weeks, the theater manager could evict the production) to pull the plug on productions that were not doing well. In the 1950s, though, the Justice Department began investigating, and Shubert signed a consent decree promising to divest several theaters and to cut their connection with United Booking Office.[65]

With the industry as concentrated as it was, Jack Poggi wonders why producers did not raise ticket prices more than they did. He speculates that they worried about competition from movies (theater tickets were $6.60 in 1928, more than three times the charge for a box seat at Yankee Stadium for a regular-season baseball game and more than the $0.50 to $1.00 charged at first-run movie theaters). He thinks the theater owners worried about public reaction to higher ticket prices, especially for popular shows, but he then describes how people would pay ticket arbitragers (scalpers) more than the top box office price for tickets to the most popular shows. He fails, therefore, to explain why theater owners worried about higher prices, when patrons willingly purchased tickets from scalpers.[66]

## Wholesome or Rebellious Audiences

Twentieth-century Americans spent much of their leisure time consuming mass entertainment. Theater, vaudeville, motion picture, radio, and television producers worked to create large audiences. Richard Butsch demonstrates that for some Americans, large gatherings of their fellow citizens were suspect.

Gathering large numbers of potentially unruly people together often made the pillars of society nervous. Since there are usually only small numbers of the upper crust, getting crowds of them together to run amuck was almost impossible by definition. The unruly were generally identified with the working class, immigrants, the "other." Such fears were not completely baseless, as mediums with live audiences, such as vaudeville, theater, music concerts, movies, and sporting events have on occasion erupted in violence.

Because the upper crust comprised so few people, entertainment entrepreneurs faced a difficult decision for many years: cater to the large, rowdy masses or to the small, genteel upper class. With the growth of a prosperous middle class, though, entrepreneurs had a new option. For owners of theaters and baseball teams, the quest for respectability often rested on attracting the growing middle classes during the late 1800s.

One tactic was to consciously shift from a young male audience to a mixed audience of men, women, and children. Theater owners hoped that the presence of women would temper male behavior, a hope they shared with baseball owners. In order to attract proper ladies, theater owners offered matinees and enforced reasonable decorum from the males. Many theater owners succeeded in transforming their clientele; women were undoubtedly pleased, as they now had another safe and respectable venue for their leisure time.[67]

The owners of vaudeville and theaters sometimes found that attracting women and children had drawbacks. As early as the 1890s, affluent teenage females attended these venues in hopes of mingling with popular stars, especially leading men. The *Ladies Home Journal,* a bastion of respectability, chided these girls for behaving so, as the girls "harmed themselves as well as the theater." The *Journal* ran, as a public service but undoubtedly also to attract buyers, a series of articles informing young girls about the theaters, ostensibly to protect them from their fascination.[68]

The development of respectable, family-oriented theaters, such as Tony Pastor's, held another benefit for women. Men often patronized saloons and other unsavory places en route to home. Many of these venues received support from city leaders, who may have deemed them useful safety valves for restless males. With the advent of respectable theaters, though, wives and husbands could share a safe evening out, watching reasonably wholesome entertainment.[69]

Audiences became larger and more diffuse in the 1920s, thanks to new technologies. Butsch believes that radio and television "privatized entertainment and provided a reason to stay home . . . the family replaced the community as the group sharing the experience. This carried the process of privatization beyond privatizing public space to withdrawing to private space, raising greater barriers to community identity and participation."[70] These technologies, then, created a reversion to private entertainment after motion pictures and other forms of entertainment had created a switch away from family-based entertainment, such as the piano. After World War II, private forms of leisure surged, while many forms of public leisure stagnated.

The rise of the nickelodeons, although castigated for allegedly being a lowbrow, immigrant working-class venue, had defenders. Temperance reformers believed that the nickelodeons provided a good substitute for alcohol. Instead of patronizing the saloon, fathers went home and retrieved the family to go attend a nickelodeon. A saloon-keeper in Middletown moaned: "The movies killed the saloon. They cut our business in half overnight."[71] While the nickelodeon was rarely a hotbed of political rabble-rousing, the fact that children, particularly working-class children, attended raised questions of whether the content of the films affected their behavior. Many people expressed concerns, although a few hoped that films could prove uplifting and educational.[72]

After the nickelodeon stage, as movie exhibitors began building ornate theaters, they consciously sought middle-class clientele. The full-length films allowed directors to insert art into the medium; the full-length films also allowed theater owners to charge higher prices, which eliminated many of the poorer, scruffier attendees. As with theater, movie theater owners hired uniformed ushers to serve customers and to maintain order.[73]

## The Rise of Commercial Entertainment

These early leisure industries grew into mass entertainment, although not necessarily mass entertainment where large numbers of consumers viewed or listened simultaneously to the same performance, such as radio, motion pictures, or television. Thousands of Americans could now hear the same song on their phonographs, but not necessarily simultaneously and certainly not in proximity with each other. Americans voted with their nickels for recorded music and, later, for motion pictures, forcing inventors and promoters to continually scramble to ascertain and to meet their patrons' demands. For those industries with large audiences viewing simultaneous showings of the same performance, we turn to the next chapter.

# Mass Entertainment to the Fore

Americans could have used their burgeoning leisure time to produce homemade leisure. Commercialized, mass leisure proved a popular alternative, however, and became a prominent way to fill leisure time. Although crowds of a few thousand attended a given theater and some tens of thousands attended a particular sporting event in the largest cities at the turn of the century, the twentieth century witnessed the rise of truly mass entertainment. Millions could watch the same movie, albeit in hundreds of theaters and over several days, by the 1910s. Radio shows captivated millions of American listeners by the 1930s. By the early 1950s, millions of Americans could collectively experience the birth of "little Ricky Ricardo" on *I Love Lucy* on television.

Americans could collectively share entertainment experiences, thanks to entrepreneurs and inventors seeking fame and profits. The government, too, shaped the mass media, although not always to the benefit of consumers.

## America's Love Affair with Professional Sports

Americans have enjoyed ball games for centuries. Baseball and football evolved from earlier games. Basketball was invented in the United States, but the concept of throwing a sphere through a target has antecedents (such as the Mayans). With more free time for leisure on their hands, many Americans have invested much time and emotional energy into rooting for their favorite sports teams.

Part of the transformation of leisure in America has been the professionalization of play activities, such as sports. Johan Huizinga suggests that "[t]he spirit of the professional is no longer the true play-spirit; it is lacking in spontaneity and carelessness. . . . This affects the amateur too, who begins to suffer from an inferiority complex. Between them they push sport further and further away from the play-sphere proper until it becomes a thing *sui generis*; neither play nor earnest."[1]

Entrepreneurs recognized how popular sporting events featuring top talent were among fans. They realized that organizing sports leagues could please fans and fill coffers. The growing prevalence of sports sections in newspapers was evidence of the popularity of sports. Newspapers provided, in essence, free advertising for sports teams, while fan interest in sports helped sell newspapers. Newspapers, radio, and television magnified professional sports' reach. For the millions of fans who rarely, if ever, saw a game, these media made it convenient for them to follow their favorite teams. Radio and television became valuable sources of revenue for the owners and eventually led to higher player salaries.

Major league baseball (MLB) was a popular commercial sport by 1903. Attendance at all professional games, major and minor leagues, as well as amateur games, was in the tens of millions per year. College football experienced rapid gains in attendance during the 1920s and may well have been the glamour sport of the decade.[2]

Baseball began its transformation into a commercialized activity prior to the Civil War. The players and their supporters found that other people were willing to pay to watch the games. The initial men's club teams were composed of amateurs, but the desire to field successful teams led to surreptitious payments to top players, some of whom would not be considered gentlemen.[3]

Businessmen and town promoters believed that having a successful team would lend prestige and attract business to their town. Cincinnati city leaders asked Harry Wright, a successful cricket and baseball player, to form a team of superior players. The revolutionary aspect of the Cincinnati Red Stockings was the team's overt professionalization: every player was paid. The Red Stockings were successful on the field, beating all comers during 1869 and turning a modest profit. Reflecting America's economic growth, Wright used the burgeoning rail lines and telegraph system to arrange games and travel.

Entrepreneurs sought the potential profits from owning a baseball team and staging games. In order to prevent people from watching games for free, owners built enclosed stadiums, usually with wooden grandstands. Eventually, the owners erected stadiums of steel and concrete.

Along with the growing popularity of MLB, the market for sporting goods became concentrated in the hands of a few firms. Albert Spalding, the top-flight baseball pitcher, recognized the growing demand for sporting goods and entered the business. Spalding exemplified the concentration of an industry; he expanded his sporting goods efforts to include the publication of sports guides and books. Stephen Hardy examined the case of Spalding and his associates in the sporting goods industry: "the spread of standardized goods does reflect and support the spread of standardized behaviors and values. Providers do make buying or adopting packaged goods and games easier than 'free play.' Control in the marketplace does make a difference. A relative handful of rules committees do

control the game forms played by most Americans, and relatively few manufacturers do supply the goods used at all levels."[4]

Although MLB was the apex of America's national pastime for most of the
first half of the twentieth century, fans in only 10 cities witnessed such games.
Cities and towns across the country, though, had professional baseball at the
minor league level.

MLB attendance was dwarfed by motion picture attendance. In 1903, the two
baseball leagues had fewer than 5 million attendees. By the 1920s, attendance
fluctuated between 8 and 10 million per season, as compared with the tens of
millions of fans attending motion picture theaters *weekly* by the 1920s. By century's end, though, MLB attendance had surpassed 70 million per season by century's end.[5]

The National Football League (NFL) and National Basketball Association
(NBA) were about a generation or two behind the major leagues. The NFL was
an unwieldy, ramshackle organization for almost a quarter century before stabilizing during the 1950s. After World War II, the NFL had a West Coast presence
and preceded MLB as a truly national organization. The NBA did not reach the
West Coast until the early 1960s. These leagues eventually measured attendance
in millions per season, but television expanded their audiences greatly.

By 2000, Americans could indulge their passion for professional sports
during their leisure time via a variety of mediums. They could also easily keep
track of their favorite teams even during their working hours, thanks to the ubiquity of personal and laptop computers.

## Movies Become a Dominant Medium

Thomas Edison invented the motion picture camera. Other inventors came up
with similar devices and auxiliary equipment. These inventors hoped to dominate the motion picture industry through ownership of patent rights. Unlike
phonographs and other in-home technology, with their outlays for durable
equipment, poorer Americans could immediately afford to patronize the new
medium. Entrepreneurs with very little capital and access to a storefront could
enter the business. The Warner brothers, for instance, decided to invest a few
hundred dollars to purchase a projector and other equipment. Poorer Americans, then, were both the crucial consumers for and the exhibitors of motion
pictures; the industry was not initially dominated by moneyed businessmen or
upper-class elites.

Nickelodeons soon sprouted across America; nickelodeon operators pioneered the new way for Americans to spend their leisure time. Many were located in arcades or other places of amusement. The accommodations were

quite sparse: a darkened room, a few chairs, and a screen. Because males and females could mingle in the audience, upper-class society was scandalized by the nickelodeons, and, of course, the sheer cheapness of a nickel admission implied a less-than-genteel audience. Nickelodeons were more profitable in amusement arcades than in vaudeville theaters, and John Izod writes that this "suggests they appealed more consistently to a working-class than a middle-class audience." The operators of the nickelodeons quickly noticed that narrative films were more popular.[6] In some vaudeville theaters, managers used the primitive one-reel films as "chasers" to encourage the audience to leave in order to bring in another group of patrons.[7] The distribution of a few hundred reels of the same film nationwide meant that, for the first time, Americans had a mass entertainment medium.[8]

The nickelodeon audience differed from other stage entertainment in that the audience appeared to attend more frequently than for theater and vaudeville. Of course, the low cost of attending nickelodeons was a factor, as one could attend a nickelodeon many times before expending the amount needed to attend a theater even once.[9] Initially, movie patrons saw a few reels of film, lasting a total of 30 minutes or so, for their nickels; sometimes they saw brief live performances between reels or joined in communal song-fests. By the 1910s, the films were getting longer, and exhibitors pushed for higher admission prices. One observer argued that people were willing to pay more to see a higher-quality motion picture, especially if the higher admission price eliminated "uncleanly people."[10]

The primitive nature of films belied its potential. Had the film producers failed to advance beyond simply showing people engaged in mundane activities, the medium would have been less likely to have become the dominant mass entertainment medium of the first half of the twentieth century, nor would it have maintained a sizable audience into the twenty-first century. Motion-picture producers quickly grasped that audiences wanted plot lines and recognizable actors. The industry's success could be seen by the fact that 15,000 theaters were in operation by the end of the 1930s. By the late 1920s, weekly movie attendance hovered around 100 million.[11]

The American nickelodeon was unique. France was an example of a country where the motion picture was aimed at sophisticated audiences rather than the masses. "European theater-goers enjoyed the novelty of living pictures, but as no arcade halls and back rooms were opened as cheap show-shops, the masses abroad had little opportunity to become acquainted with the new amusement."[12] Foreign producers often made superior films that appealed to artistic standards, but American producers supplanted the foreign producers with films that had mass appeal.[13]

The American motion picture both grew and evolved rapidly in the first two decades of the twentieth century. The entrepreneurs were dazed by the rush of nickels that was transpiring: "Everyone in the film business worked in feverish haste to grab a share of the golden flood of nickels before the inevitable day of reckoning."[14]

Motion picture producers initially resisted identifying their players for fear that a popular actor would begin demanding more money. Baseball owners had demonstrated a similar thinking; it took them years to put numbers on uniforms, so fans could identify the players. According to popular belief, Florence Lawrence was usually recognized as the first "star." Carl Laemmle, an early producer, realized that by publicizing a popular actor, he could boost box office appeal. Movie studios began proclaiming their stars and also started developing new ones. Movie patrons enjoyed reading about the stars and about newcomers. The producers became adept at trying out new talent to see whether such newcomers would be popular with audiences.[15]

Eileen Bowser, though, disputes this popular version. She describes how patrons quickly recognized specific performers and began urging studios to feature these favored performers. The groundswell of support for the "Biograph Girl" (Lawrence) gave even anonymous performers leverage in salary negotiations. Because of motion pictures' ability to reach a much larger audience than traditional theater or vaudeville, motion picture stars soon commanded salaries in excess of most performers.[16]

The longer films and higher ticket prices reflected a changing audience— the poor, nickelodeon crowd was being displaced by more prosperous patrons. The increased revenue allowed theater owners to build newer, grander theaters.[17]

Many of these new theaters were built in downtown areas. Some exhibitors also started acquiring a number of such theaters. Many of the successful owners of chains of theaters, such as the Warner brothers, were recent eastern European, Jewish immigrants. Other entrepreneurs, such as the Balaban & Katz company, exploited the combination of suburbs and mass transit to build theaters in the center of outlying business and recreational centers. In addition to choosing convenient locations, Balaban & Katz carefully hired its employees and trained them to project a classy image while keeping costs low. "All [employees] were assigned specific routine tasks so that the management of the chain could regulate their actions like an assembly line, run with a labor efficiency Henry Ford would have surely been proud of."[18]

Balaban & Katz also pioneered the use of air conditioning; many early theaters simply closed during the hot months, but with air conditioning, theaters could remain open year-round. Because of their meticulous attention to attracting a desirable audience of patrons, Balaban & Katz found suitors among the motion picture production companies; the company eventually aligned with Famous Players Lasky, later renamed Paramount.[19]

Even with tens of millions of motion theater patrons per week, the motion picture industry was not a particularly large industry in terms of gross income, ranking in the middle of the 94 industry groups categorized by the Statistics of Income, Bureau of Internal Revenue. Within the general category of "commercial amusement," however, the motion picture industry assumed a much greater importance, accounting for 78 percent of the gross income and 92 percent of the total net income of the group. The motion picture industry, though, experienced a remarkably rapid improvement in total factor productivity growth and helped boost US gross domestic product growth between 1900 and 1938.[20]

The producers scrambled to keep movie patrons excited. During the 1920s, Americans had more ways to spend their leisure time than before. After Warner Bros.' success with *The Jazz Singer*, other film companies gradually produced sound pictures. The companies confronted a major hurdle to transforming their output: the large capital investment required to produce and to exhibit sound pictures. In the end, the cost of installing sound equipment knocked out some of the smaller movie houses or else forced these theaters to sell out to larger chains that had sufficient capital to convert the houses.[21]

Warner Bros. also innovated by using color. The studio's *Gold Diggers of Broadway* and *Robin Hood* were outstanding early attempts of using color. The use of color had one advantage over the introduction of sound: it did not require capital investment in converting theaters. Since Technicolor had already incurred the research and development cost, Warner Bros. risked only the additional cost of filming a movie in color. The other studios followed, but color did not become prevalent until decades later. Pioneering in color was similar to "belling the cat." Being first meant taking the risk. If the audience responded well to color films, then all the rival firms would start using color film. If the audience disdained color, then the pioneering firm alone suffered losses. By 1949, the relatively expensive Technicolor was joined by the cheaper Eastman-Kodak color film; in 1952, 100 color films were made, whereas in previous years only a fraction as many movies used color.[22]

In 1950, Leo Handel wrote a report on film audience research. He quoted Eric Johnston, president of the Motion Picture Association of America, as admitting, "The Motion Picture Industry probably knows less about itself than any other major industry in the United States. The industry had grown so fast that it hardly has had a time to measure its own growth. . . . Much of the statistical data published about this industry is based on hearsay, personal opinion, the casual impressions of persons unfamiliar with the business or the natural exuberance of born promoters."[23]

At the time Handel wrote his report, commercialized motion pictures were barely a half century old; many older Americans had not grown up with motion pictures. Audience Research, Inc., estimated from its survey data that 81 million people over the age of 12 in 1946 had attended a motion picture at least once in their lifetime. This left roughly 30 million Americans who described themselves as only occasionally or never attending movies; movie producers had scant knowledge of why these people were not regular moviegoers. African-Americans comprised about 5 or 6 percent of the weekly film attendance, with many attending theaters in predominantly black neighborhoods; this proportion was less than their proportion of the population.[24]

The fact that future audiences would contain increasing proportions of Americans who had grown up with movies augured well for the industry: "It may be safely assumed that a larger proportion of older people will attend motion pictures in the years to come because of conditioning to this form of entertainment in their youth."[25]

The available research suggested that there was a positive correlation between radio listening, movie attendance, and news reading. Apparently, people who used one medium were likely to use the other mediums. Indeed, the mediums could reinforce each other; people might buy newspapers to read about movies.[26] On the other hand, the baby bust of the 1930s may have contributed to the slump in movie attendance after World War II.

In terms of admissions prices, Handel admitted the data was scant. The US Department of Labor collected ticket price information for its Consumer Price Index. The price data suggested that ticket prices rose during World War II, but some of the fluctuation in ticket prices may have resulted from the imposition of or changes in amusements taxes. Compared to the general price level, though, movie admission prices rose more slowly immediately after World War II.[27]

Attendance at movies, as with attendance at MLB games, did not immediately slide in the wake of the stock market crash of October 1929. Movie attendance held relatively steady for 1930 and 1931, buoyed, perhaps, by the novelty of sound.[28] After the war, Audience Research, Inc., reported that average weekly, full-price admissions were 66 million at the start of 1946; US Treasury tax figures showed that 95 million attended weekly, but the difference may have emanated from varying definitions of an attendee. During 1930–1933 and again in 1937–1938, both periods of economic downturns, "films' share of total consumer expenditures increased, while those of some so-called necessities were losing ground. . . . Films, as the largest single economic factor in recreation and entertainment, can be expected to absorb nearly a fifth of all money spent on recreation."[29]

During the Great Depression, theater owners began allowing patrons to purchase concessions. Prior to this decision, most theaters kept their theaters dark and employed ushers. The theater owners felt that the formality precluded selling concessions. The exigencies of the 1930s, though, induced owners to fire their ushers and to raise lighting, so patrons could seat themselves. Double features provided an interim for patrons to get up and purchase the now-available concessions. Popcorn proved popular, both with patrons and owners. With suitable machinery, popcorn was easy to make and included a good markup. Its salty nature induced patrons to purchase beverages.[30]

Some owners introduced "Bank Night," whereby a lucky patron would win a cash prize. Bank Night originated in the mind of Charles Yaeger, a theater manager. Movie patrons signed up for a number in the theater lobby. On a Monday or Tuesday, normally the slowest day of the week, a number was drawn by a child from the audience. The patron with the drawn number had a certain amount of time to show up to claim the prize; hence, the bromide "need not be present to win" was in force, but only for a few moments. The theater announced the number via outside loudspeakers or at the box office. If no one claimed the prize in time, the jackpot rolled over. The "no purchase necessary" aspect of the scheme kept Yaeger and his attorney-partner, Henry "Rick" Ricketson, from running an illegal lottery; they prevailed in several court cases. Observers credited Bank Night with large increases in audiences on the night of the drawings. Yaeger and Ricketson were clever enough to take out trademarks on 1,400 similar-sounding names to protect their Bank Night from imitators.[31] Not everyone was pleased with Bank Night, of course. An anonymous writer for *The New Republic* deplored Bank Nights, as the innovation introduced "innocent viewers, very often women and children, to gambling, poor quality films, and rampant materialism."[32]

Other observers felt that movies—particularly gangster movies, which were popular during the 1930s—were corrupting children via depictions of criminal behavior, easy money, and sexual licentiousness. Researcher Henry Forman's more sensational claims were repudiated by other researchers involved with him on the Payne Fund studies; many researchers concluded there was no direct link between delinquency and movie watching.[33] One study showed that children in Chicago had little interest in educational movies; what they remembered were "the thrilling parts and the dramatic details, not the lessons or morals."[34]

Some owners of movie theaters decided to cut admission prices during the Great Depression. Given the 25 percent fall in the general price level, such price cutting was understandable. The five major studios, burdened by their recent spree in buying theaters, struggled to maintain solvency and resorted to loans and selling off some theaters. With outstanding loans and increased banker scrutiny, the major studios staggered through the first half of the 1930s.[35]

Another tactic used by theater owners to generate crowds was to show double features, mimicking, perhaps, baseball's doubleheaders. The motion picture version of the double feature, though, did not consist of two high-quality films but usually an "A" picture and a "B" one (analogous, perhaps, to a hypothetical MLB and minor league twinbill). Handel's data showed that double features had

mixed effects. A majority of filmgoers surveyed, especially upper-income patrons, preferred single features; if the survey question was reworded to indicate
a choice between a single high-quality feature or double high-quality features,
then a majority supported double features.[36]

The motion picture industry suffered upheaval after World War II. Despite a
banner year in 1946, the industry suffered declines in both attendance and real
ticket receipts after World War II. The average weekly attendance fell by half between 1946 and 1956, while the Department of Commerce supplied figures
showing a reduction of 42 percent in inflation-adjusted gate receipts. Because
other leisure and recreation spending tended to rise in inflation-adjusted dollars,
the motion picture industry's share of total consumer purchases fell from 1.15
percent to 0.49 percent. Although many observers and historians have made the
quick and easy conclusion that television was the culprit responsible for the
movies' decline, some alternative explanations included changing consumer
spending patterns, with a boom and then a retrenchment immediately after the
war; the move to suburbia; the rise of drive-in theaters; worsening traffic congestion; and lower quality of motion pictures.[37]

The suburban flight thesis revolved around the increased time needed for and
transportation costs incurred by suburbanites in reaching downtown theaters;
suburban leisure alternatives not found in urban areas; and higher babysitting
costs in the suburbs—which Fredric Stuart does not document. He used Census
of Business data for 1948 and 1954 (Table 2–3 in his book) to demonstrate sizable decreases in motion picture attendance in cities of all sizes and rural areas,
although the largest declines occurred in cities with more than 500,000 people,
where traffic congestion was worse. However, these large cities also had the highest rates of television ownership.[38] The New England states displayed significant
drops in admissions receipts, while the West showed increases. Thirty states had
increases in per capita motion picture receipts between 1948 and 1954.[39] Another researcher discovered that "the movie audience was thinning out long
before the number of TV sets started to climb, but the decline in movie attendance accelerated at the same time that the TV buildup became apparent."[40]

Americans tied up their incomes and savings in buying houses and supporting their growing families. People with more education and higher income
attended movies more frequently; these were also the likely candidates for
purchasing suburban homes. Finally, historian Douglas Gomery believes that
radio and television, what I've termed "private leisure," were complementary
with suburban living; television eventually deepened the trend away from attending movie theaters.[41]

The drive-in theater argument largely fails, because most of the drive-in theaters were not located in the same general vicinity as the walk-in theaters. The
increase in drive-in theaters very nearly offset the decrease in walk-in theaters,

but there was no significant correlation between the two, once the population differences were eliminated.[42]

Elaine Tyler May coined the term "domestic containment" to describe the focus on marriage, home, and children during the 1950s. This focus reduced the emphasis on going out to bars or motion picture theaters, and shifted the emphasis to leisure-time activities at home; television's popularity was complementary to this change in focus: "It enhanced and encouraged the cultural preference for the private by what it offered in the home. The choice of television over movies was not a narrow economic choice between media, but a larger cultural choice between public and private."[43]

One other factor stands out, though. *Business Week* pointed out that there was a 13 percent drop in the number of Americans aged 15–19 between 1940 and 1950, which boded ill for the motion picture industry, since teenagers were the most frequent moviegoers.[44]

The industry was also affected by antitrust edicts. With the courts' mandated severing of its theaters as an antidote to the industry's antitrust violations, motion picture companies sought to reduce costs and to lease their facilities. One common method was to lease the studio for a percentage of the gross receipts—a system surprisingly similar to sharecropping in agriculture. Actors enjoyed the breakup of the studio system, as they were no longer tied to one company, with its sole-employer bargaining power, and they could look around for desirable projects. The actors also gained from tax advantages.[45]

The motion picture industry sought ways to remain profitable. One stillborn alternative was theater television, or closed-circuit television. The few real successes with theater-television were sporting events, where very few fans could attend games in person. Baseball owners arranged to show the World Series in several theaters in large cities.[46] Pay-television was viable by the mid-1950s. The potential was breathtaking: if just a small percentage of television households were willing to pay a dollar per game, the owners would have reaped considerable sums. Some motion picture executives, gradually accepting the proposition that most Americans preferred sitting in their living rooms to venturing to a local theater, considered showing movies on a pay-per-view basis; such a system could have reduced distribution costs while promising potentially greater receipts than those obtained at theaters.[47]

Another innovation was widescreen cinema. Cinerama required a curved screen and hi-fi stereo sound. Audiences approved of it, but the technology required major overhauls to existing theaters. CinemaScope was relatively expensive to film (more so than 3-D), but required modest installation costs. Some cinema owners did not want to absorb the cost of installing stereophonic sound, and Twentieth-Century Fox printed CinemaScope films with stereo and monaural soundtracks. In order to encourage other studios to use CinemaScope, Fox leased CinemaScope equipment to its rivals. These developments may not have stanched the decline in attendance, but because they were premium films, the theaters using the new technologies were able to charge higher admission prices for them.[48]

Motion picture theaters found another revenue source to help offset the sagging box office receipts: advertising in the theater. Theater advertisers formed a trade association, Theater-Screen Advertising Bureau, which pointed out that advertising costs per thousand viewers were just slightly higher in the theater than on network television. Theater advertising held advantages over television; it could be tailored to a more selected audience; the screen was larger; the audience had fewer distractions; and color and stereophonic sound were becoming common in theaters. In addition, the advertisements could be reinforced "by immediate distribution of samples, literature, premium coupons."[49]

## Radio Industry and Simultaneous Leisure

Radio introduced a new leisure-time activity phenomenon: millions of Americans listening simultaneously to the same program. Radio was born in a welter of patents. Since President Woodrow Wilson deemed radio an important industry for national defense, he induced the patent holders, including American Telephone & Telegraph (AT&T), Westinghouse, American Marconi, and General Electric, to pool their patents under a new entity: the Radio Corporation of America (RCA), headed by David Sarnoff.[50]

Historian Douglas Gomery places the seminal date for radio broadcasting, not on November 2, 1920, with the broadcast of the 1920 presidential election to a small group of radio aficionados, but, rather, to the Jack Dempsey–Georges Carpentier fight of July 2, 1921. Not only did hundreds of thousands of radio enthusiasts hear the fight, but the New York Times made it a front-page item with a transcription of the announcer's words.[51] There was one important but unanticipated aspect from the broadcast: many women listened.

Pittsburgh radio station KDKA was the first broadcasting station, starting regularly scheduled programming in 1915. Other stations followed after the war ended, but many of the stations used the same frequency, which led to overlapping broadcasts. The Department of Commerce opened another frequency in 1922 while also setting standards of operation, including a prohibition on the use of recorded music.[52]

Radios were initially inconvenient to use, requiring technical know-how and ability and a battery source, such as an automobile battery. Because of the limited broadcasting range, most stations broadcast material to appeal to the locals, with country music and church programs being popular in rural areas. The radio networks that people remember, the National Broadcasting Company (NBC) and the Columbia Broadcasting System (CBS), took years to create. The networks depended upon AT&T telephone lines to distribute programs nationally; they remained among AT&T's biggest customers for decades to come. The necessity of working out a deal with AT&T served as a barrier to entry against other prospective networks, although the Mutual Network eventually developed.[53]

In terms of producing radios, RCA quickly receded in importance. Even though Philco had to pay royalties for using RCA patents, it became the leading supplier of radio sets. The company devised a radio that was powered by household electricity, while developing its products to appeal to female consumers.[54]

Radio's diffusion was sudden and swift. By 1930, Americans owned 12 million radios; despite the Great Depression, the number almost doubled by 1935. The average radio receiver cost $35, which was more than two weeks' average earnings in manufacturing during the late 1920s.[55]

Similar to phonographs and motion pictures, the early radio users were excited simply to hear any sound from their apparatus. The early radio stations broadcast unpolished entertainers, although professional entertainers began to think of radio as a useful means of publicizing their performances. As time passed, though, vaudeville and musical venues began to suffer declines in their attendance and receipts. The owners of these venues began to demand payment for their performers' appearances on radio; some went so far as to prohibit their performers from appearing on radio. The radio stations balked, naturally, arguing that the broadcasts were payment enough.

The question of how to pay for radio broadcasts was controversial. The Europeans relied on a user tax; a buyer paid a tax for each receiving set purchased. Some Americans believed a voluntary contributory system was desirable, and traces of this persist today with regard to public and religious broadcasting. The third method, commercialized radio, entailed stations selling air time for advertisers to tout their products.[56]

Because the radio stations and the performers could not agree on compensation, Congress eventually became involved. Senator C. C. Dill (WA) introduced a bill to amend the Copyright Act, denying copyright control to public performances made via radio, whether for profit or without profit. Senator Dill claimed that he wanted to ensure free radio broadcasts, since he believed the public had a right to receive radio programming for free. The broadcasting industry, in a shortsighted move, testified on behalf of the bill. They sanctimoniously argued that broadcasting was a public service provided by non-profit entities and that the free publicity was sufficient remuneration for performers. Had this thinking prevailed, one can only assume that radio would have developed in a very different and probably less satisfactory way. As Marian Spitzer, *Saturday Evening Post* writer, pointed out in 1924, "Nobody knows, and only a few people suspect how far radio will go as a form of amusement." She speculated that radio would develop its own stars, performers with a skill set particularly suited to radio.[57]

Senator Dill's bill met fierce opposition from musicians and publishers. They argued that many broadcasting stations were for-profit companies. They also claimed that frequent repetition of their songs and performances on the radio hurt their attendance and box office receipts, as well as sales of sheet music and records.[58]

The musicians and publishers wanted payment for the use of copyrighted songs over the radio. Musicians and publishers, operating through the American Society of Composers, Authors and Publishers (ASCAP), negotiated an agreement with broadcasting stations, by which the stations paid a license fee, based on the station's characteristics, for the use of musical numbers. This system was far more convenient than charging fees for each number used.[59]

Radio and, later, television did provide benefits for song writers and performers. The national networks enabled publishers and performers to rapidly disseminate their songs and renditions across the country; instead of relying on national tours and travel by rail, the new medium afforded some artists almost instantaneous national coverage.[60]

For one group, the motive behind their purchases of radios was not only to have entertainment but also for practical reasons. Farmers found that radio supplied crucial market information that enabled them to bargain for better prices for their crops, as well as weather reports. The radio also alleviated some of the crushing loneliness and isolation of rural areas.[61]

Radio developed as a commercialized medium. David Sarnoff of RCA/NBC was a ruthless businessman. While telling the public that NBC was not a monopoly, he was using RCA's patents and NBC's exclusive contract with AT&T to knock out smaller stations and to block other networks during the 1920s and 1930s. Sarnoff's plan was to sell blocks of time to advertisers. The advertisers would create and produce the shows, thereby absolving NBC of any criticism regarding programming. Sarnoff's toughness extended to NBC's affiliates, where he had driven hard bargains for stations to become NBC affiliates. Eventually, he ran afoul of Federal Communications Commission (FCC) scrutiny, so Sarnoff split NBC into the Red and Blue networks.[62]

CBS was NBC's chief competition. Unlike more recent times, where CBS was the premier network for decades, the company struggled for most of two decades. CBS did not have radio patents, and it had to resort to political influence to get AT&T lines. The company received a boost from a partnership with Paramount, the motion picture company and distributor. William S. Paley assumed command and worked to keep the network afloat; in this he was quickly and spectacularly successful, as by 1931 CBS was earning more profits than NBC. The network scored coups by broadcasting the World Series, the Kentucky

Derby, and Army-Navy football games. Initially, most sports entrepreneurs did not charge for broadcasting rights, so sports were a boon for CBS. Still, CBS did not ascend to superiority over NBC in terms of ratings until after World War II.[63]

The FCC monitored the radio industry, almost from the beginning of network radio. The antitrust investigators recognized the sham competition provided by NBC's Red and Blue networks. Historian Laurence Bergreen pointed out, "As anyone with a radio could attest, NBC used its Blue network as a 'buffer' for the Red, allocating its high-rated, high-priced entertainment to the Red while loading the Blue's schedule with public-service programs, where they would do the least damage to company profit. They did not compete. . . . NBC was in the enviable position of being able to counterprogram against itself to achieve an overall competitive advantage against non-NBC networks." Bergreen identified an ironic outcome of the FCC's edict forcing NBC to divest its Blue network: with three commercial networks, the incentive to broadcast public service programs vanished: "[James L.] Fly's [FCC chairman] dilemma pointed up a classic problem with governmental regulation of industry. With only limited powers, an agency, in trying to rectify the abuses of a current situation, can, unintentionally, instigate an even worse situation."[64] The American Broadcasting System (later the American Broadcasting Company) purchased the Blue network in 1943.

After NBC's divestiture, CBS began eroding Sarnoff's dominance. Sarnoff was distracted by his efforts to develop television. Paley innovated by producing and owning radio programs, rather than having sponsors provide programming. He also altered advertising, so that firms could buy 60-second or shorter spots. CBS quickly convinced many large corporations, such as the American Tobacco Company, of the profits to be made by advertising their products on radio. Sales of Lucky Strike cigarettes soared in the wake of a clever advertising campaign. Some corporations decided to produce programs "allied with their selling thought," including many soap operas.[65]

Paley's efforts were complemented by Lew Wasserman and the Music Corporation of America (MCA). Wasserman was looking for projects for his performers to participate in. Wasserman, Paley, and Frank Stanton, Paley's trusted and able lieutenant, figured out a clever tax angle. If entertainer Jack Benny were to incorporate himself and his troupe, then CBS would buy his corporation. Benny would benefit by paying only capital gains tax (then 25 percent) instead of personal income tax (at a rate of 77 percent). This tactic revolutionized Hollywood, radio, and television. With this carrot to offer, CBS raided NBC's stars, shifting ratings almost overnight.[66]

Radio executives quickly learned that advertisers focused on the middle class, since, with exceptions, the rich had other entertainment alternatives and the poor lacked the purchasing power to interest advertisers. This left the vast middle class, whose programming preferences tended to variety shows, although music, drama, and serials were also popular.[67]

Even the Great Depression did not halt the spread of radio; declining prices for radios helped maintain the volume of sales. By the mid-1930s, even poorer Americans could afford radios. The development of radio networks with regularized schedules began to habituate listeners to arrange their activities around their favorite shows.[68]

Radio broadcasting eventually felt the worsening economic climate. Radio sales fell 40 percent from their 1929 levels in 1930. In the 1930s, to buoy their industries, radio and motion pictures gradually worked out a mutually beneficial working relationship. Radio publicized motion pictures and sometimes provided well-known personalities to movies; movies introduced songs that were played on the radio, and the studios had their stars perform on radio. The interactions between radio and movies, though, were not always harmonious. Hollywood executives decided to offset dwindling movie receipts by increasing royalty charges on their music played on the radio; radio fought back by a boycott of movie music. This temporary abeyance of playing music from movies lent an impetus to country and western and rhythm and blues being played on the radio. The Hollywood studios later relented, but their influence on radio waned.[69]

Radios eventually became semi-portable. Once American homes were saturated with radio, manufacturers sought out new ways to keep Americans buying radios. They discovered that people loved having radios in their automobiles. The manufacturers also encouraged people to buy second radios for their houses, allowing for more individual choice, if less family togetherness.[70]

Bell Laboratory's invention of the transistor led to the miniaturization of radios. The Sony Corporation's quick grasp of the advantages of miniaturization led it to introduce a transistor radio during the 1950s that the company gradually reduced in size until it could fit into a shirt pocket. Americans could now bring music to their leisure-time activities in a variety of venues. The ease of portability made these radios quite popular, especially among the young. Sony's recognition that people wanted to take their music with them was revolutionary. In the subsequent decades, Sony carried the concept forward by reducing the size of a cassette player to also fit in a shirt-pocket. By the early 1990s, Sony had introduced the mini-disc digital player. This time, the idea did not catch on.[71]

## Television Becomes Leisure's 600-Pound Gorilla

By the 1940s, radio and motion pictures reigned as America's most popular forms of mass entertainment. Their dominance, though, was about to end. Television would come to dominate leisure-time activities.

Although television dated back to the 1930s, with early telecasts of baseball and football games, among other programming, only a tiny number of households owned one. The sets were expensive, and programming was sporadic and certainly not around-the-clock as today. World War II intervened and suspended television's development for civilian uses.

Television's diffusion eventually proved astoundingly rapid, although it got off to a slow start after the war. David Sarnoff and NBC wanted to establish a television network similar to their radio stations. Their efforts were hampered by AT&T's slowness in extending its coaxial cable and microwave relay network across the country; AT&T would complete the process only in 1952.

The early days of television were dominated by New York City and the Northeast. During television's infancy, the vast majority of sets were in New York City; *Business Week* estimated that 43,000 of the existing 60,000 sets were in New York City in 1947. The periodical described how advertisers scrambled to secure time during peak viewer hours, a sort of 1940s gold rush. Advertisers knew that the current audience was minuscule but would quickly mushroom. A second advantage of being an early advertiser on television was to be first on the learning curve for advertising on television.[72]

Advertising on television, though, was going to be more expensive than on radio. National advertisers frequently bought a block of time from a network and produced their own show. The advertiser, therefore, faced three major costs: buying airtime for telecasts; the network cost, including sending the program over AT&T's coaxial cable, which was more expensive for television than for radio; and the cost of producing a program, which again was more expensive for television than for radio. In terms of sponsoring a sporting event, television was more expensive than radio, because a larger crew and different equipment were required. There was also the issue of property rights: Who owned the telecast? These were not insuperable problems, of course, but they needed to be resolved before television became a mass medium.[73]

Milton "Mr. Television" Berle exemplified television's early years; his Texaco Star Theater debuted in 1948. His Borscht-belt humor played best in New York City. As television spread to Midwestern cities, Berle's humor quickly wore thin. Because New York City was also the center of live theater, as long as the city dominated the production of television programming, live drama would appear during prime time. Once television spanned the country, live drama did not please the masses as much as did Hollywood-produced situation comedies and drama.[74] Exit live theater. New York City critics and theater folks undoubtedly lamented the change.

Although some retailers sold 10-inch tabletop televisions for $100 in 1948, the larger sets, 20-inch or more, costs hundreds of dollars and represented a real investment in entertainment for a family. Families purchasing televisions, even accounting for the flow of services provided by the set, presumably had less to spend on other leisure activities. Men wanted televisions to watch sporting events, while women wanted to view dramas; the twin demands for televisions ensured a brisk market.[75]

Television was the fortunate recipient of rising incomes across America. Manufacturers also produced an adequate supply of televisions. Many producers of radios converted to producing televisions, ensuring sufficient production, unlike the early days of radio. "As a result, technological advances, in the direction of clear reception, length of life of the receiver, reduced size and cost of sets, low cost of repairs, and increased transmission distances, came much more rapidly for television than they had for radio."[76]

In 1947, DuMont, Philco, and RCA (who were or had been leading radio manufacturers) did three-quarters of the business, but this percentage was about to fall. It was important to get more producers in order to lower the cost of televisions, which was an impediment to the sets' diffusion. The networks, television station owners, and advertisers, of course, were impatient for a larger audience. In late 1947, Hallicasters Co. and Motorola, Inc., announced plans to sell sets for $200.[77] In 1947 the average hourly earnings for production workers in manufacturing were $1.22, so such a $200 set would require 164 hours of work, ignoring taxes.[78] Since many Americans had accumulated savings during the war, they had the financial means to purchase televisions. More likely, most Americans purchasing televisions in the late 1940s paid significantly more than $200, so a television cost well over a month's wages. An American today can buy a large-screen, high-definition, color television for $800. Even at an unskilled-labor wage of $10 per hour, such a television would cost only two weeks' wages, again ignoring taxes.

Americans bought television sets at a dizzying pace. *Sales Management* devoted most of an issue to television in 1955. The motor-car industry needed 40 years to get 32 million car-and-truck registrations, while Americans bought 46 million TV sets between 1946 and 1955. Many Americans had already purchased a second set.[79]

The number of television stations rose from 108 to 425, mostly after the FCC ended a freeze on licenses. With the increased number of stations, 96 percent of all homes had access to television signals; those still lacking signals were primarily in the Plains and Rocky Mountain states. Americans spent more for television sets and repairs than "for all our new school and college buildings" in the postwar decade. Articles written in 1955 provided data showing that even the lowest income group's rate of television ownership had jumped from 45 percent to 81 percent since 1952.[80]

As television sets and stations proliferated, some network executives grappled with how to exploit the new medium's popularity. David Sarnoff wanted

NBC to continue its long-standing policy of selling advertisers blocks of air time and having them produce programs. CBS and Lew Wasserman started developing television shows. Wasserman's talent agency, Music Corporation of America (MCA), provided the actors and production personnel. Wasserman was one of the first to realize that the real profits were not in simply producing a show but in producing a show that proved durable and popular enough to generate re-runs in syndication.[81]

Sarnoff's ability to discern trends in the television broadcasting market failed him during the 1950s and 1960s, and Paley's CBS superseded the older network. CBS dominated network ratings for most of two decades, relying on a changing roster of hit shows. From the western *Gunsmoke* to corn-pone humor in the *Beverly Hillbillies* to the controversial *All in the Family*, CBS kept finding hit programs. NBC and ABC had sporadic hits. ABC demonstrated that synergy existed between network television and other entertainment venues, such as Walt Disney's weekly show and Disneyland (in which ABC had an ownership share), but these networks consistently fell behind CBS. Years later, in 1995, Disney purchased ABC.

NBC's racial integration of and colorization of television (it was the first network to go "all-color" but found the move stymied by the high costs of color television sets) were not sufficient to wrest away CBS's hold on the top rung.[82] According to *Sales Management*, in 1955, less than one-half of one percent of new televisions were color sets. The networks televised very few programs in color, which, in turn, dampened the demand for color televisions. *Sales Management* reported that advertisers anticipated ever-more effective ads, as televisions became larger and more sets were in color: "a TV executive recently told a group of broadcasters, 'the effect will be almost hypnotic.'"[83] Since the majority of movies were still filmed in black and white, audiences were still accustomed to the absence of color.

Television may have affected the market for magazines. Although one magazine, *TV Guide*, undoubtedly benefited, quickly becoming one of the biggest sellers among weekly periodicals, many other magazines struggled against television's competition. An article in *Business Week* detailed the growing competition for advertising dollars. Although *Life* and *Saturday Evening Post* maintained their holds on the top rungs of circulation and advertising revenue, other general magazines were declining. Fan and romance magazines also suffered. After all, why should Americans read about star-crossed lovers, when they could watch them? The home magazines performed well, as millions of Americans were fixing up their suburban homes. Another genre, supermarket magazines, also fared well. As *Business Week* noted, supermarket magazines were "a natural medium for some of the heaviest advertising business—food and cosmetics."[84]

By September 1951, advertising revenue for television surpassed that of radio. During 1951, television "put on more plays, hired more actors, and spent more money on drama than all the producers and backers of Broadway. In a precursor of the future, two of the smaller, independent motion picture studios announced they would produce movies for television."[85]

More companies began advertising on television. *Sales Management* reported that a diminution in the top 25 advertisers' share of television advertising from 71.2 percent in 1949 to 58 percent occurred by early 1955.[86] Advertisers obviously believed that television advertising was effective for the dollars paid. NBC issued the results of a study showing that products advertised on television experienced a 19 percent increase in the number of buyers, compared with non-television brands' loss of 11 percent. Advertising's effect was cumulative, as the more television spots a producer got, the greater number of its buyers. Owning a television was associated with greater purchases of televised brands. Television advertising also helped companies get their products on store shelves. Of course, one might wonder about the objectivity of a network-sponsored study, but *Sales Management* did not reveal any skepticism.[87]

Television saturation reached 90 percent of American households by the 1960 census, an astounding rate of diffusion. Manufacturers, worried about saturation, began a strategy of persuading families of the need for a second television or for a portable television as early as 1952. Lynn Spigel details how "advertisements in the home magazines increasingly depicted family members enjoying television alone or else in subgroups." A General Electric advertisement claimed: "When Dad wants to watch the game . . . Mom and Sis, the cooking show . . . there's too much traffic for one TV to handle."[88]

Television's dominance of leisure-time activities was quickly established. Possibly due to better reception and more channels, the A. C. Nielsen surveys implied an increase in television usage from 32 to 50 hours per week between the early 1950s to the mid-1980s. Television use often crowded out other activities, especially those that required leaving the house.[89]

Legislators and activists wrung their hands over the perceived sorry state of television and the networks' near-monopolization of the medium, but a change was going to come. The diffusion of VCRs and cable television in the 1980s provided home owners with alternatives to network television. Although motion picture producers initially opposed selling prerecorded movies to consumers instead of renting them, the practice of purchasing favorite movies quickly caught on with consumers. Along with video players, cable television finally fulfilled its potential during the 1980s, partially through legislation unleashing cable companies to compete with the networks for sporting events and by the development of satellites that allowed cable stations to avoid AT&T's monopoly on landlines. The networks' stranglehold was loosened during the 1980s, as witnessed by their declining ratings. All three networks were sold to other firms, and Sarnoff, Paley, and Leonard Goldenson (of ABC) exited the industry.[90]

VCRs allowed viewers to time shift; viewers were no longer governed by network schedules. Viewers could now watch their favorite shows during more convenient hours for taking leisure. The time shifting affected advertising, since, as Richard Butsch writes, "[t]ime-shifting eliminates the connection between scheduled air time and the demographics of the audience . . . even more threatening to television advertising is the VCR user's ability to skip commercials, a process known as 'zapping.'"[91] VCRs gained acceptance more rapidly than had color television.[92]

The VCR, similar to other entertainment devices, was initially a toy for the wealthy, as prices were around $1,000 or more in 1980. A few years later, the prices were way down and the quality was significantly improved. VCRs were similar to phonographs in that it wasn't enough to purchase a machine; consumers had to further acquire or rent videocassettes to play. The rise of video rental stores boosted the sales of video players. In recent years, Netflix and other Internet sources have shattered the video/DVD-rental industry, with industry giant Blockbuster closing most of its stores.

With regard to cable television, three factors were listed as major reasons that households subscribed in the early 1980s: availability of recently released movies, more choices, and the absence of commercials (which would soon change). A study revealed that cable subscribers were more likely to own a home computer, VCR, large-screen television, and video games. While there were few significant demographic differences between the cable and non-cable groups, subscribers had "somewhat higher incomes, a slightly younger median age for working adults, a somewhat higher proportion of home ownership, and a somewhat larger household size."[93]

Butsch identifies two events that revealed the power of consumers versus producers: the rental rebellion against Hollywood studios and the disdain of the videodisc. He writes, "audiences as individual consumers determined the prevailing technology and shaped how they could use their television."[94]

## The Interaction Between Leisure Industries

The various entertainment mediums jostled for consumers' dollars. Few people grasped how the industries would interact and coexist, and how Americans' uses of leisure time would change.

At first, motion pictures did not directly compete with live theater. The nickelodeons attracted crowds of working-class people, who often did not wish to or could not afford to pay the higher admission prices charged by theaters in down-town locations. The nickelodeons also did not show films with well-developed plots. With the advent of full-length feature movies, though, the competition heated up. At the same time, live theaters were squeezed by rapidly escalating costs. When sound was added to motion pictures, the competition became even fiercer, and by the end of the 1920s, live theater was reeling, as demonstrated by the reduction in the number of theaters.[95]

Theaters that hosted the so-called "one-night stands" also suffered. In a survey in *Billboard*, theater owners voiced their opinions as to why theater was declin-ing during the 1920s. Some claimed that the automobile and the radio provided competition for theaters. The automobile widened the radius of entertainment options, including traveling to larger cities for theater instead of patronizing the local theater, while radio, of course, came right into one's home.[96]

Theater executives weighed the effects of radio on their industry. William A. Brady, a spokesman for theater groups, claimed that radio was a formidable menace for theater and that theater owners were putting up little resistance. Other theater owners, though, applauded radio's ability to publicize produc-tions, with one gushing about how radio publicity boosted attendance at "Abie's Irish Rose" in Chicago.[97]

Radio also threatened the phonograph industry. The phonograph industry might have reach an accommodation with RCA, but RCA's management real-ized that it held the stronger bargaining position. Eventually, RCA bought out Edison's Victor company, ending his participation in phonographs.[98]

Using radio as a medium for broadcasting music was not a new idea in the 1920s. Lee De Forest attempted to use radio waves to broadcast music; Reginald Fessenden had already succeeded in doing so in 1906. David Sarnoff, though, later claimed credit for recognizing radio's potential as a "Radio Music Box."[99] The radio networks initially eschewed playing canned music. The phonograph industry viewed radio stations playing their records as a copyright violation, a piracy of sorts, but the activity provided free publicity for records.[100] The radio broadcasters wanted to air live music and entertainment but found that doing so was expensive. The radio stations would often record the live performances for repeated playback.

As another example of using recorded music, the motion picture industry began using sound equipment and loudspeakers. Warner Bros. and other movie companies decided to install loudspeakers in their smaller theaters that could not afford live musicians, an intermediate step toward jettisoning the live musicians in all theaters. Apparently Warner Bros. did not initially envision combining the sound technology with motion pictures. Harry Warner, the chief executive of Warner Bros., said, "Who the hell wants to hear actors talk? The music—that's the big thing about this."[101]

Warner Bros. owned a radio station and eventually bought out Brunswick Records. The company was now a multimedia conglomerate.[102] The Columbia Broadcasting System purchased the American Recording Corporation to get the name and plant of the Columbia Phonograph Company. The reversal in relationship between radio and phonograph was revealed by these acquisitions: "In 1927 it had been the record company that had bought the radio organization, but recorded sound was no longer the profitable business it had once been. Now radio was the king of the entertainment industry."[103] The phonograph industry was now subsumed within a larger industry.

Executives in the three media gradually realized that cross-pollination was useful. Entertainers now needed to be skillful performers across media.[104]

The advent of radio threatened the motion picture industry's dominance of the entertainment industry. The increased competition may have spurred movie makers to produce more spectacular features.[105]

With the advent of network television, network radio began to fade out. Radio networks proved vulnerable to television. Television was "a more direct substitute for radio than for motion pictures, from the consumer viewpoint." There were similarities between television and radio: the audience was located at home; the consumer needed to purchase a durable good; the marginal cost (in dollars) of listening was minimal; and the programming on network radio was similar to network television. The motion pictures' disadvantages were that they required people to leave their homes; people paid an explicit price to watch; and the entertainment material was specialized.[106]

As a sign of the times, David Sarnoff gave permission to NBC radio affiliates to play "canned music": records instead of live music. The remaining stations sought to revamp the industry. Several factors enabled many radio stations to survive. Some radio stations opted for "Top Forty" formats, whereby a disc jockey played the same records over and over. Coincident with "Top Forty" was local advertising. The network stations lost much of their national advertising to television, but the shortfall was, at least partially, offset by increased local advertising. Some stations began specializing in musical genres, such as country and western, which was becoming popular even in New York City and Chicago. News and talk radio formats also proved viable.[107]

The rise of FM radio, with its superior stereophonic sound quality, also proved a valuable asset. FM was stymied by the need for radio stations and listeners to convert to stereophonic radios. At first it was relegated to stations catering to young affluent audiences. David Sarnoff had long tried to suppress FM radio, but Newton Minow and the FCC eventually approved FM stereo broadcasting. By the 1970s, ownership of AM/FM station combinations proved popular with radio station operators, as the operations were largely automated. FM stations received a boost when Detroit started putting stereo radios in cars.

Many Americans facing lengthier commutes to work greatly appreciated having a radio to listen to.[108]

Some of television's rapid diffusion was due, in part, to its older media siblings. The radio industry helped television by providing experienced technicians, producers, managers, and lobbyists. The television industry thus avoided much of the trial-and-error, birth pangs of new industries. The movie industry also helped by providing television with a backlog of old films.[109]

Although television's effects on the radio industry were not dire—radio simply confronted a decreased rate of growth in revenue instead of an absolute decline—radio executives initially underestimated the new medium's effects. The radio *networks* suffered disproportionately. Television cut into the radio audience, especially prime-time network radio programming. However, some parts of the radio audience were largely immune from television—automobile radio listeners, for instance. As NBC Vice President M. J. Culligan stated, "Living-room radio died eighteen months ago. But while television was driving radio out of the living room, radio was winning the battle of the highway, the kitchen, and the bathroom."[110]

Sports historians attribute the decline of minor league baseball to the diffusion of television. They appear to believe that telecasts of big-league baseball games crowded out attendance at minor league baseball games. Of course, Milton "Uncle Miltie" Berle and other television shows proved to be strong competitors to watching callow, minor league players. The reality, though, was that the diffusion of televisions lagged the declines in attendance at motion picture theaters and at ballparks. Small-town operators of minor league teams may have misjudged the postwar boom; many, if not most, of the minor league teams that folded played in very small towns.[111]

In 1950, when baseball began to see persistent declines in attendance, television ownership was still quite rare, and the televisions were concentrated in the largest Northeastern and Midwestern cities where MLB teams played. Parts of the Great Plains and Rocky Mountain regions, as well as some areas in the South, had spotty television coverage until the mid-1950s. Teams in these regions often folded, too. The story that televised MLB games "killed" baseball's minor leagues therefore suffers from a lack of synchronicity in timing. Television certainly affected minor league baseball, but it wasn't the sole culprit.

Television affected sports in another way. Because television created a vast market of lukewarm fans, willing to pay perhaps 25 cents to watch baseball slugger Ted Williams or football quarterback Otto Graham in the 1950s, the demand for sports contests increased. True, the demand was wide but shallow (many people willing to pay a small amount), but the increased demand for games spurred the demand for top athletic talents. In the end, television boosted professional athletes' salaries. A similar argument held for musicians and actors, whose performances could now be viewed by millions. Economist Sherwin Rosen noted in his seminal article, "The Economics of Superstars," that the changing marketplace for professional sports created disproportionate rewards for the top performers; his argument also applied to musicians and actors.[112]

Television's relationship with movies proved complex. The postwar peak in motion picture theater attendance began receding by 1948, and studios were losing money on some films. Television was slowly spreading during the late 1940s, but its development worried movie companies (Table 11.1). Audience Research, Inc., a research agency, showed that those people with televisions reduced their attendance at movies by 20 to 30 percent. The question remained: Was television the culprit or the manifestation of other changing factors? An observer noted that the relationship between television ownership and movie attendance was not clear-cut: "The decline [in movie attendance] has taken place as much in the areas in which television is not available as in those where it is."[113]

Some theater owners hoped that once televisions saturated the market, people would return to theaters. They viewed this as likely, believing that people enjoyed being in a crowd watching a movie; people would tire of advertisements on television; housewives would want to get out of the house; and motion pictures were of better quality than television shows. The movie executives based the latter argument on three factors: the television screens were tiny; television producers had smaller budgets; and there weren't enough good writers and actors to fill television's demand. To buttress this belief of movies' superiority over television shows, motion pictures began concentrating on fewer but bigger and better films.[114]

*Table 11.1*  **Diffusion of Radio and Television Ownership (First 15 Years) (Thousands)[a]**

| Year | Households with Radio Sets | | Year | Households with TV Sets | |
|------|----------|-----------|------|----------|---------|
|      | *Produced* | *Radio Sets* |      | *Produced* | *TV Sets* |
| 1922 | 100 | 60 | 1946 | 6 | 8 |
| 1925 | 2,000 | 2,750 | 1949 | 3,000 | 940 |
| 1928 | 3,250 | 8,000 | 1952 | 6,096 | 15,300 |
| 1931 | 3,594 | 16,700 | 1955 | 7,757 | 30,700 |
| 1934 | 4,479 | 20,400 | 1958 | 4,920 | 41,924 |
| 1937 | 8,083 | 24,500 | 1961 | 6,178 | 47,200 |

[a] US Department of Commerce, *Historical Statistics of the United States, Part 2*, 796.

The attendance at motion pictures began falling before television was wide-spread, but a Stanford Research Institute study attributed most of the industry's attendance woes of 1948–1954 to television. Fortunately for the motion picture industry, drive-in theaters offset part of the decrease in attendance. The drive-ins mushroomed throughout the country during the late 1940s and throughout the 1950s. Given the baby boom and suburbanization, one can easily envision why drive-ins proved so popular. With a proliferation of automobiles in the suburbs, it was easier to load small children into a family vehicle and head to a drive-in rather than to arrange for a babysitter and to go downtown to a walk-in theater. By 1956, attendance at drive-in theaters occasionally surpassed that for walk-in theaters.[115]

The phenomenon altered patterns of moviegoing, with summer now becom-ing the most popular movie season. In addition, drive-ins were popular with un-escorted teenagers driving the family or their own car. Drive-in theaters were gaining attendance, and one observer speculated that many of these people were not regular moviegoers. John Houseman also addressed the oft-heard criticism of drive-ins, which were known as "passion pits." He noted one drive-in manag-er's defensive remark that nothing happened in a parked car that could not occur in a theater balcony.[116] The drive-in theater audience was not a simple shift of venue but a different group of patrons: families with young children and teenag-ers. The drive-ins were well suited for the new widescreen productions, as well as films aimed at teenage audiences, a prominent 1950s genre.[117]

An article in *Variety* pointed out that building a drive-in theater was much cheaper than a walk-in theater on a per-seat basis. In addition, people tended to buy more food at drive-ins than at walk-in theaters.[118] Decades later, though, drive-ins became almost extinct. Rising land values may have triggered the demise of most drive-in movie theaters. The drive-ins were often built on cheap land, but as suburbs expanded and encroached upon the drive-ins, land values went up. During the 1970s, rising fuel costs also hurt drive-ins. The burgeoning shopping malls began including multi-screen movie theaters.[119]

The motion picture studios sold thousands of their older films to television stations and networks during the 1950s. Showing these films on television proved sufficiently popular, but, from the motion picture industry's perspective, the programming was a mixed blessing, as it spurred television viewing. The tel-evision networks, too, viewed the stockpile of old movies with ambivalence. The public's demand for these old movies undercut the network's domination of pro-gramming. Smaller stations found the old films an attractive and cheap form of programming. David Sarnoff worried that the process of using old movies threat-ened to transform television into a "national movie screen."[120]

By 1953, roughly one-third of the cinemas made a profit based on the sale of tickets alone; another slightly larger group lost money on the film but recouped enough at the concessions stand to turn a profit; and the remaining third lost money. Most of these theaters were marginal venues, showing late-run and B movies.[121]

## Market Provision of Cheap Leisure Activities

By the 1960s, most Americans had access to one or more of the mass media. Television and radio, in particular, were well-nigh ubiquitous by 1960, and most Americans had attended motion pictures at some point in their lives. Although fewer Americans witnessed the highest levels of professional team sporting events, almost all Americans could hear or see ball games on television and radio. Americans had to sacrifice fewer and fewer hours of labor in order to purchase these leisure-time options, while the options were improving in technical quality. Rather than completely supplanting one another, radio, television, and sporting events often aided each other in the search for consumer dollars.

By century's end, Americans devoted their increased leisure time to watching television. In fact, they devoted more than 100 percent of their gains, suggesting that displacement of other leisure activities occurred. Even college-educated men and women devoted more time to watching television, although not as many hours as less-educated Americans. Some of the activities that were crowded out included socializing. This finding may coincide with Robert Putnam's concern that Americans were turning away from social activities and toward private forms of leisure. Then again, by 2000, cable-television, DVDs, and videocassettes offered a cornucopia of choices.[122]

The profit-seeking entrepreneurs may have often failed to anticipate many of the consumers' responses to the new forms of commercialized leisure, but these business owners continually sought to improve existing products, to create new products, and to cut costs and prices. They succeeded in transforming American leisure patterns.

Americans, it is true, may not have relied upon their own efforts for amusement and leisure as much as in the past, but they freely chose the newer forms of commercialized leisure. They also gained more control over what and when they watched or listened to programming, thanks to various recording devices. The advent of cable television also gave them many more choices of programming. Producers could profitably afford to cater to niche genres, such as the Sci-Fi channel.

What about the children? They, too, now have many more entertainment choices on television than in the past; PBS no longer monopolizes high-quality children's offerings, as Nickelodeon and the Disney Channel offer around-the-clock programming for children.

# 12

# Improved Infrastructure and Leisure

Improvements in transportation played an important role in the evolving patterns of leisure activities. By 1900, railroads girded America, and passenger trains dominated intercity travel. Within the cities, trolley lines and elevated trains were appearing. The automobile, though, became the dominant twentieth-century mode of transportation, as it provided convenience and independence. The nation's obsession with automobile travel may have reached its apogee with the Interstate Highway System, begun in the 1950s.

## Improving Infrastructure Boosts Leisure

Leisure industries also benefited from improved transportation, as it "provided even the poorer classes with new opportunities for leisure. In urban areas motorbuses were increasingly used to transport workers to cinemas, pubs and other places of leisure."[1]

Spreading trolley systems affected leisure activities. Many owners of trolley companies built amusement parks and other leisure venues at the end of their lines. A few purchased baseball teams, such as the Brooklyn (Trolley) Dodgers. Many urban residents worked near where they lived and rarely ventured to see the rest of the city. The cheap trolley ride itself became a source of amusement and leisure.[2]

In vaudeville, the Keith-Albee organization dominated the industry. Vaudeville was centered in New York City. Vaudeville theater owners followed the growth of the city's subway system, placing vaudeville houses at desirable stops, although they concentrated their efforts at Times Square.[3]

Along with the subway lines, vaudeville and theater troupes used railroads to tour the country. Railroad travel was both more convenient and often cheaper than alternative transportation means. Because of this reliable and cheap transportation network, entire productions traveled across the country; previously, only the star traveled, as the star could earn more profit by traveling alone than with a troupe.[4]

As mentioned earlier, Americans appeared to have turned toward private forms of leisure activities during the late 1940s and 1950s. With their move to the suburbs into single-family dwellings, coupled with a rising number of young children and the jump in proportion of automobile ownership, Americans reduced their consumption of public forms of leisure activities and transportation, such as motion pictures, sporting events, and rides on mass transit. The rise of the drive-in theater in the late 1940s and 1950s demonstrates the desire for "private" leisure: families could sit in the privacy of their automobiles, while watching a movie.

## Electricity Makes Life Easier

Electricity provided a cheap source of power, enhancing productivity and affecting leisure choices. The increased productivity contributed to less arduous and often safer working conditions. Electricity, in effect, lengthened the day by reducing the cost of illumination and allowing people to do tasks that required adequate illumination even at night. Widespread electrification, though, required safe, reliable generators. Thomas Edison and George Westinghouse's competing currents exemplified the contentious and controversial efforts by the rivals to gain supremacy. The state prison in Auburn, New York, decided to install the "humane" electric chair using Westinghouse's alternative current (AC), which proved a temporary publicity coup for Edison's advocacy of direct current (DC).[5]

J. Pierpont Morgan became the first New Yorker to solely illuminate his house by electricity.[6] His electrified house in 1882 preceded Edison's technicians' attempt to produce a satisfying home system. Other wealthy Americans turned to electricity, not only for illumination but as "a status symbol for the very wealthy and the adventurous."[7]

Electricity remained affordable only for the wealthy for a few decades after Morgan's choice—only 3 percent of American homes had electric lighting by 1900. By 1950, though, 94 percent of American homes had electrical illumination.[8]

Aside from providing extended hours, especially during the winter, for activities, electricity also affected leisure and recreational activities. Electrical lighting allowed football and baseball owners to stage games in the cooler evening hours after work, helping to maintain or to boost attendance. In addition, amateur athletes now had more hours in which to practice or to stage games. Electricity also made operating phonographs and radio easier than relying on hand-powered motors or batteries. Entertainment venues such as New York's Broadway, Coney Island, and other large cities' downtown theater districts became a riot of electric lighting, signifying new and exciting leisure-time activities.

Rural electrification and roads must have been godsends to people living on isolated farms. Gone were the unendurable isolation and loneliness that bedeviled farmers on the Great Plains, as poignantly described by Willa Cather in her novels *O Pioneers!* and *My Antonia*. Since the population density of much farmland was not sufficient to support privately financed electrical service, farmers often created cooperatives or enlisted federal assistance in the form of information and subsidies. Western European governments aided electrification of their farmlands, resulting in a much greater diffusion of electricity by the 1920s than in much of the rural United States, but differences in population densities of the regions' farmland may have been an explanation. In the case of England, most farmers lived in a village and walked to their fields, while American farmers were diffused. As American farms gained electricity, their productivity quickly rose; they also quickly accumulated many electrical appliances enjoyed by their urban cousins. Instead of keeping younger rural Americans on the farm, electrification and the ensuing productivity gains helped push them off the land.[9]

Not all observers were pleased with rural electrification, and an article in *The Literary Digest* lamented or criticized farmers and their families' desires for electrical appliances. The author appeared to be sarcastic in writing, "Will [the farmer] continue his commendable habit of early rising if he can milk a dozen cows at a time by simply turning on the juice? Will not the farmer's wife lose the well-rounded arms that she developed by long hours at the churn and the rosy complexion that she acquired over the cook-stove. . . . In short, will those whose hardest labor has been to press a button or jerk a switch acquire those sterling qualities which have made us what we are."[10]

## Automobiles Transform the American Economy

The automobile certainly loomed large in the changing patterns of leisure endeavors. The American Automobile Association estimated that 45 million Americans took vacation motor tours as early as 1929.[11] The increased mobility and flexibility of auto travel made national parks and national forests popular destinations. Almost 30 million people visited the national forests in 1930, while 900,000 private automobiles entered the national parks. Assuming multiple persons per automobile, automobiles provided the bulk of the transportation in traveling to both the national parks and national forests.[12]

Before the automobile, there was the bicycle. Both forms of transportation needed good roads. Engineers in England began developing better road construction techniques in the early 1800s, but the railroads crowded out this development. Bicycle enthusiasts in the United States, too, began petitioning for better roads. They were soon joined by other people interested in better roads, including farmers who were battling railroads and seeking an alternative transportation system. The first effort to lobby for better roads foundered on class conflict. The League of American Wheelmen, founded in 1880, was comprised of relatively well-to-do members, since bicycles were relatively expensive. As the price of bicycles fell, though, bicycle ownership spread throughout the population, creating a more potent political force. Americans railroads were also early proponents for road improvement, believing that better roads meant a wider range of territory from which they could draw business.[13]

The bicycle reflected changing mores for women's leisure. By the late 1890s, women were beginning to escape the confining clothes that dominated fashion. Corsets and crinolines were prisons made of fabric, limiting women's mobility and occasionally proving dangerously flammable. With new recreational opportunities, including tennis and cycling, becoming available to ever-larger numbers of women, the "Gibson Girl" ideal gained acceptance. Coincident with cycling was a change in women's fashions to tailored skirts and looser blouses—shirtwaists—that provided more comfort and mobility. A writer for *Cosmopolitan* observed: "the bicycle is an unmixed blessing [for men], but to women it is deliverance, revolution, salvation. It is . . . impossible to overestimate the potentialities of this exercise in the curing of . . . ills of womankind, both physical and mental, or to calculate the far-reaching effects of its influence in matters of dress and dress reform."[14]

Although the first cars were primitive in performance, reliability, and safety, Americans quickly sought them. As new production techniques—especially mass rather than custom production—reduced prices, purchases soared. James Flink suggests that although European-style regulation of automobiles had advantages of standardization and better safety through inspecting drivers' abilities, the American laissez-faire policy was conducive to a more rapid diffusion of car ownership.[15]

The automobile was "the most important force for change in American society . . . [while] many consequences of the automobile revolution have proved either illusory or deleterious . . . the American automobile movement was democratic in its inception . . . automobility was until recently a progressive force as well as the predominant one in American historical development."[16] Cars were more convenient and versatile; they were not restricted to rails (but to more widespread roads).

Mass production of cars was beneficial for consumers, but for assembly-line workers, the benefits were mixed. Henry Ford famously introduced the $5 workday, a daily rate well above the average unskilled or semi-skilled worker's wage. In return, though, workers were, in effect, chained to a perpetually moving assembly belt. Because workers had to synchronize their efforts, Ford stated, "Without the most rigid discipline we would have the utmost confusion." Toward eliciting that discipline, Ford factories severely restricted worker behavior on the line, including prohibitions on talking, smoking, whistling, singing, and myriad other actions. Ford justified this draconian work regime: "The men do their work and go home—a factory is not a drawing room."[17]

Once the men left work, they were still subject to Ford scrutiny. Ford, similar to many businessmen of his era, worried that the higher wages he paid his workers would be squandered on alcohol and other vices, so he created a "Sociological Department to monitor and spy upon his workers; workers could be fired, if they violated one of the Ford precepts."[18]

The deadening work environment altered employees' attitudes toward work and leisure. With nothing to look forward to at work, except the $5 per day, men focused on their free time. Flink argues that the dreary monotony of the assembly line transformed the Protestant ethic into a reward of monetary remuneration only, and the monetary reward sloughed off thrift and prudence, as mass consumption gained dominance.[19]

As more Americans owned cars, political pressure built for better roads. Legislators in Oregon, New Mexico, and Colorado hit upon the happy idea of imposing a gasoline tax in addition to the license fee to fund building roads. Automobile drivers probably perceived the tax as fair in the sense that they were using the roads. Initially, the tax was quite low, and did not incite much opposition; even when the tax increased, falling gasoline prices mitigated the tax increase. In addition, John Burnham points out that "the vocal and literate classes enjoyed general prosperity . . . and apparently were not sensitive to the increases," before adding, "never before in the history of taxation has a major tax been so generally accepted in so short a period." The idea of a popular tax surprised government officials.[20]

Even though the Federal Highway Act of 1921 only proposed to build a small fraction of the nation's roads, improved roads spread like tentacles across America, with the miles of improved roads surpassing the number of unimproved roads by 1945. In the end, road building proved a Sisyphean task; drivers often matched or surpassed road builders' efforts at building more roads and lanes by driving more miles. Flink observed that road building assumed an air of futility, as new roads never quite satisfied the growing demands of motorized vehicles.[21]

Roads had earlier been built by a combination of property taxes, poll taxes, and mandatory labor by citizens. Once the gasoline tax and license registration fees displaced these earlier sources and became widespread, they provided over half of the funds for building highways. The federal government helped in financing highway construction via the Federal Aid Act (1921), which provided matching funds for such construction.[22] Once the gasoline tax became a pot of gold, various groups lobbied for their favored uses. Farmers wanted improvements in rural roads, so they could more cheaply transport their crops to market, while other groups, such as bus companies, favored intracity or intercity roads. Farmers' initial hesitance in supporting better roads may have arisen partially from their ignorance of what a good road meant in terms of hauling goods. In later years, some legislators wanted to tap the gasoline tax funds for other, non-road purposes, but they were usually rebuffed by a powerful coalition.[23]

The petroleum industry initially opposed the gasoline tax, fearing a reduction in the amount they would sell. Some people sought to circumvent the gasoline tax by bootlegging, but the petroleum industry and state tax officials squelched this rebellion. Petroleum interests eventually decided that the tax might initially adversely affect the amount of gasoline sold, but, in the long run, better highways were conducive to greater demand for gasoline.[24]

Why did the automobile dominate American transportation? E. H. Holmes, a director of the Office of Policy Planning in the Federal Highway Administration, pointed out, "highway transportation is different. It is a personalized form of transportation primarily involving people moving themselves and their goods in their own vehicles."[25]

The automobile and motorized bus ended the dominance of railroads for intercity travel. Intercity automobile mileage kept pace with and frequently exceeded the growth of population and the economy. John Rae asserted that the impressive automobile mileage for intercity trips represented not just a replacement for rail travel but trips that were made only because of the existence of personal mobility. Another attribute of the automobile was that "the motor vehicle offered 'extensive and varied outlets' for travel of all kinds ... it pinpoints a feature of automobile travel that cannot be effectively demonstrated statistically. The private car is a multipurpose vehicle. ... It is impossible to separate intercity automobile trips by type; some are for business, some are for pleasure, but many, probably most, combine various purposes so that the participants themselves are not quite sure how to reply if they are questioned in a traffic survey."[26]

The growing use of automobiles and increased miles of improved road created new industries: service stations, motels, and roadside eateries. Motels originated in roadside camps, cabins, and private homes; by the 1950s, chains such as Holiday Inn were promoting standardization and brand recognition to gain significant shares of the motel industry revenues.[27]

Even during the Great Depression, motor-vehicle registrations continued to increase. Although most retailers suffered reduced revenues, the filling stations suffered only modest downturns. The automobile was so ingrained that Muncie residents told Robert and Helen Lynd, "People give up everything in the world but their car," and "So long as they have a car and can borrow or steal a gallon of gas, they'll ride around . . . and if they can't get gas, they're busy trying to figure out some way to get it."[28]

The burgeoning Interstate Freeway Act, passed by Congress in 1956 at the behest of President Eisenhower, grew out of a plan to accommodate intercity traffic only. Helen Leavitt describes how the original concept just grew and grew, as highway boosters chose to make the private automobile the focus for urban transportation. She points out that the highway system allowed automobile owners to, in effect, have their own individual "private transportation systems." She chided this situation for its inefficiency, especially since most trips covered short distances. Alternative forms of transportation systems might have been more efficient but possibly less convenient. The interstate freeways were not supposed to pass through the heart of major cities or to serve intracity traffic. Because the interstate freeways eventually went into and through cities, they often disrupted neighborhoods, usually of poorer residents. After the interstate freeways, poorer urban residents often found themselves isolated within large cities.[29]

The rise of the automobile, though, made demands on parents, especially mothers. Mothers often became chauffeurs for children, spending time ferrying them to events.[30] As we've seen, women's hours of domestic work entailed a switch from drudgery to less onerous, but still time-consuming, tasks such as driving to supermarkets and other shopping.

## The Automobile as Leisure Provider

The automobile eventually widened Americans' choices of leisure-time activities. Rural Americans gained from improved roads and automobiles. Many young rural Americans left the farms to escape the isolation of farm life. Thomas MacDonald, chief of the Federal Bureau of Public Roads, knew about America's terrible roads, having grown up in rural Iowa with its endless morass of mud. He hoped that improved transportation would end rural isolation and induce more youth to remain on farms. In order to realize his vision of a strong road system, he created a coalition—oil companies, cement manufacturers and contractors, automobile manufacturers, road builders, chambers of commerce, and other industries. Henry Ford's ability to mass produce relatively cheap automobiles was also crucial in the effort to build a road system; early automobiles cost a lot of money and required continual outlays of money, which just a few Americans could afford.[31] Youth, however, confounded MacDonald by not remaining on the farms.

The automobile proved irresistible for those Americans who wanted to roam the country in search of adventure. There was enough room to store camping gear, and one could even sleep in the car. The individualistic, independent auto travel provided relief from daily worries and chores. "The evolution took thirty-five years. In the first stage, 1910–1920, several hundred thousand middle-class families toured the countryside, camping each night in a different spot along the road, sleeping in cars or in tents, cooking meals over smoky campfires. Auto campers called this squatter-anarchist stage 'gypsying.'" Some auto campers may have felt an independence from the prevailing cross-country modes of transportation and lodging—railroads and hotels—but, in the end, most returned to their respectable positions in society.[32] There were, of course, drawbacks to this style of travel. One might trespass on an overly possessive farmer's land or drink contaminated water.

By the 1920s, when automobile ownership filtered past the middle class and into the lower class, the democratization process probably had gone too far, in many auto campers' opinions. The less-wealthy automobile travelers often found auto camps their sole choice. Instead of hundreds of thousands of car owners, now there were millions and soon tens of millions of car owners in America. New elements started using auto camps. One group was the year-round tourists; these people violated the unspoken norm of motor traveling—it was intended to be a temporary, rejuvenating tour making one ready to resume his or her responsibilities. Those who became permanent tourists were suspect. For Americans with lesser means, auto camps were an easy transition. Rather than deal with a formal hotel, the auto camps were informal and usually self-service and therefore were less intimidating. As the hoi polloi began crowding the auto camps, the middle- and upper-class campers sometimes felt condescension, believing, in some cases, that the poorer people owning cars had made unreasonable sacrifices to maintain their installment payments.[33]

As middle- and lower-class Americans began owning new and used cars, the death toll on the roads escalated rapidly. By the 1920s, drivers killed 25,000 people per year, most of them pedestrians and many children under age 15. The upper crust undoubtedly looked on in disgust and commented that most accidents were caused by low-born people. Auto campers contributed to the carnage, including many farm animals (road kill, in the parlance of rural Americans).[34]

Town merchants urged the development of free auto camps that would provide clean water and other amenities. In return, the merchants hoped to capture some business. Towns started building auto camps. The conditions of these camps varied widely, but they proved popular. The arrangement worked until indigent travelers wore out their welcome, and municipalities began charging small fees. The small fees created an opportunity for private venders to offer similar, if not better, services. Some of these private camp owners built some cabins with beds, clean linens, and other conveniences.[35] Eventually, private auto camps and motor inns displaced the municipally run auto camps.

Many of the original camp owners were rural property owners with spare land situated near a road. People touring by automobile often wanted a respite from the rigors of auto camping. During the early years of the Great Depression, as housing starts fell, lumber and plumbing suppliers sought new markets. The camp cabins proved a good market, and the manufacturers offered good credit terms and often devised prefabricated cottages. Since auto touring's popularity proved largely impervious to the Great Depression, the market for auto camps and cottages grew. National manufacturers joined the building suppliers in providing camps with name-brand products, running from mattresses to soap. Camps often advertised the availability of these national brands in an effort to attract tourists. As the motel industry grew in popularity, the increased competition and rising demand for higher standards pressed hard against profit margins, and many motel pioneers could not endure until the better times after World War II.[36]

Traditional hotels viewed motels with alarm. In order to undercut this new competition, state hotel associations tried to get legislators to pass tough sanitation requirements that would raise costs and prices for motels. The hotels also used calumny against motels, accusing the newer industry of harboring vice and corruption. J. Edgar Hoover even weighed in with a typically bombastic but largely baseless tirade against motels. Several Hollywood movies, though, depicted the motor inn as a place to hide out while on the lam, such as Humphrey Bogart's character in High Sierra and the star-crossed lovers in They Drive by Night. The motels, though, had sufficient political allies to weather the storm. Legislators passed tougher regulations that redounded to the benefit of higher-quality motels, as they forced out competition on the lower end of the trade. Motel trade associations also began to create alliances between higher-quality motels, who then attempted to fix prices and standards. These attempts were sometimes hindered by many motel owners' stubborn independence, cheating on prices by members and non-members, and growing skepticism of motel advertising. At times, the Roosevelt administration helped industries create and enforce price fixing and standards through the National Recovery Administration.[37]

After World War II, national chains such as Best Western and Holiday Inn eased travelers' concerns. These national chains' key selling point was standardization. Often the chains enlisted owners through franchising. The owner operated the motel according to chain standards and gained the benefits of national advertising and brand-name recognition. Readers familiar with the Alfred Hitchcock movie Psycho may well conclude that Marion Crane, the ill-fated protagonist, should have sought a national-chain motel instead of the

Bates Motel.[38] The more or less simultaneous development of national chains of roadside restaurants complemented motels. Many early auto campers cooked their own food, but other tourists wanted food service. Eating locally was an adventure with perhaps high variability in quality and in healthiness.[39] While some motels offered food service, large restaurant chains enjoyed economies of scale in advertising and distribution costs. Tourists could depend upon a McDonalds in Kalamazoo, Michigan, being similar to one in Walla Walla, Washington.

By the 1960s, the interstate freeway system combined well-designed, fast roadways with convenient and standardized motels and restaurants. Although some social critics bemoaned the sameness and blandness of the national chains, these entities made long-distance travel, whether for business or for pleasure, more convenient and predictable.[40]

## The Rise of Suburbs and New Leisure Patterns

Longer commutes were closely tied to suburbanization. Economist John Owen considered the effects of commuting: "This activity is not only an important use of time but also one which may gave rise to economies of scale in the work day. Hence, it may tend to increase the length of the effective work day and thus reduce the demand for leisure time. . . . Thus, one would expect commuters to have less leisure but would not necessarily expect them to have longer hours of paid work."[41] Commuters have options in taking this change in leisure time, whether by working fewer days per week, taking longer vacations, or retiring from work, rather than reducing work hours per day. He concludes, "Insofar as weekend leisure is a good substitute for a shorter work week, a commuting work force can have both high wages and more leisure. In that case commuting would affect the distribution of leisure time more than it would affect the aggregate level of leisure."[42]

Reliable, fast transportation was needed to make early suburbs feasible for white-collar workers, whose jobs were usually downtown. The trolley car was an integral part of early suburbanization. Horses were the initial motive power, but electrification rapidly supplanted the horse. The electric streetcars quickly caught on, especially because of their much greater speed than horse cars, and became "one of the most rapidly accepted innovations in the history of technology."[43] Many owners of trolley companies became land speculators. The experiences of Francis "Borax" Smith, who dreamed of using his commuter line, the Key System, and land purchases in the California Bay area to make millions of dollars, was an example. He hoped the reigning Southern Pacific Railroad would ignore his operations. Instead, Smith suffered large losses on the commuter line and lost his battle with the powerful railroad. Other trolley operators cum real estate developers fared better.[44]

Not only did the trolley operators build lines into sparsely inhabited areas in hopes of developing communities, they used a fare system that differed from European lines. The American trolley operators charged a flat five-cent fare and often had free transfers, while the Europeans used high variable fares depending upon the distance traveled. The latter system was designed to capture patronage from wealthier citizens, while the Americans hoped for heavy volume. The cheap flat fare encouraged entrepreneurs to build on cheaper land on the periphery of the urban area.[45]

The cheaper, reliable transportation system, inexpensive land, and the rise of the balloon-frame method of building houses meant that, as Kenneth Jackson puts it, "for the first time in the history of the world, middle-class families in the late nineteenth century could reasonably expect to buy a detached house on an accessible lot in a safe and sanitary environment." Not all were pleased with the development. As with many mass consumption commodities, suburban housing drew the ire of social and architectural critics. Charlotte Perkins Gilman before World War II and many critics in the postwar era denigrated the "bloated buildings, filled with a thousand superfluities."[46] Malvina Reynolds and Pete Seeger, with their song, "Little Boxes," created a memorable image for 1960s Americans. True, many of the homes had a numbing similarity to neighboring houses, but compared to living in an apartment in a decaying city, Leavittown homes were greatly desired. Most suburban residents paid little heed to Gilman and her ilk. Many apartment buildings in urban areas had a numbing similarity, too.

The trolley lines served to bring suburban shoppers downtown. Large department store owners quickly realized that locating their stores near trolley lines, especially intersections where multiple lines crossed, meant a steady stream of customers from the suburbs. The land value of the one-half square mile of the Chicago Loop at one point reportedly accounted for two-fifths of the total assessed land value of the city. The trolley lines' nickel fare eventually became an albatross, as prices in general rose. City politicians refused to permit the trolley lines to raise their fares, in effect dooming the lines.[47]

Before motorized buses could replace the trolley lines, though, many changes were needed. While the trolley's rapid diffusion was astounding, the automobile, now a symbol of suburbanization, faced obstacles. One was the horse. Apparently enough horses were spooked by the noisy early automobiles that many cities enacted laws requiring automobiles to move very slowly; Jackson cites cases where a man on foot carrying a red flag had to precede an automobile. As was discussed in the section on automobiles, American roadways were generally abominable. City streets were hardly better, becoming a morass of mud during rainy weather and an unsavory concoction of dust and dried manure in the summer. The impetus for paved city streets came from a coalition of automobile manufacturers and their suppliers, road builders, oil companies and gas stations, merchants, and land developers. Much of the citizenry, no doubt, approved of this coalition's efforts. Many of these advocates claimed that the municipalities would gain financially, since the cost of paving the streets would be more than offset by taxes on increasing land values.[48]

Not only automobiles, but also trucks proliferated on the improved city streets and highways. Trucks affected suburbanization by allowing manufacturing, warehousing, and distribution to relocate to cheaper land on the outskirts of cities. Trucks also delivered beer and liquor, allowing establishments selling alcohol and brothels to locate outside downtown areas.[49]

The American family of the 1950s, with its suburban house and automobile, was a throwback to the Victorian cult of domesticity: "the new suburban Victorianism was part of the 'long amnesia'—the years between 1930 and 1960 when earlier debates about the position of women seemed to have been forgotten, and the traditional conceptions of gender roles dominated public and private life. It's not the domesticity of the 1950s that is puzzling . . . but the exaggerated form it assumed: a birthrate that approached that of India, the insistence that marriage and motherhood take up the whole of a woman's identity, and the increased emphasis on gender difference." Families spent much of their time at home; they produced their own leisure goods and services.[50] Affordable suburban houses helped foster this domesticity.

The burgeoning suburbs induced many American males to take up do-it-yourself household repairs and improvements. In 1952, *Business Week* proclaimed the "age of do-it-yourself." More people owned their own homes, and the war had familiarized both men and women with power tools. Whether or not the do-it-yourself activities were leisure activities was in question. *Business Week* surmised that the high cost of labor (construction workers' wages had outpaced many other workers' wages) drove many men to undertake such projects. Reflecting the growing interest in do-it-yourself was the prosperity of *Better Homes & Garden* magazine, whose circulation and advertising revenue shot up rapidly after the war. The magazine's editors were quick to recognize trends, such as the large numbers of unfinished attics. They devoted articles on how to improve attics, which proved popular.[51]

A couple of years later, *Time* magazine also recognized the do-it-yourself movement, stating that the industry was booming, earning $6 billion per year in revenue; the do-it-yourself hobby was now the biggest hobby in the country. The article pointed out that homeowners were doing much of the painting, wallpapering, and asphalt tile work for their homes, all the while looking at a variety of specialty magazines and publications. Economic necessity combined with greater amounts of leisure to generate the boom, and observers predicted that as homeowners felt confident enough to tackle bigger projects, the boom in do-it-yourself would continue.[52]

The do-it-yourself concept had existed before the 1950s but became almost de rigueur during that decade. Steven Gelber dubs the male assumption of re-pairs and improvement as "masculine domesticity."[53] Although many of the new home power tools could have been wielded by women, the ethos required men to assume these duties; in addition, the tools raised expectations for men's work in maintaining their house's repair. Gelber isolates a subtle distinction: "[the workshop] had to remain not only a male realm but a voluntary one as well. In good times craftsmanship was a sign of manly self-reliance, but in bad times it could be a sign of economic impotence."[54]

During the Great Depression, Business Week cited the motivation of making better use of spare time. Craftsmen were repairing or remodeling their homes, building furniture, and doing other crafts projects. These were lumped under the category of "hobby" but were just precursors of a boom just decades away.[55]

For the Americans occupying higher rungs on the economic ladders, a home with a large yard was greatly desired. One of suburban males' household chores was maintaining the lawn. Expansive lawns were a marker of "gracious living" and "an impression of wealth and social standing." The drawback, of course, was the difficulty in maintaining such an expanse. Lawn mowers had existed since the 1830s, but the early model required a horse. Gradually the concept was suf-ficiently improved that women or boys could push the mower.[56]

The availability of relatively cheap land outside the central city allowed coun-try clubs to develop. Thorstein Veblen had argued that recreational activities in America, circa 1900, were the preserve of the rich, but Kenneth Jackson points out that prior to the Civil War, many leisure activities, such as hunting, had been frowned upon by men of culture. He believes that only in postbellum America did "sport take on profoundly aristocratic connotation."[57] In any events, country clubs with their mix of recreational offerings appealed to middle- and upper-class families. Golf was prevalent at these country clubs and, for many decades, playing on private courses was a marker of social prestige.[58]

The federal government also assisted the rise in suburbanization, through its subsidization of both the national highway system and of homeownership, whether in suburbs, urban, or rural areas. Many legislators felt that private own-ership was superior to public ownership of houses, the latter being tainted with "socialism"; homeownership supposedly motivated thrift and good citizenship. Americans' dream of homeownership perked up during the waning years of the 1930s but exploded after World War II. Although new, mass-production tech-niques reduced construction costs, the federal government provided subsidized mortgages through the Federal Housing Administration and tax deductions for mortgage interest payments. Renters did not receive any such subsidies. These factors helped make monthly outlays for homeownership comparable or even lower than such outlays for renting. Rates of homeownership rose; Americans not only bought homes, but with the incentives provided by the mortgage interest deduction, they bought larger homes than they might have otherwise.[59]

Federal largesse sometimes came with stipulations, including limiting consumer choice to suburbs instead of city neighborhoods. There were, of course, fraud and shoddy craftsmanship in some of the newly constructed homes, but, overall, Americans gained both quantity and quality in their living spaces.[60]

If social critics hated the suburban housing developments, they missed the point. Many young couples were not choosing between upper-class housing and the suburban tract home; they were more often choosing between renting an apartment in a crowded tenement with no place for their children to play and the tract home with a backyard. The Levittowns of America offered backyards, new schools, and safety. As Jackson puts it, "whatever its aesthetic failings, [suburban houses] offered growing families a private haven in a heartless world."[61] Suburbanites socialized and held backyard parties, while the old sociability of sitting on the front streets of the tenement house or on the front porch receded. The diffusion of home air conditioning also fostered the trend towards "cocooning."[62]

## Air Conditioning Improves the Leisure Environment

For the first decades of air conditioning, the emphasis was not on cooling but on controlling the indoor environment. Air-conditioning technicians demanded control of the indoor air, including keeping windows closed. Workers and other groups resisted this control; in many industrial processes, skilled craftsmen manipulated humidity and temperature by adroit opening and closing of windows.[63] Workers worried about how environmental conditions affected not only product quality but also worker comfort.

The motion picture industry has often been cited as pioneers in installing air conditioning. A crowded theater generated heat, smell, and discomfort. For the motion pictures' first two decades, theaters often closed during the summer months. Air conditioning helped make exhibiting motion pictures a year-round endeavor. By 1938, the vast majority of theaters had air conditioning of some sort. Air-conditioning technicians and theater owners struggled for control of the air environment. Many theater owners fixated on room temperature, while many air-conditioning technicians highlighted humidity.[64]

Although motion picture theaters led the way, air conditioning in homes lagged. Just before America's entry into World War II, less than one percent of

American homes had air conditioning. Part of the delay in diffusing residential air conditioning was the price of installing a system in an existing structure. After the war, when home builders and lending institutions cooperated in installing air conditioners into new construction, the price of air conditioners fell as mass production became profitable. Home builders found it relatively cheap to build in air conditioning during construction. "Architects, builders, and bankers accepted air conditioning first, and consumers were faced with a fait accompli that they had merely to ratify."[65] The cheaply built tract homes were environmentally unsound with respect to heat, so the air conditioners proved popular and necessary with homeowners.[66]

## The Changed Environment and Leisure

Within the span of a century, Americans gained the ability to determine their own transportation schedules via the automobile. The automobile provided cheaper and more convenient transportation for families than did the railroads, with its requirement of multiple fares and stopovers for long trip. Most Americans lived in their own homes and drove to work. Their homes provided more space, interior and exterior, than the crowded urban tenements. With the diffusion of air conditioning, Americans found it more comfortable to stay at home during the hottest days of the summer. The automobile, tract home, and air conditioning affected leisure choices and, in many cases, reduced the cost of many choices, although traveling to downtown venues in the evening may have become less attractive.

# Government and Leisure

Governments affect leisure in America via a variety of ways. Richard Butsch characterizes the growth of commercialized leisure as shifting "from local leisure entrepreneurs to leisure oligopolies—in some cases stimulated by state policy—and with it a shift from labor- to capital-intensive leisure . . . these corporations built new marketing strategies to attract middle-class audiences."[1]

The federal government was involved in the rise of commercialized leisure through copyright laws that raised the commercial value of motion picture films, music, plays, and fiction, and through favorable antitrust rulings or legislation that allowed, for instance, radio patent holders to form a pool, thereby leaving the radio broadcasting and, later, television industries in the control of a few.[2]

Governments at federal, state, and local levels played other roles in recreation and leisure, whether through the provision of goods and services or by the regulation of working hours. Some of governments' effect on leisure was indirect. Governments affected leisure industries by establishing legal institutions, such as limited liability. For example, the introduction of limited liability in 1862 helped the commercialization of leisure in Great Britain and led to a boom in building large music halls with significant capital investment by reducing risk.[3]

## Rationales for Government Involvement with Leisure

Two historians described the governments' effects on leisure. Historian Peter Borsay asks, "Why should it [the state] have involved itself so much in a field [leisure] where, on the face of it, there was little need to intervene?" He lists areas where governments were concerned: image, economy, security, and order. "Spending on leisure was not only about image building." Legislators worried about the common people's willingness to work or to rely on welfare. Would the working class deteriorate in the face of urbanization and industrialization?[4]

Chris Rojek makes a more forceful argument that without the state, modern leisure would be very different. The state uses taxations, licensing, policing, and propaganda to affect leisure activities. The state, though, also began supplying the needs of communities.[5] He notes that only recently had governments considered leisure as a right of citizenship and something worth funding in order to create good citizens and a good society.[6] He posits that leisure is rarely, if ever, free of political implications, citing anthropologist Victor Turner's definition: "leisure is: '(1) *freedom to enter*, even to generate new symbolic worlds of entertainment, sports, games, diversions of all kinds. It is furthermore, (2) *freedom to* transcend social structural limitations, freedom to play . . . with ideas, with fantasies, with words, with social relationships [emphasis in original].'"[7]

Governments were interested in leisure for another reason: providing able-bodied men for military service. Many American males in 1917 were unfit for military service. Private voluntary organizations such as the Boy Scouts recognized the utility of training a corps of boys in rugged living and physical exercise. Leisure leaders of that era advocated for Muscular Christianity and self-improvement. These efforts sought to counterbalance, if not roll back, "the feral, infected world of prostitution, alcohol abuse, drug dependence, street violence, crime and the other types of vice and degradation that undisciplined leisure brought in its train."[8]

Rojek suggests that the state went through phases with regard to leisure. Personal Growth and Enrichment, the Beautification of Life, and Moral Reform were the first three phases. Under the fourth phase, during World War II, the state and middle class used leisure to improve the population. These forces focused on at-risk youth. "Their solution was to introduce organized sports, cultural events and educational facilities."[9]

If the public sector had no special capabilities relative to voluntary or commercial provision of leisure, then the question would be "whether the public sector performed better or worse than one of the alternatives." Instead, Ken Roberts suggests a third, not-so-desirable, possibility: the state could deter voluntary and commercial enterprise by usurping provision of goods and services, often with no direct charge or heavily subsidized rates to users, or by taxing or prohibiting certain goods and services.[10]

Roberts dispels some myths surrounding public provision of leisure facilities. "First, public provisions are unable to redistribute leisure opportunities in favour of the socio-economically disadvantaged . . . we find that it is nearly always the better-off who make the most use of free-to-use and subsidized facilities." People with higher incomes have better access to publicly provided recreation activities. He does acknowledge that, in a few instances, such as the British Broadcasting Corporation, the poor and the rich both use the provision. More generally, though, government-provided recreational activities are a regressive poll tax. In addition, state provision of leisure is, at best, an unreliable method for dictating people's use of their leisure: "If people were susceptible to leisure education and state-promoted opportunities, we would now be a nation of church-goers and Shakespeare readers." Social control arguments, though, are a good way to gain public funds, but "the willingness of the authorities to act on a manifestly false premise suggests that the official rationale of the relevant measures may perform latent functions. It enables governments to be seen to be 'doing something' about conditions in 'problem areas.'"[11]

This perception is actually harmful to the poor and other groups dealing with problems, as the general public may believe that the government has solved the target population's problems, and that any residual ill-health or problems are the result of individual choices rather than societal and economic conditions. "The crucial fact of this matter is that when people have a choice of commercial, voluntary and public sector leisure provisions, they will use the latter only if the provisions coincide with their own inclinations."[12]

Free admission to public libraries, museums, and art galleries are defended as a matter of public service. The free admission allows access by all citizens (assuming they can easily get to the facilities), gives a sense of national ownership, and performs educational functions.[13]

## Other Drawbacks of Government Provision of Leisure

There are several other inconvenient outcomes of government provision of leisure activities. National and state lotteries provide both entertainment and leisure, but people with lower incomes tend to spend a greater proportion of their incomes on lotteries: "As a pseudo-tax, the Lottery is regressive. It is an amazingly successful method of persuading the poor to pay for the rich's good causes and pleasures."[14] Roberts admonishes over-zealous government intervention into commercial provision of leisure, arguing that leisure programs designed to redress economic disadvantages, to cure "bad" behavior, to "please everyone," or to provide prestige are poor uses of resources.[15]

In terms of providing outdoor leisure and recreation opportunities at little or no costs, various government agencies crowd out potential private provision of such opportunities. Economists Terry Anderson and Donald Leal observe that one-third of the land in the continental United States is controlled by the federal government. Politicians gain support from constituents—ranchers, miners, farmers, and outdoor enthusiasts—by doling out natural resources for minimal or no user fees. This largesse often precludes private provision of recreational and environmental amenities.[16]

## Government Regulation of Labor

Federal and state governments set rules pertaining to labor, from limiting the number of hours of work to safety regulations. The governments' efforts, though, may not have been as much of an instrument of change as presumed. As economist Claudia Goldin argues, "government intervention often reinforced existing trends, the decline of child labor, the narrowing of the wage structure, and the decrease in the hours of work."[17] An example of this government reinforcement was Federal Order 213, passed in 1932. This order "mandated that executive branch officials, in the face of layoffs, fire workers whose spouses were employed by the federal government. The regulation almost always entailed the firing of married women, although many husbands could have been furloughed." Goldin points out that the order gave credibility to discriminatory hiring and retaining policies of the past, while, "[t]he [marriage] bar was extended to occupations and sectors, such as manufacturing, where it was not extensively found before the Depression. The Depression served to reinforce social norms that kept married women, particularly the emerging middle class, out of the labor force."[18]

The federal government often led the way to shorter hours. In 1840, President Martin Van Buren issued an order stipulating that government manual laborers toil for just 10 hours a day. By 1868, labor groups pressured Congress to enact an eight-hour day for federal employees. During World War I, the federal government mandated an eight-hour day for war workers.[19]

Labor union's struggles for shorter hours were tumultuous; strikes proved divisive and bloody. An alternative to strikes and direct confrontation with owners and management was to seek legislative mandates covering workers in industries. During the years before and after 1900, some of the legislation was aimed at reducing women's and children's hours of labor to a 5.5-day workweek. The fight eventually evolved as a campaign for a five-day workweek, which, for many workers, would not be realized until the Great Depression gave a final impetus to changes in labor practices. Just prior to the Great Depression, a study conducted in 1929 showed that roughly half of workers worked more than 48 hours per week, which were longer hours than typical workweeks throughout the industrialized world.[20]

Legislative attempts to reduce the workweek below 40 hours failed, including Franklin Roosevelt's opposition to the 36-hour workweek proposal of 1933 mentioned earlier. The Fair Labor Standards Act of 1938 stipulated that employers working for the government on contracts greater than $10,000 work a maximum eight-hour day, 40-hour week, with overtime for hours beyond the eight and 40 limits. Early in 1964, President Lyndon Johnson came out against a 35-hour workweek during his State of the Union address that was largely devoted to the "War on Poverty." Johnson, as had John Kennedy before him, worried that the proposed legislation would drive up labor costs and create inflation. Organized labor split with regard to the proposal. United Auto Workers president Walter Reuther opposed the measure, while American Federation of Labor-Congress of Industrial Organizations president George Meany supported it. In fact, Meany wanted a 30-hour workweek—but with 40 hours pay.[21]

The Fair Labor Standards Act may have had modest effects on workers' choice of hours. Prior to the act, many workers were already working fewer hours than state-mandated maximums. In addition, "the more dramatic reductions in hours of work in the United States occurred before the passage of the Fair Labor Standards Act. Moreover, while the Fair Labor Standards Act brought about a short-term reduction in hours of work in those industries where it was applied, there is some evidence that, in the years following the passage of the F.L.S.A., reductions in hours were larger in industries not covered by the act than in covered industries."[22]

Government-imposed minimum wage laws affected unskilled workers' choices between leisure and labor. Although unskilled workers who retained their jobs gained a higher wage, other unskilled workers lost their jobs. Unskilled workers not originally in the labor force may have entered the labor force, resulting in more workers competing for fewer jobs. Unemployed workers faced longer searches with the attendant waste of time and travel expenses searching for jobs.

## Government Provision of Leisure and Recreation

Various government agencies provide a wide range of leisure and recreational amenities, ranging from federal national parks to local community centers and swimming pools. The National Park system—including national parks, monuments, recreation centers, and other areas—drew 286 million visits in 2000, while state parks and recreation areas had 725 million visitors in 2005. The latter figure was roughly double the combined attendance at Major League Baseball, National Football League, National Hockey League, and National Basketball Association games that year.[23] Although people may not drive long distances to state parks, many trips to National Parks entail considerable expenditures and time.

With the removal of government restrictions on gambling, state-run lotteries, Native American–run casinos, and private gambling industries have burgeoned. Americans now enjoy an array of gambling venues. State-run lotteries sold $37 billion worth of tickets in 2000, while gross revenues from amusement taxes amounted to about $5 billion in 2004. The gaming industry took in $62 billion in revenues. Clearly, Americans liked various games of chance.[24] Tribal gaming revenue was about $13 billion in 2001. The windfall from running casinos have benefited many tribes, but the windfalls have mixed effects, as the distribution and investment of such profits can prove contentious.[25]

The state-run lotteries, though, raise a number of troubling questions, including the aforementioned disproportionate number of lower-income Americans playing the lotteries. Federal agencies have granted state-run lotteries exemptions from regulations pertaining to advertising, while media networks afford state-run lotteries with impressive amounts of publicity through stories purporting to be news regarding huge jackpots. The lotteries' misleading statements regarding winnings, which are not always stated in present value (discounted because dollars received in the future are not as valuable as dollars received today, since you can invest today's dollars), are also troubling. Lottery revenues are directed toward education and economic development projects, but often there is no *net* increase in the state revenues going to education. The canard that lottery revenues help fund education is inaccurate.[26]

## Government Taxation Policies and Leisure

If the government levies a percentage tax on, say, labor income, the effective, take-home wage falls. Workers are worse off, so they will cut back on leisure hours. But because the price of leisure has fallen, workers will substitute toward taking more leisure hours and working fewer hours. The net result is that workers may or may not increase their hours worked. The question of whether they will work more or less in response to a change in the income tax rate was crucial in the 1980 presidential campaign, when economist Arthur Laffer asserted that the existing rate was so high that a reduction would spur people to work more. By working more, workers would earn sufficiently increased incomes to afford both increased consumption and higher taxes. Because the American income tax system is progressive, workers in different income brackets may, on average, have different responses in their hours worked.[27]

Although governments may invest in recreational capital, they also need to raise revenues to pay for these investments. In the United States, the federal government and down to local governments placed taxes on amusement, such as baseball games and motion pictures. Stephen Jones relates how such government policies shaped the "economic structure of the leisure industry. Furthermore, the tax [in Britain] hindered the development of those smaller commercial concerns and voluntary organizations without the means to meet fiscal demands, as well as increasing the price of entertainment to consumers."[28]

## Government Involvement during the Great Depression

The Great Depression provided an impetus for government involvement in recreation and leisure. Even before the Great Depression, recreation experts advocated for public facilities. Some of the larger cities were building playgrounds, parks, and other recreational facilities, but many small towns lagged in imitating their larger counterparts.[29]

There were two other trends. The growing government support of public recreation was complementing the earlier private efforts to build playgrounds and other recreational areas for children and, later, for adults. During this early push for expanded free recreational areas for working-class families, playground reformers encouraged schools to open their playgrounds during non-class times. The growing acceptance of leisure time also led to increased demand for repealing Sunday restrictions on leisure activities, since lax enforcement had already loosened Sunday leisure activities.[30]

Unlike previous economic downturns, during the Great Depression, most Americans had accepted leisure time as being legitimate and necessary. A few even hoped that commercialized leisure activities might lead the country out of the economic downturn. The federal government began getting involved with leisure and recreation, advised by social scientists, such as Louis Walker. Walker believed the government should take responsibility for promoting an equitable distribution and organization of leisure time via a "division of leisure." He feared that without government involvement, limits to the workweek would spawn ever more unregulated leisure time. He espoused the belief that leisure was now a product, the new American product: "we here in America face the necessity of studying our new product."[31]

Carrying this concept of leisure as a product and the desirability of producing it efficiently, W. Lou Tandy, an economist who applied economic concepts to the issue, wrote: "Even though most people may not use leisure to their degradation, they are not prepared to use it most proficiently. Proficiency in the art of using leisure may be acquired, however, by careful attention to and application of the principles of economics which pertain to its use."[32]

The Works Progress Administration surveyed its recreation projects and advocated, unsurprisingly, making the government responsible for providing and overseeing recreation. Roosevelt's "fatherly" intimacy with Americans fostered "a newfound notion that the happiness of the masses and their psychological well-being was now definitely one of the government's responsibilities." The government-financed Civilian Conservation Corps built trails, campsites, lodges, and other outdoor facilities; the program created jobs and new recreational facilities.[33]

Roosevelt's National Industrial Recovery Act indirectly affected the leisure issue. By mandating shorter workweeks in industry in order to spread jobs among more workers, the administration was exacerbating the problem of unwanted leisure time.[34] The discussion of regulating leisure time and activities attracted opposition: "Modern recreational leaders, especially in group work, are rejecting superimposed programs of activity and are, instead, studying the interest of people for the purpose of helping individuals engage in leisure time venture which enlist their wholehearted activity."[35] As Howard Brauscher wrote in *Recreation*, "some of us would rather live in a bad world than a in a world made good by compulsion."[36]

By the middle of the Great Depression, recreation experts could identify gains in the numbers of municipally provided playgrounds, swimming pools, sports fields, and other spaces and activities. Robert and Helen Lynd, though, warned that vigilance was needed to maintain these gains, as they worried that a return to prosperity would erode taxpayers' willingness to finance such public spaces. Susan Currell argues that the "recreation reform of the thirties was a last-ditch attempt to stem the tide of changing social roles and mores associated with increased sexual liberty and social mobility. At the same time, it was also an attempt to create a better society outside of the capitalist work ethic that had dominated life for the past century."[37]

## Governments' Myriad Roles in Leisure and Recreation

Federal, state, and local governments were involved in leisure and recreation, starting with setting hours of work. Even if these entities did not enact any legislation or provide any recreational or leisure goods and services, they would still play a role. Government definitions of property rights alone affected commercial leisure. The federal government, though, has created and defined property rights and antitrust regulations that deeply affect leisure and recreation businesses. Television, radio, motion pictures, and professional team sports provided examples of interaction between governments and business people, as will be described in the next chapter. Government officials, too, helped shaped the work week, provided goods and services directly to Americans, and offered advice about judicious uses of leisure time. Various government entities provide playgrounds, parks, and other amenities. Whether government provision of these amenities was superior to market-based provision remains a hotly debated issue.

# 14

# Antitrust Issues and the Leisure Industries

In the late nineteenth centuries, Americans worried about the concentration of power in the hands of a few industrialists. The era witnessed the formation of combinations and trusts. In response, Congress passed the Sherman Antitrust Act in 1890. The act states, in part:

> Section 1: Every contract, combination in the form of trust or otherwise, or conspiracy, in restraint of trade or commerce among the several States, or with foreign nations, is declared to be illegal.

> Section 2: Every person who shall monopolize, or attempt to monopolize, or combine or conspire with any other person or persons, to monopolize any part of the trade or commerce among the several States, or with foreign nations, shall be deemed guilty of a felony.[1]

Although the language seems clear, the interpretation was often ambiguous, and the courts have developed a "rule of reason" approach.[2] The early history of the Sherman Antitrust Act saw the breaking up of Standard Oil, Northern Trust, and other industrial trusts, but U.S. Steel escaped this fate. Sometimes concentration and cooperation between firms created efficiencies and benefited consumers. In these cases, the courts did not find an antitrust violation.[3]

Because some of the industries producing leisure goods and services were concentrated in the hands of a few firms, Congress and the Department of Justice repeatedly investigated these industries for possible antitrust violations. Federal authorities, however, sometimes (wittingly and unwittingly) aided and abetted firms in their attempts to dominate industries via patents and regulations. The dominance of some firms and cartels allowed them to exploit their skilled labor. Athletes and actors, while often earning several times the average salary for Americans, were among the most economically exploited Americans.

This chapter examines some antitrust issues concerning leisure industries. The resolution of antitrust issues often led to unexpected outcomes.

## The Music Industry's Antitrust Sour Notes

The recorded sound industry experienced waves of domination by a handful of firms. The federal government aided inventors in their quest to dominate the sound recording industry via patents. Technological innovations often gave their firms an advantage; however, sheer technical superiority was rarely the only way to gain dominance. Consumers demanded other amenities and product characteristics. Consumers, not just the industrial leaders, determined the mass appeal of musical genres.[4]

Phonographs, vaudeville, theater, motion picture theaters, and radio had an unquenchable thirst for new songs, while songwriters needed to get their music played. One attempt to control the industry arose when the Music Publishers' Contact Employees and the music publishers considered such an agreement. The American Federation of Musicians opposed the proposal.[5]

The music publishing industry was roiled when the radio broadcasters formed Broadcast Music Incorporated (BMI) to compete with the older American Society of Composers, Authors, and Publishers (ASCAP). The two leading music associations' struggles were intertwined with the rise of new musical genres after World War II. BMI held rights to most of the popular new music of the 1950s. For the first half of the twentieth century, the song was paramount; after 1950, the performer, who often wrote his or her own songs, assumed dominance.[6]

For the independent record companies, rhythm and blues and rock 'n' roll were a potent brew. The time was propitious; radio networks were jettisoning their regular programming and needed material to fill the time. Playing recorded music became ever more important. The radio stations' transformation into music jukeboxes was a boon to both record companies and phonograph manufacturers. The move toward all-canned-music formats on the radio, though, triggered FCC concern, and the agency refused to renew some stations' licenses for their embrace of total music and news formats while forsaking their public service responsibilities.[7]

Rock 'n' roll was a valuable filler; young people spent hours listening to their favorite hits on the radio. If a record label could get its records played on radio, chances were that sales would jump. The keen competition for air time induced some independent producers to encourage radio disc jockeys to play their records in return for gifts-in-kind or cash.

The Top 40 began to be dominated by rock 'n' roll. Once the major labels realized that rock 'n' roll was not a passing fad, they quickly signed up young musicians or purchased independent labels. Steve Chapple and Reebee Garofalo suggest that "the payola investigations of 1959–60 were simply a highlight of a long-running argument and legal controversy between ASCAP and BMI. The music industry has moved squarely from publisher domination that favored ASCAP writers to record and radio domination that uses a looser structure, like BMI's."[8]

When ASCAP filed an antitrust suit against BMI, Brooklyn representative Emanuel Celler, chair of the Antitrust Subcommittee, agreed to investigate. The original subject of the investigation was the television quiz show scandal, but ASCAP also played on conservatives' fears pertaining to rock 'n' roll. The committee members found the payola question useful: "Many conservative congressmen were connected with legions of public decency back in their home districts. They saw themselves as moral guardians who represented parents back home who were quite simply appalled by the loud sexual music."[9]

Radio listeners probably never thought about how certain songs were introduced to radio jockeys. It was not as though disc jockeys attended a national convention, heard music, and selected the ones they wished to play. If a music publisher had a promising song, the real task was to expose the song to popular disc jockeys and induce them to play it. Until 1960, it was not against the law to offer a payment of cash or gifts to disc jockeys in return for their playing a song. Many social commentators and politicians expressed outrage and surprise that such a practice existed. The mixture of payola and rock 'n' roll confirmed many people's fears and prejudices against the new musical genre.

Payola is actually a fascinating story about economics and business. Nobel Prize–winner Ronald Coase analyzed the practice. His findings suggested that payola deserves a more sympathetic response. He defined payola as "undisclosed payments (or other inducements) which are given to bring about the inclusion of material in broadcast programs."[10]

Although the American public gasped in indignation at the exposed practice of payola, payola predated rock 'n' roll by decades. Music publishers had long offered cash or gifts to get popular singers or radio programs to play particular songs.[11]

During Senate hearings in 1958, there was mention of payola to disc jockeys, but the senators were unconcerned; Senator John Pastore (RI) likened it to paying "a headwaiter $5 to get a desirable table."[12] It wasn't until composer Burton Lane, who was serving as president of the American Guild of Authors and Composers, sent a letter to the Investigation of Television Quiz Shows hearings that payola received prominence. Lane alleged that the practice of deception was not limited to game shows, but that the promotion of music was heavily influenced by commercial bribery that clandestinely induced customers to buy specific recordings. Representative Oren Harris (ARK), who had already made up his mind, opened the House hearings by stating, "these practices constitute unfair competition with honest businessmen who refuse to engage in them.

They tend to *drive out of business small firms* [italics mine] who lack the means to survive this unfair competition."[13]

Some witnesses testified that without payola, "this so-called junk music, rock and roll stuff" would "never get on the air." A key issue surrounding payola was its concealment, which, according to the Federal Trade Commission (FTC), constituted a deceptive act and could lead to unfair competition. Before 1960, the FTC's only authority to regulate payola came from Section 317 of the Communications Act of 1934, whereby any direct or indirect payment in return for broadcasting needed to be "announced as paid for or furnished . . . by such person." The 1950s-style payola involved payments to disc jockeys and not to stations, so the applicability of the rule was dubious. If the radio station, however, knew of and condoned its disc jockeys receiving payola, then it could not constitute a bribe.[14] Because radio stations received their licenses from the government, though, Congress felt justified in interfering with payola.

The music publishers were the foremost proponents of the anti-payola laws. Years earlier, they had tried to stop payola through a collusive agreement but had failed. If they could get the government to enforce such a rule, then the practice would be curbed, if not eliminated. Many in the music industry, however, tacitly approved of payola.[15]

The resulting legislation did not eliminate payola. Reports of the practice recurred. Government enforcers found that a more effective way to combat the policy was to seek out tax evasion or perjury violations.[16] Record companies reacted by placing greater emphasis on promotional staff. Coase observes that this gave major labels a competitive edge over the independents, since the majors had promotional organizations that were superior to those of the independents. Representative Harris's allegation was stood on its head: elimination of payola protected the established firms and hurt the smaller, new ones. Coase surmises that the purpose of the Senate hearings and resulting legislation was "to obtain confessions of guilt from the witness and to demonstrate the high moral standards of the congressmen. . . . In the circumstances it is hardly surprising that widely held misconceptions about payola were perpetuated by the enquiry."[17]

The payola case is instructive, especially from an economics perspective. Station managers and owners likely approved of payola. First, the prospect of collecting payola would have increased the number of people wanting to be disc jockeys, leading to a reduction in the requisite salaries paid. Disc jockeys had to carefully consider which records to play, since pleasing listeners led to higher ratings and greater advertising revenues. A disc jockey, therefore, would not accept payola for a record likely to displease the audience. Payola probably only moderately affected the selection of records.[18]

Certainly ASCAP and BMI paid attention to payola. The shifting popularity of genres was advantageous to BMI, with its stable of country and western and rhythm and blues artists. With rock 'n' roll's rise, ASCAP's share of the *Billboard* top hits sank. ASCAP and the devotees of "good music" would not accept the verdict of the consuming public; there had to be chicanery involved, and payola was identified as the culprit in the shift toward "bad music." Coase concludes, "There can be no doubt that the new companies, which entered the business in the 1950s and succeeded in securing such an important share of the record market, relied on payola to obtain 'exposure' for their records."[19]

Coase compares ASCAP and the government's actions to professional groups (lawyers and physicians) prohibiting advertising for many years. He observes that if payola was outlawed, then record companies would have had to devote more money to the production and distribution of records; consumers would not have gained from these expenditures. Such expenditures naturally favored incumbent and larger firms, so consumers might end up being deprived of new talent and musical styles.[20]

Payola, therefore, offers an instructive example of the ironies of the legislative process. Rather than help new entrants and independent producers compete, the hearings contributed to concentration of the music industry into the hands of a few, large firms.

## The Motion Picture Seven Violate Antitrust Laws

The distribution of motion pictures may have been destined to be concentrated into a few firms, because the minimum optimal scale for distribution was national in order to efficiently schedule the movement of prints and the coordination of local and national advertising. A national distributor needed scores of films to be cost effective, as distributing only a handful of films on a national basis was inefficient; therefore it should not be surprising to find only 10 national distributors in the industry.[21]

The patent holders in the Motion Picture Patents Company (MPPC) initially dominated the film industry, but they failed to match the innovations spawned by other firms.[22] These innovations included the star system and the feature picture. Those exhibitors who were the first to show better films gained valuable reputations and often ended up having their theaters classified as first-run. Adolph Zukor also began grading films depending upon the attractions of the actors and the quality of the story. By doing so, he created a system compatible with charging different prices for individual films, rather than the old standard of selling film by the foot.[23]

The MPPC was never one big happy family. Its members continued to contest patent rights. The federal government broke up the cartel under the

Sherman Act, citing the cartel's attempt to monopolize the trade in films and film equipment.[24]

The MPPC was the parent company of the General Film Company. The General Film Company sought to organize theaters by quality and assigned runs, fixed release dates, and differential rentals. These policies were the groundwork underlying Hollywood's distribution policies for decades to come. The company used its discriminatory powers via the assignments of runs to cultivate theaters in middle-class and downtown business districts. These theaters were better equipped and more lavish than the neighborhood theaters and nickelodeons. To attract a better clientele, the company began publicizing movies in newspapers and magazines while censoring the movies for offensive content.[25]

The MPPC quickly dominated the industry, but there were holdouts. William Fox's Greater New York Film Rental Company proved nettlesome. When the trust cut off his supply of films, he reacted by establishing film production and filing an antitrust lawsuit. The film production quickly began reaping benefits, while the antitrust lawsuit took years to confer benefits. In the end, the antitrust lawsuit may have been irrelevant as the trust's patents began expiring. The moviegoing public demonstrated a preference for the films Fox and his allied exhibitors were showing. Fox was not alone in contesting the dominance of the MPPC. W. W. Hodkinson established a national distribution company, Paramount Pictures Corporation. The company arranged to distribute the films of Adolf Zukor's Famous Players and those of Jesse Lasky, Samuel Goldfish (or Goldwyn), and Cecil B. DeMille. With a steady supply of films, Paramount was able to guarantee exhibitors sufficient films to fill their bill, especially when such films were shown for more than one night.[26]

Although patents were one source of monopoly power in the motion picture industry, there was another, longer lasting, source: copyright. In the motion picture industry, manufacturing is called production, whereby the producer assembles all of the personnel and story required to make a film. The producer owns the copyright to his film and will license the negative or a number of positive prints to a distributor or market it himself. "The copyright on the film, the greatest single source of monopoly power in the industry, enables the producer to prevent unlicensed duplications of his prints and to control their distribution." So far, so good—one would expect nothing else from the process; the producer should have rights to his intellectual property. Producers, however, were not always satisfied with monopolizing their own movie; "It was the illegal extension of the monopoly power given by film copyright—its use for the purpose of controlling admission prices and the marketing of other films—that facilitated the creation of the industry-wide combinations," which facilitated much of the monopolization of the motion picture industry.[27]

Building upon a concept used in vaudeville—the exchange—the motion picture company distributed its product through the exchanges into the theaters. A film exchange served as a middle man, creating a large demand and renting large numbers of films from producers, often for higher prices. The exchange then offered exhibitors a wider variety of films, often for lower prices. The exchange's large volume helped reduce negotiating costs for all three parties.[28]

At once, the industry devolved into three separate branches: production, distribution, and exhibition. These branches became dominated by a few firms; some of the more audacious or far-seeing business minds realized that it was even better to control all three branches under one controlling interest. The film distributor gained copyright to his films and rented or leased the films to the exhibitor, who gained no ownership stake in the film. The exhibitor paid a fee for the right to screen the film; the exhibitor then charged a fee to the patron for the right to watch the film. By owning the copyright, the distributor retained control over the conditions of exhibition, allowing the distributor to dictate the admission price, the days of the week that the film can be shown, the advertising, and other aspects.[29]

In 1917, 26 of the largest, first-run exhibitor circuits created a combine that they named First National Exhibitors Circuit. The combine was able to bargain for exclusive rights to pictures; it then apportioned costs among members according to the expected gross rentals of circuit. First National began producing films in 1923, while Zukor's Famous Players-Lasky decided to start buying theaters in response.[30] Zukor also purchased Paramount, but in 1921 the Federal Trade Commission (FTC) charged the companies with unlawful restraint of trade in attempting to monopolize production and distribution of motion pictures in 1914. Famous Players-Lasky's purchase of Paramount and other companies was alleged to be part of a conspiracy. The FTC's charges were repudiated in a later court action, in which the court argued that a "state of free competition [existed] in the industry."[31]

The upshot of these movements was the formation of firms integrating all three aspects of the industry. By subsuming exhibition, distribution, and production under one parent firm, film companies could increase profits.

Movie officials quickly recognized that the large theaters in the major metropolitan centers accounted for a disproportionate amount of the film rentals. Control of these large theaters meant the ability to control exhibition. The five major studios scrambled for large theaters in the major cities in the late 1920s.[32]

There was little direct competition between the eight leading producers (the five majors included Loew's-MGM, Warner Bros., Paramount, Fox, and RKO, while the three minors were Universal, Columbia, and United Artists). The eight largest producers monitored each other's output, which "grows out of the interdependent relationship of the major companies. Any attempt on the part of one major to deviate from the accepted method of doing business involves the danger of reprisal in the form of joint action by the other majors. This action may consist of a double-edged refusal to deal with the dissident company."[33]

Mae Huettig suggests that the motion picture industry's product was "the right to look at a film, in a given type of theatre, at a given time with reference to the original release date of the film." As she points out, the film itself is "but a part of the commodity sold." By her reckoning, seeing *Gone With the Wind* within a week of its release in a New York City or Chicago palatial downtown theater was a different product from seeing it several months later in a suburban theater.[34] In other words, the time and the location were important facets of the product, aside from the picture itself.

Why was this so? After the marketing and publicity buildup, movie patrons may have simply been impatient to see the new film. There may have been a status associated with being one of the first to see a film; the reader can easily imagine that a moviegoer who saw the latest film on the first day of its release gained satisfaction from being able to describe it to friends, coworkers, and family members who had yet to see the film. Whatever the motivation, filmgoers were willing to pay a premium to see a film on its initial release. The movie companies exploited this preference by establishing first-run theaters. These theaters, although a minority of all theaters, received the opportunity to screen new releases. Second-run and lower-run theaters screened a film as it worked its way down the theater hierarchy. At each lower rung, the theaters were smaller or were located in less desirable neighborhoods; the admission price also tended to diminish. First-run theaters generated over 50 percent of the total revenue.[35]

The five major studios and their distributors used a variety of tactics to manipulate the industry in their favor. Adolph Zukor introduced "block booking," whereby exhibitors who wanted Mary Pickford movies had to rent a set of movies in order to get the Pickford ones. As anyone who has collected baseball cards via bubblegum packets knows, the process entails buying a bunch of obscure players in the hopes of getting a Mickey Mantle or Miguel Cabrera card.[36]

Block booking might have been defended as an economical way of distributing motion pictures, as negotiating for a block of films was more convenient than negotiating for individual films. However, the FTC repeatedly investigated block booking. In 1927, the FTC declared the practice unfair and issued a case-and-desist order. A US Circuit Court of appeals reversed the decision in 1932. In 1938, the Justice Department tried again, gaining a consent decree.[37] Michael Conant suggests that another rationale for block booking was the majors' desire to curb independent exhibitors and to deter entry by independent distributors.[38]

Block booking involved "blind buying," since the distributor was offering exhibitors movies that had not even been filmed. The distributors liked the system, since it shifted the risk pertaining to audience acceptance of the un-completed movies onto the exhibitor. Block booking also deterred independ-ent producers, who might have filled the gaps between the good films and the mediocre ones.[39]

Another distributor tactic was "designated play dates." Because the producer owned the copyright to the films, he could dictate which days of the week the exhibitor must screen the films. The distributor wanted to ensure that his best pictures would be shown on the most lucrative days: Saturdays, Sundays, or holidays.[40]

The owners of small, independent theaters realized the onerous nature of block booking, blind buying, and designated play dates. They chafed under these mandatory strictures and saw them as discriminatory and injurious. These owners claimed that mandatory block booking and other restrictions were not always levied on large chains or on the producers' own theaters.[41]

Clearance and zoning were other key parts of the majors' domination. A the-ater owner wanted as much clearance (period between runs) and as extensive zoning (geographical territory) as possible, since these would grant considera-ble protection from competition in showing a particular picture. Distributors typically wanted shorter clearance and less-restrictive zoning than did the ex-hibitors. To adjudicate disputes regarding clearance and zoning, the industry formed local film boards of trade. The film boards of trade were perhaps inevi-table. The five major studios, though, dominated these trade associations.[42]

Producers had to develop an allocation method for their films. They found it economically infeasible to print enough copies of a film to service no more than a tiny fraction of the theaters willing to show the movie. Producers typically printed only a few hundred copies of their movies; each print might last 200 showings (40 to 60 runs). The majors and their allied minors created a pricing scheme both to allocate the limited number of prints and to maximize revenues and profits.

The distribution system, naturally, relegated independently owned theaters to the lowest priority in the system. The eight majors and minors therefore fun-neled most of the rentals of their films to their own first-run theaters. Setting ticket prices was crucial. If exhibitors set too high a price, people would wait for a later run. If customers' demands were perfectly known to the producers and ignoring transportation costs and the inconvenience of traveling to motion pic-ture theaters, then "customers should be allocated among the runs so that no one who would have paid a higher price to see a film in an earlier run will wait to see it in a later run at a lower price." Of course, there is no way to perfectly know customers' demand curves, and Conant suggests, "[t]he problem is essentially analogous to the interdependent demand curves of different classes of railway travel."[43]

The Department of Justice accepted a decree that prohibited most of these practices. Huettig remarks, "it is noteworthy that one of the principal results of the action was an agreement by the government to refrain from disturbing in any way the status quo with respect to theatre holdings of the majors. This was apparently the quid pro quo required from the government in exchange for the concessions offered by the majors. The concessions themselves are not very substantial."[44]

Warner Bros.' introduction of the "talkies" upset the industry's status quo of the 1920s. The large investments needed to convert film studios and movie houses increased the large chains and studios' advantages relative to independent houses and producers. The five major studios swooped in to purchase hundreds of theaters by 1930; in doing so, they incurred large debts.[45]

By the 1930s, the five major studios controlled the majority of first-run theaters in the larger cities. The three minors did not own theaters. The majors needed the minors' output of films in order to complete their listings, as the majors failed to produce enough films per year to fill their demand. The majors owned chains of theaters, but there was little geographical overlap of theaters; therefore, the majors' theaters rarely competed directly with each other. Although the majors owned a significant number of theaters, they did not own the majority of all theaters. They did, however, own the bulk of the first-run theaters that skimmed the cream of the business.[46]

To understand the industry, one must view the five majors and three minors as operating under a cooperative atmosphere. The firms cooperated not only in terms of sharing their films, they also shared their star performers. By doing so, they largely shut out the independent theaters and producers from films and from talent. The major studios controlled a key labor input: actors. The movie studios' "star system" had many similarities to professional team sports' reserve clauses. The movie studios used the actors' contracts to control them. The studio determined which productions would use the actors, thus gaining discipline over the more free-spirited actors. The studios could protect or destroy their actors by judicious choice of productions. The studios, unlike most sports team owners, frequently loaned their stars to other studios among the eight studios. The studios rarely loaned their star players to independents, and when they did so, they charged a price well above the actor's contract terms.[47]

The cooperation among the eight studios might be thought to raise profits above the average, but Huettig argues that movie studio bosses distributed its earnings above costs by distributing bonuses (often self-awarded) or by paying lavish salaries to executives. Given the income tax structure of the 1930s, in which corporate tax rates were higher than individual income tax rates, studio executives usually preferred bonuses and higher salaries instead of dividends.[48]

Motion pictures, as with music and, later, comic books, created controversy. Many of the early 1930s movies were quite risqué. Some politicians and social activists protested the declining morality they claimed films were promoting. Under pressure, the movie industry instituted self-censorship as early as 1922 (the Motion Picture Producers and Distributors of America, Inc.). On the surface, the industry's capitulation might be seen as a victory for the moral crusaders. Beneath the surface, however, the movie production code became a vehicle for the majors and their allies to increase their control of the industry. The major studios dominated the Production Code and used it to deter entry by independents, who were trying to attract audiences by filming new and daring plot lines. Some industry observers felt the Production Code was a private government—but one without an "equal protection clause."[49]

Former postmaster of the United States, Will Hays, ran what became known as the Hays Office. The ostensible purpose of his office was to monitor and censor motion pictures; however, the office served a second, covert role. Hays organized the Association of Motion Picture Producers, which was charged with intervening in industrial relations. Stars received high salaries, although not as high as if they had been free agents, but the rank and file of Hollywood workers were worked hard and paid as little as possible. These workers began to form unions, and Hays's other office was charged with dealing with these issues.[50]

All of these methods of control gave the majors and their allies the ability to make it very difficult for an independent to screen his film. The federal government filed an antitrust suit against the five majors and two of the minors. United Artists was not one of the defendants. The government's case rested upon the allegation that the defendants controlled acting and technical personnel and only rarely lent them to independents. By the time of the trial, however, some of the defendants were increasing their lending of talent to the independents, as the majors and the two minors were cutting back on production. In addition, several of the studios rented their production facilities to independents. The evidence showed that the seven producer-defendants made a majority of features during World War II, although independent studios produced a large minority. The seven defendants and United Artists, though, made 80 percent of the A-quality pictures.[51]

The government failed to establish that the seven defendants monopolized the inputs of motion picture production. The defendants did not control the raw materials and machinery needed to produce movies. "Had there been effective combined control of supply at that level [production], much of the combination in distribution and exhibition would have been unnecessary. Monopoly power sufficient to control supply could be enforced only at the exhibition level when supplemented by the distribution combine. For this reason, the real barriers to independent producers were created in the marketing of films."[52]

The government did demonstrate that the majors controlled a large majority of first-run theaters in the largest cities. Of the 92 largest cities, only five did not have any theaters affiliated with the major circuits. In 38 cities, there were no independent first-run theaters, while in the remaining cities, there was rivalry between the majors' and independents' first-run theaters. The majors' first-run theaters rarely competed against one another. The owners had not purposely divided geographical territories, but they willingly maintained such divisions to forestall competition.[53]

The distributor-defendants were convicted of illegally combining in motion picture distribution but not in monopolizing inputs. Although several of the defendants did distribute promising independent films, their ownership of a large number of key theaters afforded them the ability to shut out independents. Even those independents who gained access to the defendants' theaters often paid a higher distribution fee and had to adhere to the Production Code.[54]

The eight defendants fixed admission prices. Any single theater that cut its admission price threatened the entire optimal price-discrimination scheme (charging different prices based on runs). "For example, admission prices from 60 cents to $1.00 were maintained for first-run evening performances [probably 1930s and 1940s]. Later-run prices ranged as low as 10 cents in last run.... The effect was to eliminate all price rivalry among theaters."[55]

Given the established system dictating run, clearance, zoning, and admission price, the only remaining factor for bargaining was the film rental, which helped keep bargaining costs low; the system also had the advantage that the number of prints of any given film could be kept low.[56] The two basic choices for setting film rentals—flat rate or a percentage of the gross admissions receipts—had drawbacks for either the exhibitor or the distributor. If the exhibitor paid a flat rate, he was assuming the risk of the film's popularity. From the distributor's point of view, a flat rate had one big advantage: there was no need to monitor the ticket receipts. Distributors paid significant sums checking theater receipts and admission records when percentage rentals were used. Despite this drawback, most distributors wanted exhibitors to pay on the basis of a percentage of gross revenue. The distributors used two independent firms to audit the gross admissions, as theater owners sometimes attempted to defraud distributors.[57]

The majors' and minors' actions came under antitrust scrutiny in the *Paramount* case, filed in 1938. The five majors were charged "with combining and conspiring to restrain trade unreasonably and to monopolize the production, distribution, and exhibition of motion pictures."[58]

The three minor defendants were "charged with combining with the five majors to restrain trade unreasonably and to monopolize commerce in motion pictures." The defendants used tactics to exclude or deter independents from screenings in first- and other run theaters. The lawsuit asked for the majors to divest themselves of their theaters, as well as other remedies. The five majors and the government agreed to a consent decree in which the government agreed not to force divestiture in return for a system of rules for bargaining and settling disputes; the system was similar to that used by the five majors under the National Recovery Act. In essence, the decree caused little change in the industry.[59]

The government again pursued the *Paramount* case in 1944 by requesting the District Court to modify the decree by forcing divestiture by the majors of their theater holdings. The three-judge court decreed that the distribution system violated the Sherman Act. A decree issued in December 1946 prohibited a variety of the majors' practices. On remand from the Supreme Court, RKO and Paramount agreed to divest some theaters from the circuits. The other six defendants awaited the court's final decision, filed on July 25, 1949. The court found that the defendants' actions violated Sections 1 and 2 of the Sherman Act and ordered divestiture, along with prohibiting block booking and other tactics, albeit allowing sufficient time for an orderly divestiture. The majors slowly and grudgingly obeyed. In some cases, they evaded the intent of the decree by shifting theaters to other family members.[60]

The divestiture decree allowed the majors to decide which theaters to sell; naturally, the defendants sold the least-desirable of their holdings. Conant suggests, "In retrospect, it would seem that the major theater circuits, by being forced to sell their weaker houses, gained more from their divestitures than they lost."[61]

The evidence for antitrust violations against the three minors was ambiguous. The minors may have been more sinned against than sinners, as they often had less bargaining power than the majors. Conant argues that the film boards of trade should have been named as defendants, since they were the vehicles allowing the majors to conclude agreements pertaining to runs, clearances, and prices at the local level. The failure to name the boards of trade as defendants meant that their records were not subpoenaed, forcing the government to make an argument based on circumstantial evidence. The board of trade records, subpoenaed in other cases, very clearly showed illegal action. Conant agrees with the court's decision mandating divorcement by producers and distributors of their theaters. However, he does not believe that the court should have ordered divorcement between *distributor and producer*, citing cost advantages of consolidated distribution due to the need to launch national marketing campaigns. He suggests, though, that the concentration of distributors would lead to greater monopoly power within the industry.[62]

Conant criticized the court's decrees because it did not break up the circuits of theaters into small enough units. In addition, the court's scrutiny was temporary, and the circuits could have arisen again. He thought the court should have forced the industry to use competitive bidding for films, but the Supreme Court rejected this solution.[63] Another possible remedy was to prohibit clearance that allowed for a gap between runs and to end exploiting price discrimination, which might have led to lower ticket prices.[64]

There may have been another motive for the court's ruling. The court, recognizing its limited understanding of the industry, may have hesitated to impose restrictions and changes that might inadvertently harm industrial efficiencies and render the industry worse off than before the divestiture. Such a possibility could have displeased millions of leisure-seeking Americans.[65]

Historian John Izod summarized the effects of the Supreme Court's decision on the industry. The majors opted to charge higher rental fees but needed to ensure that each "A" film delivered a sizable audience. The "B" picture gradually disappeared. In order to generate large crowds, especially in the face of competition from television, movies had to exhibit different characteristics from television programming. Producers began to shoot in color, on location, using 3-D, widescreen, and other innovations; plot lines gravitated to the spectacular and epic. Each individual film carried risk; in a sense, movie producers and professional sports team owners faced uncertainty in the quality or popularity of their output. Because the major studios were producing fewer films, they cut back on personnel. Independent producers picked up some of the slack; given that many actors, directors, and technicians ached for more freedom of expression, many new independent producers entered the market. In addition, the government's tax treatment encouraged independent production.[66]

After the war, changes in the audience dampened the demand for movies. The majors responded by reducing the number of films produced from 243 in 1940 to 116 by 1956. The court's prohibition on block booking helped the minors and the independents; the majors' theaters needed more movies from these sources, so block booking may have become irrelevant over time. Since theaters could now pick and choose among the movies offered by the majors, there might have been a presumption that overall quality improved. Exhibitors, though, found that negotiating for individual movies was too time-consuming and continued to buy films in groups.[67]

In terms of pricing, the decrees may not have benefited consumers much. Although distributor control of admission prices ended, most exhibitors hesitated to engage in price competition, lest they be relegated to a later run. The theaters that had been assigned late runs now were free to raise prices and exploit their local monopoly power. In the wake of the decrees, motion picture producers began charging higher film rentals, up to 70 percent of gross admissions, but they also guaranteed the exhibitor a 10 percent profit after expenses.[68]

Television, too, changed the economics of the movie industry. The movie industry eventually reached an accord with the new medium. The motion picture companies may have felt constrained in getting involved with television because of continued antitrust scrutiny.[69]

By the 1970s, although some of the eight majors and minors still existed and dominated the industry, they did so under parent companies. These parent companies were usually multinational corporations with diverse products. J. C. Strick believes that "it has been argued that the conglomerates have had positive effects on the industry such as adding stability . . . by providing financial backing to sustain production programs on a planned basis."[70]

## Television and Antitrust Confusion

The television industry, the dominant leisure-time activity by 1960, was shaped by government policies ranging from patent laws to licensing of stations. The federal government claimed ownership of the airwaves for both radio and television. It decided to apportion stations by licensing rather than through direct regulation controlling programming (similar to the British BBC model), which might have led to government interference with free speech. The Communications Act of 1934 listed three goals for broadcasting and, later, telecasting: promote competition, provide service for the entire country, and have as many local stations as possible. The government granted a license in return for the station owner's promise to program in the public interest of his community. Station owners who failed to promote the public interest could lose their licenses or face fines, although very few ever lost their licenses. In later years, economists would criticize the government's failure to auction off such licenses; by the 1990s, government officials finally started listening to economists and began auctioning licenses. The federal government reaped tens of billions of dollars from these auctions.[71]

Regulation, though, was no guarantee that consumers would fare well. The Federal Communications Commission (FCC) allowed television networks to own up to seven stations, of which up to five could be VHF stations, just like any other prospective owners. CBS, NBC, and ABC each owned five VHF stations located in the largest markets. The FCC's willingness to allow networks to own stations created a vertical structure for the industry. The vertical integration, in itself, need not have been baneful for consumers, if it resulted in more efficient operation.[72]

Barry Litman studied the television industry with respect to antitrust issues involved in the vertical integration of the networks. While the American broadcasting system was supposed to foster dissemination of news and information from as many sources as was possible, for over a quarter-century, three television networks dominated the industry and "have determined to a great extent what would flow through this important marketplace of ideas."[73]

Television network executives, many of whom had worked in the radio industry, were undoubtedly keenly aware of the volatility of mass entertainment industries. New technologies kept disrupting their well-developed oligopolies.
Economist Joseph Schumpeter famously wrote of the "gale of creative destruction" that frequently overturned the market power of incumbent firms. In order
to protect themselves, incumbent firms strove to prevent the entry of new firms,
continued to develop and patent new ideas to protect existing patents, and tied
one good with another. These endeavors clashed with the owners' goal: "They
want to lead the quiet life."[74]

An early threat to the networks' efforts to dominate television came from
Allen B. DuMont, who suggested that the FCC help develop powerful regional
stations via switching to an all-UHF system. Since the FCC, via its freeze on licenses, had virtually given monopoly power to the 108 early licensees, most of
whom had VHF stations, the UHF stations, with their limited transmitting
range, had difficulty competing. The FCC rejected DuMont's proposal and allowed CBS and NBC to solidify their dominance. Almost all television stations
were affiliated with one of the three networks, while a majority of radio stations
were unaffiliated.[75]

The rise of networks was probably inevitable. There were efficiencies arising
out of what economists call economies of scale. In other words, it was much
cheaper for multiple stations to share a program than for each station to produce
separate programming. The average costs would decline, assuming low intercon-
nection costs between stations. The other reason for industry concentration arose
out of the "public good" characteristic of television programs. The program's
quality was not affected by the number of people watching. If you watched an ep-
isode of the Public Broadcasting System's (PBS's) *Masterpiece Theater*, it did not
lessen the quality of my viewing. Stations and consumers gained from this aspect
of networking. A network also benefited producers and advertisers by acting as a
broker. The network connected programs with stations and with advertisers.[76]

The FCC's freeze on issuing licenses, though, had the unhappy effect of allowing two networks, CBS and NBC, to dominate television. The other two networks, DuMont and ABC, were barely able to survive. In recognition of these
networks' weakness and losses, the FCC urged the Justice Department to allow
ABC to merge with Paramount Pictures. DuMont exited the industry in 1955,
leaving two big players and ABC (the "third network"). Although this result was
hardly desirable and various committees criticized the outcome, no legislation
ensued to alter the situation.[77]

Most people believe that regulatory agencies such as the FCC worked to benefit the citizenry. In many, if not most, situations, though, the FCC often danced
cheek to cheek with the industries it regulated. The television networks lobbied
diligently to get favorable legislation or interpretation and implementation of

regulations. Many industries, from television to professional team sports, facing unfavorable regulations, testified that their industry would be in mortal peril should such regulations be implemented. Litman pointed out that the television networks fought hard to get the FCC to enact restrictions on cable television, slowing its diffusion by years and even decades.[78] The networks often complained, apparently without irony, of cable television's "unfair" advantages.

The regulatory agencies proved bumbling at times. When the FCC reduced "prime time" by 30 minutes each night, it inadvertently helped the networks and their affiliated stations. With fewer advertising spots available during prime time, advertisers began paying more money per spot, while the networks cut their costs of programming. No single network was likely to be the first to reduce their prime-time offerings (due to fears that the other networks might not follow suit), so the government's regulation imposed the necessary coordination and benefited the networks. "Time and again, the FCC, in its zeal to preserve the spirit of free enterprise, proved to be the best friend a network, and especially ABC, ever had."[79]

Even well-intentioned legislation backfired. President Lyndon Johnson pushed for legislation establishing the Public Broadcasting System, in response to a perceived lack of interest by the networks in public-service programming. The networks supported PBS, because it further absolved them of the responsibility to program generally low-rated educational and cultural programs. Because PBS was not directly supported by advertising dollars, it would not compete with the three networks.[80]

The networks' vertical structure gave them many advantages, and sparked conflicts of interest that did not satisfy the public interest. Because of network dominance, local affiliated stations usually cleared all of the network programs, regardless of quality or content. If a show was offensive to the vast majority of viewers in Poughkeepsie, New York (to take a whimsical example, since Poughkeepsie is a fun name), the affiliated station would have been hard pressed to substitute another show, given the nature of its contract with the network. The networks were, in essence, imposing a considerable uniformity upon programming. If a new show proved a hit, most viewers could anticipate that imitation shows would pop up on the rival networks. This imitation process was inimical to the FCC's stipulation that stations program in the public interest.[81]

One of Litman's more provocative assertions was his interpretation of the fact that "the percentage of households watching prime-time television remains virtually fixed . . . it suggests that television is the opiate of the masses, and their habits do not change regardless of quality." If this is true, then the networks did not need to upgrade quality: "the incentive lies in the other direction, to collude to downgrade quality. Therefore the networks were constrained to operate at highest profits during only five hours of the day, and this placed a second type of restriction on the number of advertising minutes available for sale."[82]

The networks also controlled the supply of minutes by agreeing to show only three minutes of advertising per half hour of programming; such a limitation on advertising pleased fans and placated government overseers, while benefiting the networks, who could now charge higher prices for advertising. In this, the television industry differed from most other industries, where vertical integration may create savings that are passed on to customers. In the television industry, the networks retained the savings instead of passing them on to the advertisers.[83]

The vertical integration of broadcasting and telecasting may have limited the diffusion of ideas. The networks chose their own made-for-TV movies instead of other programming. Given that there were only three networks for decades, the ability to shut out novel or threatening ideas was a barrier to the diffusion of ideas. At the time that Litman was writing his book, cable and pay television were still struggling to gain significant inroads into the television market. He noted that "cable, the medium of abundance, possesses none of the classic economic reasons for being regulated; yet this infant industry has been saddled with extremely rigid rules which could not help but deter entry."[84]

Donald Baker, deputy assistant attorney general, Antitrust Division, suggested that the viewing public desired cable television, if they could gain access, since cable and pay television promised to cater to specialized tastes; however, these industries had to fight unfavorable publicity promulgated by incumbent television networks: "cable television represents what has been alternatively described as 'the devil incarnate' or even more flamboyantly as 'a piranha tearing at the flesh of broadcasting.'"[85]

## Professional Team Sports' Antitrust Foul Balls

At first glance, the owners of professional sports teams would seem to be at a disadvantage relative to their leisure-industry peers in recorded music, motion pictures, radio, and television. The sports owners had no protection via patent rights. They had to, instead, create their own protection from competition. They did so by forming leagues that had collusive aspects.

William Hulbert's creation of the National League in 1876 had antitrust implications, although the Sherman Act was still years off.[86] The baseball league afforded territorial protection for the owners in the sense that other league owners could not encroach upon an owner's territory. Although it is understandable that owners would not want the internal squabbling resulting from invading each other's territory, when owners began to interpret the territorial protection as restricting any potential owners, even those in other leagues, from a league member's territory, the antitrust issues arose.

By assuming territorial protection, owners gained price-setting power (the ability to set price as opposed to price taking, where the market determines the price) over ticket prices. With price-setting power, an owner could charge a price above the competitive-market price.

The owners chronically complained of player salaries, even when such salaries comprised less than 20 percent of a team's expenses during the mid-1950s. By the early 1880s, baseball owners implemented a reserve clause, tying a player to the team unless traded, sold, or released. The reserve clause gave an owner disproportionate leverage over the player in negotiating salaries and resulted in player salaries below what a competitive market would have paid. Baseball owners interpreted the reserve clause to be perpetual, lasting for the player's entire professional career. The Clayton Act exempted labor unions from antitrust. Because the players formed unions, legal observers suggested that the way to resolve disputes over rights to players' labor was via negotiation. Baseball players gained limited free agency in the 1970s, and players in the other leagues eventually won similar rights.[87] Even motion picture moguls limited their control over actors to just seven years. Although these controls suppressed their salaries, baseball players and motion picture stars still made incomes well above those of average Americans. Despite their higher incomes, though, these highly talented performers were likely to be among the most exploited workers in America, in terms of the proportional difference between their actual salaries and potential free-market salaries.

With the territorial protection offering monopoly power within each owner's city and the reserve clause enhancing bargaining power over players, professional sports team owners had to be inept not to earn profits, as long as the demand for their games remained adequate. Few business owners have had the same advantages as the owners of sports teams.

Incumbent owners loathed newcomers. New leagues posed dual threats to their cozy arrangements. New leagues often placed teams in the largest cities, New York and Chicago, thereby offering fans new choices for entertainment. New teams also meant increased competition for players, resulting in rising salaries. Whether it was the threat of the Federal (Baseball) League, the All-America Football League, the American Football League, or the American Basketball Association, the incumbent leagues fought hard and sometimes dirty to squelch the newcomers (notwithstanding the fact that the American League and National Basketball Association were once interlopers).

Major league baseball (MLB) owners owned stadiums, controlled large numbers of players, and maintained alliances with teams in the minor leagues. These barriers to entry made it difficult for an upstart league, such as the Federal League, to gain playing venues, well-known players, and fan support. The Federal League (1913–1915) raided existing teams' rosters with mixed success. The

Federal League owners hurriedly built some ballparks, including Chicago's famed Wrigley Field. The league ultimately failed after two seasons, although some of its owners were allowed to purchase shares of National and American League franchises. One Federal League franchise, though, refused to go quietly into oblivion. The Baltimore team filed a lawsuit against MLB. The Supreme Court eventually ruled that MLB was not commerce. Many subsequent commentators have professed bemusement at the Court's decision, but a few writers have pointed out that the ruling was in line with the conservatism of the era, as exemplified by the E. C. Knight case and previous baseball cases adjudicated at the state level.[88] With the advent of radio broadcasts and telecasts of ball games across state lines, the argument that baseball was not commerce became ever more dubious.

The National Football League (NFL) proved successful in getting partial antitrust exemptions for certain of their television policies, including local blackouts of telecasts of home games and the ability to negotiate national TV contracts; the partial exemptions extended to the other professional team sports, too. When the American Football League (AFL) would not disappear, in large part due to the league's national TV contract with ABC, NFL owners negotiated with their AFL counterparts to effect a merger. Such a merger would normally run afoul of antitrust laws, so the owners petitioned congressional legislators to enact a bill permitting such a merger.

The Senate passed the NFL-AFL merger with little consideration. The House committee on Antitrust Subcommittee of the Committee on the Judiciary held hearings in 1966. Committee chairman Emanuel Celler of Brooklyn was skeptical about the propriety of the merger, based on his previous experiences with professional team sports. He noted that the AFL owners had unsuccessfully sued the NFL for antitrust violations, but now those owners wanted to join the NFL.[89]

Football team owners argued that without a merger, owners of financially weaker teams would go out of business due to those pesky player salaries. Because there were teams in each league holding draft rights to individual players, the owners had engaged in a spirited bidding war for top collegiate talent. The graduating seniors benefited from the competition. Team owners and sportswriters also argued that fans wanted to see a championship game between the two leagues' best teams. Some legislators pointed out that a merger was not necessary to establish such a championship game. When the House subcommittee hesitated to recommend approval of the merger, professional football enlisted the help of Louisiana legislator Hale Boggs, who shepherded the bill as a rider on a popular tax bill, in return for NFL commissioner Pete Rozelle's promise that New Orleans would get a franchise.[90]

The American Basketball Association (ABA) and National Basketball Association (NBA) owners also decided to end their internecine struggle and accompanying bidding war for talented college seniors by seeking a merger. These owners justifiably felt confident that legislators would approve their proposed merger, given football owners' successful attempt in 1966. This time, however, both the House and the Senate held hearings. The legislators chided ABA owners for seeking a merger with the NBA, since the ABA owners had sued the NBA for antitrust violations. The legislators were more skeptical than in 1966, because NFL owners used their merger agreement to forestall expansion, to sign contracts with all three major television networks, and to continue their abuse of player rights. The legislators agreed to the basketball merger but with stipulations, including loosening the reserve and option clauses to allow a semblance of free agency. The ABA and NBA owners disliked the stipulations and refused the legislation. The NBA eventually absorbed four ABA teams.[91]

The specter of pay television haunted many people in the 1950s, when the technology first became viable. Congressional hearings into professional team sports focused on the possibility of pay television replacing network (free) television. A coalition of broadcast, telecasters, advertisers, legislators, and fans wrung their hands over this potential development.[92] Cable and pay television allowed sports fans many more opportunities to watch their favorite team, albeit sometimes with pay-per-view or monthly charges.

## Are Mass Entertainments Antitrust Abusers?

Americans enjoyed mass entertainment; they seemed to care little about how such entertainment was provided. They did not appear unduly upset that such entertainment often occurred under conditions of market concentration, but antitrust regulators did care. The major movie studios, radio and television networks, and sports leagues frequently ran afoul of antitrust laws. Legislators and jurists, though, hesitated in prohibiting many of these industries' questionable practices, fearing that by doing so, consumers would be worse off.

Until cable television revealed the benefits from a fragmented market for programming, many Americans may not have worried about the limited choices that television networks offered during primetime or the constricted numbers of big league sports teams. They may, indeed, have deemed the national audience for a particular radio or television show to be a benefit: the next day, most Americans could share their collective experience of watching *I Love Lucy* or *Gunsmoke* the night before.[93]

Few Americans, too, wrung their hands over the exploitation of actors and ballplayers, who performed under a rigged market. Americans wanted their games and programming to continue without interruption.

# Epilogue
## More Leisure, Better Leisure, Cheaper Leisure

Given that the rich have always had their leisure time, the workers' gain in leisure time during the twentieth-century American experience was a triumph. The rise of leisure was a triumph shared by Europeans and some other countries around the world, but many workers in other countries did not enjoy such gains.

A comparison between leisure opportunities for working-class Americans in 1900 and those of 2000 is stark. Assuming a working-class male of 1900 had a job, he worked 9 or 10 hours per weekday and some hours on Saturday. On his time off, he might stop in for a drink at the local saloon. He might make an occasional trip to a theater. Within a few years, nickelodeons provided competition for his nickel beer. Now he could watch short, often plotless, motion pictures in a converted storefront. He could even bring his wife and children.

By 1930, working-class Americans were attending motion pictures on a frequent basis. The theaters were far more comfortable, and the quality of the movies, not only with regard to technical quality but with respect to acting and storyline, was vastly improved. Indeed, Americans could now hear Greta Garbo talk, as the famous advertisement boasted. If a worker wasn't interested in or had tired of motion pictures, automobile and radio ownership were percolating down the income strata and provided a myriad of leisure options. As producers became more efficient in producing them, these commodities often gradually required the worker to sacrifice fewer hours' earnings to obtain them.

Americans now had weekends off, and a growing number enjoyed paid vacations. Americans were enjoying longer and healthier lives. Retirement transformed from being a quiet, playing-out-the-string endeavor to being devoutly desired. The baby boomers will undoubtedly reshape retirement in their own inimitable way.

Seventy years later, American workers enjoyed television, compact discs, DVDs, Internet, cell phones, and many other gadgets, courtesy of risk-taking, profit-seeking entrepreneurs and inventors. Americans could listen to a mind-boggling array of musicians from the famous to the obscure. Many of them could listen not only at home but at their workplace, in their automobiles, and at the beach. Leisure activities invaded workplaces and became portable. Americans could watch Peyton Manning, LeBron James, Albert Pujols, and other top athletes perform, even if they lived hundreds of miles from the nearest big league team.

Despite the cornucopia of leisure options facing Americans at the turn of the millennium, some people expressed fears similar to those voiced throughout the twentieth century. *Business Week* published a survey of the theme park, casino, sports, and interactive television industries in 1994 that it labeled "America's Growth Engines." The publication included a commentary by Mark Landler. Landler fretted about the burgeoning gambling industry, whose tentacles were just about to enter the home through interactive television and computers. He acknowledged that the gaming industry could create hundreds of thousands of jobs, which he characterized as low paying. He wondered about the ramifications of Americans spending more on entertainment and recreation in 1993 than public and private spending on elementary and secondary education and also on their tumbling savings rate (which had halved between 1980 and 1993).[1]

American workers gained new freedoms, although these often revolved around work. According to an article in *USA Today*, most workers had the opportunity of telecommuting by 2011. Telecommuting held the promise of alleviating, to some degree, traffic congestion and saving workers commuting time. Workers also gained the freedom to wear more casual clothes. Although the American Movie Channel's hit *Mad Men*, a show about Madison Avenue advertising executives in the 1960s, depicts a culture of suits and dresses, a contemporary version of *Mad Men* might display polo shirts and khakis for both men and women.[2]

## New Concerns about Leisure and Recreational Activities

As the twentieth century ended, concerns about leisure activities changed. With the greater popularity of national parks and wilderness, Americans confronted over-crowding and pollution. Jet and car travel for recreational purposes added to pollution. A quick Google search reveals articles debating whether jet plane pollution is serious or not so serious.[3]

Leisure activities can sometimes work to protect the environment. Samuel Hays chronicles American's changing attitudes toward the environment. Leisure

activities affect people's attitudes. He points out that the growing interest in hunting and fishing inspired more Americans to consider how to preserve enough wilderness to maintain a sustainable yield of game. The sportspeople's desires for
using the wilderness has often clashed with lumber and mining interests. "The
search for environmental quality was an integral part of this rising standard of
living. Environmental values were based not on one's role as a producer of goods
and services but on consumption, the quality of home and leisure. Such environmental concerns were not prevalent at earlier times. But after World War II, rising
standards of living led more people to desire qualitative experiences as well as
material goods in their lives."[4]

The Hetch Hetchy water project, for instance, became an issue between the
few wealthy sportsmen who could travel to the Hetch Hetchy Valley and the potentially millions of Californians needing cheap water and power. But even leisure users of wilderness areas have clashed, as some sought peace and solitude,
while others opted for more noisy activities such as snowmobiling or motor
boating.[5]

## Leisure as a Reflection of American Economic Growth

Americans have long felt ambivalent about leisure. They worried about its effects
on personal salvation or about the effects of leisure activities on other people. If
Americans have not devoted their discretionary time to contemplation in an Aristotelian manner, at least they have more opportunity to do so than Americans
in the past. Even so, more than many people in other developed countries,
Americans choose to use some of their discretionary time participating in religious activities; perhaps religious services are their times for reflection and
contemplation.

The glory of American economic growth is that Americans enjoy more discretionary time than in the past and greater financial ability to employ such
discretionary time in enjoyable, even carefree ways. No longer living at subsistence levels, few Americans today have to worry that an hour spent in leisure
means less food on the table and deprivation. Modern Americans rarely need to
spend time worrying about assuaging their children's chronic cries of hunger or
their children's death from mysterious diseases, as all too many parents did in
the past and even do today in other parts of the world. Fewer Americans today
than in the past have to worry that a moment daydreaming will result in their
maiming or death from machinery in the workplace, or that their working conditions will reduce their longevity. Although Americans may chafe at working
for a boss, they are not slaves, as in Aristotle's time. Their discretionary time is
voluntarily sold.

Even poorer Americans have a wider range of leisure activities to choose from and often much greater amounts of disposable income with which to purchase leisure goods and services than even in the recent past. Americans with little disposable income can still hear classical music played by virtuoso musicians and can see supremely talented actors on television and at the motion picture theaters. They have access to reading material and can watch top athletes.

Many older Americans now enjoy years of discretionary time in retirement. Older people in many cultures reap veneration, but they may be an economic drain for their families; with prudence and/or good fortune, older Americans can enjoy their retirement, with little concern that they are burdening their children with their upkeep and care. Older Americans today are also generally blessed with better health, so they are more likely to enjoy years of active retirement.

The twentieth century marked a transformation in American society in many ways, but the widespread diffusion of leisure time and consumption ranks high among the country's economic achievements. Our ancestors would marvel at our lives. Indeed, today's grandparents may have regaled their children and grandchildren about how difficult their lives were in the 1950s. Barring unforeseen economic, political, or environmental catastrophes, our descendants are likely to enjoy even greater levels of material comfort and more time to pursue contemplation, if they choose to contemplate. I suspect and hope that our descendants will be in the enviable position of looking back at twentieth-century America and thinking how tough our lives were.

# CITATIONS

*Prelims*

1. Marshall, *Principles of Economics*, 1.
2. See Hutchison, *Religious Pluralism in America*, 4.
3. *Discover Magazine*, 2008, http://blogs.discovermagazine.com/gnxp/2008/05/religion-pub-lic-attitudes-europe-vs-usa/.
4. Etzioni, "A Crisis of Consumerism," 155–162.
5. Weber, *Protestant Ethic*, 85.
6. Weber, *Protestant Ethic*, 95.
7. Weber, *Protestant Ethic*, 100.
8. Weber, *Protestant Ethic*, 101.
9. Quoted in Weber, *Protestant Ethic*, 116.
10. Weber, *Protestant Ethic*, 125; emphasis in the original.
11. Weber, *Protestant Ethic*, 127.
12. Weber, *Protestant Ethic*, 132.
13. Weber, *Protestant Ethic*, 161.
14. Weber, *Protestant Ethic*, 159.
15. Weber, *Protestant Ethic*, 163–164; Weber's emphasis.
16. Weber, *Protestant Ethic*, 164.
17. Weber, *Protestant Ethic*, 173.
18. Weber, *Protestant Ethic*, 172–173; Weber's emphasis.
19. Wesley, *Free Grace*, 6–7.
20. Veblen, *Instinct of Workmanship*, 6.
21. Veblen, *Theory of the Leisure Class*, 15.
22. Veblen, *Theory of the Leisure Class*, 110.
23. Veblen, *Theory of the Leisure Class*, 14.
24. Veblen, *Instinct of Workmanship*, 183–184.
25. Veblen, *Theory of the Leisure Class*, 231–232.
26. Veblen, *Theory of the Leisure Class*, 36.
27. Veblen, *Theory of the Leisure Class*, 43.
28. Veblen, *Theory of the Leisure Class*, 84.
29. Veblen, *Theory of the Leisure Class*, 85.
30. Veblen, *Place of Science in Modern Civilization*, 391.
31. Veblen, *Theory of the Leisure Class*, 32.
32. Marshall, *Principles of Economics*, 3.

## Introduction

1. GDP is now more widely used than GNP, but during most of the period discussed in this book, GNP was used.
2. Table 1.3 shows only from 1900 to 1969, because later *Statistical Abstracts* appear to use a different set of figures.
3. *Listen to the Story*, "Trillions Earned under Table as More Work Off Radar," http://www.npr.org/2013/03/26/175361658/trillions-earned-under-table-as-more-work-off-radar.
4. Fogel, *Political Arithmetic*, 5.
5. Gendell and Siegel, "Trends in Retirement Ages," 23.
6. *Wall Street Journal*, "Americans, Especially Baby Boomers, Voice Pessimism for Their Kids' Economic Future," A14. Politicians like to tell voters that the current and future generations of young Americans may not attain the same living standards as their parents. Creating fear and anger can help politicians, as long as they can deflect any blame upon themselves. The long-term trends in leisure belie such claims.
7. Ernst Engel discovered this tendency for expenditures on food to increase less rapidly than increases in incomes; economists now denote it as Engel's Law.

## Chapter 1

1. De Grazia, *Time, Work, and Leisure*, 31. Greek slavery differed in many ways from slavery in the United States; the former version limited the masters' rights to physically abuse slaves. Many Greek slaves were obtained through warfare.
2. De Grazia, *Time, Work, and Leisure*, 388.
3. De Grazia, *Time, Work, and Leisure*, 15, see also 13–14. John Owen also highlights Aristotle's delineation of leisure and amusement, but he points out that many recent commentators dispute Aristotle's belief that amusement is not leisure (Owen, *Price of Leisure*, 3).
4. De Grazia, *Time, Work, and Leisure*, 15–16.
5. De Grazia, *Time, Work, and Leisure*, 8.
6. Dumazedier, *Sociology of Leisure*, 71.
7. De Grazia, *Time, Work, and Leisure*, 91, 246.
8. De Grazia, *Time, Work, and Leisure*, 134, 274. By de Grazia's reckoning, some of the males in the Plains tribes had copious amounts of free time. For them, much or most of the day was devoted to hunting, raiding, conversing with friends, or other activities. Agricultural labor was not a male's métier (de Grazia, *Time, Work, and Leisure*, 249). Denys Harding also expressed the residual concept during the 1930s (Harding, "Varieties of Work and Leisure," 104).
9. Currell, *March of Spare Time*, 187.
10. Jones, *Workers at Play*, 116.
11. McTell's lyrics can be found at http://www.metrolyrics/stranger-to-the-season-lyrics-ralph-mctell, viewed May 4, 2013, 9:33 a.m.
12. De Grazia, *Time, Work, and Leisure*, 91, 327.
13. De Grazia, *Time, Work, and Leisure*, 63.
14. Kaplan, *Leisure in America*, 36.
15. Kaplan, *Leisure in America*, 22, 33, 43.
16. Huizinga, *Homo Ludens*, 9–10 and Foreword, no page number.
17. Huizinga, *Homo Ludens*, 18–19.
18. Huizinga, *Homo Ludens*, 132.
19. Huizinga, *Homo Ludens*, 43.
20. Pieper, *Leisure: The Basis of Culture*, 45.
21. Pieper, *Leisure: The Basis of Culture*, 56.
22. Huizinga, *Homo Ludens*, 148.
23. Lundberg, et al., *Leisure: A Suburban Study*, 19.
24. De Grazia, *Time, Work, and Leisure*, 19.
25. Pieper, *Leisure: The Basis of Culture*, 22, see also 20. De Grazia did not resolve whether children attending school should be counted as going to work or engaging in leisure; instead he

consciously drops the problem by leaving youth under 20 from the discussion (De Grazia, *Time, Work, and Leisure*, 67).

26. Pieper, *Leisure: The Basis of Culture*, 42.
27. Schultz, *Investment in Human Capital*, 82–83.
28. Denney, *Astonished Muse*, 11.
29. Wilensky, "Orderly Careers and Social Participation," 522.
30. Wilensky, "Orderly Careers," 532; Rojek, *Labour of Leisure*, 27. Rojek notes that the accumulation of emotional intelligence and the management of emotional labor blur the distinction between work and leisure. "Leisure and emotional intelligence go hand in hand, which acutely compromises traditional connotations of 'free time' and 'time off' in the literature on leisure forms and practice."
31. Mannell and Iso-Ahola, "Work Constraints on Leisure," 160; see also Stebbins, *Serious Leisure: A Perspective for Our Time*, 4; Wade, "Preface," *Constraints on Leisure*, ix.
32. Thompson, "Time, Work Discipline and Industrial Capitalism," 90–91.
33. Rojek, *Labour of Leisure*, 2.
34. Rojek, *Labour of Leisure*, 4.
35. Rojek, *Labour of Leisure*, 4.
36. Roberts, *Leisure Industries*, 4–5.
37. Roberts, *Leisure Industries*, 5–6.
38. Owen, *Price of Leisure*, 5–6.

## Chapter 2

1. Matthew, vi:26 and 28, King James version.
2. De Grazia, *Time, Work, and Leisure*, 26.
3. De Grazia, *Time, Work, and Leisure*, 31.
4. Pieper, *Leisure: The Basis of Culture*, 35.
5. De Grazia, *Time, Work, and Leisure*, 45.
6. De Grazia, *Of Time, Work and Leisure*, 47.
7. Weber, *Protestant Ethic*, 24, Routledge Edition.
8. http://www.quotationspage.com/quote/117.html.
9. Miller, *New England Mind*, 40–41; Daniels, *Puritans at Play*, 7.
10. Morgan, *Puritan Family*, 16; see Daniels, *Puritans at Play*, 8. Before wags suggest that Daniels' book is full of empty pages or is the world's briefest book, let's remember that the Pilgrims, at least, had a day of celebration.
11. Rutman, "The Mirror of Puritan Authority," 149, 164; see also Daniels assessment of Rutman's work, *Puritans at Play*, 9–10.
12. Daniels, *Puritans at Play*, 93 and 105, see also 218.
13. Daniels, *Puritans at Play*, 218, see also xii.
14. Daniels, *Puritans at Play*, 120–121.
15. Daniels, *Puritans at Play*, quote on 181, see also 83, 143, 151–153, 176–178.
16. Daniel, *Puritans at Play*, 165, 167; see 52 and 67 for discussion of elaborate music and theater.
17. Daniels, *Puritans at Play*, 76. It is jarring to consider sermons as the first mass entertainment in America.
18. Daniels, *Puritans at Play*, 221.
19. Butsch, *Making of American Audiences*, 100.
20. Steiner, *Americans at Play*, 2–3, 6.
21. Steiner, *Americans at Play*, 6.
22. De Grazia, *Time, Work, and Leisure*, 283.
23. Brown, *Life Against Death*, 16, 33. John Stuart Mill hoped that industrial progress would produce more than mere wealth but also an abridgment of labor (Mill, *Principles of Political Economy*, 751).
24. Kirsch, *History of the End of the World*, 193. Fortunately, the Fundamentalists did not have access to a time machine, so they could view early twenty-first-century recreation. Think of their conniptions.
25. Gutman, "Protestantism and the American Labor Movement," 88–89.

26. Gutman, "Protestantism," 113–114.
27. Aron, *Working at Play*, 36.
28. Aron, *Working at Play*, 37.
29. Aron, *Working at Play*, 39; see 40 for a discussion of Henry Ward Beecher's changing attitudes toward vacations.
30. Dulles, *America Learns to Play*, 288.
31. Dulles, *America Learns to Play*, ix.
32. Ramsaye, *Million and One Nights*, 259; Dulles, *America Learns to Play*, 290.
33. Surdam, *Wins, Losses, & Empty Seats*, 188–193.
34. Borsay, *History of Leisure*, quote on 81, see also 97–98.
35. Aiken, "A Laborer's Leisure," 272–273. Modern readers might ask if robotics can displace human labor, what will the unemployed do in 2050 and how will they subsist? Allport worried that without work, people would become "like children" (Allport, "This Coming Era of Leisure," 642–651).
36. Chase, "Play," 347. Chase deplored the "thrills, excitement and intense stimulation of prize fights, ball games, race courses, roller coasters, tabloid murder stories, gambling, gin, and 'torrid screen dramas of sexy souls.'"
37. Borsodi, *This Ugly Civilization*, 16–17.
38. Chase, *Men and Machines*, 256.
39. Chase, "Play," 335.
40. Currell, *March of Spare Time*, 22–23.
41. Nash, *Spectatoritis*, 4.
42. Nash, *Spectatoritis*, 88, 98.
43. Nash, *Spectatoritis*, 63, 221–222.
44. Kaplan, *Leisure in America*, 301–302.
45. Kaplan, *Leisure in America*, 297.
46. Kaplan, *Leisure in America*, 295
47. Kaplan, *Leisure in America*, 246.
48. Kaplan, *Leisure in America*, 293.
49. Kaplan, *Leisure in America*, 155.
50. Kerr, *The Decline of Pleasure*, 39–40.
51. Wilson, "Happy Idle Hours," 120–121, 123.
52. Havemann, "The Task Ahead: How to Take Life Easy," 92.
53. Havemann, "Task Ahead," 93. Norman Brown worried: "There is no country and no people, who can look forward to the age of leisure and abundance without a dread" (Brown, *Life Against Death*, first quote 36).
54. Riesman, *Lonely Crowd*, 74–75, 96–98, 116–123; see also Hunnicutt, *Work Without End*, 45.
55. Illich, *Toward a History of Needs*, 11.
56. Fromm, *Sane Society*, 136.
57. Pack, *Challenge of Leisure*, 64–66.
58. Wyrwa, "Consumption and Consumer Society," 436–437. Chris Rojek, too, discusses "positional goods" whereby one person's enjoyment of a good deprives someone else's ability to enjoy the good. The scarcity of, say, a highly popular concert in a small venue confers great status upon the ticket holders. He concludes, "However egalitarian a society becomes there will always be a ranking of positional goods that conveys high prestige to those who are able to enjoy them" (Rojek, *Labour of Leisure*, 17).
59. Lobsenz, "Pleasure Neurotics," 38. Margaret Mead argued that Americans believed "leisure should be earned before it is enjoyed. The function of recreation is to prepare man for further work" (Mead, "Pattern of Leisure in Contemporary American Culture," 11–15). See also O'Connor, *Leisure Wasters*, 15–16, 44.
60. Kreps, *Lifetime Allocation of Work and Income*, 20.
61. Barzun, *God's Country and Mine*, 38.
62. Barzun, *God's Country*, 88.
63. Roberts, *Leisure Industries*, 18–19.
64. Sowell, *Ethnic America*, 286.
65. Rojek, *Labour of Leisure*, 79.

66. Marcuse, *Essay on Liberation*, 13, see also 20.
67. Rojek, *Labour of Leisure*, 80.
68. Roberts, *Leisure Industries*, 159.
69. Roberts, *Leisure Industries*, 128–130, 160–162.
70. Rojek, *Labour of Leisure*, 29–30. See 32 and 40 for a discussion of the evolution of leisure studies.
71. Rojek, *Labour of Leisure*, 72.
72. Rojek, *Labour of Leisure*, 44.
73. Rojek, *Labour of Leisure*, 45.
74. Rojek, *Labour of Leisure*, 136–137.
75. Rojek, *Labour of Leisure*, 49–52, 69–70.
76. Rojek, *Labour of Leisure*, 73.
77. Rojek, *Labour of Leisure*, 165. In the movie *Battleground*, the young replacement soldier eschews cigarettes at first, but lights up after a fire-fight; he ignored Hitler's campaign against smoking, although the US government supplied cigarettes to the troops.
78. Rojek, *Labour of Leisure*, 112.
79. Rojek, *Labour of Leisure*, 91.
80. Rojek, *Labour of Leisure*, 181.
81. Rojek, *Labour of Leisure*, 189.
82. Zuzanek, "The Work Ethic: What Are We Measuring?" 675.
83. Club of Rome, *Limits to Growth*, 175; see also Hunnicutt, "Economic Constraints," 259–260, 265, 270–271, 276.

## Chapter 3

1. Kuznets, *Modern Economic Growth*, 58; see also his Nobel Prize address, "Modern Economic Growth."
2. Simon, *Ultimate Resource*, 9–10.
3. Researchers in the 1950s identified changes in technology as being responsible for much of per capita growth (Solow, "Contribution to the Theory of Economic Growth," 65–94).
4. Johnson, "Agriculture and the Wealth of Nations," 1–12.
5. Cain and Hong, "Survival in 19th Century Cities," 451, 461–462; Floud et al., *Changing Body*, 325.
6. Floud et al., *Changing Body*, 28, see also 22, 31, 125–126, 129. Late eighteenth-century France's lack of caloric production left many people unable to do much more than beg in the streets, as they lacked the energy to work. Economic growth has also allowed people to undertake energy-intensive leisure-time activities: "The great technological advances since 1700 have not freed humankind from toil; today, we toil not just out of necessity, but out of choice, and largely in activities we relish" (Floud et al., *Changing Body*, 76–77).
7. Floud et al., *Changing Body*, 41, see also 43.
8. Floud et al., *Changing Body*, 129–130.
9. Rosen, *History of Public Health*, 381, 390. Eventually the US Department of Agriculture began establishing guidelines and the infamous food pyramids that those of us who attended elementary school during the 1960s can recall.
10. Floud et al., *Changing Body*, 317.
11. Floud et al., *Changing Body*, 298, 326. Joel Mokyr and Rebecca Stein argue that technological progress at the household level was a major contributor to declining mortality rates (Mokyr and Stein, "Science, Health, and Household Technology," 145).
12. Kuznets, *Modern Economic Growth*, 57. Greenwood, Seshadri, and Vandenbroucke cite improvements in household technology for creating the conditions underlying the Baby Boom of 1946–1964 (Greenwood, Seshadri, and Vandenbroucke, "Baby Boom and Baby Bust," 197, 205).
13. Stanley Jevons recognized that people worked in order to afford consumption and that work, although possibly enjoyable in moderate doses, eventually became onerous (Jevons, *The Theory of Political Economic*, 5th ed., 167–169).

14. In equilibrium, people equate the marginal utility of an hour of leisure to the sum of the marginal utility of an hour of work and the marginal utility of the income earned. This formulation does not need to assume that the marginal utility of leisure and the marginal utility of leisure be either positive or negative, so it allows for people to love or hate either (or both) their work or their leisure (Owen, *Price of Leisure*, 7).

15. Although Thoreau "opposed luxuriousness and materialism, in some ways he was anything but puritanical. Walden rejected the Protestant virtues of hard work, steadfast habits, moderate comfort, and restrained feelings and opted instead for intense pleasures achieved not though material comforts but through transcendence" (Horowitz, *The Morality of Spending*, 5). Kleiber and Dirkin suggest that some people may be "leisure addicts" or "workaholics" or somewhere in between (Kleiber and Dirkin, "Interpersonal Constraints," 17–19, 23, 25–26; see also Iso-Ahola and Mannell, "Social and Psychological Constraints on Leisure," 112–143).

16. Kleiber and Dirkin, "Intrapersonal Constraints," 38. The author personifies Kleiber and Dirkin's observations. Why a boy, small in size relative to his classmates, would choose basketball as his favorite sport had much to do with an older brother, who was a star player on the high school team.

17. Owen, *Price of Leisure*, 36. Owen found support for the thesis that, "the neglect of the fatigue factor . . . tends to obscure the role of other factors, such as the price of recreation, in the determination of the work week" (Owen, *Price of Leisure*, 111).

18. One can adjust this for after-tax, take-home wage. Such an insight, though, raises questions about the opportunity cost of leisure for people who are retired or unable to work. Here one could use an alternative use of time as an implicit cost—two hours of television means giving up two hours of playing bridge.

19. Owen, *Price of Leisure*, 37.

20. Owen, *Price of Leisure*, 37.

21. Rapoport and Rapoport, *Leisure and the Family Life Cycle*, 16, 27.

22. Maslow, "A Theory of Human Motivation," 370–396. Economists have applied the individual choice model to addiction, using the insight that people choosing behavior that may end up becoming addictive believe that the immediate gains outweigh the long-term losses (Becker and Murphy, "Theory of Rational Addiction," 694–695). Other economists have studied how individuals respond to "status goods."

23. Becker, *Treatise on the Family*, 4–9; Becker, "Theory of the Allocation of Time," 493–517.

24. Michael Grossman adapted Becker's model to address health issues. One of his key insights was the importance of health capital and the demand for health (Grossman, "On the Concept of Health Capital and the Demand for Health," 224–226, 247). Theodore W. Schultz made this connection clear, too: "The additional health capital . . . tend[s] to increase the productivity of workers. . . . Better health and vitality in turn lead to more productivity per man-hour at work" (Schultz, *Investing in People*, 14).

25. Owen, *Price of Leisure*, 72–73.

26. Lebergott, *American Economy*, 90–91.

27. Owen, *Price of Leisure*, 13. British economist M. A. Bienefeld uses the example of workers wanting Saturday afternoons off, so they could attend football matches; employers acquiesced and granted the five-and-a-half-day workweek (Bienefeld, "Normal Week under Collective Bargaining," 188). Another institution affecting workers' choices of weekly hours is fringe benefits. From the employer's perspective, fringe benefits are a large, fixed cost of hiring a particular worker (Bienefeld, "Normal Week," 189).

28. Hunnicutt, "Economic Constraints on Leisure," 253; Owen, *Price of Leisure*, 1969. Since longevity has only roughly doubled, as compared to a much greater proportional increase in productivity, the shift toward using goods and services in the production of leisure and recreational activities should not be surprising.

29. Ram and Schultz, "Life Span, Health, Savings, and Productivity," 402, 409.

30. Schultz, *Investing in People*, 14.

31. Owen, *Price of Leisure*, 45.

32. Owen, *Price of Leisure*, 45, footnote 38.

33. Owen, *Price of Leisure*, 46–47. Owen suggests that analyzing the labor-leisure trade-off in the short run, such as for the upcoming week or year, is affected by preferences across the long run (Owen, *Price of Leisure*, 8–9).

34. Kreps, *Lifetime Allocation*, 76–77. Per capita income rose much faster than did years of longevity across the twentieth century. We now have relatively more consumption than leisure.

35. Linder, *Harried Leisure Class*, 8–9.

36. Linder, *Harried Leisure Class*, 10.

37. Linder, *Harried Leisure Class*, 5, 7, 77, 79, 94–95, 97, 126–127.

38. Linder, *Harried Leisure Class*, 54, 144.

39. Linder, *Harried Leisure Class*, 18. On a less exalted level, Owen found that while eating and sleeping were less important for Americans than for people in other cultures, unemployed people spent more time eating and sleeping than working Americans and housewives, with one exception: white-collar men spent more time eating than unemployed men (Owen, *Price of Leisure*, 5).

40. Linder, *Harried Leisure Class*, 47. This is not a modern phenomenon: Europeans remarked on how fast Americans ate, especially with respect to rail and stagecoach travelers.

41. Biddle and Hamermesh found that, contrary to the Protestant work ethic, Protestants slept longer (Biddle and Hamermesh, "Sleep and the Allocation of Time," 922–943, Protestant/Catholic differences found on 927).

42. Keynes, "Economic Possibilities for Our Grandchildren," 364–365.

43. Gordon, "Why Innovation Won't Save Us," no pagination.

## Chapter 4

1. Roediger and Foner, *Our Own Time*, vii–viii, 31, 184–185; Lebergott, *Americans: An Economic Record*, 68–69.

2. John Owen presented estimated hours of work per week for 1901, 1929, and 1956. He adjusted the 1956 estimate for paid vacations and holidays. The hours of work fell from 58.4 in 1901 to 48.7 in 1929 and 41.9 in 1956. While the reduction slowed down between 1929 and 1956, the increase in real hourly wages accelerated. He estimated that the relative price of recreation fell sharply between 1901 and 1929 and only modestly between 1929 and 1956 (Owen, *Price of Leisure*, 76–77).

3. Robert Fogel suggests that people will enjoy significantly greater amounts of leisure in the future, based on past trends (Fogel, *Fourth Great Awakening*, 184, 189; see his Tables 5C.1 and 5C.2 on 265–266 for uses of income). Ramey and Francis believe that Fogel's estimates are flawed, as he relied upon hours worked in manufacturing and he assumes a constant amount of time spent by men on household production (Ramey and Francis, "Century of Work and Leisure," 193–194, 210).

4. Hunnicutt, *Work Without End*, 1, see also 2–3.

5. Hunnicutt, *Work Without End*, 15.

6. Hunnicutt, *Work Without End*, 7.

7. Hunnicutt, *Work Without End*, 7, see also 3, 6.

8. Hunnicutt, *Work Without End*, 80.

9. Hunnicutt, *Work Without End*, 86.

10. Millis and Montgomery, *Economics of Labor*, I:491, see also 3:423; Hunnicutt, *Work Without End*, 11.

11. De Grazia, *Time, Work, and Leisure*, 193; others have made this argument.

12. Hunnicutt, *Work Without End*, 73. Academic researchers have more recently begun to shift their focus from leisure in the context of economic aspects toward leisure as a cultural factor. Leisure allows workers to express traditional values and customs and class consciousness within family and religious communities, even when workers have not embraced the dominant work ethic (Hunnicutt, *Work Without End*, 12).

13. Hunnicutt, *Work Without End*, 116.

14. Hunnicutt, *Work Without End*, 111, see also 110.

15. Adams, *Our Business Civilization*, 191–192.

16. Hunnicutt, *Work Without End*, 40.

17. *New York Times*, "Senate Votes 30-Hour Work Week, 53–30; Robinson 36-Hour Amendment Is Beaten," 1 and 7; *New York Times*, "For Reconsidering Five-Day-Week Bill," 8.

18. Rifkin, *End of Work*, 28–29.

19. Hunnicutt, *Work Without End*, 26, see also 17.

20. National Recreation Association, *Leisure Hours of 5,000 People*, 4.
21. National Recreation Association, *Leisure Hours*, Summary page, 2, 8–9, 15. While these surveys supposedly confirmed that workers spent their leisure time responsibly, presumably there were no queries regarding time devoted to drunken revelry or dissipation.
22. National Recreation Association, *Leisure Hours*, 3, 12.
23. National Recreation Association, *Leisure Hours*, 20.
24. Commons, *History of Labor in the United States*, 1:170–172, 384–385; Hunnicutt, *Work Without End*, 10.
25. Keynes, "Economic Possibilities for Our Grandchildren," 367.
26. Robbins, "Elasticity of Income in Terms of Effort," 123–129.
27. Hunnicutt believed a key ramification of Lionel Robbins's insights was the idea that leisure was a commodity, like all others (Hunnicutt, *Work Without End*, 54–55).
28. Veblen quote in Hunnicutt, *Work Without End*, 56; Kyrk, *Theory of Consumption*, 263, 292–293.
29. Owen, "Workweeks and Leisure," 4.
30. Owen, "Workweeks and Leisure," 6.
31. Owen, "Workweeks and Leisure," 5.
32. Havemann, "Emptiness of Too Much Leisure," 76, 84–85.
33. Havemann, "Emptiness of Too Much Leisure," 80; he is quoting Martin Clawson.
34. Havemann, "The Task Ahead: How to Take Life Easy," 86.
35. De Grazia, *Time, Work, and Leisure*, 143.
36. De Grazia, *Time, Work, and Leisure*, 84, see also 66, 72–86.
37. *Business Week*, "Outdoor Power Tools," 58–59, 62.
38. Cordell et al., "United States," *World Leisure Participation*, 226.
39. Zuzanek, "Canada," *World Leisure Participation*, 64.
40. Jones, "New Estimates of Hours of Work," 374.
41. Kreps, *Lifetime Allocation of Work and Income*, 23.
42. Schor, *Overworked American*, 1, 29.
43. Schor, *Overworked American*, quote on 7, see also 5, 13, 66, 126–128.
44. Robinson and Godbey, *Time for Life*, xix.
45. Robinson and Godbey, *Time for Life*, 3–4.
46. Robinson and Godbey, *Time for Life*, 4–5.
47. Robinson and Godbey, *Time for Life*, 11.
48. Robinson and Godbey, *Time for Life*, quote on 59; see 89.
49. Robinson and Godbey, *Time for Life*, 94.
50. Robinson and Godbey, *Time for Life*, 16; Levine and Wolff, "Social Time: The Heartbeat of Culture," 28–35.
51. Robinson and Godbey, *Time for Life*, 38.
52. Robinson and Godbey, *Time for Life*, 39.
53. Robinson and Godbey, *Time for Life*, quote on 48, see also 38–40. This author says, "Amen!" for bottled orange juice.
54. Lengfelder and Dallen, "Leisure Time in the 1990's and Beyond," quote on 16, see also 17–18.
55. Robinson and Godbey, *Time for Life*, quote on 8; see 96.
56. Hamilton, "Work and Leisure," 354–355; Robinson and Godbey, *Time for Life*, 50. For people in Schor's probable social network, the possibility of women working longer hours at jobs and at domestic work might have been realistic. People with higher educational attainments and higher wages often work longer hours than people with lower education and lower wages. These highly educated, highly paid Americans are among the most articulate people in the society, and they have better access to the press.
57. Rifkin, *End of Work*, 13.
58. Rifkin, *End of Work*, 242.
59. Rifkin, *End of Work*, 19, 27.
60. Rifkin, *End of Work*, 257–257, 271.
61. Aguiar and Hurst, "Measuring Trends in Leisure," 978.
62. Aguiar and Hurst, "Measuring Trends in Leisure," 78, 982.
63. Aguiar and Hurst, "Measuring Trends in Leisure," 980.

64. Aguiar and Hurst, "Measuring Trends in Leisure," 970.

65. Aguiar and Hurst, "Measuring Trends in Leisure," 983.

66. Aguiar and Hurst, "Measuring Trends in Leisure," 971, 994.

67. Ramey and Francis, "Century of Work and Leisure," 190–191, see also 201; Ramey, "Time Spent in Home Production," 32.

68. Ramey and Francis, "Century of Work and Leisure," quote on 206, 210.

69. Aguiar and Hurst, "Measuring Trends in Leisure," 972; Ramey and Francis, "Century of Work and Leisure," 210.

70. Owen, *Price of Leisure*, 72. Some leisure activities have a fixed cost. Going to an amusement park has a fixed cost, such as a travel time. You incur the same cost of getting to the amusement park, whether you are going to stay three hours or eight hours.

71. Owen, *Price of Leisure*, 71–72.

72. See, for instance, *New York Times*, "Paid Vacation Spreads to Manual Labor Ranks," XXII; Bowers, "Nesday Chemical Company," 162–170; *Monthly Labor Review*, "Vacations for Factory Workers," 212–213; *Monthly Labor Review*, "Vacations with Pay for Production Workers," 35–36; see also Aron, *Working at Play*, 198–201.

73. Aron, *Working at Play*, 200–201.

74. Aron, *Working at Play*, 7, see also 5.

75. Aron, *Working at Play*, 41.

76. Aron, *Working at Play*, 49; Weiss, "Tourism in America," 300.

77. Aron, *Working at Play*, 67–68, 111, 181, 220.

78. Aron, *Working at Play*, 128, 155, see also 112.

79. Aron, *Working at Play*, 145.

80. Aron, *Working at Play*, 155.

81. Aron, *Working at Play*, 204–205.

82. De Grazia, *Time, Work, and Leisure*, 306; see 87 for number of holidays on the calendar.

83. Lebergott explains how the number of holidays was increasing in the twentieth century, after most of the religious holidays were dropped from the secular calendar (Lebergott, *American Economy*, 91).

## Chapter 5

1. Weber, *Protestant Ethic*, 104–108, Routledge edition.

2. Weber, *Protestant Ethic*, 114, Routledge editions.

3. Costa, *American Living Standards*, 3. Housing, transportation, and other services appeared to be complementary with non-market time, while durables were substitutes with non-market time (Abbott and Ashenfelter, "Labour Supply, Commodity Demand and the Allocation of Time," 408).

4. Costa, *American Living Standards*, 10; Costa, *Evolution of Retirement*, 142.

5. Costa, *Evolution of Retirement*, 151–152, see also 144.

6. Costa, *American Living Standards*, 5, 27, 34.

7. *Business Week*, "A Big Fast-Growing Market: The Leisured Masses, Part I," quotes on 142 and 145.

8. John Owen believes the expenditure estimates "understate the growth of commercial recreation relative to other goods in the 1901 to 1929 period, since recreation prices relative to cost of living indexes dropped by 20 percent in those years." The index continued to fall during the 1930s, then rose during the immediate postwar period before stabilizing. He attributes this decline to changes in radio production and distribution: "If radios were excluded from the index, one would see rising relative prices for recreation goods and services in the 1929 to 1935 period" (Owen, *Price of Leisure*, 84–86).

9. Owen, *Price of Leisure*, 90.

10. De Grazia, *Time, Work, and Leisure*, 96, see also 98, 102, 110.

11. Steiner, "Recreation and Leisure Time Activities," 947–948; Steiner, *Americans at Play*, 181–182.

12. Kaplan, *Leisure in America*, 76, 79.

13. Kaplan, *Leisure in America*, 79–80.

14. Kaplan, *Leisure in America*, 86.
15. Kaplan, *Leisure in America*, 87.
16. Kaplan, *Leisure in America*, 90, see also 88. Among the ways to conceal monetary inequality was the department store, which he characterizes as "a highly important contributor to class-lessness" and the installment plan, whereby people can conceal their lack of wealth.
17. De Grazia, *Time, Work, and Leisure*, 223.
18. Mitchell, "The Backward Art of Spending Money," 267–276.
19. McGovern, "Consumption and Citizenship," 51; Lynd, "People as Consumers," 2:881.
20. Lears, *Fables of Abundance*, 47, 49.
21. Kaplan, *Leisure in America*, 206.
22. Kaplan, *Leisure in America*, 220, see also 213.
23. Houseman, "Hollywood Faces the Fifties, Part II," 51; Kaplan, *Leisure in America*, 222–223, 225, 239.
24. Horowitz, *Morality of Spending*, xvii.
25. Horowitz, *Morality of Spending*, xviii–xix. Stephen Jones suggests that British Communists neglected to see or to admit that capitalism provided workers with more leisure choices: "To neglect this fact and in failing to see that the prevailing culture was genuinely popular with the workers was to marginalize their own critiques" (Jones, *Workers at Play*, 141).
26. Horowitz, *Morality of Spending*, 131.
27. Bogart, *War Costs and Their Financing*, 285, 291, 294.
28. Horowitz, *Morality of Spending*, 116.
29. Horowitz, *Morality of Spending*, 122.
30. Bruere, "Savings or Efficiency," 194–195.
31. Horowitz, *Morality of Spending*, 62–63.
32. Chapin, *Standard of Living*, 198; Byington, *Homestead*, 149, 151.
33. Horowitz, *Morality of Spending*, 65–66.
34. Horowitz, *Morality of Spending*, 32.
35. Peixotto, "How Workers Spend a Living Wage," 201; Horowitz, *Morality of Spending*, 140.
36. Lynd, "People as Consumers," 867.
37. Lynd, "People as Consumers," 867–868, see also 869.
38. Currell, *March of Spare Time*, 114; Horowitz, *Morality of Spending*, 153; Vaile and Canoyer, *Income and Consumption*, 28, 114–115, 175, 232; Vaile, *Research Memorandum on Social Aspects of Consumption in the Depression*, 28.
39. Lynd, "People as Consumers," 860. It is interesting that he cited movies, given the nickelodeon phenomenon.
40. Lynd, "People as Consumers," 862, 864. Veblen predicted such an outcome.
41. Lynd, "People as Consumers," 866.
42. *Literary Digest*, "The Current Fad for Picture Mags," 20, 30.
43. Peterson, *Magazines in the Twentieth Century*, 92; Nyberg, *Seal of Approval*, 125. Magazines relied upon a distribution system that was largely controlled by the American News Company and its subsidiary, Union News Company. The Department of Justice eventually broke up this combination.
44. *Business Week*, "Food-Store Magazines Hit the Big Time," 108.
45. Steiner, *Americans at Play*, 50; Steiner, "Recreation and Leisure Time in America," 913.
46. Steiner, *Americans at Play*, 70, see also 55; Steiner, "Recreation," 925 for motorboats and 927 for golf equipment.
47. Steiner, *Americans at Play*, 81–82.
48. Steiner, *Americans at Play*, 148–151.
49. Lynd, "People as Consumers," 865, 902, 905, 907; Hinman, "Inventory of Housing in a Suburban City," 174. This insight was provided by an anonymous referee.
50. *New York Times*, "Nation's Play Bill $10,165,857,000 a Year," 1.
51. *Business Week*, "We Spend about as Much for Fun as for Running the Government," 20.
52. Weinberger, "Economic Aspects of Recreation," 448.
53. Weinberger, "Economic Aspects of Recreation," 450, 455–456.
54. Weinberger, "Economic Aspects of Recreation," 461, see also 459–460.
55. Weinberger, "Economic Aspects of Recreation," 449–450.

56. Weinberger, "Economic Aspects of Recreation," 452–453, 454–455.

57. Quote in Belasco, *Americans on the Road: From Autocamp to Motel, 1910–1945*, 142–143; Weinberger, "Economic Aspects of Recreation," 455. Given the deflation of the early 1930s, the 1933 figure was higher in real terms.

58. Lundberg et al., *Leisure: A Suburban Study*, 4.

59. Borsay, *History of Leisure*, 133.

60. Lundberg et al., *Leisure*, 112–113 177–178, 187.

61. Lundberg et al., *Leisure: A Suburban Study*, 187.

62. Olney, *Buy Now, Pay Later*, 1–2, 47–52, 76. Olney noted that the Department of Commerce defined purchases of a durable good as an act of household consumption (Olney, *Buy Now*, 47).

63. Olney, *Buy Now*, 22, 42.

64. Olney, *Buy Now*, 86.

65. Olney, *Buy Now*, 92, 95.

66. Olney, *Buy Now*, 179–180; see Schudson, *Advertising, The Uneasy Persuasion*, 9–10. Did advertising change consumers' tastes? "The answer depends largely on how broadly or narrowly we define 'tastes.'" (Olney, *Buy Now*, 180)

67. The question becomes: "What caused income elasticity of demand for appliances to increase?" (quote in Olney, *Buy Now*, 186–187; see also Oshima, "Consumer Asset Formation," 31–33).

68. Oshima, "Consumer Asset Formation," 24.

69. Lynd and Lynd, *Middletown*, 39, 47, 80, 226, 260; Horowitz, *Morality of Spending*, 148.

70. Horowitz, *Morality of Spending*, 162.

71. Scott, *Influencing Men in Business*, 132, see also 154.

72. Ewen, *Captains of Consciousness*, 78, see also 35.

73. Nystrom, *Economics of Fashion*, 1928, 103, cited by Ewen, *Captains of Consciousness*, 79.

74. Ewen, *Captains of Consciousness*, 79.

75. Owen discusses the importance of newspapers, magazines, and books in the commercial recreation industry, although some of these expenditures may have been for non-leisure purposes (Owen, *Price of Leisure*, 91).

76. Potter, *People of Plenty*, first quote on xxv, second quote on 30.

77. Potter, *People of Plenty*, 83.

78. Potter, *People or Plenty*, 200–201, see also 199–200. Potter appears to have missed the baby boom.

79. Potter, *People of Plenty*, 126.

80. Potter, *People of Plenty*, 136; Lundberg, "World Revolution, American Plan," 38–46.

81. Coughlan, "A $40 Billion Bill Just for Fun," 69–70, 72–74.

82. Owen, *Price of Leisure*, 110.

83. Owen, *Price of Leisure*, 141–142.

84. Brown, *Life Against Death*, 256; Lears, "Reconsidering Abundance: A Plea for Ambiguity," 455.

85. Lears, "Reconsidering Abundance: A Plea for Ambiguity," 460. Lasch, for instance, wrote in the late 1970s, a period of ennui for Americans. "Having trivialized the past by equating it with outmoded styles of consumption, discarded fashions and attitudes, people today resent anyone who draws on the past in serious discussions of contemporary conditions or attempts to use the past as a standard by which to judge the present" (Lasch, *Culture of Narcissism*, xvii).

86. O'Leary and Dottavio, "Outdoor Recreation Expenditures," 46–47.

87. Roberts, *Leisure Industries*, 61, see also 63.

88. Roberts, *Leisure Industries*, 80.

89. Cox and Alm, "Time Well Spent," 3, Exhibit 1, 15–16.

90. *US News and World Report*, "Leisure: Where No Recession Is in Sight," 41, 44; Dupont and Weiss, "Variability in Overseas Travel by Americans," 325.

91. Quote in *Business Week*, "The Entertainment Economy," 59–60, 63; US Department of Commerce, *Statistical Abstract of the United States: 1998*, cited by Lengfelder and Dallen, "Leisure Time in the 1990's and Beyond," 19.

## Chapter 6

1. Kreps, *Lifetime Allocation*, 80.
2. Kreps, *Lifetime Allocation*, 8, 14–15.
3. *Business Week*, "Marriages Make a Market," 42.
4. *Business Week*, "Who Are Tomorrow's Customers?" 146.
5. Costa, *Evolution of Retirement*, 97.
6. Tom Brokaw anointed the generation born during World War I and most of the twenties as the "Greatest Generation." The baby boomers started appearing in 1946, so the group born between 1929 and 1945 might be dubbed the "tweeners." While baby boomers liked to claim credit for rock 'n' roll, student protests, and other groovy activities, the "tweeners" were the original practitioners.
7. Gendell and Siegel, "Trends in Retirement Age by Sex," 26, see also 23–25.
8. *Business Week*, "The Leisured Masses: Where Leisure Time—and Money—Goes, Part II," 151.
9. Costa, *Evolution of Retirement*, 26; Fischer, *Growing Old in America*, 122; Haber and Gratton, *Old Age and the Search for Security*, 160–161.
10. Costa, *Evolution of Retirement*, 1, 20, 26–27.
11. Costa, *Evolution of Retirement*, 81–82; see also Owen, *Price of Leisure*, 10.
12. Costa, *Evolution of Retirement*, 101.
13. Costa, *Evolution of Retirement*, 91.
14. Gratton, "Poverty of the Impoverishment Theory," 61; see also Haber and Gratton, *Old Age*, 42.
15. Graebner, *History of Retirement*, 200.
16. Costa, *Evolution of Retirement*, 106, 108, 128–129, 133.
17. Michelon, "The New Leisure Class," 371, 373–374; Kaplan, *Leisure in America*, 47.
18. Havemann, "The Task Ahead: How to Take Life Easy," 86, 88.
19. Bennett, "Constraints on Leisure in Middle Age," 332.
20. Bennett, "Constraints on Leisure in Middle Age," 322.
21. McGuire, "Constraints in Later Life," 337, 342.
22. Balazs, "Toward a Better Understanding of the Nature Traveler," 6–7.
23. Fisk, "American Labor in the 20th Century," no pagination.
24. US Department of Commerce, *Historical Statistics, Pt. 1*, 368–370, 385–386.
25. Kleiber and Rickards, "Leisure and Recreation in Adolescence," 295–296.
26. Braden, "'The Family That Plays Together, Stays Together,'" 145, 151–156.
27. Dawson, *Laboring to Play*, 16.
28. Dawson, *Laboring to Play*, 30.
29. Knapp and Hartsoe, *Play for America*, cites Butler, *Introduction to Community Recreation*, 4th ed., 10–11.
30. Rainwater, *Play*, 36–43, 50–51; Knapp and Hartsoe, *Play for America*, 15–16, 20. William Gleason believed that proponents held another rationale for playgrounds: "Properly guided play . . . would 'fit' the city child with the physical, intellectual, and moral skills formerly best developed in the countryside" (Gleason, *Leisure Ethic*, 100). Industrial recreation blossomed during World War II, when manufacturers realized that offering recreational facilities in lieu of prohibited pay increases proved useful (Knapp and Hartsoe, *Play for America*, 56, 137).
31. Gilbert, *A Cycle of Outrage*, 4, 6.
32. Fass, *Damned and the Beautiful*, 22, see also 300.
33. Fass, *Damned and the Beautiful*, 306.
34. Gauss, *Life in College*, 16; see also Fass, *Damned and the Beautiful*, 46, 191.
35. Fass, *Damned and the Beautiful*, 56.
36. Fass, *Damned and the Beautiful*, 227–228, see also 126.
37. Fass, *Damned and the Beautiful*, 262–263.
38. Fass, *Damned and the Beautiful*, 88–90.
39. Wartella and Mazzarella, "Historical Comparison of Children's Use of Leisure Time," 176–177.
40. Wartella and Mazzarella, "Historical Comparison," 183, see also 179.

41. Wartella and Mazzarella, "Historical Comparison," 183, see also 189.
42. Gilbert, *Cycle of Outrage*, 13–14, 19.
43. Gilbert, *Cycle of Outrage*, first quote on 201, second quote on 212–213.
44. Riesman, "Listening to Popular Music," 361; second quote on 369. See also Osgerby, "'A Caste, a Culture, a Market,'" 20.
45. Chapple and Garofalo, *Rock 'N' Roll*, 12–14, 57. Before angry readers inundate me with outrage, the author asserts that he personally enjoys the above-named artists.
46. Chapple and Garofalo, *Rock 'N' Roll*, 22.
47. Chapple and Garofalo, *Rock 'N' Roll*, 43.
48. MacDonald, "Profiles: A Caste, a Culture, a Market, Part I," 70.
49. Miles, *Youth Lifestyles in a Changing World*, 85; Osgerby, "'A Caste, a Culture, a Market,'" 20–21.
50. Joel, "New, $10-Billion Power: The U.S. Teen-age Consumer," 78.
51. *Newsweek*, "Teen-Age Tasters," 77–78; MacDonald, "Profiles, Part 1," 57, 70, 77.
52. MacDonald, "Profiles, Part 2," 62. Lindner's explanation smacks of a 1950s science fiction movie, where the scientist mouths some dire mumble-jumble.
53. MacDonald, "Profiles, Part 2" 76.
54. Wartella and Mazzarella, "Historical Comparison," 173.
55. Hajdu, *Ten-Cent Plague*, 110, 155, 326; Abelson, "Comics Are a Serious Business, Part I," 41–42.
56. Abelson, "Comics Are a Serious Business, Part II," 80, 82.
57. Abelson, "Comics Are a Serious Business, Part II," Nehi official T. H. Stanley quote on 82.
58. *Ladies Home Journal*, "A Crime Against American Children," 5.
59. North, "National Disgrace," 21; Nyberg, *Seal of Approval*, 3–4; for other denunciations of comics, see page 12. Marya Mannes, a mother of comic-book reading children, raised the key concern, "I don't know what future and enduring harm, if any, comic-book reading will do to my own child. . . . Every hour spent in reading comics is an hour in which all inner growth is stopped." Her lament echoes in a recent issue of *The Atlantic* regarding very young children's use of electronic media in early twenty-first century America (Mannes, "Junior Has a Craving," 22; Rosin, "Touch-Screen Generation," 57–58).
60. Denney, *Astonished Muse*, 27.
61. *New York Times*, "Many Doubt Comics Spur Crime, Senate Survey of Experts Shows," quote on 1, see also 61.
62. Hajdu, *Ten-Cent Plague*, 63. Perhaps McDonald's took a cue from Biro in their "More than X hamburgers served" signs.
63. Hajdu, *Ten-Cent Plague*, 154–155.
64. Nyberg, *Seal of Approval*, 7–8. Author's note: the author gained much of his knowledge about the literary greats from *Gold Key Classics Illustrated*.
65. Nyberg, *Seal of Approval*, 15; see Abelson, "Comics, Part II," 92 for another example.
66. Gruenberg, "The Comics as a Social Force," 206–211; Frank, "What's in the Comics?" 215–220; Kihss, "Senator Charges 'Deceit' On Comics," *New York Times*, 29.
67. Zorbaugh, "Editorial," 194; Zorbaugh, "The Comics—There They Stand!" 201–203.
68. Hajdu, *Ten-Cent Plague*, 6, 37.
69. Deutsch, *Our Rejected Children*, 214.
70. Nyberg, *Seal of Approval*, 18.
71. Nyberg, "Comic Book Censorship in the United States," 42–43.
72. Gilbert, *Cycle of Outrage*, 92–94, Nyberg, "Comic Book Censorship," 51.
73. Gilbert, *Cycle of Outrage*, 167.
74. Gilbert, *Cycle of Outrage*, first quote 175, second quote 162–163.
75. Quote in *Newsweek*, "Purified Comics," 56; Nyberg, "Comic Book Censorship," 46. *Newsweek* published the ACMP code in "Purified Comics," 56; US Congress, Senate, *Juvenile Delinquency*, 128.
76. *New York Times*, "Many Doubt Comics Spur Crime," 1; Nyberg, "Comic Book Censorship," 48, 52–53; Gilbert, *Cycle of Outrage*, 150.
77. Barker, "Fredric Wertham—The Sad Case of the Unhappy Humanist," 216–218.
78. Wertham, "The Comics . . . Very Funny!" 6, 27–29; Nyberg, *Seal of Approval*, 156.

79. Nyberg, *Seal of Approval*, 124. William was Max Gaines's son. Readers should note Gaines's testimony. Senator Kefauver: "This seems to be a man with a bloody ax holding a woman's head up which has been severed from her body. Do you think that is in good taste?" Gaines: "Yes, sir; I do, for the cover of a horror comic. A cover in bad taste, for example, might be defined as holding the head a little higher so that the neck could be seen dripping blood from it and moving the body over a little further so that the neck of the body could be seen to be bloody." Gaines also pointed out that Wertham didn't get comic books: "it would be just as difficult to explain the harmless thrill of a horror story to a Dr. Wertham as it would be to explain the sublimity of love to a frigid old maid," http://www.thecomicbooks.com/gaines. html, viewed March 3, 2014, 8:54 a.m.

80. Nyberg, "Comic Book Censorship," 54. The senators, apparently, were happy to bandy such terms as "nuclear weapons" and "mutually assured destruction."

81. Nyberg, *Seal of Approval*, 109.

82. Nyberg, "Comic Book Censorship," 56.

83. Nyberg, *Seal of Approval*, 116.

84. Hajdu, *Ten-Cent Plague*, 314; see also Nyberg, *Seal of Approval*, 125–126.

85. Hajdu, *The Ten-Cent Plague*, 291; Nyberg, *Seal of Approval*, 156.

86. Nyberg, *Seal of Approval*, 116–117.

87. Kline, "Toys, Socialization, and the Commodification of Play," 340; *Business Week*, "The Entertainment Economy," 60.

88. Schwartzman, *Transformations: The Anthropology of Children's Play*, 328.

89. Sutton-Smith, *Toys and Culture*, 6; Kline, "Toys, Socialization, and the Commodification of Play," 340.

90. Kline, "Toys, Socialization," 357.

91. Kline, "Toys, Socialization," 348, 355; Graham, "Kids Gain Power of Purse," 1.

92. Osgerby, *Playboys in Paradise*, 9; see also Osgerby, "'A Caste, a Culture, a Market,'" 25–26.

93. Osgerby, *Playboys in Paradise*, 14.

94. Chudacoff, *Age of the Bachelor*, 67; Osgerby, *Playboys in Paradise*, 28.

95. Osgerby, *Playboys in Paradise*, 58.

96. Osgerby, *Playboys in Paradise*, 67–70.

97. Wilson, "Happy Idle Hours," 123; Osgerby, *Playboys in Paradise*, 113.

98. Osgerby, *Playboys in Paradise*, 115.

99. Osgerby, "'A Caste, a Culture, a Market,'" 27.

100. Frank, *Conquest of Cool*, 29.

101. Butsch, "Introduction: Leisure and Hegemony in America," 12–13.

102. Alvarez, *Power of the Zoot*, 96.

103. Samuelson, "Paul A. Samuelson on Social Security," 88.

## *Chapter 7*

1. Songwriter Tom Lehrer expressed such in his song, "Pollution," referring to 1960s America.

2. Centers for Disease Control, "CDC on Infectious Diseases in the United States," 636–637, see also 635.

3. Wolman and Peck, "Labour Groups in the Social Structure," 827; see also Rosen, *History of Public Health*, 361.

4. Hoy, *Chasing Dirt*, 99.

5. Rosen, *History of Public Health*, 326–327, 334; Hoy, *Chasing Dirt*, 109, 134; see also Floud et al., *Changing Body*, 327.

6. Rosen, *History of Public Health*, 338–339.

7. Higginson, "Saints and Their Bodies," 582–595; Higginson, "Gymnastics," 283–302; Aron, *Working at Play*, 42.

8. www.brainyquote.com/quotes/quotes/s/sophietuck145824.html, viewed July 28, 2013, 7:38 p.m.

9. Fogel, *Egalitarianism: The Economic Revolution of the Twentieth Century*, Simon Kuznets Memorial Lectures presented at Yale University, April 22–24, 1992, 30.

10. *Economist*, "Unhealthy Poor," 55–56; Konner, "Still Invisible and Dying in Harlem," 25.

11. Floud et al., *Changing Body*, 361; BMI defined on page 21.
12. Fischer, *Growing Old in America*, 56.
13. Mulhall and 1756 quote cited in Lebergott, *Pursuing Happiness*, 78–80.
14. Fogel, *Fourth Great Awakening*, 76–77.
15. Bension, "Poliomyelitis and the Rockefeller Institute," 85.
16. Centers for Disease Control, "CDC on Vaccines and Children's Health, 392–393.
17. Floud et al., *Changing Body*, 130–131.
18. Rosen, *History of Public Health*, 463.
19. Floud et al., *Changing Body*, 324.
20. Costa, *Evolution of Retirement*, 62, 64.
21. Floud et al., *Changing Body*, first quote on 344, second quote on 367.

## Chapter 8

1. Thompson, "Time, Work-Discipline, and Industrial Capitalism," 81–82, see also 75.
2. Thompson, "Time, Work-Discipline, and Industrial Capitalism," 86.
3. Owen, *Price of Leisure*, 23.
4. Owen, *Price of Leisure*, 28.
5. Rojek, *Labour of Leisure*, 62.
6. Dreisler, *Sister Carrie*, 26–29.
7. Lundberg et al., *Leisure: A Suburban Study*, 7.
8. Cox and Alm, "Have a Nice Day!" 16; see also "Regulations to Be Observed in the Lewiston Mills, circa 1867 posted at http://invention.smithsonian.org/centerpieces/whole_cloth/u2ei/u2images/act9/Lew_rules.html, viewed May 8, 2013, 1:50 p.m. Readers may recall their school days, when hall passes were required to use the restrooms.
9. Wendt and Kogan, *Give the Lady What She Wants!* 220–223.
10. Thompson, "Time, Work-Discipline, and Industrial Capitalism," 81.
11. Gutman, "Work, Culture, and Society," 37–38.
12. Gutman, "Work, Culture, and Society," 30.
13. Faith, *World the Railways Made*, 200; see also Holbrook, *The Story of American Railroads*.
14. Faith, *World the Railways Made*, 201.
15. US Department of Commerce, *Historical Statistics, Part 2*, 740. For a detailed account of improvements in railroad safety technology, see Usselman, *Regulating Railroad Innovation*, 117–139.
16. O'Neill, *A Democracy at War*, 208–209.
17. US Department of Commerce, *Statistical Abstract: 1999*, 450–451.
18. US Department of Commerce, *Statistical Abstract: 1999*, 450–451.
19. Rosen, *History of Public Health*, 408–412.
20. US Department of Commerce, *Historical Statistics*, Pt. I, 139. Cox and Alm, "Have a Nice Day!" 18–20. The five best jobs included financial managers; securities and financial services salespeople; mathematical and computer scientists; computer programmers and equipment operators; and legal assistants. The five worst jobs included timber cutters and logger; oil field and coal mine workers; fishers, hunters, and trappers; structural metalworkers; and construction laborers. Garbage collectors ranked sixth.
21. Wolman and Peck, "Labor Groups in the Social Structure," 804–805.
22. Edwards, *Contested Terrain*, quote on 97, see also 101.
23. Gutman, "Work, Culture, and Society," 5–6.
24. McConnell, "Riveting to Rhythm," quote on SM17; Roell, *Piano in America*, 11–12.
25. Millard, *America on Record*, 3–4.
26. Day, *Century of Recorded Music*, 215.
27. Cooper, *Air-Conditioning America*, 157, see also 158–159, 162.
28. *Business Week*, "A Big Fast-Growing Market, Part I," 146.
29. Miller, "Time-off Benefits in Small Establishments," 3–7; "Economic News Release, Table 5, Average paid holidays and days of vacation and sick leave for full-time employees, 1996," http://www.bls.gov/news.release/ebs.t0.5htm, viewed April 19, 2013, 10:30 a.m.
30. Kerr, *The Decline of Pleasure*, 32.

31. Havemann, "Emptiness of Too Much Leisure," 89.
32. Tooley, "Personal Internet Usage in the Workplace—A Serious Epidemic," January 17, 2010, http://voices.yahoo.com/personal-internet-usage-workplace-serious-5284153html?cat=15, viewed June 12, 2013, 3:01 p.m.
33. Conner, "Employees Really Do Waste Time at Work," July 17, 2012, http://www.forbes.com/sites/cherylsnappconner/2012/07/17/employees-really-do-waste-time-at-work, viewed June 12, 2013, 3:03 p.m.
34. Edwards, *Contested Terrain*, quote on 114, see also 53, 119, 147–148.
35. Edwards, *Contested Terrain*, 109–110. Edwards could just as well have called them "incentives."
36. Edwards, *Contested Terrain*, 146.
37. Edwards, *Contested Terrain*, 97.
38. Edwards, *Contested Terrain*, 58, 60.
39. Edwards, *Contested Terrain*, 124; Don Peck, "They're Watching You at Work," 72–84 (quote is from the cover).
40. Garber, "Perks and Recreation," 30.
41. Malcolm, "Unlimited vay-k? I want to work here," 5B.

## Chapter 9

1. Mincer, "Labor Force Participation of Married Women," 66–69.
2. Rotella, "Women Labor Force Participation," quote on 97–98, see 112.
3. *Time*, "The Richer $ex," March 26, 2012, cover.
4. *Virginia Magazine of History and Biography*, "Boundary Line Proceedings, 1710," 10.
5. Abbott, *Women in Industry*, 11.
6. Degler, *At Odds*, 155, 181.
7. Rotella, "Women's Labor Force Participation," 115.
8. Pidgeon, *Women in the Economy of the United States*, 25; Hooks, "Women's Occupations Through Seven Decades," 25–26; Degler, *At Odds*, 379, 415.
9. Abramovitz, *Regulating the Lives of Women*, 184–185.
10. Abramovitz, *Regulating the Lives of Women*, 188; Perkins, "Do Women in Industry Need Special Protection?" 530.
11. Goldin, *Understanding the Gender Gap*, 6, see also 198–199. Goldin provides a concise description of the case on page 192. She suggests that support exists for the two conflicting interpretations of protective legislation. She notes that many conservatives were in favor of the ERA between the 1920s and 1960s (Goldin, *Understanding the Gender Gap*, 199).
12. Campbells, *Women Wage-Earners*, 91.
13. Degler, *At Odds*, 422. The question was: "Should a married woman earn money if she has a husband capable of supporting her?" http://www.pbs.org/fmc/book/2work9.htm, viewed June 20, 2013, 4:03 p.m.
14. Degler, *At Odds*, 415.
15. Goldin, *Understanding the Gender Gap*, 116, 159, 174–175.
16. Degler, *At Odds*, 420–421; Goldin, *Understanding the Gender Gap*, 153–154.
17. Degler, *At Odds*, 420.
18. Degler, *At Odds*, 422–423.
19. Blau and Kahn, "Gender Differences in Pay," 75.
20. Lebergott, *Pursuing Happiness*, 57–58; Lebergott, *The Americans: An Economic Record*, 168–169; see also Greenwood, Seshadri, and Yorukoglu, "Engines of Liberation," 109–133.
21. Peiss, *Cheap Amusements*, 22–23.
22. Peiss, *Cheap Amusements*, 35, see also 38, 41–42.
23. Peiss, *Cheap Amusements*, 75.
24. Peiss, *Cheap Amusements*, 62–63.
25. Peiss, *Cheap Amusements*, 102, see 88–89. Peiss interprets the tough dance as allowing "young women to use their bodies to express sexual desire and individual pleasure in movement that would have been unacceptable in any other public arena."
26. Peiss, "Commercial Leisure and the 'Woman Question,'" 108, see also 105; Peiss, *Cheap Amusements*, 186.

27. Peiss, *Cheap Amusements*, 135–137, see also 128. Peiss notes, "The commercialization of leisure, at least in the amusement parks, made playing with heterosexual expressiveness not only respectable but a privilege for which women and men gladly paid."

28. Peiss, "Commercial Leisure and the 'Woman Question,'" first quote on 112, see also 111 and 114.

29. Peiss, *Cheap Amusements*, 139–140.

30. Peiss, *Cheap Amusements*, 148–151, 161.

31. Peiss, *Cheap Amusements*, 153, 159.

32. Peiss, *Cheap Amusements*, first quote on 165 and second quote on 178.

33. Peiss, *Cheap Amusements*, 184.

34. Lundberg et al., *Leisure: A Suburban Study*, 99, see also 89 and 96.

35. Lebergott, *Pursuing Happiness*, 58; Ramey, "Time Spent on Household Production," 3–4, 10.

36. Robinson and Godbey, *Time for Life*, 100. Juster and Stafford, in their comment on Hamilton's critique of the Harris Poll findings, found that, "The data on total work hours in the society, including both house-work and work for pay in the market . . . show a substantial decline in total work time, with men showing a decline of a little over 5 hours a week between the mid-1960s, and the early 1980s, women showing a decline of about 6.5 hours per week." They noted that men experienced fewer hours on the job but more at home, while women had more hours on the job but fewer at home (Juster and Stafford, "Comment," 358–359).

37. Graham, "Kids Gain Power of Purse," 15.

38. Lebergott, *Pursuing Happiness*, 50–51.

39. Lebergott, *Pursuing Happiness*, 57–58.

40. Hoy, *Chasing Dirt*, quote on 11, see 158–159.

41. Hoy, *Chasing Dirt*, 26–27.

42. Hoy, *Chasing Dirt*, 65–68, 74; Werner Troesken argues that municipal water supplies quite likely disproportionally aided blacks, due to the lower level of segregation in American cities of 1900; this lower level of segregation meant that attempting to deny publicly provided clean water and sewer lines to blacks would have meant denying it to some whites, too (Troesken, *Water, Race, and Disease*, 204).

43. Richmond, "American Attitudes Toward the Germ Theory of Disease," quote on 60, see also 77, 79–81.

44. Mokyr and Stein, "Science, Health, and Household Technology," 143–206, quote on 195; Mokyr, "Why 'More Work for Mother?'" 35; Rosen, *History of Public Health*, 84–85, 270.

45. Rosen, *History of Public Health*, 314, see also 190–191, 222, 253, 265–266, 316; see Chapin, "End of the Filth Theory of Disease," 236–238 for an assessment of public health efforts.

46. Rosen, *History of Public Health*, 317.

47. Cooper, *Air-Conditioning America*, 174.

48. Hoy, *Chasing Dirt*, 173, see also 107.

49. Lears, *Fables of Abundance*, first quote on 164, second quote on 172.

50. Americans did not have a complete monopoly on cleanliness. Lucy Maud Montgomery's *Anne of Green Gables* books chronicle Prince Edward Island women's attempts to maintain tidy homes.

51. Morris, "Homes Get Dirtier as Women Seek Jobs," 33.

52. Lebergott, *Pursuing Happiness*, 114.

53. Lebergott points out that the shift away from salt pork, salt beef, and lard and toward fresh meat, butter, and fresh vegetables indicates Americans' dietary preferences (Lebergott, *American Economy*, 293).

54. Juliet Schor paints a more pessimistic picture; see Schor, *Overworked American*, 8, 84, 87–88.

55. Strasser, "'Convenience Is Out of This World,'" 275.

56. Thrall, "Conservative Use of Modern Household Technology," 175–194.

57. Strasser, "'Convenience Is Out of This World,'" 275; Hoy, *Chasing Dirt*, 170.

58. Lindquist, *Family in the Present Social Order*, 1931, 49–50.

59. Cowan, *More Work for Mother*, 4–5; Mokyr, "Why 'More Work for Mother?'" 3.

60. Cowan, *More Work for Mother*, 13–14.

61. Cowan, *More Work for Mother*, 45, see also 41–42, 61, 66.

62. Cowan, *More Work for Mother*, 52, 61–62.

63. Cowan, *More Work for Mother*, 66, see also 63–65.
64. Cowan, *More Work for Mother*, 79.
65. Cowan, *More Work for Mother*, 79–81. The modern-day grocery store delivery service offered by Peapod and similar companies uses another technology, the Internet, in helping harried people buy groceries.
66. Cowan, *More Work for Mother*, 83–85.
67. Cowan, *More Work for Mother*, 97–99.
68. Cowan, *More Work for Mother*, 99–100.
69. Cowan, *More Work for Mother*, 100–101.
70. Owen, *Price of Leisure*, 9
71. Vanek, "Time Spent in Housework," 116–117. David Nye emphasized the dismal prospect facing farm women in Texas, where the well "was 250 feet from the house." His description of laundry competes with the descriptions provided by Lebergott. Nye suggests that electrification meant more to farm women than their urban sisters (Nye, *Electrifying America*, 303).
72. Vanek, "Time Spent in Housework," 117.
73. Vanek, "Time Spent in Housework," 119–120.
74. Ramey, "Time Spent in Home Production," 39–40; Cox and Alm, "Have a Nice Day!" 2.
75. Lebergott, *American Economy*, 93–95. Carson McCullers's *The Heart Is a Lonely Hunter* (1940) is just one of many novels revolving around a boarder.
76. Benson, "Gender, Generation, and Consumption," 224.
77. *Business Week*, "The Weird Economics of the Washing Machine," 79; Schor, *Overworked American*, 84, 88.
78. Hoy, *Chasing Dirt*, 156. Heidi Hartmann also noticed the anomaly that commercialized laundry services were often cheaper than home laundry, but families rarely turned to commercialized service, if they could afford their own washer (Edwards, *Contested Terrain*, 196–197).
79. Schor, *Overworked American*, 101–102.
80. Cowan, *More Work for Mother*, 108–109; Gilman, *Women and Economics*, 242–252.
81. Cowan, *More Work for Mother*, 101.
82. Cowan, *More Work for Mother*, 149.
83. Cowan, *More Work for Mother*, 191.
84. Cowan, *More Work for Mother*, 208
85. Greenwood, Seshadri, and Yorukoglu, "Engines of Liberation," 130.
86. Kreps, *Sex in the Marketplace*, 24.
87. Schor, *Overworked American*, 96–97, 115.
88. Currell, *March of Spare Time*, 159, 169.
89. Currell, *March of Spare Time*, 180. Shades of *The Stepford Wives*!
90. Currell, *March of Spare Time*, quote on 107, see also 109.
91. Ramey, "Time Spent in Home Production," 23.
92. Johnson, "Until Dust Do Us Part," 41.

## Chapter 10

1. "Kids, be the first on your block to own . . ." a fondly remembered shibboleth from the baby boomers' youth, actually was a disadvantage for many owners of new leisure commodities. True, the first owner of a radio or a television gained some social prestige (Veblen, again), but within a few years, their original purchase was technologically obsolete, and their less well-to-do friends could buy superior products, often at a fraction of the original price.
2. Butsch, *Making of American Audiences*, 296–297.
3. Jones, *Workers at Play*, 83; Lovell, "The Social Relations of Cultural Production," 232–256.
4. Jones, *Workers at Play*, 81–82.
5. Steiner, *Americans at Play*, 9–10.
6. Adams, *American Amusement Park Industry*, 27, 43, 66; Trachtenberg, *Incorporation of America*, 1982, 215.
7. Adams, *American Amusement Park Industry*, 96.
8. Adams, *American Amusement Park Industry*, 101, 133.
9. Adams, *American Amusement Park Industry*, 110.

10. Adams, *American Amusement Park Industry*, 165, see also 112–113, 121–122, 154, 168. Thomas Weiss provides an economic history of the tourism industry prior to 1941 (Wiess, "Tourism in America before World War II").

11. US Department of Commerce, *Statistical Abstract: 2008*, 752, Table 1201.

12. Courtwright, *Violent Land*, 41–42. Too bad he wasn't named David Cartwright—Adam's, Hoss's, and Little Joe's long-lost half-brother, perhaps. Then he could have not only been an observer but a participant in the weekly mayhem at *Bonanza's* Ponderosa.

13. Courtwright, *Violent Land*, 203; see also Mintz and Kellogg, *Domestic Revolutions*, 153, for a discussion of wartime marriage patterns.

14. Kingsdale, "The 'Poor Man's Club,'" 473, 476–477; Butsch, "Introduction: Leisure and Hegemony in America," 12–13; Peiss, *Cheap Amusements*, 17.

15. Roberts, *Leisure Industries*, 165.

16. Cressey, *Taxi-Dance Hall*, 262; Currell, *March of Spare Time*, 145.

17. Erenberg, *Steppin' Out*, 9, 36–37, 79.

18. Erenberg, *Steppin' Out*, xi, 75.

19. Erenberg, *Steppin' Out*, 200, 214, 220.

20. Erenberg, *Steppin' Out*, 258.

21. Butsch, *Making of American Audiences*, 238–239; McCarthy, "The Front Row Is Reserved for Scotch Drinkers," 31–32, 34–35; *Business Week*, "Television's Audience Problem," 70; *Newsweek*, "Television in the Tavern," 64.

22. McCarthy, "'The Front Row Is Reserved for Scotch Drinkers,'" 40–43. The *Newsweek* article stated that a 25" x 19" large-screen television cost $1,995, plus $100 for installation and three months' service charge (*Newsweek*, "Television in the Tavern," 64).

23. *New York Times*, "'Dry' Club Renews Video Appeal," 12; *New York Times*, "'Angels' Seeking Television's Aid," 23; *Time*, "Pub Crawlers," 43; McCarthy, "'The Front Row Is Reserved for Scotch Drinkers,'" 38. The *Time* article also mentioned a Hoboken bar owner who made 6 p.m. to 7 p.m. a children's hour. He cleared out the drinkers for that hour and let children and their mothers in to watch children's programming for an hour. The State Beverage Control Commissioner put the kibosh on the arrangement, citing a state law prohibiting minors in a bar.

24. *Time*, "Barrooms with a View," 63; McCarthy, "'The Front Row Is Reserved for Scotch Drinkers,'" 36–37.

25. Barzun, *God's Country and Mine*, 87–88.

26. Roell, *Piano in America*, quote on 5, see also 186. Modern Americans may find it difficult to believe, but sales of pianos and their associated products dwarfed talking machines and records as late as 1913: $593.5 million to $60 million.

27. Day, *Century of Recorded Music*, 61.

28. Roell, *Piano in America*, 72, 77, 93.

29. Roell, *Piano in America*, 144.

30. Roell, *Piano in America*, 43–44, see also 42, 46.

31. Roell, *Piano in America*, 151.

32. Roell, *Piano in America*, 50–51.

33. Roell, *Piano in America*, 34; Sanjek, *American Popular Music*, Vol. II, 296.

34. Roell, *Piano in America*, 61, see also 59–61.

35. Roell, *Piano in America*, 62–64.

36. Roell, *Piano in America*, 153, 212–213, 215, 259.

37. Gelatt, *Fabulous Phonograph*, 44, 60; Millard, *America on Record*, 43–44.

38. Gelatt, *Fabulous Phonograph*, 42.

39. Millard, *America on Record*, 40–42.

40. Gelatt, *Fabulous Phonograph*, 46–47; Day, *Century of Recorded Music*, 11.

41. Gelatt, *Fabulous Phonograph*, 122, 125; Millard, *America on Record*, 59–62.

42. Yorke, "The Rise and Fall of the Phonograph," 2; Millard, *America on Record*, 123–124.

43. Millard, *America on Record*, 129.

44. Gelatt, *Fabulous Phonograph*, 193.

45. Millard, *America on Record*, 65, 72, 74; see Gelatt, *Fabulous Phonograph*, 132–133 for the formation of the patent pool.

46. Millard, *America on Record*, 57–58.
47. Millard, *America on Record*, 74–75; Gelatt, *Fabulous Phonograph*, 188–189.
48. Gelatt, *Fabulous Phonograph*, 146, 148.
49. Day, *Century of Recorded Music*, 16; Millard, *America on Record*, 142–143, 207.
50. Gelatt, *Fabulous Phonograph*, 313; Day, *Century of Recorded Music*, 20; Millard, *America on Record*, 221–222, 317, 320, 325.
51. Izod, *Hollywood and the Box Office*, 104.
52. Gelatt, *Fabulous Phonograph*, 255–256, 265.
53. Gelatt, *Fabulous Phonograph*, 272. Millard claims 500,000 jukeboxes were in operation during the 1930s and that half of the record discs sold were used in jukeboxes (Millard, *America on Record*, 169; Gustatis, "The Jukebox: America's Music Machine," 44–46; Sanjek, *American Popular Music*, 2: 136).
54. Gelatt, *Fabulous Phonograph*, 300. Millard emphasizes the wartime research and its effect upon sound reproduction (Millard, *America on Record*, 199).
55. Gelatt, *Fabulous Phonograph*, 324–325.
56. Hamill, "Record Business—'It's Murder,'" 149–150. Hamill pointed out that Americans bought far more classical records than people in any other country.
57. Gelatt, *Fabulous Phonograph*, 300, 305; Frank, *Winner-Take-All Society*.
58. Millard, *America on Record*, 342, see 339–341.
59. Millard, *America on Record*, 5. Digital and Internet technology enables independents to compete again in the new millennium.
60. Butsch, *Making of American Audiences*, 111, see 108–109; Snyder, "Big Time, Small Time," 119.
61. Poggi, *Theater in America*, 5. The theater producers' argument was eerily similar to baseball and other sports owners' complaints about stars.
62. Poggi, *Theater in America*, xv.
63. McConachie, "Pacifying American Theatrical Audiences," 65; Poggi, *Theater in America*, 10, 12–13; Butsch, *Making of American Audiences*, 113.
64. Poggi, *Theater in America*, 17.
65. Poggi, *Theater in America*, 24–26.
66. Poggi, *Theater in America*, 42, 72; Surdam, *Wins, Losses & Empty Seats*, 51–53.
67. Butsch, *Making of American Audiences*, 67, 69–70, 74, 80.
68. Butsch, *Making of American Audiences*, 117.
69. Butsch, *Making of American Audiences*, 96, 106.
70. Butsch, *Making of American Audiences*, 2, 16–17.
71. Bustch, *Making of American Audiences*, quote on 148; Elaine Bowser, *Transformation of the Cinema, 1907–1915*, 1990, 2.
72. Butsch, *Making of American Audiences*, 149–152, 156.
73. Butsch, *Making of American Audiences*, 158.

## Chapter 11

1. Huizinga, *Homo Ludens*, 197. Some readers might find Huizinga a bit of a crank for his criticism of modern sports: "It results in the puerilism of the lowest order; yells or other signs of haberdashery, walking in marching order or at a special place and the whole rigmarole of collective voodoo and mumbo-jumbo," before he castigates mass meetings, mass-demonstrations, and parades (Huizinga, *Homo Ludens*, 205).
2. Steiner, *Americans at Play*, 86, 90, 97.
3. US Congress, House, 1952, *Organized Baseball, Report*; Pietrusza, *Major Leagues*, 2–20; see also Seymour, *Baseball: The Early Years*, for general histories of professional baseball.
4. Levine, *A. G. Spalding*, 82; Hardy, "'Adopted by All the Leading Clubs,'" 93.
5. Thorn, Palmer, and Gershman, *Total Baseball, Seventh Edition*, 75–78.
6. Izod, *Hollywood and the Box Office*, 8–9. Butsch presented evidence painting a more nuanced picture of nickelodeon audiences; research implied that while immigrant working-class neighborhoods were fervent patrons, small-town and middle-class clientele also patronized the early films. In addition, children comprised a large proportion of the audience (Butsch, *Making of American Audiences*, 141–145).

7. Butsch, *Making of American Audiences*, 140. This may have been a precursor to using music to increase turnover of customers in restaurants.
8. Bowser, *Transformation of Cinema*, 8–9.
9. Butsch, *Making of American Audiences*, 146–147.
10. Bowser, *Transformation of Cinema*, 133, see also 84.
11. US Department of Commerce, *Places of Amusement*, 5.
12. Hampton, *History of the Movies*, 25.
13. Dulles, *America Learns to Play*, 292.
14. Hampton, *History of the Movies*, 57.
15. Izod, *Hollywood Box Office*, 28, 47.
16. Bowser, *Transformation of Cinema*, 107, 109.
17. Izod, *Hollywood Box Office*, 28–29, 35.
18. Gomery, "The Movie Palace Comes to America's Cities," 144, see also 137–138.
19. Gomery, "Movie Palace," 145–146.
20. Gomery, *Hollywood Studio System*, 6; Huettig, *Economic Control of the Motion Picture Industry*, 56–57; for total factor productivity growth and GDP, see Bakker, "How Motion Pictures Industrialized Entertainment," 1,038.
21. Millard, *America on Record*, 153, 158; Izod, *Hollywood Box Office*, 76.
22. Izod, *Hollywood Box Office*, 83, 138.
23. Handel, *Hollywood Audience*, 93.
24. Handel, *Hollywood Audience*, 94–95.
25. Handel, *Hollywood Audience*, 98.
26. Handel, *Hollywood Audience*, 96, 155–156.
27. Handel, *Hollywood Audience*, 215–216.
28. Bergman, *We're in the Money*, xix.
29. Handel, *Hollywood Audience*, 96–98. In economic terms, necessities are goods and services where expenditures rise, but proportionally less rapidly than the growth in incomes.
30. Gomery, *Hollywood Studio System*, 21; Izod, *Hollywood Box Office*, 101.
31. Bergman, *We're in the Money*, xxii; *Time*, "Bank Night," 57–58; Parkhill, "Bank Night Tonight," 20–21, 82; Kusell, "Bank Night," 363–365. His name was spelled Yeager in the Kussell article.
32. Kusell, "Bank Night," 363; Currell, *March of Spare Time*, 129.
33. Forman, *Our Movie Made Children*, 185; Currell, *March of Spare Time*, 140–141.
34. Rugg, *Problems of American Culture*, 499.
35. Izod, *Hollywood Box Office*, 96–98; Bordwell, Thompson, and Staiger, *Classical Hollywood Cinema*, 315.
36. Handel, *Hollywood Audience*, 131, 133.
37. Stuart, *Effects of Television*, 10, 15. Using data from the *Historical Statistics of the United States*, I calculated a decline of 40.5 percent, as receipts fell from $1,692 to $1,394 million between 1946 and 1956, while the C.P.I. rose from 58.5 to 81.4, or a 38.5 percent increase; the deflated gate receipts for 1956 becomes $1,006.97 (US Department of Commerce, *Historical Statistics, Pt. 1*, 210 and 401).
38. Stuart, *Effects of Television*, 15, 19.
39. Stuart, *Effects of Television*, 24. He discusses a multiple correlation procedure with Per-capita Motion Picture Receipts as the dependent variable; Per-capita Personal Income and percent of Households with Television Sets were positively and negatively, respectively, related to the dependent variable (Stuart, *Effects of Television*, 31).
40. *Printers' Ink*, "Magazine Readership Unaffected by TV Starch Finds," 40.
41. Gomery, *Shared Pleasures*, 87–88; Gomery, "Who Killed Hollywood?" 106–112.
42. Stuart, *Effects of Television*, 37.
43. May, *Homeward Bound*, 1988, 14, ch. 1.
44. *Business Week*, "Who Are Tomorrow's Customers?" 151.
45. Stuart, *Effects of Television*, 54–55.
46. Bill Paddock, "Video's Vital Role in Series Shown by Survey," 11; Stuart, *Effects of Television*, 80–81. Even before the war ended, theater owners were considering installing television in their theaters (*Variety*, "Bulk of Expected Postwar Theatre Bldg. Boom Seen," 5).
47. Surdam, *Postwar Yankees*, 132–135; Stuart, *Effects of Television*, 82–84, 87, 92.

48. Izod, *Hollywood Box Office*, 139–141.
49. Stuart, *Effects of Television*, 100–101.
50. Bergreen, *Look Now, Pay Later*, 34.
51. Gomery, *History of Broadcasting*, 1, 6; *New York Times*, "Wireless Telephone Spreads Fight News over 120,000 Miles," 6.
52. Bergreen, *Look Now, Pay Later*, 24, 26.
53. Gomery, *History of Broadcasting*, 13–14, 29.
54. Gomery, *History of Broadcasting*, 22–23.
55. Millard, *America on Record*, 170; US Department of Commerce, *Historical Statistics, Pt. 1*, 171.
56. Spitzer, "Freedom of the Breeze," 74, 82.
57. Spitzer, "Freedom of the Breeze," 80, see also 76, 78.
58. Spitzer, "Freedom of the Breeze," 78.
59. Spitzer, "Freedom of the Breeze," 76.
60. Millard, *America on Record*, 109.
61. Wik, "The USDA and the Development of Radio in Rural America," 178–182; Butsch, *Making of American Audiences*, 209–211.
62. Gomery, *History of Broadcasting*, 17, 21–22; see also Bergreen, *Look Now, Pay Later*, 41.
63. Gomery, *History of Broadcasting*, 23–26; Bergreen, *Look Now, Pay Later*, 62.
64. Bergreen, *Look Now, Pay Later*, quote on 131, see also 132.
65. Gomery, *History of Broadcasting*, 39–41.
66. Gomery, *History of Broadcasting*, 32, 39–41; Bergreen, *Look Now, Pay Later*, 162–163.
67. Gomery, *History of Broadcasting*, 54, 98.
68. Butsch, *Making of American Audiences*, 196–197.
69. Millard, *America on Record*, 164; Izod, *Hollywood Box Office*, 103–104.
70. Butsch, *Making of American Audiences*, 205.
71. Millard, *America on Record*, 217–218, 364. The author should know, as he purchased a minidisc system in the late 1990s; he finds it quite useful and has never purchased an i-Pod.
72. *Business Week*, "Television's Audience Problem," 71, 74.
73. *Business Week*, "A Hard Look at TV's Future," 72.
74. Gomery, *History of Broadcasting*, 108–110; Bergreen, *Look Now, Pay Later*, 214. Baughman describes the divergent views of what television programming should be: "an extraordinary cultural opportunity" or a "much more imitative [of radio] medium" based on entertainment (Baughman, *Same Time, Same Place*, 3).
75. Gomery, *History of Broadcasting*, 109–110.
76. Stuart, *Effects of Television*, 49.
77. *Business Week*, "Video Visions," 39; *Business Week*, "A Hard Look at TV's Future," 72.
78. US Department of Commerce, *Historical Statistics, Pt. 1*, 169.
79. Hughes's comparison, of course, neglected the difference in population between the two periods.
80. Hughes, "TV in 10 Years Transforms America," 30–32; *Sales Management*, "Two-Thirds of U.S. Homes Now Boast Television Sets," 32.
81. Gomery, *History of Broadcasting*, 110–112, 185–188. Gomery lauds Wasserman as worthy of mention alongside the network bosses, Sarnoff, Paley, and Leonard Goldenson of ABC, see page 134.
82. Gomery, *History of Broadcasting*, 168–169, 173–177, 235; Bergreen, *Look Now, Pay Later*, 205.
83. *Sales Management*, "Will Color Television 'Hypnotize Customers?'" 42–43. Apparently CBS cultivated color television in the early 1940s, before American's entry into the war. According to Bergreen, CBS's system failed, since it was based on a mechanical system and was not compatible with RCA's color system. RCA out-maneuvered CBS and had FCC backing. In addition to stymieing CBS's color television system, Sarnoff and NBC manufactured televisions without UHF capability, further injuring CBS's attempt to implement color television (Bergreen, *Look Now, Pay Later*, 140–142).
84. *Business Week*, "Competition—From Inside and Out—Grips Magazines," 38, 40, 42.
85. Willingham, "Television: Giant in the Living Room," 114.
86. *Sales Management*, "How Much TV Does a Dollar Buy?" November 20, 1955, 36–37.
87. *Sales Management*, "TV-Sold Brands Become Consumer-Dealer 'Choice,'" 38.

88. Spigel, *Make Room for TV*, quote and advertisement on 69; *Business Week*, "TV Slump: The Old One-Two," 91.

89. Sahin and Robinson, "Beyond the Realm of Necessity: Television," 92; *Television/Radio Age*, "Viewing Trends: From '50s to '80s," 49 for increase in usage; Butsch, *Making of American Audiences*, 251.

90. Gomery, *History of Broadcasting*, 301–313. James Baughman describes the sad state of CBS by the end of the millennium (Baughman, *Republic of Mass Culture*, 247).

91. Butsch, "Home Video and Corporate Plans," 219.

92. Nulty, "Matsushita Takes the Lead in Video Recorders," 110.

93. Rothe, Harvey, and Michael, "The Impact of Cable Television," 17–19.

94. Butsch, *Making of American Audiences*, 270. Elsewhere, he marveled that a group of large corporations "would have the market power to create a demand for a new product and thus shape the leisure practices of millions of people. But just such a group of companies was unsuccessful in doing so with the videodisc and consequently wrote off several hundred million dollars in losses" (Butsch, "Home Video and Corporate Plans," 223).

95. Poggi, *Theater in America*, 29, 78, 81–82.

96. *Billboard*, "The Present Status of the Legitimate Theater in the United States," 51.

97. *Literary Digest*, "The Theater Flings Down the Glove to Radio," 29.

98. Yorke "The Rise and Fall of the Phonograph," 12.

99. Millard, *America on Record*, 136.

100. Court cases ruled that "property rights to a recording ended when it was sold" (Millard, *America on Record*, 186).

101. Warner and Jennings, *My First Hundred Years in Hollywood*, 168–169; Millard, *America on Record*, 152.

102. Millard, *America on Record*, 161; Izod, *Hollywood Box Office*, 82.

103. Millard, *America on Record*, 174, cites Gelatt, *Fabulous Phonograph*, 268, 274.

104. Millard, *America on Record*, 172, 177–78.

105. Izod, *Hollywood Box Office*, 74; Everson, *American Silent Film*, 1978, 290–291.

106. Stuart, *Effects of Television*, 200–201.

107. Gomery, *History of Broadcasting*, 143, 150–155.

108. Gomery, *History of Broadcasting*, 159, 281–290; Bergreen, *Look Now, Pay Later*, 120–121.

109. Stuart, *Effects of Television*, 194–195.

110. *Printers' Ink*, "The Tape Threat," 27; Stuart, *Effects of Television*, 182–183, see also 105, 114, 147–149.

111. Surdam, "Television and Minor League Baseball," 67.

112. Rosen, "Economics of Superstars," 845–858.

113. Houseman, "Hollywood Faces the Fifties, Part II," quote on 55, see also 51–52. An augur of the more distant future, pay television, received FCC permission for a test of a pay-as-you-see device, Phonevision, in the state of Illinois (Houseman, "Hollywood Faces the Fifties, Part II," 57).

114. Stuart, *Effects of Television*, 51–52, 56.

115. Conant, *Motion Picture Industry*, 14–15.

116. Houseman, "Hollywood Faces the Fifties, Part I," 55.

117. Izod, *Hollywood Box Office*, 143–147; Handel, *Hollywood Audience*, 210.

118. *Variety*, "Hardtops Lag in Suburbia" 19; Conant, *Motion Picture Industry*, 147.

119. Jackson, *Crabgrass Frontier*, 255.

120. Stuart, *Effects of Television*, 78–79.

121. Izod, *Hollywood Box Office*, 143. In Peter Bogdanovich's *The Last Picture Show*, the town's only theater closed. It did not appear to be a first-run theater.

122. Aguiar and Hurst, "Measuring Trends," 986, 995; Putnam, *Bowling Alone*, 27.

## Chapter 12

1. Jones, *Workers at Play*, 21.

2. Adams, *American Amusement Park Industry*, 57–58; Jackson, *Crabgrass Frontier*, 112.

3. Snyder, "Big Time, Small Time," 120–122.

4. Poggi, *Theater in America*, 6.
5. Jonnes, *Empires of Light: Edison, Tesla, and Westinghouse, and the Race to Electrify the World*, 185–214.
6. Jonnes, *Empires of Light*, 4–10.
7. Jonnes, *Empires of Light*, 11.
8. Lebergott, *Pursuing Happiness*, 40; see also Nye, *Electrifying America*, for a history of electrification.
9. Nye, *Electrifying America*, 287, 292, 319. My thanks to an anonymous reviewer for pointing this out.
10. *Literary Digest*, "Electric Farming," 23.
11. Steiner, "Recreation and Leisure Time Activities," 921–922.
12. Steiner, "Recreation and Leisure Time Activities," 920.
13. Flink, *Car Culture*, 7–8; Leavitt, *Superhighway-Superhoax*, 22–23; Rae, *Road and the Car in American Life*, 30–31.
14. Zeitz, *Flapper: A Madcap Story*, 138–140.
15. Flink, *Car Culture*, 18, 23, 33.
16. Flink, *Car Culture*, 40.
17. Ford and Crowther, *My Life and Work*, 111–112.
18. Flink, *Car Culture*, 87–89. The reader might ask, "If Ford thought workers would spend wages on alcohol, why didn't he open up liquor stores and taverns?"
19. Flink, *Car Culture*, 87–88.
20. Quotes from Burnham, "The Gasoline Tax and the Automobile Revolution," 445, 448–449; Flink, *Car Culture*, 150; Paxson, "The Highway Movement, 1916–1935," 239–242; Rae, *Road and the Car*, 62–63.
21. Flink, *Car Culture*, 175; Rae, *Road and the Car*, 68.
22. Burnham, "Gasoline Tax," 435–436.
23. Rae, *Road and the Car*, 28; Burnham, "Gasoline Tax," 441, 449, 455.
24. Burnham, "Gasoline Tax," 450–454; Paxson, "Highway Movement," 249. The issue of who gained and who lost under the gasoline tax revolved around who bore the burden of the tax. Even if the gasoline stations bore the legal responsibility for paying the tax, consumers would share the burden of the tax if the pump price increased. The distribution of the burden of the tax depended upon, in economic parlance, the relative price elasticities between buyers and sellers.
25. Rae, *Road and the Car*, 88.
26. Rae, *Road and the Car*, 90–91.
27. Rae, *Road and the Car*, 102–106; Paxson, "Highway Movement, 1916–1935," 248–249.
28. Lynd and Lynd, *Middletown in Transition*, 26, 265. If Americans took car ownership as almost a God-given right, people around the world marveled at such ownership. Soviet authorities used John Ford's movie version of John Steinbeck's *The Grapes of Wrath* to demonstrate how bad things were under capitalism. Apparently the move backfired, when Russian audiences were impressed that the Joad family owned a car—a run-down jalopy to Americans—and wore shoes (Jackson, *Crabgrass Frontier*, 187). During World War II, the fact that almost every American GI, from officers down to the lowliest private, could hop into a motor vehicle and drive astounded Europeans.
29. Leavitt, *Superhighway-Superhoax*, 7–9. Leavitt chronicles how the interstate freeway system became popular, even with governors, who had initially opposed it, since they wanted to control road building within their states. Secretary of Commerce Sinclair Weeks cynically identified the real reason behind the program's political popularity—not defense, safety, or economy—but because the system "touches or crosses 406 of the 435 congressional districts" (Leavitt, *Superhighway-Superhoax*, 44, see also 390). Mark Rose describes the changing methods for determining Interstate freeway routes (Rose, *Interstate: Express Highway Politics*, 102).
30. Lewis, *Divided Highways*, 243.
31. Lewis, *Divided Highways*, 8, 12–13, 31.
32. Belasco, *Americans on the Road*, 3, 20. Trailers or caravans were the descendants, of a sort, of auto camping (Belasco, *Americans on the Road*, 167).
33. Belasco, *Americans on the Road*, 106–115.

34. Belasco, *Americans on the Road*, 116; US Department of Commerce, *Historical Statistics, Part 2*, 719–720.
35. Steiner, *Americans at Play*, 45–46, 59; Belasco, *Americans on the Road*, 4, 76, 103–105.
36. Belasco, *Americans on the Road*, 125–131, 140, 142–143.
37. Belasco, *Americans on the Road*, 148, 153–154, 168.
38. Belasco, *Americans on the Road*, 170–172. Or else she should have used a different surname than her bird-motif Crane. The question of what proportion of the hotel/motel industry's business came from business, convention, or pleasure appeared to be highly variable. Wyckoff and Sasser presented figures showing that these percentages changed considerably just between 1976 and 1977 (Wyckoff and Sasser, *U.S. Lodging Industry*, xxxii).
39. Belasco, *Americans on the Road*, 166–167.
40. Lewis, *Divided Highways*, 212–213.
41. Owen, *Price of Leisure*, 47–48. Owen suggested that there are two ways to think about this: "One way to analyze commuting activity is to regard the worker's residence as fixed and his daily travel trip as a method of finding better-paying work. Alternatively, one might regard his place of work as fixed, and his commuting as an effort to obtain lower prices for a number of items in his budget, especially housing, schools, and recreation, and thus to raise his real wage rate. . . . These economies of scale in work may induce him to take less leisure than if he were a non-commuter."
42. Owen sees a parallel between commuting and "that of 'education for consumption.'" There is a critical difference between education and commuting, "which may influence the effect of commuting on the labor-leisure choice. . . . An investment in commuting is made each day and is repaid each day by the daily wage. Since the investment is not large and fixed, the commuter is permitted a flexibility denied to the student" (Owen, *Price of Leisure*, both quotes on 49).
43. Hilton, "Transport Technology and the Urban Pattern," 126; Jackson, *Crabgrass Frontier*, 111. Hilton also pointed out that because "power from any one generating station could be sent freely to any line in a city, the electric streetcar had an economy of scale, relative to either the horse car or the cable car, which was a powerful anti-competitive force, and it was not long before all street railways in most, but not all, American cities were brought under a single firm" (Hilton, "Transport Technology," 126).
44. Jackson, *Crabgrass Frontier*, 112.
45. Jackson, *Crabgrass Frontier*, 119. The San Francisco Bay Area BART and Washington, D.C., Metro systems mirror the French, while Chicago's "el" system reflects the American system.
46. Jackson, *Crabgrass Frontier*, 136, 236–237. See Warner for a discussion of what the new homes in the suburb meant to people (*Streetcar Suburbs*, 156–157).
47. Hoy, *One Hundred Years of Land Values in Chicago*, 337; Jackson, *Crabgrass Frontier*, 114, 168. Sam Bass Warner describes Boston horsecar manager Henry Whitney's belief in the five-cent fare (Warner, *Streetcar Suburbs*, 26).
48. Jackson, *Crabgrass Frontier*, 158, 164.
49. Jackson, *Crabgrass Frontier*, 184.
50. Skolnick, *Embattled Paradise*, 52.
51. *Business Week*, "The New Do-It-Yourself Market," 60–61, 71.
52. *Time*, "Modern Living: The Shoulder Trade," 62–66.
53. Gelber, *Hobbies*, 205, 287.
54. Gelber, *Hobbies*, 240, 278.
55. *Business Week*, "Industrious Leisure," 14–15.
56. Jackson, *Crabgrass Frontier*, 60.
57. Jackson, *Crabgrass Frontier*, 97. Early baseball clubs, though, were made up of young white-collar men, probably clerks.
58. Jackson, *Crabgrass Frontier*, 98.
59. Jackson, *Crabgrass Frontier*, 191–192, 205, 293–294. Jackson points out many of the distortions created by the mortgage interest deduction. He recalls presidential candidate George McGovern's quixotic proposal to abolish the deduction and to replace it with a lower overall tax policy (see 294).
60. Jackson, *Crabgrass Frontier*, 206–207, 293; see Keats, *Crack in the Picture Window*, for example.
61. Jackson, *Crabgrass Frontier*, 244.

62. Jackson, *Crabgrass Frontier*, 280–281.
63. Cooper, *Air-Conditioning America*, 2, 44, 52.
64. Cooper, *Air-Conditioning America*, 80–82, 85.
65. Cooper, *Air-Conditioning America*, 142, see also 122, 138, 147.
66. Cooper, *Air-Conditioning America*, 152, 156–157.

## Chapter 13

1. Butsch, "Leisure and Hegemony in America," 14.
2. Butsch, "Leisure and Hegemony in America," 15.
3. Jones, *Workers at Play*, 34; Bailey, *Leisure and Class in Victorian England*, 149.
4. Borsay, *History of Leisure*, 58, 62–63.
5. Rojek, *Labour of Leisure*, 133–134.
6. Rojek, *Labour of Leisure*, 54.
7. Rojek, *Labour of Leisure*, 60.
8. Rojek, *Labour of Leisure*, 87.
9. Rojek, *Labour of Leisure*, 89.
10. Roberts, *Leisure Industries*, 38.
11. Roberts, *Leisure Industries*, 50, 53.
12. Roberts, *Leisure Industries*, 53. In other words, you can lead a person to a recreational site, but you cannot make him recreate (in a socially desirable manner).
13. Roberts, *Leisure Industries*, 189. Presumably this was what was meant by Portland, Oregon's "Expose Yourself to Art," whose model eventually became mayor of the city.
14. Roberts, *Leisure Industries*, 180.
15. Roberts, *Leisure Industries*, 204.
16. Anderson and Leal, *Free Market Environmentalism*, 62.
17. Quoted in Fisk, "American Labor in the 20th Century," no pagination, from Goldin, "Labor Markets in the Twentieth Century," 6.
18. Goldin, *Understanding the Gender Gap*, 165–166.
19. Roediger, *Our Own Time*, 40, 177; Cahill, *Shorter Hours*, 21–22.
20. Roediger, *Our Own Time*, 228.
21. Roediger, *Our Own Times*, 237–243, 253; Cutler, *Labor's Time*, 1–4.
22. Owens, *Price of Leisure*, 14–15.
23. US Department of Commerce, *Statistical Abstract: 2008*, 760, 765.
24. US Department of Commerce, *Statistical Abstract: 2008*, 281, 767.
25. US Department of Commerce, *Statistical Abstract: 2008*, 767.
26. See, for instance, Goodman, *The Luck Business*, 143–145; Walters, "Taking a Chance on Education," 10.
27. Owen, *Price of Leisure*, 51.
28. Jones, *Workers at Play*, 99.
29. Steiner, "Recreation and Leisure Time Activities," 946.
30. Steiner, *Americans at Play*, 172, 180.
31. Walker, *Distributed Leisure*, 152; Currell, *March of Spare Time*, 5, 7, 68.
32. Currell, *March of Spare Time*, 68.
33. Currell, *March of Spare Time*, 72.
34. Currell, *March of Spare Time*, 33, 50.
35. Busch, "Contributions of Recreation," 308–309.
36. Brauscher, "Freedom in Leisure," 401.
37. Currell, *March of Spare Time*, 188; Chase, "Play," 344–345.

## Chapter 14

1. Archive.org/stream/ShermanMotion Picture Industry024534mbp/shermanantirust024534mbp_djvu.text, viewed July 22, 2013, 9:01a.m.
2. A leading textbook on industrial organization and *Motion Picture Industry* observed that the language in Section 1 of the Sherman *Motion Picture Industry* Act led courts to make

"illegal *per se* all agreements among competing firms to fix prices, to restrict or pool output, or otherwise directly to restrict the force of competition. Such agreements have been singled out for judicial treatment different from under the *rule of reason* approach taken with respect to a variety of other practices" (Scherer and Ross, *Industrial Market Structure*, 317).

3. Scherer and Ross, *Industrial Market Structure*, 450–452.
4. Millard, *America on Record*, 6–7.
5. Coase, "Payola in Radio," 283, 285.
6. Millard, *America on Record*, 294.
7. Stuart, *Effects of Television*, 181–182.
8. Millard, *America on Record*, 231–232, 333; Chapple and Garofalo, *Rock 'N' Roll*, 62, 66.
9. Chapple and Garofalo, *Rock 'N' Roll*, 65.
10. Coase, "Payola in Radio," 269.
11. Coase, "Payola in Radio," 276, see also 278.
12. Coase, "Payola in Radio," 286.
13. Coase, "Payola in Radio," 291.
14. Coase, "Payola in Radio," 295–297.
15. Coase, "Payola in Radio," 307. Once it became clear that Congress was going to do something about payola, other industries became concerned. The motion picture industry asserted that the FCC regulations pertaining to payola were not applicable to films produced for theater distribution. In that industry, firms had often supplied products, such as automobiles, for use in films. If movies had to announce in the credits that Firm XYZ supplied a car, then sponsors making similar products would not use the films (Coase, "Payola in Radio," 302).
16. Coase, "Payola in Radio," 304–305.
17. Coase, "Payola in Radio," 306. Payola resembled campaign donations. Of course, when a Congressional legislator accepted a campaign donation, this would not affect his or her decisions.
18. Coase, "Payola in Radio," 308.
19. Coase, "Payola in Radio," 315.
20. Coase, "Payola in Radio," 318–319.
21. Conant, *Motion Picture Industry*, 118–119; Gomery, *Hollywood Studio System*, 11–12.
22. Huettig, *Economic Control*, 29.
23. Conant, *Motion Picture Industry*, 21–22.
24. Huettig, *Economic Control*, 15–16.
25. Izod, *Hollywood Box Office*, 19–20.
26. Izod, *Hollywood Box Office*, 24–26.
27. Conant, *Motion Picture Industry*, 2.
28. Izod, *Hollywood Box Office*, 15.
29. Huettig, *Economic Control*, 113–114.
30. Conant, *Motion Picture Industry*, 24.
31. Conant, *Motion Picture Industry*, 27–28, 33.
32. Huettig, *Economic Control*, 69–75; Izod, *Hollywood Box Office*, 50–51.
33. Huettig, *Economic Control*, 115.
34. Huettig, *Economic Control*, 3.
35. Huettig, *Economic Control*, 79, 81, 114, 143.
36. Huettig, *Economic Control*, 30–32, 35.
37. Cassady, "Some Economic Aspects of Motion Picture Production and Marketing," 120; he describes the advantages and economics of block booking on 123; see also Huettig, *Economic Control*, 119; Conant, *Motion Picture Industry*, 77–78. Block booking is similar to De-Beer's distribution of diamonds to jewelers, a set of diamonds on a "take it or leave it" basis.
38. Conant, *Motion Picture Industry*, 79; *Variety*, "Next Metro Block to be Seven Pictures," 3.
39. Huettig, *Economic Control*, 120.
40. Huettig, *Economic Control*, 124.
41. Huettig, *Economic Control*, 123.
42. Conant, *Motion Picture Industry*, 65. Cassady argues that without some system of exclusivity, "every theater in the country would have a right to demand a picture immediately upon release. Under such conditions the market would be in a turmoil because a theater purchasing a picture might find after purchase that the competitor across the street was playing it. . . .

Reasonable protection is such a device. But it is quite obvious that in such a system there is excellent opportunity for favoritism" (Cassady, "Some Economic Aspects," 122).

43. Conant, *Motion Picture Industry*, 60, see also 58–59, 68.
44. Huettig, *Economic Control*, 140.
45. Huettig, *Economic Control*, 51, 53. The struggle to dominate theater sound systems led to the creation of RCA's Radio-Keith-Orpheum Corporation RKO (see Izod, *Hollywood*, 77–78; Conant, *Motion Picture Industry*, 29–30; Gomery, *Hollywood Studio System*, 8).
46. Huettig, *Economic Control*, 60, 84–85.
47. Huettig, *Economic Control*, 94, 146.
48. Huettig, *Economic Control*, 100–101, 111–112.
49. *Variety*, "Mary Pickford Charges Prod. Code Favors Big 5 at Expense of Indies," 3; Gomery, *Hollywood Studio System*, 11. Howard Hughes, for instance, failed in court to enjoin the code's revocation of approval of his film, *The Outlaw*, a film emphasizing Jane Russell's generous cleavage (Conant, *Motion Picture Industry*, 42).
50. Izod, *Hollywood Box Office*, 70–71.
51. Conant, *Motion Picture Industry*, 38–39, 55, 81. Earlier Department of Justice investigations of the motion picture industry concluded that "most activities of the film boards of trade were legal" (Conant, *Motion Picture Industry*, 202).
52. Conant, *Motion Picture Industry*, 38–39, 47.
53. Conant, *Motion Picture Industry*, 50–53.
54. Conant, *Motion Picture Industry*, 47, 62.
55. Conant, *Motion Picture Industry*, 69–70.
56. Gomery, *Hollywood Studio System*, 18.
57. *Variety*, "Par and Metro Sue Mass. Indie on %," 9; *Variety*, "20th, Par, Loew's, WB Ask 180 G Judgments on 'False' B.O. Reports," 13; *Variety*, "Ralph E. Snider, New England Exhib, Sued by Majors on 'False Grosses,'" 10; *Variety*, "Settlement Negotiations Go on Quietly on Falsified Grosses," 21; Conant, *Motion Picture Industry*, 70–71; Strick, "Economics of the Motion Picture Industry," 413. In the movie, "Matinee," John Goodman plays an independent producer; he is shown looking at the box office receipts with a theater owner.
58. Izod, *Hollywood Box Office*, 108.
59. Conant, *Motion Picture Industry*, 94, 202–203.
60. Conant, *Motion Picture Industry*, 98–100, 102, 110–112; Izod, *Hollywood Box Office*, 122–123.
61. Conant, *Motion Picture Industry*, 140. This may have been a Prisoners' Dilemma situation, where no major was willing to sell any of its theaters, unless all of them sold. By being forced to by the government, the issue was solved.
62. Conant, *Motion Picture Industry*, 207.
63. Conant, *Motion Picture Industry*, 219.
64. Conant, *Motion Picture Industry*, 214.
65. Scherer, *Industrial Market Structure*, 467.
66. Izod, *Hollywood Box Office*, 124–126.
67. Conant, *Motion Picture Industry*, 145, see also 122, 128–129.
68. Conant, *Motion Picture Industry*, 135, 145, 150, 201.
69. Izod, *Hollywood Box Office*, 135–136.
70. Strick, "Economics of the Motion Picture Industry," 415. While ambitious executives hoped to create media conglomerates, Hollywood often foiled their plans. Even in 2000, no one knew how to create sure-fire hits on the small or large screens (Baughman, *Republic of Mass Culture*, 255).
71. Litman, *Vertical Structure*, 19–20; McMillan, *Reinventing the Bazaar*, 80–82.
72. Efficiency might have been improved if production costs fell due to operating two stages under combined ownership rather than under separate ownership; coordinating control of the combined production process; and avoiding selling costs by developing captive markets. The networks, though, have frequently used the vertical integration to deter entry of new networks (Litman, *Vertical Structure*, 5–6). Many owners of newspapers sought licenses for television stations, hoping to compensate for any losses in newspaper revenues (Baughman, *Same Time, Same Place*, 41). One ramification of the Telecommunications Act

of 1996, which relaxed restrictions on the number of stations an individual corporation could own, was concentration of stations into fewer hands (Baughman, *Republic of Mass Culture*, 241–242).

73. Litman, *Vertical Structure*, 1.

74. Litman, *Vertical Structure*, 12; Schumpeter, *Capitalism, Socialism, and Democracy*, 83–84.

75. Litman, *Vertical Structure*, 22; Bergreen, *Look Now, Pay Later*, 202. Bergreen describes how the freeze hurt ABC's ability to sign affiliates; ABC's few affiliates were in urban areas and this factor affected the network's programming choices. In the 1970s, ABC executive Fred Silverman decided to program shows that appealed to young, urban audiences; these younger viewers were highly desired by advertising firms (Bergreen, *Look Now, Pay Later*, 202, 225).

76. Litman, *Vertical Structure*, 23–24.

77. U.S. Congress, Senate, 1956, *Network Monopoly*, 1; Litman, *Vertical Structure*, 44. The television show *Get Smart* cleverly spoofed the "third network" idea with its "Third Spy Network," an upstart between Control and K.A.O.S.

78. Litman, *Vertical Structure*, 27.

79. Bergreen, *Look Now, Pay Later*, 235.

80. Bergreen, *Look Now, Pay Later*, 254, 258.

81. Litman, *Vertical Structure*, 52, 109–110.

82. Litman, *Vertical Structure*, 99.

83. Litman, *Vertical Structure*, 105–107. The overall effect upon revenues from selling advertising spots depended upon whether the prices increased proportionally more than the proportional decrease in the number of advertising minutes.

84. Litman, *Vertical Structure*, 138.

85. Donald I. Baker testimony in US Congress, House, 1975, *Pay Cable Television Industry*, 232; *Wall Street Journal*, "Limit of One Over-the-Air Pay-TV Station," 5; Litman, *Vertical Structure*, 99, 119.

86. Meacham, "The Professional Base Ball Association," 12.

87. Surdam, *Postwar Yankees*, 72; US Congress, House, 1952, *Organized Baseball, Report*, 22–24; Surdam, *Big Leagues Go to Washington*, 15–22.

88. US Congress, House, 1952, *Organized Baseball, Report*, 197–198; Nathanson, "The Sovereign Nation of Baseball," 75; US Congress, House, 1977, *Inquiry into Professional Sports, Report*, 54; Wolohan, "Curt Flood Act of 1998," 351.

89. US Congress, House, 1966, *Professional Football League Merger*, 2–3.

90. US Congress, House, 1972, *Proposed Merger*, 243; Harris, *The League*, 17.

91. US Congress, Senate, 1972, *Authorizing the Merger*.

92. *Sales Management*, "Free-vs-Toll Forces Gird for Big Battle," 43.

93. The movie *Tin Men* had a scene where the aluminum siding salesmen were drinking coffee in a diner; they discussed the previous evening's episodes of *Bonanza* and *The Flintstones*.

## Epilogue

1. Landler, "Are We Having Fun Yet?" 66.

2. Malcolm, "Unlimited vay-k? I want to work here," 5B.

3. *USA Today*, "Concern Grows over Pollution from Jets," posted December 18, 2006, http://usatoday30.usatoday.com/money/biztravel/2006-12-18-jet-pollution, viewed April 17, 2013, 1:51p.m.; US Government Accounting Office, "Global Pollution from Jet Aircraft Could Increase in the Future," January 29, 1992, http://ww.gao.gov/products/RCED-97-72, viewed April 17, 2013, 1:51 p.m.

4. Hays, *Beauty, Health, and Permanence*, 34, see also 19, 539–541.

5. Starr, *Endangered Dreams*, 280; Hays, *Beauty, Health, and Permanence*, 116.

# BIBLIOGRAPHY

Abbott, Edith. *Women in Industry: A Study in American Economic History* (New York: Arno and *New York Times*, 1969).

Abbott, Michael, and Orley Ashenfelter. "Labour Supply, Commodity Demand and the Allocation of Time." *The Review of Economic Studies* 43(3), October 1976, 389–411.

Abelson, Nathan R. "Comics Are a Serious Business, Part I." *Advertising & Selling* 39(7), July 1946, 41–42, 80, 82, 84.

Abelson, Nathan R. "Comics Are a Serious Business, Part II." *Advertising & Selling* 39(8), August 1946, 80, 82, 84, 86, 90, 92.

Abramovitz, Mimi. *Regulating the Lives of Women: Social Welfare Policy from Colonial Times to the Present* (Boston: South End Press, 1996).

Adams, James Truslow. *Our Business Civilization: Some Aspects of American Culture* (New York: Albert & Charles Boni, 1929).

Adams, Judith A. *The American Amusement Park Industry: A History of Technology and Thrills* (Boston: Twayne Publishers, 1991).

Aguiar, Mark, and Erik Hurst. "Measuring Trends in Leisure: The Allocation of Time over Five Decades." *Quarterly Journal of Economics* 122(3), August 2007, 969–1006.

Aiken, Ralph. "A Laborer's Leisure." *North American Review* 232(3), September 1931, 268–273.

Allport, Floyd H. "This Coming Era of Leisure: Will It Be Worth Having?" *Harpers Magazine* 163, November 1931, 641–652.

Alvarez, Luis. *The Power of the Zoot: Youth Culture and Resistance during World War II* (Berkeley: University of California Press, 2008).

Anderson, Terry, and Donald Leal. *Free Market Environmentalism* (Boulder, CO: Westview Press, 1991).

Aron, Cindy S. Working at Play: A History of Vacations in the United States (Oxford: Oxford University Press, 1999).

Bailey, Peter. *Leisure and Class in Victorian England: Rational Recreation and the Contest for Control, 1830–1885* (London: Routledge & Kegan Paul, 1978).

Bakker, Gerben. "How Motion Pictures Industrialized Entertainment." *Journal of Economic History* 72(4), December 2012, 1036–1063.

Balazs, Anne L., "Toward a Better Understanding of the Nature Traveler." *Visions in Leisure and Business* 9(4), 1991, 5–13.

Barker, Martin. "Fredric Wertham—The Sad Case of the Unhappy Humanist." In *Pulp Demons: International Dimensions of the Postwar Anti-Comics Campaign*, edited by John A. Lent (Cranbury, NJ: Associated University Presses, 1999) 215–233.

Barzun, Jacques. *God's Country and Mine: A Declaration of Love Spiced with a Few Harsh Words* (Boston: Little, Brown and Company, 1954).

Baughman, James. *The Republic of Mass Culture: Journalism, Filmmaking, and Broadcasting in America since 1941* (Baltimore, MD: Johns Hopkins University Press, [1992, 1997] 2006), 3rd edition.

Baughman, James. *Same Time, Same Station: Creating American Television, 1948–1961* (Baltimore, MD: Johns Hopkins University Press, 2007).

Becker, Gary S. "A Theory of the Allocation of Time." *The Economic Journal* 75(299), 1965, 493–517.

Becker, Gary S. *A Treatise on the Family* (Cambridge, MA: Harvard University Press, 1981).

Becker, Gary S., and Kevin Murphy. "A Theory of Rational Addiction." *Journal of Political Economy* 96(4), August 1988, 675–700.

Belasco, Warren James. *Americans on the Road: From Autocamp to Motel, 1910–1945* (Cambridge, MA: MIT Press, 1979).

Benison, Saul. "Poliomyelitis and the Rockefeller Institute: Social Effects and Institutional Response." In *Theory and Practice in American Medicine*, edited by Gert H. Brieger (New York: Science History Publications, 1976), 85–103.

Bennett, M. Jeanine. "Constraints on Leisure in Middle Age." In *Constraints on Leisure*, edited by Michael G. Wade (Springfield, IL: Charles C. Thomas, 1985), 319–333.

Benson, Susan Porter. "Gender, Generation, and Consumption in the United States: Working-Class Families in the Interwar Period." In *Getting and Spending: European and American Consumer Societies in the Twentieth Century*, edited by Susan Strasser, Charles McGovern, and Matthias Judt (Cambridge, UK: Cambridge University Press, 1998), 223–240.

Bergman, Andrew. *We're in the Money: Depression America and Its Films* (New York: New York University Press, 1971).

Bergreen, Laurence. *Look Now, Pay Later: The Rise of Network Broadcasting* (Garden City, NY: Doubleday, 1980).

Biddle, Jeff, and Daniel Hamermesh. "Sleep and the Allocation of Time." *Journal of Political Economy* 98(5), October 1990, 922–943.

Bienefeld, M. A. "The Normal Week under Collective Bargaining." *Economica* 36(142), May 1969, 172–192.

*Billboard.* "The Present Status of the Legitimate Theater in the United States." August 14, 1926, 52–53, 129.

Blau, Francine, and Lawrence Kahn. "Gender Differences in Pay." *Journal of Economic Perspectives* 14(4), Autumn 2000, 75–99.

Bogart, Ernest Ludlow. *War Costs and Their Financing: A Study of the Financing of the War and the After-War Problems of Debt and Taxation* (New York: D. Appleton, 1921).

Bordwell, David, Kristin Thompson, and Janet Staiger. *The Classical Hollywood Cinema: Film Style and Mode of Production to 1960* (New York: Columbia University Press, 1985).

Borsay, Peter. *A History of Leisure: The British Experience since 1500* (Hampshire, UK: Palgrave Macmillan, 2006).

Borsodi, Ralph. *This Ugly Civilization* (New York: Harper & Brothers, 1933).

Bowers, Glenn A. "Nesday Chemical Company." *Harvard Business Reports* 4(1927), 162–170.

Bowser, Eileen. *The Transformation of Cinema, 1907–1915.* History of the American Cinema. Charles Harpole, General Editor (New York: Charles Scribner's Sons, 1990).

Braden, Donna R. "'The Family That Plays Together Stays Together': Family Pastimes and Indoor Amusements, 1890–1930." In *American Home Life, 1880–1930: A Social History of Spaces and Services*, edited by Jessica H. Foy and Thomas J. Schlereth (Knoxville: University of Tennessee Press, 1992), 145–161.

Brauscher, Howard. "Freedom in Leisure." *Recreation* 27(9), December 1933, 401.

Brown, Norman O. *Life Against Death: The Psychoanalytical Meaning of History* (Middletown, CT: Wesleyan University Press, 1959).

Bruere, Martha. "Savings or Efficiency?" *The Outlook*, January 27, 1912, 392–397.

Burnham, John Chynoweth. "The Gasoline Tax and the Automobile Revolution." *The Mississippi Valley Historical Review* 48(3), December 1961, 435–459.

Busch, Henry. "Contributions of Recreation to the Development of Wholesome Personality." *Recreation* 27(7), October 1933, 307–311.

*Business Week.* "A Big Fast-Growing Market: The Leisured Masses, Part 1." September 12, 1953, 142–143, 145–146, 148, 150, 152.

*Business Week.* "A Hard Look at TV's Future." October 30, 1948, 72, 74, 78.

*Business Week.* "Competition—From Inside and Out—Grips Magazines." July 12, 1952, 38, 40, 42.

*Business Week.* "Food-Store Magazines Hit the Big Time." February 9, 1952, 108, 110.

*Business Week.* "Industrious Leisure." February 23, 1935, 14–15.

*Business Week.* "Marriages Make a Market." May 31, 1952, 42.

*Business Week.* "Outdoor Power Tools: Coming Up Fast." April 4, 1953, 58–59, 62.

*Business Week.* "Television's Audience Problem." September 13, 1947, 70–71, 74–75.

*Business Week.* "The Entertainment Economy." March 14, 1994, 58.

*Business Week.* "The Leisured Masses: Where Leisure Time—and Money—Goes, Part II." September 19, 1953, 144–146, 148, 150–152, 154.

*Business Week.* "The New Do-It-Yourself Market." June 14, 1952, 60–62, 64, 66, 69–70, 72, 74, 76.

*Business Week.* "The Weird Economics of the Washing Machine." June 14, 1952, 79.

*Business Week.* "TV Slump: The Old One-Two." May 5, 1951, 86, 88, 91.

*Business Week.* "Video Visions." November 29, 1947, 39, 41.

*Business Week.* "We Spend about as Much for Fun as for Running the Government." July 3, 1932, 20–23.

*Business Week.* "Who Are Tomorrow's Customers?" December 8, 1951, 146–148, 151–152.

Butler, George D. *Introduction to Community Recreation* (New York: McGraw-Hill Book Company, 1976), 5th edition.

Butsch, Richard. "Home Video and Corporate Plans: Capital's Limited Power to Manipulate Leisure." In *For Fun and Profit: The Transformation of Leisure into Consumption*, edited by Richard Butsch (Philadelphia: Temple University Press, 1990), 136–151.

Butsch, Richard. "Introduction: Leisure and Hegemony in America." In *For Fun and Profit: The Transformation of Leisure into Consumption*, edited by Richard Butsch (Philadelphia: Temple University Press, 1990), 3–27.

Butsch, Richard. *The Making of American Audiences: From Stage to Television, 1750–1990* (Cambridge, UK: Cambridge University Press, 2000).

Byington, Margaret. *Homestead: The Households of a Mill Town* (New York: New York Charities Publication, 1910).

Cahill, Marion. *Shorter Hours: A Study of the Movement since the Civil War* (New York: Columbia University Press, 1932).

Cain, Louis, and Sok Chul Hong. "Survival in 19th Century Cities: The Larger the City, the Smaller Your Chances." *Explorations in Economic History* 46(2009), 450–463.

Campbell, Helen. *Women Wage-Earners* (Boston: Roberts Brothers, 1893).

Cassady, Ralph, Jr. "Some Economic Aspects of Motion Picture Production and Marketing." *Journal of Business of the University of Chicago* 6(2), April 1933, 113–131.

Centers for Disease Control and Prevention. "CDC on Infectious Diseases in the United States: 1900–99." *Population and Development Review* 25(3), September 1999, 635–640.

Centers for Disease Control and Prevention. "CDC on Vaccines and Children's Health: United States 1900–98." *Population and Development Review* 25(2), June 1999, 391–395.

Chapin, Charles V. "The End of the Filth Theory of Disease." *Popular Science Monthly* 60(3), July 1902, 234–239.

Chapin, Robert C. *Standard of Living among Working Men's Families in New York City* (New York: Charities Publication Committee, 1909).

Chapple, Steve, and Reebee Garofalo. *Rock "N" Roll Is Here to Pay* (Chicago: Nelson-Hall, 1977).

Chase, Stuart. "Play." *Whither Mankind: A Panorama of Modern Civilization* (New York: Longmans, Green, 1928).

Chase, Stuart. *Men and Machines* (New York: Macmillan, 1929).

Chudacoff, Howard. *The Age of the Bachelor: Creating an American Subculture* (Princeton, NJ: Princeton University Press, 1999).

Clark, John M. "Recent Developments in Economics." *Recent Developments in the Social Sciences* (Philadelphia: J. B. Lippincott, 1927), 213–306.

Club of Rome. *The Limits to Growth: A Report for the Club of Rome's Project on the Predicament of Mankind* (New York: Universe Books, 1972).

Coase, Ronald H. "Payola in Radio and Television Broadcasting." *Journal of Law and Economics* 22(2), October 1979, 269–328.

Commons, John, R. *History of Labour in the United States*, Vol. 1 (New York: Macmillan, 1918).

Conant, Michael. *Antitrust in the Motion Picture Industry: Economic and Legal Analysis* (Berkeley: University of California Press, 1960).

Conner, Cheryl. "Employees Really Do Waste Time at Work." July 17, 2012, http://www.forbes.com/sites/cherylsnappconner/2012/07/17/employees-really-do-waste-time-at-work, viewed June 12, 2013, 3:03 p.m.

Cooper, Gail. *Air-Conditioning America: Engineers and the Controlled Environment, 1900–1960* (Baltimore, MD: Johns Hopkins University Press, 1998).

Cordell, H. Ken, Barbara L. McDonald, Burt Lewis, Morgan P. Miles, Jack K. Martin, and James J. Bason. "United States." In *World Leisure Participation: Free Time in the Global Village*, edited by Grant Cushman and Jiri Zuzanek (Oxon, UK: CAB International, 1996), 215–235.

Costa, Dora. *American Living Standards: Evidence from Recreational Expenditures* (Cambridge, MA: National Bureau of Economic Research, 1999).

Costa, Dora. *The Evolution of Retirement: An American Economic History, 1880–1990* (Chicago: University of Chicago Press, 1998).

Coughlan, Robert. "A $40 Billion Bill Just for Fun." *Life*, December 28, 1959, 69–70, 72–74.

Courtwright, David T. *Violent Land: Single Men and Social Disorder from the Frontier to the Inner City* (Cambridge, MA: Harvard University Press, 1996).

Cowan, Ruth Schwartz. *More Work for Mother: The Ironies of Household Technology from the Open Hearth to the Microwave* (New York: Basic Books, 1983).

Cox, W. Michael, and Richard Alm. "Have a Nice Day!: The American Journey to Better Working Conditions." *Federal Reserve Bank of Dallas Reprint from Annual Report 2000* (Dallas, TX: Federal Reserve Bank of Dallas, 2001).

Cox, W. Michael, and Richard Alm. "Time Well Spent: The Declining *Real* Cost of Living in America." *1997 Annual Report of the Federal Reserve Bank of Dallas* (Dallas, TX: Federal Reserve Bank of Dallas, 1998).

Cressey, Paul. *The Taxi-Dance Hall: A Sociological Study in Commercialized Recreation and City Life* (New York: AMS Press, [1932] 1971).

Currell, Susan. *The March of Spare Time: The Problem and Promise of Leisure in the Great Depression* (Philadelphia: University of Pennsylvania Press, 2005).

Cutler, Jonathan. *Labor's Time: Shorter Hours, the UAW, and the Struggle for American Unionism* (Philadelphia: Temple University Press, 2004).

Daniels, Bruce C. *Puritans at Play: Leisure and Recreation in Colonial New England* (New York: St. Martin's Press, 1995).

Dawson, Melanie. *Laboring to Play: Home Entertainment and the Spectacle of Middle-Class Cultural Life, 1850–1920* (Tuscaloosa: University of Alabama Press, 2005).

Day, Timothy. *A Century of Recorded Music: Listening to Musical History* (New Haven, CT: Yale University Press, 2000).

Degler, Carl. *At Odds: Women and the Family in America from the Revolution to the Present* (Oxford: Oxford University Press, 1980).

De Grazia, Sebastian. *Of Time, Work, and Leisure* (New York: The Twentieth Century Fund, 1962).

Denney, Reuel. *The Astonished Muse* (Chicago: University of Chicago Press, 1957).

Deutsch, Albert. *Our Rejected Children* (Boston: Little, Brown, 1950).

*Discover Magazine.* May 22, 2008, http://blogs.discovermagazine.com/gnxp/2008/05/religion-public-attitudes-europe-vs-usa/html.

Dreiser, Theodore. *Sister Carrie* (New York: W. W. Norton, [1900] 2006), 3rd edition.

Dulles, Foster Rhea. *America Learns to Play: A History of Popular Recreation, 1607–1940* (New York: D. Appleton-Century, 1940).

Dumazedier, Joffre. *Sociology of Leisure* (Amsterdam: Elsevier, 1974).

Dupont, Brandon, and Thomas Weiss. "Variability in Overseas Travel by Americans, 1820–2000." *Cliometrica* 7(3), 2013, 319–339.

*Economist*. "The Unhealthy Poor." June 4, 1994, 55–56.

Edwards, Richard. *Contested Terrain: The Transformation of the Workplace in the Twentieth Century* (New York: Basic Books, 1979).

Erenberg, Lewis. *Steppin' Out: New York Nightlife and the Transformation of American Culture, 1890–1930* (Westport, CT: Greenwood Press, 1981).

Etzioni, Amitai. "A Crisis of Consumerism." In *Aftershocks: Economic Crisis and Institutional Choice*, edited by Anton Hemerilck, Ben Knapen, and Ellen van Doorne (Amsterdam: Amsterdam University Press, 2009), 155–162.

Everson, William. *American Silent Film* (New York: Oxford University Press, 1978).

Ewen, Stuart. *Captains of Consciousness: Advertising and the Social Roots of the Consumer Culture* (New York: Basic Books 2001, 1976), 25th anniversary edition.

Faith, Nicholas. *The World the Railways Made* (London: Pimlico, [1990] 1994).

Fass, Paula. *The Damned and the Beautiful: American Youth in the 1920's* (New York: Oxford University Press, 1977).

Federal Reserve Bank of Dallas. *These Are the Good Old Days: A Report on U.S. Living Standards* (Dallas, TX: Federal Reserve Bank of Dallas, 1994).

Fischer, David Hackett. *Growing Old in America* (New York: Oxford University Press, 1978).

Fisk, Donald M. "American Labor in the 20th Century." *Compensation and Working Conditions*, Fall 2001, http://www.bls.gov/opub/cwc/cm20030124ar02pl.html, viewed April 19, 2013, 10:28 a.m.

Flink, James J. *The Car Culture* (Cambridge, MA: MIT Press, 1975).

Floud, Roderick, Robert W. Fogel, Bernard Harris, and Sok Chul Hong. *The Changing Body: Health, Nutrition, and Human Development in the Western World since 1700* (Cambridge, UK: Cambridge University Press, 2011).

Fogel, Robert W. *Egalitarianism: The Economic Revolution of the Twentieth Century*, Simon Kuznets Memorial Lectures presented at Yale University, April 22–24, 1992.

Fogel, Robert W. *The Fourth Great Awakening and the Future of Egalitarianism* (Chicago: University of Chicago Press, 2000).

Fogel, Robert W. *Political Arithmetic: Simon Kuznets and the Empirical Tradition in Economics* (Chicago: University of Chicago Press, 2013).

Ford, Henry, and Samuel Crowther. *My Life and Work* (Garden City, NY: Doubleday, Page, 1923).

Forman, Henry James. *Our Movie Made Children* (New York: Arno Press Reprint [1935] 1970).

Frank, Josette. "What's in the Comics?" *Journal of Educational Sociology* 18(4), December 1944, 214–222.

Frank, Robert. *The Winner-Take-All Society* (New York: Penguin Books, 1996).

Frank, Thomas. *The Conquest of Cool: Business Culture, Counterculture, and the Rise of Hip Consumerism* (Chicago: University of Chicago Press, 1997).

Fromm, Erich. *The Sane Society* (New York: Rinehart, 1955).

Garber, Megan. "Perks and Recreation: In Silicon Valley, a New Breed of Tech Company Tries to Enforce Fun." *The Atlantic*, December 2012, 28–32.

Gauss, Christian. *Life in College* (New York: Charles Scribner's Sons, 1930).

Gelatt, Roland. *The Fabulous Phonograph, 1877–1977* (New York: Macmillan, [1954] 1977), 2nd revised edition.

Gelber, Steven M. *Hobbies: Leisure and the Culture of Work in America* (New York: Columbia University Press, 1990).

Gendell, Murray, and Jacob S. Siegel. "Trends in Retirement Age by Sex, 1950–2005." *Monthly Labor Review* (July 1992), 22–29.

Gilbert, James. *A Cycle of Outrage: America's Reaction to the Juvenile Delinquent in the 1950s* (New York: Oxford University Press, 1986).

Gilman, Charlotte P. *Women and Economics: A Study of the Economic Relation Between Men and Women as a Factor in Social Evolution* (Berkeley: University of California, [1898] 1998).

Gleason, William A. *The Leisure Ethic: Work and Play in American Literature, 1840–1940* (Stanford, CA: Stanford University Press, 1999).

Goldin, Claudia. *Understanding the Gender Gap: An Economic History of American Women* (New York: Oxford University Press, 1990).

Goldin, Claudia. "Labor Markets in the Twentieth Century." Working Paper H0058, NBER, June 1994.

Gomery, Douglas. *A History of Broadcasting in the United States* (Malden, MA: Blackwell Publishing, 2008).

Gomery, Douglas. *Shared Pleasures: A History of Movie Presentation in the United States* (Madison: University of Wisconsin Press, 1992).

Gomery, Douglas. *The Hollywood Studio System* (New York: St. Martin's Press, 1986).

Gomery, Douglas. "The Movie Palace Comes to America's Cities." In *For Fun and Profit: The Transformation of Leisure into Consumption*, edited by Richard Butsch (Philadelphia: Temple University Press, 1990), 136–151.

Gomery, Douglas. "Who Killed Hollywood?" *Wilson Quarterly* 16(3), Summer 1991, 106–112.

Goodman, Robert. *The Luck Business: The Devastating Consequences and Broken Promises of America's Gambling Explosion* (New York: Free Press, 1995).

Gordon, Robert. "Why Innovation Won't Save Us." *Wall Street Journal.com*. December 21, 2012.

Graebner, William. *A History of Retirement: The Meaning and Function of Retirement in America, 1885–1978* (New Haven, CT: Yale University Press, 1980).

Graham, Ellen. "As Kids Gain Power of Purse, Marketing Takes Aim at Them." *Wall Street Journal*, January 19, 1988, 1, 15.

Gratton, Brian. "The Poverty of Impoverishment Theory: The Economic Well-Being of the Elderly, 1890–1950." *Journal of Economic History* 56(1), 1996, 39–61.

Greenwood, Jeremy, Ananth Seshadri, and Guillaume Vandenbroucke. "The Baby Boom and Baby Bust." *American Economic Review* 95(1), March 2005, 183–207.

Greenwood, Jeremy, Ananth Seshadri, and Mehmet Yorukoglu. "Engines of Liberation." *Review of Economic Studies* 72(1), January 2005, 109–133.

Grossman, Michael. 1972. "On the Concept of Health Capital and the Demand for Health." *Journal of Political Economy* 80(2), 223–255.

Gruenberg, Sidonie Matsner. "The Comics as a Social Force." *Journal of Educational Sociology* 18(4), December 1944, 204–213.

Gustaitis, Joseph. "The Jukebox: America's Music Machine." *American History Illustrated*, November/December 1989.

Gutman, Herbert G. "Protestantism and the American Labor Movement: The Christian Spirit in the Gilded Age." In *Work, Culture, and Society in Industrializing America: Essays in American Working-Class and Social History* (New York: Alfred A. Knopf, 1976), 79–117.

Gutman, Herbert G. "Work, Culture, and Society in Industrializing America, 1815–1919." In *Work, Culture, and Society in Industrializing America: Essays in American Working-Class and Social History* (New York: Alfred A. Knopf, 1976), 3–78.

Haber, Carole, and Brian Gratton. *Old Age and the Search for Security: An American Social History* (Bloomington: Indiana University Press, 1994).

Hajdu, David. *The Ten-Cent Plague: The Great Comic-Book Scare and How It Changed America* (New York: Farrar, Straus and Giroux, 2008).

Hamill, Katharine. "The Record Business—'It's Murder.'" *Fortune*, May 1961, 148–151, 178, 182, 187.

Hamilton, Richard. "Work and Leisure: On the Reporting of Poll Results." *Public Opinion Quarterly* 55(3), Autumn 1991, 347–356.

Hampton, Benjamin. *History of the American Film Industry: From Its Beginnings to 1931* (New York: Dover Publications, [1931] 1970).

Handel, Leo A. *Hollywood Looks at Its Audience: A Report of Film Audience Research* (Urbana: University of Illinois Press, [1950] 1974).

Harding, Denys. "Varieties of Work and Leisure." *Occupational Psychology* 12(2), Spring 1938, 104–115.

Hardy, Stephen. "'Adopted by All the Leading Clubs': Sporting Goods and the Shaping of Leisure, 1800–1900." In *For Fun and Profit: The Transformation of Leisure into Consumption*, edited by Richard Butsch (Philadelphia: Temple University Press, 1990), 71–101.

Harris, David. *The League: The Rise and Decline of the NFL* (New York: Bantam Books, 1986).

Havemann, Ernest. "The Emptiness of Too Much Leisure: Automation and a Shrinking Work Week Bring a Real Threat to All of Us." *Life*, February 7, 1964, 76–90.

Havemann, Ernest. "The Task Ahead: How to Take Life Easy: Raised on a Diet of Success Through Hard Work, Americans Now Face a Glut of Leisure." *Life*, February 21, 1964, 84–94.

Hays, Samuel P. *Beauty, Health, and Permanence: Environmental Politics in the United States 1955–1985* (Cambridge, UK: Cambridge University Press, 1987).

Higginson, Thomas Wentworth. "Gymnastics." *Atlantic Monthly* 7, March 1861, 283–302.

Higginson, Thomas Wentworth. "Saints and Their Bodies." *Atlantic Monthly* 1, March 1858, 582–595.

Hilton, George. "Transport Technology and the Urban Pattern." *Journal of Contemporary History* 4(3), July 1969, 123–135.

Hinman, Albert. "An Inventory of Housing in a Suburban City." *Journal of Land & Public Utility Economics* 7(2), May 1931, 169–180.

Holbrook, Stewart. *The Story of American Railroads* (New York: Crown Publishers, [1947] 1981).

Hooks, Janet. "Women's Occupations Through Seven Decades." *Women's Bureau Bulletin*, No. 218 (Washington, DC: Government Printing Office, 1951). US Department of Labor.

Horowitz, Daniel. *The Morality of Spending: Attitudes Toward the Consumer Society in America, 1875–1940* (Baltimore, MD: Johns Hopkins University Press, 1985).

Houseman, John. "Hollywood Faces the Fifties. Part I. The Lost Enthusiasm." *Harper's*, April 1950, 50–59.

Houseman, John. "Hollywood Faces the Fifties. Part II. Battle over Television." *Harper's*, May 1950, 51–59.

Hoy, Suellen. *Chasing Dirt: The American Pursuit of Cleanliness* (New York: Oxford University Press, 1995).

Hoyt, Homer. *One Hundred Years of Land Values in Chicago* (Chicago: University of Chicago Press, 1933).

Huettig, Mae D. *Economic Control of the Motion Picture Industry: A Study in Industrial Organization.* Ph.D. dissertation (University of Pennsylvania, 1944).

Hughes, Lawrence M. "TV in 10 Years Transforms America." *Sales Management*, November 20, 1955, 30–31.

Huizinga, Johan. *Homo Ludens: A Study of the Play Element in Culture* (Boston: Beacon Press, 1955 reprint).

Hunnicutt, Benjamin K. "Economic Constraints on Leisure." In *Constraints on Leisure*, edited by Michael G. Wade (Springfield, IL: Charles C. Thomas, 1985), 243–286.

Hunnicutt, Benjamin Kline. *Work Without End: Abandoning Shorter Hours for the Right to Work* (Philadelphia: Temple University Press, 1988).

Hutchison, William R. *Religious Pluralism in America: The Contentious History of a Founding Ideal* (Ann Arbor, MI: Sheridan Books, 2003).

Illich, Ivan. *Toward a History of Needs* (New York: Pantheon Books, 1977).

Iso-Ahola, Seppo, and Roger C. Mannell. "Social and Psychological Constraints on Leisure." In *Constraints on Leisure*, edited by Michael G. Wade (Springfield, IL: Charles C. Thomas, 1985), 111–151.

Izod, John. *Hollywood and the Box Office, 1895–1986* (New York: Columbia University Press, 1988).

Jackson, Kenneth T. *Crabgrass Frontier: The Suburbanization of the United States* (New York: Oxford University Press, 1985).

Jevons, William Stanley. *The Theory of Political Economy* (New York: Augustus M. Kelley, [1957] 1965), 5th edition.

Joel, Yale. "A New, $10-Billion Power: The U.S. Teen-age Consumer." *Life*, August 31, 1959, 78.

Johnson, D. Gale. "Agriculture and the Wealth of Nations: Richard T. Ely Lecture." *American Economic Review* 87(2), May 1997, 1–12.

Johnson, Dirk. "Until Dust Do Us Part: In a New Study the Dirty Truth Is Revealed about Men, Women and Housework: Nobody Really Wants to Do It." *Newsweek*, March 25, 2002, 41.

Jones, Ethel B. "New Estimates of Hours of Work per Week and Hourly Earnings, 1900–1957." *Review of Economics and Statistics* 45(4), November 1963, 374–385.

Jones, Stephen G. *Workers at Play: A Social and Economic History of Leisure, 1918–1939* (London: Routledge & Kegan Paul, 1986).

Jonnes, Jill. *Empires of Light: Edison, Tesla, and Westinghouse, and the Race to Electrify the World* (New York: Random House, 2003).

Juster, F. Thomas, and Frank P. Stafford. *Time, Goods, and Well-Being* (Ann Arbor, MI: Survey Research Center, 1985).

Juster, F. Thomas, and Frank P. Stafford. "Comment." *Public Opinion Quarterly* 55(3), Autumn 1991, 357–359.

Kaplan, Max. *Leisure in America: A Social Inquiry* (New York: John Wiley & Sons, 1960).

Keats, John. *The Crack in the Picture Window* (Boston: Houghton Mifflin Company, 1956).

Kerr, Walter. *The Decline of Pleasure* (New York: Simon and Schuster, 1962).

Keynes, John Maynard. "Economic Possibilities for our Grandchildren." In *Essays in Persuasion* (New York: Harcourt, Brace, 1932), 358–373.

Kihss, Peter. "Senator Charges 'Deceit' On Comics." *New York Times*, April 23, 1954, 29.

Kingsdale, Jon M. "The 'Poor Man's Club': Social Functions of the Urban Working-Class Saloon." *American Quarterly* 25(4), October 1973, 472–489.

Kirsch, Jonathan. *A History of the End of the World* (New York: HarperCollins, 2006).

Kleiber, Douglas A., and Guy R. Dirkin. "Intrapersonal Constraints to Leisure." In *Constraints on Leisure*, edited by Michael G. Wade (Springfield, IL: Charles C. Thomas, 1985), 17–42.

Kleiber, Douglas A., and William H. Rickards. "Leisure and Recreation in Adolescence: Limitation and Potential." In *Constraints on Leisure*, edited by Michael G. Wade (Springfield, IL: Charles C. Thomas, 1985), 289–317.

Kline, Stephen. "Toys, Socialization, and the Commodification of Play." In *Getting and Spending: European and American Consumer Societies in the Twentieth Century*, edited by Susan Strasser, Charles McGovern, and Matthias Judt (Cambridge, UK: Cambridge University Press, 1998), 339–358.

Knapp, Richard F., and Charles E. Hartsoe. *Play for America: The National Recreation Association, 1906–1965* (Arlington, VA: National Recreation and Park Association, 1979).

Konner, Melvin. "Still Invisible and Dying in Harlem." *New York Times*, February 24, 1990, 25.

Kreps, Juanita M. *Lifetime Allocation of Work and Income: Essays in the Economics of Aging* (Durham, NC: Duke University Press, 1971).

Kreps, Juanita M. *Sex in the Marketplace: American Women at Work* (Baltimore, MD: Johns Hopkins Press, 1971).

Kusell, H.O. "Bank Night." *The New Republic*. May 6, 1936, 363–365.

Kuznets, Simon. "Modern Economic Growth: Findings and Reflections." Nobel Prize Lecture. http://www.nobelprize.org/nobel_prizes/economics/laureates/1971/kuznets-lecture.html. Viewed June 5, 2013, 9:42 a.m.

Kuznets, Simon. *Modern Economic Growth: Rate, Structure, and Spread* (New Haven, CT: Yale University Press, 1966).

Kyrk, Hazel. *A Theory of Consumption* (Boston: Houghton Mifflin).

*Ladies Home Journal*. "A Crime Against American Children." January 1909, 5.

Landler, Mark. "Are We Having Fun Yet? Maybe Too Much." *Business Week*, March 14, 1994, 66.

Lasch, Christopher. *The Culture of Narcissism: American Life in an Age of Diminishing Expectations* (New York: W. W. Norton, 1978).

Lears, Jackson. *Fables of Abundance: A Cultural History of Advertising in America* (New York: Basic-Books, 1994).

Lears, Jackson. "Reconsidering Abundance: A Plea for Ambiguity." In *Getting and Spending: European and American Consumer Societies in the Twentieth Century*, edited by Susan Strasser, Charles McGovern, and Matthias Judt (Cambridge, UK: Cambridge University Press, 1998), 449–466.

Leavitt, Helen. *Superhighway—Superhoax* (Garden City, NY: Doubleday, 1970).

Lebergott, Stanley. *The American Economy: Income, Wealth, and Want* (Princeton, NJ: Princeton University Press, 1997).

Lebergott, Stanley. *The Americans: An Economic Record* (New York: W. W. Norton, 1984).

Lebergott, Stanley. *Pursuing Happiness: American Consumers in the Twentieth Century* (Princeton, NJ: Princeton University Press, 1993).

Lengfelder, Julie, and Dallen J. Timothy, "Leisure Time in the 1990's and Beyond: Cherished Friend or Incessant Foe?" *Visions in Leisure and Business* 19(1), Spring 2000, 13–26.

Levine, Peter. *A. G. Spalding and the Rise of Baseball: The Promise of American Sport* (New York: Oxford University Press, 1985).

Levine, Robert, and Ellen Wolff. "Social Time: The Heartbeat of Culture." *Psychology Today*, March 1985, 28–35.

Lewis, Tom. *Divided Highways: Building the Interstate Highways, Transforming American Life* (New York: Penguin Books, 1997).

Linder, Staffan B. *The Harried Leisure Class* (New York: Columbia University Press, 1970).

Lindquist, Ruth. *The Family in the Present Social Order: A Study of Needs of American Families* (Chapel Hill: University of North Carolina Press, 1931).

*Listen to the Story*. "Trillions Earned under Table as More Work Off Radar." Michel Martin, Host. http://www.npr.org/2013/03/26/175361658/trillions-earned-under-table-as-more-work-off-radar. Viewed June 5, 2013, 9:40 a.m.

*Literary Digest*. "The Theater Flings Down the Glove to the Radio." January 24, 1925, 29.

*Literary Digest*. "Electric Farming." August 7, 1926, 23.

*Literary Digest*. "The Current Fad for Picture Mags." January 30, 1937, 20–22.

Litman, Barry Russell. *The Vertical Structure of the Television Broadcasting Industry: The Coalescence of Power* (East Lansing: Michigan State University Press, 1979).

Lobsenz, Norman. "The Pleasure Neurotics." *Science Digest* 52(2), August 1962, 36–42.

Lovell, Terry. "The Social Relations of Cultural Production: Absent Centre of a New Discourse." In *One-Dimensional Marxism*, edited by Simon Clarke, Victor Jenleniewski Seidler, Kevin McDonnell, Kevin Robins, and Terry Lovell (London: Allison & Busby, 1980), 232–256.

Lundberg, George A., Mirra Komarovsky, and Mary Alice McInerny. *Leisure: A Suburban Study* (New York: Columbia University Press, 1934).

Lundberg, Isabel. "World Revolution, American Plan." *Harper's Magazine*, CXCVII, December 1948, 38–46.

Lynd, Robert S. "The People as Consumers." *Recent Social Trends in the United States: Report of the President's Research Committee on Social Trends* (New York: McGraw-Hill, 1933), 857–911.

Lynd, Robert S., and Helen Merrell Lynd. *Middletown in Transition: A Study in Cultural Conflicts* (New York: Harcourt Brace Jovanovich, [1937] 1965).

MacDonald, Dwight. "Profiles: A Caste, A Culture, A Market." *New Yorker*, November 22, 1958, 57–94; November 29, 1958, 57–107.

Malcolm, Hadley. "Unlimited vay-k? I want to work here." *USA Today*, April 30, 2013, 5B.

Mannell, Roger C., and Seppo E. Iso-Ahola. "Work Constraints on Leisure: A Social Psychological Analysis." In *Constraints on Leisure*, edited by Michael G. Wade (Springfield, IL: Charles C. Thomas, 1985), 155–187.

Mannes, Marya. "Junior Has a Craving." *New Republic*, February 17, 1947, 21–23.

Marcuse, Herbert. *An Essay on Liberation* (Boston: Beacon Press, 1969).

Marshall, Alfred. *Principles of Economics* (New York: Macmillan, [1890] 1950), 8th edition.

Maslow, Abraham. "A Theory of Human Motivation." *Psychological Review* 50(4), 1943, 370–396.

May, Elaine. *Homeward Bound: American Families in the Cold War Era* (New York: Basic Books, 1988).

McCarthy, Anna. "'The Front Row Is Reserved for Scotch Drinkers': Early Television's Tavern Audience." *Cinema Journal* 34(4), Summer 1995, 31–49.

McConachie, Bruce A. "Pacifying American Theatrical Audiences, 1820–1900." In *For Fun and Profit: The Transformation of Leisure into Consumption*, edited by Richard Butsch (Philadelphia: Temple University Press, 1990), 47–70.

McConnell, F. H. "Riveting to Rhythm: Music, Tried Out as a Cure for Factory Boredom, Proves to Be a Stimulus to Wartime Production." *New York Times*, August 31, 1941, SM17.

McGovern, Charles. "Consumption and Citizenship in the United States, 1900–1940." In *Getting and Spending: European and American Consumer Societies in the Twentieth Century*, edited by Susan Strasser, Charles McGovern, and Matthias Judt (Cambridge, UK: Cambridge University Press, 1998), 37–58.

McGuire, Francis A. "Constraints in Later Life." In *Constraints on Leisure*, edited by Michael G. Wade (Springfield, IL: Charles C. Thomas, 1985), 335–353.

McMillan, John. *Reinventing the Bazaar* (New York: W. W. Norton, 2002).

Meacham, Lewis. "The Professional Base Ball Association—What It Must Do to Be Saved." *Chicago Tribune*, October 24, 1875, 12.

Mead, Margaret. "The Pattern of Leisure in Contemporary American Culture." *Annals of the American Academy of Political and Social Science* 313, September 1957, 11–15.

Michelon, L. C. "The New Leisure Class." *American Journal of Sociology* LIX(4), January 1954, 371–378.

Miles, Steven. *Youth Lifestyles in a Changing World* (Buckingham, UK: Open University Press, 2000).

Mill, John Stuart. *Principles of Political Economy* (Fairfield, NJ: Augustus M. Kelley, [1848] 1987).

Millard, Andre. *America on Record: A History of Recorded Sound* (Cambridge, UK: Cambridge University Press, 1995).

Miller, Michael A. "Time-off benefits in small establishments." *Monthly Labor Review* (March 1992), 3–8.

Miller, Perry. *The New England Mind: The Seventeenth Century* (Cambridge, MA: Belknap Press, 1939).

Millis, Harry, and Royal Montgomery. *Economics of Labor*, Vol. 1 (New York: McGraw-Hill, 1938).

Mills, C. Wright. *White Collar: The American Middle Classes* (New York: Oxford University Press, 1951).

Mincer, Jacob. "Labor Force Participation of Married Women: A Study of Labor Supply." *Aspects of Labor Economics: A Conference of the Universities-National Bureau Committee for Economic Research* (Princeton, NJ: Princeton University Press, 1962).

Mintz, Steven, and Susan Kellogg. *Domestic Revolutions: A Social History of American Family Life* (New York: The Free Press, 1988).

Mitchell, Wesley. "The Backward Art of Spending Money." *American Economic Review* 2(2), June 1912, 269–281.

Mokyr, Joel. "Why 'More Work for Mother?' Knowledge and Household Behavior, 1870–1945." *Journal of Economic History* 60(1), March 2000, 1–41.

Mokyr, Joel, and Rebecca Stein. "Science, Health, and Household Technology: The Effect of the Pasteur Revolution on Consumer Demand." In *The Economics of New Goods*, edited by Timothy Bresnahan and Robert Gordon (Chicago: University of Chicago Press, 1996), 143–206.

*Monthly Labor Review*. "Vacations for Factory Workers." XIII(2), August 1921, 212–213.

*Monthly Labor Review*. "Vacations with Pay for Production Workers." XXII(1), July 1926, 35–36.

Morris, Betsey. "Homes Get Dirtier as Women Seek Jobs and Men Volunteer for the Easy Chores." *Wall Street Journal*, February 12, 1985, 33.

Nash, Jay B. *Spectatoritis* (New York: Sears Publishing, 1932).

Nathanson, Michael. "The Sovereign Nation of Baseball: Why Federal Law Does Not Apply to 'America's Game' and How It Got That Way." *Villanova Sports & Entertainment Law Journal* 16, 2009, 49–98.

National Recreation Association. *The Leisure Hours of 5,000 People: A Report of a Study of Leisure Time Activities and Desires* (New York: National Recreation Association, 1934).

*Newsweek.* "Purified Comics." July 12, 1948, 56.

*Newsweek.* "Teen-Age Tasters." December 3, 1951, 77–78.

*Newsweek.* "Television in the Tavern." June 16, 1947, 64.

*New York Times.* "'Angels' Seeking Television's Aid." June 21, 1948, 23.

*New York Times.* "'Dry' Club Renews Video Appeal." July 19, 1948, 12.

*New York Times.* "For Reconsidering Five-Day-Week Bill." April 8, 1933, 8.

*New York Times.* "Many Doubt Comics Spur Crime, Senate Survey of Experts Shows." November 12, 1950, 1, 61.

*New York Times.* "Nation's Play Bill $10,165,857,000 a Year; Dr. Steiner Predicts Cut in 'Grand Scale.'" April 9, 1933, Sec. 2, 1.

*New York Times.* "Paid Vacation Spreads to Manual Labor Ranks." July 12, 1925, XXII.

*New York Times.* "Senate Votes 30-Hour Work Week, 53–30; Robinson 36-Hour Amendment Is Beaten." April 7, 1933, 1, 7.

*New York Times.* "Wireless Telephone Spread Fight News Over 120,000 Miles." July 3, 1921, 6.

North, Sterling. "A National Disgrace." *Chicago Daily News.* May 8, 1940, 21.

Nulty, Peter. "Matsushita Takes the Lead in Video Recorders." *Fortune*, July 16, 1979, 110–112, 116.

Nyberg, Amy Kiste. "Comic Book Censorship in the United States." In *Pulp Demons: International Dimensions of the Postwar Anti-Comics Campaign*, edited by John A. Lent (Cranbury, NJ: Associated University Presses, 1999), 42–68.

Nyberg, Amy Kiste. *Seal of Approval: The History of the Comics Code* (Jackson: University of Mississippi Press, 1998).

Nye, David E. *Electrifying America: Social Meanings of a New Technology, 1880–1940* (Cambridge, MA: MIT Press, 1990).

Nystrom, Paul H. *Economics of Fashion* (New York: Ronald Press, 1928).

O'Connor, Connie. *The Leisure Wasters* (New York: A. S. Barnes, 1966).

O'Leary, J. T., and F. D. Dottavio, "Outdoor Recreation Expenditures: A Nationwide Study," *Visions in Leisure and Business* 5(4), 1987, 46–52.

Olney, Martha L. *Buy Now, Pay Later: Advertising, Credit, and Consumer Durables in the 1920s* (Chapel Hill: University of North Carolina Press, 1991).

O'Neill, William. *A Democracy at War* (Cambridge, MA: Harvard University Press, 1993).

Osgerby, Bill. *Playboys in Paradise; Masculinity, Youth and Leisure-Style in Modern America* (Oxford: Berg, 2001).

Osgerby, Bill. "'A Caste, a Culture, a Market': Youth, Marketing, and Lifestyle in Postwar America." In *Growing Up Postmodern: Neoliberalism and the War on the Young*, edited by Ronald Strickland (Lanham, MD: Rowman and Littlefield, 2002), 15–33.

Oshima, Harry T. "Consumer Asset Formation and the Future of Capitalism." *Economic Journal* 71(281), March 1961, 20–35.

Owen, John D. *The Price of Leisure: An Economic Analysis of the Demand for Leisure Time* (Rotterdam: Rotterdam University Press, 1969).

Owen, John D. "Workweeks and Leisure: An Analysis of Trends, 1948–75." *Monthly Labor Review* 99(8), August 1976, 3–8.

Pack, Arthur Newton. *The Challenge of Leisure* (New York: Macmillan, 1934).

Paddock, Bill. "Video's Vital Role in Series Shown by Survey." *The Sporting News*, October 19, 1949, 11.

Parkhill, Forbes. "Bank Night Tonight." *Saturday Evening Post*, December 4, 1937, 20–21, 82.

Paxson, Frederic L. "The Highway Movement, 1916–1935." *The American Historical Review* 51(2), January 1946, 236–253.

Peck, Don. "They're Watching You at Work." *The Atlantic* 312(5), December 2013, 72–84.

Peiss, Kathy. *Cheap Amusements: Working Women and Leisure in Turn-of-the-Century New York* (Philadelphia: Temple University Press, 1986).

Peiss, Kathy. "Commercial Leisure and the 'Woman Question.'" In *For Fun and Profit: The Transformation of Leisure into Consumption*, edited by Richard Butsch (Philadelphia: Temple University Press, 1990), 105–117.

Peixotto, Jessica. "Cost of Living Studies. II: How Workers Spend a Living Wage: A Study of the Incomes and Expenditures of Eighty-Two Typographers' Families in San Francisco." *University of California Publications in Economics* 5, 1928–1931. Reprinted 1966.

Perkins, Frances. "Do Women in Industry Need Special Protection?" *The Survey* LV(10), February 15, 1926, 529–531.

Peterson, Theodore. *Magazines in the Twentieth Century* (Urbana: University of Illinois Press, 1964).

Pidgeon, Mary. *Women in the Economy of the United States of America: A Summary Report* (Washington, DC: GPO, 1937).

Pieper, Josef. *Leisure: The Basis of Culture* (New York: Mentor-Omega, 1963).

Pietrusza, David. *Major Leagues: The Formation, Sometimes Absorption and Mostly Inevitable Demise of 18 Professional Baseball Organizations, 1871 to Present* (Jefferson, NC: McFarland, 1991).

Poggi, Jack. *Theater in America: The Impact of Economic Forces, 1870–1967* (Ithaca, NY: Cornell University Press, 1968).

Potter, David M. *People of Plenty: Economic Abundance and the American Character* (Chicago: University of Chicago Press, 1954).

*Printers' Ink.* "Magazine Readership Unaffected by TV, Starch Finds." November 9, 1951, 40.

*Printers' Ink.* "The Tape Threat: Is Live TV Dead? Are Networks Through?" April 25, 1958, 25–27, 30, 32.

Putnam, Robert. *Bowling Alone: The Collapse and Revival of American Community* (New York: Simon & Schuster, 2000).

Rae, John B. *The Road and the Car in American Life* (Cambridge, MA: MIT Press, 1971).

Rainwater, Clarence E. *The Play Movement in the United States* (Chicago: University of Chicago Press, 1922).

Ram, Rati, and Theodore W. Schultz. "Life Span, Health, Savings, and Productivity." *Economic Development and Cultural Change* 27(3), April 1979, 399–421.

Ramey, Valerie. "Time Spent in Home Production in the Twentieth-Century United States: New Estimates from Old Data." *Journal of Economic History* 69(1), March 2009, 1–47.

Ramey, Valerie, and Neville Francis. "A Century of Work and Leisure." *American Economic Journal: Macroeconomics* 1(2), July 2009, 189–224.

Ramsaye, Terry. *A Million and One Nights: A History of the Motion Picture* (New York: Simon and Schuster, 1926).

Rapoport, Rhona, and Robert N. Rapoport. *Leisure and the Family Life Cycle* (London: Routledge & Kegan Paul, 1975).

Richmond, Phyllis A. "American Attitudes Toward the Germ Theory of Disease (1860–1880)," In *Theory and Practice in American Medicine*, edited by Gert H. Brieger (New York: Science History Publications, 1976), 58–84.

Riesman, David. "Listening to Popular Music." *American Quarterly* 2(4), Winter 1950, 359–371.

Riesman, David. *The Lonely Crowd: A Study of the Changing American Character* (New Haven, CT: Yale University Press, 1950).

Rifkin, Jeremy. *The End of Work: The Decline of the Global Labor Force and the Dawn of the Post-Market Era* (New York: Jeremy P. Tarcher/Putnam Book, 1995).

Robbins, Lionel. "On the Elasticity of Demand for Income in Terms of Effort." *Economica* 29, June 1930, 123–129.

Robinson, John P., and Geoffrey Godbey. *Time for Life: The Surprising Ways Americans Use Their Time* (University Park: Pennsylvania State University Press, 1997).

Roberts, Ken. *The Leisure Industries* (Hampshire, UK: Palgrave Macmillan, 2004).

Roediger, David, and Philip Foner. *Our Own Time: A History of American Labour and the Working Day* (London: Verso, 1989).

Roell, Craig H. *The Piano in America, 1890–1940* (Chapel Hill: University of North Carolina Press, 1989).

Rojek, Chris. *The Labour of Leisure: The Culture of Free Time* (Los Angeles, CA: Sage, 2010).

Rose, Mark. *Interstate: Express Highway Politics, 1939–1989* (Knoxville: University of Tennessee Press, [1990] 1979). Revised edition.

Rosen, George. *A History of Public Health*, Expanded edition (Baltimore, MD: Johns Hopkins University Press, [1958] 1993).

Rosen, Sherwin. "The Economics of Superstars." *American Economic Review* 71(5), December 1981, 845–858.

Rosin, Hanna. "The Touch-Screen Generation." *The Atlantic*, April 2013, 56–65.

Rotella, Elyce. "Women's Labor Force Participation and the Decline of the Family Economy in the United States." *Explorations in Economic History* 17(2), April 1980, 95–117.

Rothe, James T., Michael G. Harvey, and George C. Michael. "The Impact of Cable Television on Subscriber and Nonsubscriber Behavior." *Journal of Advertising Research* 23(4), August/September 1983, 15–23.

Rugg, Harold. *An Introduction to Problems of American Culture* (Boston: Ginn, 1931).

Rutman, Darrett B. "The Mirror of Puritan Authority." In *Law and Authority in Colonial America*, edited by George Athan Billias (New York: Dover Publications, 1965), 149–167.

Sahin, Haluk, and Robinson, John P. "Beyond the Realm of Necessity: Television and the Colonization of Leisure." *Media, Culture & Society* 3(1), 1980, 85–95.

*Sales Management*. "Free-vs-Toll Forces Gird for Big Battle." November 20, 1955, 43.

*Sales Management*. "How Much TV Does a Dollar Buy?" November 20, 1955, 36–37.

*Sales Management*. "TV-Sold Brands Become Consumer-Dealer 'Choice.'" November 20, 1955, 38.

*Sales Management*. "Two-Thirds of U.S. Homes Now Boast Television Sets." November 20, 1955, 32.

*Sales Management*. "Will Color Television 'Hypnotize Customers?'" November 20, 1955, 42–43.

Samuelson, Paul. "Paul A. Samuelson on Social Security." *Newsweek*, February 15, 1967, 88.

Sanjek, Russell. *American Popular Music and Its Business: The First Four Hundred Years (Part II: From 1790 to 1909)* (New York: Oxford University Press, 1988).

Scherer, F. M. *Industrial Market Structure and Economic Performance* (Chicago: Rand McNally, 1970).

Schor, Juliet B. *The Overworked American: The Unexpected Decline of Leisure* (New York: Basic Books, 1991).

Schudson, Michael. *Advertising, the Uneasy Persuasion: Its Dubious Impact on American Society* (New York: Basic Books, 1984).

Schultz, Theodore W. *Investment in Human Capital: The Role of Education and of Research* (New York: The Free Press, 1971).

Schultz, Theodore W. *Investing in People: The Economics of Population Quality* (Berkeley: University of California Press, 1981).

Schumpeter, Joseph A. *Capitalism, Socialism and Democracy* (New York: Harper Torchbooks 1970; originally published by Harper & Brothers, 1942).

Schwartzman, Helen. *Transformations: The Anthropology of Children's Play* (New York: Plenum Press, 1978).

Scott, Walter Dill. *Influencing Men in Business: The Psychology of Argument and Suggestion* (New York: Ronald Press, [1911] 1928).

Seymour, Harold. *Baseball: The Early Years* (New York: Oxford University Press, 1960).

Simon, Julian. *The Ultimate Resource* (Princeton, NJ: Princeton University Press, 1981).

Skolnick, Arlene. *Embattled Paradise: The American Family in an Age of Uncertainty* (New York: BasicBooks, 1991).

Smithsonian.com. October 2010, http://www.smithsonianmag.com/history-archaeology/Americas-True-History-of-Religious-Tolerance.html.

Snyder, Robert W. "Big Time, Small Time, All Around the Town: New York Vaudeville in the Early Twentieth Century." In *For Fun and Profit: The Transformation of Leisure into Consumption*, edited by Richard Butsch (Philadelphia, PA: Temple University Press, 1990), 118–135.

Solow, Robert. "A Contribution to the Theory of Economic Growth." *Quarterly Journal of Economics* 70(1), February 1956, 65–94.

Sowell, Thomas. *Ethnic America: A History* (New York: Basic Books, 1981).

Spigel, Lynn. *Make Room for TV: Television and the Family Ideal in Postwar America* (Chicago: University of Chicago Press, 1992).

Spitzer, Marian. "The Freedom of the Breeze." *Saturday Evening Post*, December 6, 1924, 74, 76, 78, 80, 82.

Starr, Kevin. *Endangered Dreams: The Great Depression in California* (New York: Oxford University Press, 1996).

Stebbins, Robert A. *Serious Leisure: A Perspective for Our Time* (New Brunswick, NJ: Transaction Publishers, 2007).

Steiner, Jesse F. *Americans at Play* (New York: Arno Press and *New York Times*, 1970; reprinted from McGraw-Hill, 1933).

Steiner, Jesse F. "Recreation and Leisure." *Recent Social Trends in the United States: Report of the President's Research Committee on Social Trends* (New York: McGraw-Hill, 1933), 912–957.

Strasser, Susan. "'The Convenience Is Out of This World:' The Garbage Disposer and American Consumer Culture." In *Getting and Spending: European and American Consumer Societies in the Twentieth Century*, edited by Susan Strasser, Charles McGovern, and Matthias Judt (Cambridge, UK: Cambridge University Press, 1998), 263–279.

Strick, J. C. "The Economics of the Motion Picture Industry: A Survey." *Philosophy of the Social Sciences* 8(4), December 1978, 406–417.

Stuart, Fredric. *The Effects of Television on the Motion Picture and Radio Industries* (New York: Arno Press, 1976).

Surdam, David. 2005. "Television and Minor League Baseball: Changing Patterns of Leisure in Postwar America." *Journal of Sports Economics* 6(1), 61–77.

Surdam, David. *The Big Leagues Go to Washington: Congress and Sports Antitrust, 1951–1989.* (Urbana: University of Illinois Press, 2015).

Surdam, David. *The Postwar Yankees: Baseball's Golden Age Revisited* (Lincoln: University of Nebraska Press, 2008).

Surdam, David. *Wins, Losses, and Empty Seats: How Baseball Outlasted the Great Depression* (Lincoln: University of Nebraska Press, 2011).

Sutton-Smith, Brian. *Toys as Culture* (New York: Gardner Press, 1986).

*Television/Radio Age.* "Viewing Trends: From '50s to '80s." July 22, 1985, 49–50.

Thompson, E. P. "Time, Work-Discipline, and Industrial Capitalism." *Past & Present* 38(4), December 1967, 56–97.

Thorn, John, Pete Palmer, and Michael Gershman, eds. *Total Baseball: The Official Encyclopedia of Major League Baseball* (New York: Total Sports Publishing, 2001), 7th edition.

Thrall, Charles. "Conservative Use of Modern Household Technology." *Technology and Culture* 23, April 1982, 175–194.

*Time.* "Bank Night." February 3, 1936, 57–58.

*Time.* "Barrooms with a View." March 24, 1947, 63–64.

*Time.* "Modern Living: The Shoulder Trade." August 2, 1954, 62–66, 68.

*Time.* "Pub Crawlers." August 2, 1948, 43.

*Time.* "Richer $ex." March 26, 2012. Cover page.

Tooley, Heather. "Personal Internet Usage in the Workplace—A Serious Epidemic," January 17, 2010, http://voices.yahoo.com/personal-internet-usage-workplace-serious-5284153html?cat=15, viewed June 12, 2013, 3:01 p.m.

Trachtenberg, Alan. *The Incorporation of America: Culture and Society in the Gilded Age* (New York: Hill and Wang, 1982).

Troesken, Werner. *Water, Race, and Disease* (Cambridge, MA: MIT Press, 2004).

*USA Today*. "Concern Grows over Pollution from Jets," posted December 18, 2006, http://usatoday30.usatoday.com/money/biztravel/2006-12-18-jet-pollution, viewed April 17, 2013, 1:51 p.m.

US Congress. House. *Hearings Before the Subcommittee on Antitrust and Monopoly on the Committee on the Judiciary United States Senate. Pay Cable Television Industry*. 94th Cong., 1st Sess. (Washington, DC: Government Printing Office, 1975).

US Congress. House. *Inquiry into Professional Sports. Final Report of the Select Committee on Professional Sports*. House Report No. 94–1786. 94th Congress, 2nd Sess. (Washington, DC: Government Printing Office, 1977).

US Congress. House. *Organized Baseball: Report of the Subcommittee on the Study of Monopoly Power of the Committee of the Judiciary*. House Report No. 2002, 82nd Cong., 1st Sess. (Washington, DC: Government Printing Office, 1952).

US Congress. House. *Professional Football League Merger. Hearings before Antitrust Subcommittee of the Committee on the Judiciary*. Serial no. 22. 89th Cong., 2nd Sess. (Washington, DC: Government Printing Office, 1966).

US Congress. House. *The Antitrust Laws and Organized Professional Team Sports Including Consideration of the Proposed Merger of the American and National Basketball Associations*. 92nd Cong., 2nd Sess. (Washington, DC: Government Printing Office, 1972).

US Congress. Senate. *Authorizing the Merger of Two or More Professional Basketball Leagues, and for Other Purposes. Report to the Committee on the Judiciary*. 92nd Cong., 2nd Sess. (Washington, DC: Government Printing Office, 1972).

US Congress. Senate. *Juvenile Delinquency: A Compilation of Information and Suggestions Submitted to the Special Senate Committee to Investigate Organized Crime in Interstate Commerce Relative to the Incidence of Juvenile Delinquency in the United States and the Possible Influence Thereon of So-Called Crime Comic Books During the 5-Year Period 1945 to 1950* (Washington, DC: Government Printing Office, 1950).

US Congress. Senate. *The Network Monopoly: Report Prepared for the Use of the Committee on Interstate and Foreign Commerce*. 84th Cong., 2nd Sess. Prepared by Senator John W. Bricker (Washington, DC: Government Printing Office, 1956).

US Department of Commerce, Bureau of the Census. *Historical Statistics of the United States: Colonial Times to 1970* (Washington, DC: Government Printing Office, 1975), 2 vols.

US Department of Commerce. Bureau of the Census. *Seventeenth Census of the United States, Census of Housing: 1950, Vol. I, General Characteristics, Part I, United States Summary* (Washington, DC: Government Printing Office, 1953).

US Department of Commerce. Bureau of the Census. *Sixteenth Census of the United States: 1940. Census of Business: 1939*. "Places of Amusement." (Washington, DC: Government Printing Office, 1951).

US Department of Commerce. Bureau of the Census. *Sixteenth Census of the United States: 1940, Housing, Vol. II, General Characteristics, Part 1* (Washington, DC: Government Printing Office, 1943).

US Department of Commerce, Bureau of the Census. *Statistical Abstract of the United States: 1951* (Washington, DC: Government Printing Office, 1950).

US Department of Commerce, Bureau of the Census. *Statistical Abstract of the United States: 1999* (Washington, DC: Government Printing Office, 1998).

US Department of Commerce, Bureau of the Census. *Statistical Abstract of the United States: 2008* (Washington, DC: Government Printing Office, 2007).

US Department of Commerce, Bureau of the Census. *Statistical Abstract of the United States: 2011* (Washington, DC: Government Printing Office, 2010).

US Government Accounting Office. "Global Pollution from Jet Aircraft Could Increase in the Future." January 29, 1992, http://ww.gao.gov/products/RCED-97-72, viewed April 17, 2013, 1:51 p.m.

*U.S. News & World Report*. "Leisure: Where No Recession Is in Sight." January 15, 1979, 41–42, 44.

Usselman, Steven. *Regulating Railroad Innovation: Business, Technology, and Politics in America, 1840–1920* (Cambridge, UK: Cambridge University Press, 2002).

US Treasury Department. Bureau of Statistics. *Statistical Abstract of the United States: 1900* (Washington, DC: Government Printing Office, 1901).

Vaile, Roland, and Helen Canoyer. *Income and Consumption* (New York: Henry Holt, 1938).

Vaile, Roland. *Research Memorandum on Social Aspects of Consumption in the Depression* (New York: Arno Press, 1972).

Vanek, Joann. "Time Spent in Housework." *Scientific American*, November 1974, 116–120.

*Variety*. "20th, Par, Loew's, WB Ask 180G Judgments on 'False' B.O. Reports." February 7, 1945, 13.

*Variety*. "Bulk of Expected Postwar Theatre Bldg. Boom Seen as 600–750 Seaters with Streamlined Television a Factor." December 20, 1944, 3, 18.

*Variety*. "Hardtops Lag in Suburbia." January 25, 1956, 7, 19.

*Variety*. "Mary Pickford Charges Prod. Code Favors Big 5 at Expense of Indies." September 25, 1946, 3, 29.

*Variety*. "Next Metro Block to Be 7 Pictures." December 20, 1944, 3.

*Variety*. "Par and Metro Sue Mass. Indie on %." November 15, 1944, 9.

*Variety*. "Ralph E. Snider, New England Exhib, Sued by Majors on 'False Grosses.'" January 16, 1946, 10.

*Variety*. "Settlement Negotiations Go On Quietly on Falsified Grosses." February 20, 1946, 21.

Veblen, Thorstein. *The Instinct of Workmanship* (New York: Augustus M. Kelley, [1914] 1964).

Veblen, Thorstein. *The Theory of the Leisure Class* (New York: Augustus M. Kelley, [1899] 1965).

Veblen, Thorstein. *The Place of Science in Modern Civilization* (New Brunswick, NJ: Transaction Publishers, [1919] 1990).

*Virginia Magazine of History and Biography*. "Boundary Line Proceedings, 1710." Vol. V, No. 1, July 1897, 1–21.

Wade, Michael G. "Preface." In *Constraints on Leisure*, edited by Michael G. Wade (Springfield, IL: Charles C. Thomas, 1985), ix–x.

Walker, L. C. *Distributed Leisure: An Approach to the Problem of Overproduction and Underemployment* (New York: Century, 1931).

*Wall Street Journal*. "Americans, Especially Baby Boomers, Voice Pessimism for Their Kids' Economic Future," January 19, 1996, A14.

*Wall Street Journal*. "Limit of One Over-the-Air Pay-TV Station in a Community May Be Boosted by FCC." December 22, 1977, 5.

Walter, Laurel. "Taking a Chance on Education." *The Christian Science Monitor*, August 16, 1993, 9–11.

Warner, Jack, and Dean Jennings. *My First Hundred Years in Hollywood* (New York: Random House 1964).

Warner, Sam, Jr. *Streetcar Suburbs: The Progress of Growth in Boston, 1870–1900* (Cambridge, MA: Harvard University Press, [1962] 1978), 2nd edition.

Wartella, Ellen, and Sharon Mazzarella. "A Historical Comparison of Children's Use of Leisure Time." In *For Fun and Profit: The Transformation of Leisure into Consumption*, edited by Richard Butsch (Philadelphia: Temple University Press, 1990), 173–194.

Weber, Max. *The Protestant Ethic and the Spirit of Capitalism* (London: Routledge-Classics, [1930] 2001), translated by Talcott Parsons.

Weber, Max. *The Protestant Ethic and the Spirit of Capitalism* (New York: Oxford University Press, [1920] 2011), translated by Stephen Kalberg.

Weinberger, Julius. "Economic Aspects of Recreation." *Harvard Business Review* XV(4), Summer 1937, 448–463.

Weiss, Thomas. "Tourism in America Before World War II." *Journal of Economic History* 64(2), June 2004, 289–327.

Wendt, Lloyd, and Herman Kogan. *Give the Lady What She Wants! The Story of Marshall Field & Company* (Chicago: Rand McNally, 1952).

Wertham, Fredric, M. D. "The Comics . . . Very Funny!" *The Saturday Review of Literature*. May 29, 1948, 6–7, 27–29.

Wesley, John. *Free Grace.* 1940. http://www.umcmission.org/Find-Resources/Global-Worship-and-Spiritual-Growth/John-Wesley-Sermmons/Sermon-128-Free-Grace.

Wik, Reynold M. "The USDA and the Development of Radio in Rural America." *Agricultural History* 62(2), Spring 1988, 177–188.

Wildt, Michael. "Changes in Consumption as Social Practice in West Germany during the 1950s." In *Getting and Spending: European and American Consumer Societies in the Twentieth Century,* edited by Susan Strasser, Charles McGovern, and Matthias Judt (Cambridge, UK: Cambridge University Press, 1998), 301–316.

Wilensky, Harold. "Orderly Careers and Social Participation: The Impact of Work History on Social Integration in the Middle Mass." *American Sociological Review* 24(4), August 1961, 521–359.

Willingham, Calder. "Television: Giant in the Living Room." *American Mercury,* February 1952, 114–119.

Wilson, Sloan. "Happy Idle Hours Become a Rat Race." *Life,* December 28, 1959, 118–123.

Wolman, Leo, and Gustav Peck. "Labor Groups in the Social Structure." *Recent Social Trends in the United States: Report of the President's Research Committee on Social Trends* (New York: McGraw-Hill, 1933), 801–856.

Wolohan, John. "The Curt Flood Act of 1998 and Major League Baseball's Federal Antitrust Exemption." *Marquette Sports Law Journal* 9(2), Spring 1999, 347–377.

Wyckoff, D. Daryl, and W. Earl Sasser. *The U.S. Lodging Industry* (Lexington, MA: Lexington Books, 1981).

Wyrwa, Ulrich. "Consumption and Consumer Society: A Contribution to the History of Ideas." In *Getting and Spending: European and American Consumer Societies in the Twentieth Century,* edited by Susan Strasser, Charles McGovern, and Matthias Judt (Cambridge, UK: Cambridge University Press, 1998), 431–447.

Yorke, Dane. "The Rise and Fall of the Phonograph." *The American Mercury,* September 1932, 1–11.

Zeitz, Joshua. *Flapper: A Madcap Story of Sex, Style, Celebrity, and the Women Who Made America Modern* (New York: Three Rivers Press, 2006).

Zorbaugh, Harvey. "Editorial." *Journal of Educational Sociology* 18(4), December 1944, 193–194.

Zorbaugh, Harvey. "The Comics—There They Stand!" *Journal of Education Sociology* 18(4), December 1944, 196–203.

Zuzanek, Jiri. "The Work Ethic: What Are We Measuring?" *Industrial Relations,* 33, 1978, 666–677.

Zuzanek, Jiri. "Canada." *World Leisure Participation: Free Time in the Global Village* (Oxon, UK: CAB International, 1996), 25–75.

# INDEX

Note: The letter 'n' following locators refers to notes

Adams, James, 49, 158
advertising, 12, 80–81, 142–43, 259n66; and children, 97–98, 104; and the middle class, 187–88; in movie theaters, 184; and pianos, 162–63, 165; and radio, 185, 186, 187–88, 192, 195; and television, 189, 190–92, 193, 238, 239–40, 277n75, 277n83
agriculture, 34, 44, 186; and electricity, 202; and productivity, 35–36, 38, 43, 45, 109; and road conditions, 205, 206; and working conditions, 119. see also food
Aguiar, Mark, 59–60
air conditioning, 141, 178, 213–14; and working conditions, 126, 213
alcohol consumption, 4, 19, 68, 73; expenditures on, 66, 67, 77, 78, 83. see also saloons and taverns
Alvarez, Luis, 106
American Society of Composers, Authors and Publishers (ASCAP), 186, 224–25, 226–27
amusement parks, 103, 137, 157–59, 200, 265n27. see also recreational sites
antitrust issues: and legislation, 223, 226, 228, 237, 238, 239, 240, 241, 242–43, 274n2, 275n15, 276n72; and motion pictures, 183, 227–32, 233–37, 275n37, 275n42, 276n51; and payola, 224–27, 275n15, 275n17; and radio, 187, 224–27, 275n15; and "rule of reason," 223, 274n2; and sports, 240–43; and television, 237–40, 276n72, 277n77; and theater, 170–71. see also government
Aristotle, 10, 13–14, 25, 31, 91, 250n3
automobiles, 50, 194, 201, 203–4, 214, 244; and auto camps, 207–8, 209; and commuting, 53, 196, 209, 210–11, 273nn41–42; credit purchasing of, 79–80; and radio, 188, 195–96; and status, 105, 272n28; and travel,

7, 15, 67–68, 70, 77, 78, 200, 202, 205–9; women's use of, 144, 147–48, 149, 154, 206. see also transportation

"baby boom," 52, 81, 87, 253n12, 260n6; and retirement trends, 107, 244. see also birthrates; children
bachelorhood, 104–5, 159
Baker, Donald, 240
Barzun, Jacques, 27, 162
baseball, 174, 175, 183, 200, 273n57; and antitrust issues, 240–42; and attendance, 176, 196. see also sports
basketball, 174, 176, 242–43. see also sports
Becker, Gary, 39, 42, 84
birthrates, 34, 52, 81, 107, 134, 142, 211. see also "baby boom"; children
Black, Hugo, 49
"Blue Laws" (Sunday), 23, 48, 137, 221. see also religion
Borsay, Peter, 23, 215
Bourdieu, Pierre, 104
Brady, William O., 194
Broadcast Music Incorporated (BMI), 224–25, 226–27
Burtless, Gary, 55
Bushnell, Horace, 22
Butsch, Richard, 106, 156, 171, 172, 193, 215, 268n6

cabarets, 159, 160. see also saloons and taverns
cable television, 192–93, 199, 239, 240, 243. see also television
caloric intake. see food
capitalism, x, xi, 28–29, 106, 157, 258n25, 272n28; "neat," 30; "welfare," 125, 128. see also economic growth, American

cars. *see* automobiles
"celebration," 13, 14. *see also* leisure
Celler, Emanuel, 225, 242
Channing, William, 22
Chase, Stuart, 23, 24, 68–69
child care, 134, 149; as leisure time, 8–9, 16, 59,
    60. *see also* household production
child labor, 90, 118, 218
children: care of, 8–9, 16, 59, 60, 134, 149; cost of
    raising, 52, 75–76; number of, in families,
    78–79, 82, 87, 93, 132, 145–46. *see also*
    education
class, 71, 72, 150, 187–88, 258n16; and
    bachelorhood, 104–5, 159; and cleanliness,
    140; and the counterculture, 106; and
    electricity, 201; and food, 113; and
    installment buying, 80, 258n16; and leisure
    activities, 23, 24–25, 26, 39, 54, 73, 79,
    91–92, 156, 157, 158, 160, 171–73, 176,
    177, 215, 228, 255n12, 268n62; and leisure
    expenditures, 64, 73, 74, 76; and leisure time
    increases, 1, 21, 46, 53; and longevity, 109,
    111–12; and motion pictures, 176, 177, 228,
    268n6; and proper behavior, xv, 21; and
    status, xv, xvi, 70–71, 80–81; and
    transportation, 203, 206; and travel, 61–62,
    207; and women's leisure activities, 135,
    136–37, 153; and youth culture, 94
Coase, Ronald, 225, 226, 227
Columbia Broadcasting System (CBS), 191, 238,
    270n83; on radio, 185, 186–87, 195
comic book industry, 98–103, 261n59, 262n79;
    and advertising to children, 97–98
commercialized leisure, 7, 265n27; benefits of,
    27–28; criticisms of, 26–28, 29, 30, 49, 94,
    156; dominance of, 30, 77, 199; growth of,
    155, 174; and passivity, 24, 77, 78, 156.
    *see also* leisure; leisure activities
Commons, John R., 51
compensation leisure, 14. *see also* leisure
"conspicuous consumption," xiv, xv, 25, 30–31,
    70–71, 81. *see also* consumption
consumerism, ix–x, 28, 72, 105, 139
consumption, 36–37, 40, 52, 86; and advertising,
    12, 80–81, 97–98, 104, 192, 259n66;
    attitudes toward, 64, 71–72, 73, 75, 84; and
    children, 97–98, 103–4; "conspicuous," xiv,
    xv, 25, 30–31, 70–71, 81; criticisms of,
    31–32, 48, 49, 84, 259n85; and fads, 93, 107;
    and male identity, 104–5; and the middle
    class, 74, 80, 106, 150; of non-necessities,
    26, 51; productive, 38; and status, 27, 54,
    70–71, 104, 252n58; and
    underconsumption, 51; and work hours, 37,
    38, 41–42, 51, 52, 58, 71, 253n13, 255n34;
    and youth culture, 93, 95–96. *see also* durable
    goods; expenditures; leisure expenditures

contemplation, 10, 17, 25, 31, 88, 246. *see also*
    leisure activities
Costa, Dora, 65, 88, 115
Coughlan, Robert, 83–84
counterculture, 84, 105–6
Cowan, Ruth Schwartz, 146, 147–49, 151, 152
culture: and counterculture, 84, 105–6;
    heterosocial, 105, 137, 265n27; and speed of
    consumption, 42; youth, 92–104, 107, 168,
    198
Currell, Susan, 11, 75, 222

dance halls, 74, 136, 160, 264n25. *see also* leisure
    activities
"dark leisure," 15, 30–31. *see also* leisure
debt, household, 79–80. *see also* expenditures
"decreation," 24
De Grazia, Sebastian, 10, 11–12, 18, 62; on leisure
    time measurement, 11, 53–54, 250n25
delinquency. *see* juvenile delinquency
Dill, C. C., 185, 186
Disney, Walt, 158
dissipation, 24, 25, 27, 45, 49, 61–62, 64, 74,
    159–60; and youth culture, 92–94, 96.
    *see also* juvenile delinquency; morality
do-it-yourself movement, 211–12
drive-in theaters, 182–83, 198, 201. *see also* motion
    pictures
DuMont, Allen B., 238
durable goods, 4, 52, 71, 96, 152, 165, 259n62;
    expenditures on, 66, 77–78, 79–81, 83, 146,
    185, 188, 189–90, 267n22; as substitutes for
    time, 257n3. *see also* consumption

economic growth, American, 1–5, 6, 21, 33–36,
    132, 246–47, 253n3, 253n6; and character
    of population, 81–83, 84; and economic
    indicators, 41, 82; and standards of living,
    42–43. *see also* income increases
Edgerton, John E., 49
Edison, Thomas, 165, 166, 176, 194, 201
education, 4, 13–14, 90–91, 152, 250n25; and
    longevity, 40–41, 116; and productivity, 91;
    and retirement, 88, 89; spending on, 45, 52;
    and work hours, 58, 60, 256n56
Edwards, Richard, 127–28
electricity, 7, 69, 85, 143, 167, 201–2, 209–10,
    273n43; and appliances, 75, 77, 140, 144,
    146–47, 148. *see also* technology
electric streetcars. *see* trolley cars
emotional intelligence, 15, 31, 251n30
emulation, xiii–xiv, xv, 70. *see also* status
expenditures: on alcohol, 66, 67, 77, 78, 83; on
    durable goods, 66, 77–78, 79–81, 83, 146,
    185, 188, 189–90, 267n22; on food, 5, 35,
    75, 250n7; and housing, 77; and installment
    buying, 75, 79–80, 258n16; measuring,

67–69, 72–74; "personal consumption," 66, 67; surveys studying, 72–74. *see also* consumption; leisure expenditures

farmers, 119, 186, 202, 205, 206. *see also* rural Americans

fatigue conditions, 38. *see also* working conditions

Federal Communications Commission (FCC), 275n15; and radio, 186, 187, 195, 224; and television, 190, 237–39, 270n83, 271n113. *see also* antitrust issues

fertility rates, 132, 135. *see also* birthrates; children

Fogel, Robert, 35, 36, 114–15, 141, 255n3

food, 19, 81, 83, 253n6; and diversity, 28; expenditures on, 5, 45, 250n7; and health, 35, 36, 109, 111, 113, 115, 116, 118; preparation of, 139, 144, 147, 265n53; and time spent eating, 42, 255nn39–40. *see also* agriculture

football, 174, 175, 176, 242, 243. *see also* sports

Ford, Henry, 203–4, 206

Fox, William, 228

Frank, Josette, 99–100

Frankfurt School, 28–29

Frederick, Christine, 153–54

"free time," 11–12, 51, 53, 54, 55; and demographic factors, 57–58; involuntary, 27, 42; as opposed to leisure, 10, 14, 15–16, 25, 31, 251n30; and social issues, 47. *see also* leisure time

Freud, Sigmund, 21

Fromm, Erich, 26

Gaines, Max, 99, 262n79

Gaines, William C., 98, 99, 102, 262n79

gambling, 15, 68, 85, 103, 153, 245; and lotteries, 19, 181, 217, 219–20. *see also* leisure activities

Gilbert, James, 92, 94, 100–101

Gilman, Charlotte Perkins, 151–52, 210

Godbey, Geoffrey, 55–58, 139

Goldenson, Leonard, 193, 270n81

Goldin, Claudia, 133, 218, 264n11

golf, 76, 84, 88, 212

Gordon, Robert, 43

government, 7, 45, 115, 134, 215–17, 219–22; and the comic book industry, 98–99; and home ownership, 212–13, 273n59; and labor regulations, 218–19; and lotteries, 217, 219, 220; and radio oversight, 95, 185–86, 187, 195; and recreational sites and parks, 7, 216–17, 219, 221–22; and taxes, 73, 161, 204–5, 216, 220, 236, 272n24; and television, 238–39, 277n75; and transportation, 204–5; and working conditions, 123. *see also* antitrust issues; legislation

Great Britain, ix, 5, 15, 35, 117, 134, 215, 220; longevity in, 112; and public health, 113, 114–15; and working conditions, 125–26

Great Depression, 2, 23, 46, 50, 66, 75–78, 168, 218, 221; and automobile travel, 77, 202, 205–6, 208; and birthrates, 52, 134, 153; and do-it-yourself movement, 212; and motion pictures, 180, 181; and radio, 185, 188; and unemployment, 11, 21

Greeks, 10, 12, 17, 26, 31, 250n1

gross national product (GNP), 1, 2–4, 41, 82; limitations in measurement of, 3–5. *see also* economic growth, American

Gruenberg, Sidonie, 99

guilt, xii, xiii, 26, 27, 64

Hajdu, David, 100, 103

Handel, Leo, 179, 180, 181–82

Harris, Oren, 225–26

Havemann, Ernest, 26, 53, 89, 127

Hayes, Samuel, 245–46

Hays, Will, 233

health, 48, 49, 112–14; and causes of death, 108–11, 114, 115; and food, 35, 36, 109, 111, 113, 115, 116, 118; and health care, 45, 66, 67, 108, 112; and income, 38, 112; and infant mortality rates, 34, 108, 109, 111, 114, 141, 142; and productivity, 254n24; public, 35–36, 109, 111, 113–14, 140–41; and retirement, 88, 89–90, 108, 247; and status, 112; and technology, 253nn11–12; and working conditions, 119, 120–23. *see also* longevity

health care: and longevity, 108, 112; spending on, 45, 66, 67. *see also* health

heterosocial culture, 105, 137, 265n27

Hodkinson, W. W., 228

holidays, 42, 45, 46, 53, 54, 62, 63, 126, 257n83. *see also* work hours, shorter

Horowitz, Daniel, 73, 74

hotels, 208–9, 273n38. *see also* travel

household production, 255n3; alternatives to, 150–52, 266n78; and appliances, 75, 77, 80, 140, 144, 146–47, 148, 152; and child care, 8–9, 16, 59, 60, 134, 149; and cleanliness expectations, 139–43, 145–46; and driving chores, 144, 147–48, 149, 154, 206; and gender division of labor, 53, 56, 60, 146, 148, 152, 154; hours spent on, 138–39, 145–46, 147–50, 151, 154, 265n36; and leisure time measurement, 3, 8, 11, 16, 53, 55, 59, 60; and physicality of work, 143–44; and technology, 75, 77, 82, 135, 144–47, 148–49, 150, 152, 266n65; and women, 3, 11, 53, 59, 60, 130, 131–32, 138–53, 154, 206, 265n36. *see also* consumption; work hours

housework. *see* household production

Hoy, Suellen, 140, 141–42, 146
Huettig, Mae, 230, 232
Huizinga, Johan, 12–13, 174, 268n1
Hunnicutt, Benjamin, 46–47, 49–50
Hurst, Erik, 59–60

Illich, Ivan, 26, 84
immigrants, 72, 98, 125, 157, 178; and leisure
    activities, 20, 22, 28, 62, 73, 74; and public
    health, 35, 111, 140; and work hours, 50.
    see also class
income increases, 5, 35, 69–70, 157; and the
    income effect, 51; and income elasticities,
    45, 65; and leisure time opportunity cost, 37,
    51; and longevity, 34, 255n34; and
    productivity, 27, 41; and the substitution
    effect, 38, 51; and work hours, 18, 37, 38, 41,
    43, 45, 49–50, 51, 52, 130, 255n2. see also
    leisure time
industrialization, 18, 22, 23, 24, 34, 72, 215; and
    women's work, 147–48; and working
    conditions, 119, 120–22, 123, 125
infant mortality rates, 34, 108, 109, 111, 114, 141,
    142. see also health
innovation, 64, 156, 167–68, 193, 245, 266n1.
    see also electricity; technology
Internet, 118, 127, 128, 157, 193, 266n65. see also
    technology

Jackson, Kenneth, 210, 212, 213
job types, 123–25, 263n20. see also work
Johnson, D. Gale, 34, 35
Johnson, Lyndon, 218–19, 239
Johnston, Eric, 179
Jones, Stephen, 157, 220, 258n25
"jubilee scale," 27. see also consumption
jukeboxes, 168, 268n53. see also music
Juster, Thomas, 139
juvenile delinquency, 14, 92, 94, 98–99, 100–101,
    181. see also dissipation; morality

Kaplan, Max, 12, 24–25, 29, 70–71
Kefauver, Estes, 100, 101, 102, 262n79
Kellogg, W. K., 58
Keynes, John Maynard, 43, 51
Kleiber, Douglas, 91
Kline, Stephen, 103, 104
Kreps, Juanita, 27, 41, 54, 152
Kuznets, Simon, 33, 34, 36

labor productivity, 58, 60, 85, 254n28; and
    agricultural productivity, 35–36, 38, 43, 45;
    and education, 91; and health, 254n24;
    increases in, 2–3, 12, 27, 33, 36, 41, 43, 45,
    56, 91, 148, 201; and wage increases, 27,
    41, 53, 91; and working conditions,
    125–26. see also work hours

labor unions, 22, 62, 218, 219, 233, 241; and work
    hour decreases, 46–48
Lane, Burton, 225
Lasch, Christopher, 84, 259n85
Lawrence, Florence, 178
Lears, Jackson, 72, 84, 142
Leavitt, Helen, 206, 272n29
Lebergott, Stanley, 113, 135, 138–39, 144, 147,
    150
legislation: antitrust, 223, 226, 228, 237, 238, 239,
    240, 241, 242–43, 274n2, 275n15, 276n72;
    copyright, 164, 185–86, 194, 215, 224,
    271n100; labor, 7, 18, 47, 48, 49, 90, 133,
    218–19, 264n11; and radio, 185; and
    transportation, 204–5, 206. see also
    government; taxes
leisure, 118–19; "addicts," 254n15; attitudes
    toward, 17–32, 73, 246–47; and
    "celebration," 13, 14; as commodity,
    256n27; "conspicuous," xiv–xv; definitions
    of, 8–9, 10, 11–16, 31, 216, 221; and
    freedom, 24, 29–30, 86, 90; and "free time,"
    10, 11–12, 14, 16, 31, 91, 251n30; Greek
    definitions of, 10, 12–14, 17, 26, 31, 250n1;
    as "improving force," 216; marginal utility
    of, 37, 254n14; and morality, 6, 19–20,
    21–23, 49, 73, 92, 106, 160, 161, 245; as
    "normal good," 8; and play, 12–13, 18–19,
    22, 24. see also leisure activities; leisure
    expenditures; leisure time; work hours
leisure activities: for children, 91–92, 93–94,
    98–104, 199, 221, 268n6; contemplation,
    10, 17, 25, 31, 88, 246; cost of, 50, 61,
    257n70; dance halls, 74, 136, 160, 264n25;
    and "dark leisure," 15, 30–31; disapproval of,
    17, 19, 20, 21, 22–24, 25–28, 29–32, 51,
    93–94, 171, 252n36; gambling, 15, 19, 68,
    85, 103, 153, 181, 217, 219–20, 245;
    interaction between leisure industries,
    155–56, 193–99; nickelodeons, 22, 137,
    156, 165, 172–73, 176–78, 193–94, 244,
    268n6; outdoor activities, 19, 50, 54, 57, 76,
    84, 246; and participation rates, 54, 71;
    passivity of, 24, 77, 78, 156; private vs.
    community-oriented, 79, 81, 91, 172,
    182–83, 199, 201, 211, 213; and
    productivity, 53, 56; reading, 50, 76, 98–100,
    258n43; simultaneous, 184; and single men,
    159, 160; speed of, 56–57; surveys
    regarding, 50, 57; theater, 169–71, 172, 177,
    189, 194, 268n61; vaudeville, 137, 162,
    169–70, 172, 177, 185, 200; at work, 118,
    126–27. see also leisure; leisure expenditures;
    leisure time; motion pictures; music; radio;
    sports; television; travel
leisure expenditures, 9–11, 21, 40, 45, 67–69, 156,
    257n8, 259n75; attitudes toward, 73–74, 75;

for children, 103, 104, 135; and durable goods, 66, 77–78, 79–81, 83, 146, 185, 188, 189–90, 267n22; during the Great Depression, 75–78; and income increases, 69–70, 157; increases in, 6, 64, 65, 66, 67, 78, 81, 83–85; and leisure commodities, 65, 84, 157, 257n3; on leisure industries, 158–59, 193–94; measuring, 67–69, 72–74, 77–78; on motion pictures, 75, 81, 179, 180, 182, 269n37; on music, 166, 167, 169; regional differences in, 70; and sports, 81, 82, 83, 85; and television, 190; and theater, 171; and travel, 15, 67, 72, 78; and wealth disparity, 156, 266n1; after World War II, 81, 82–83, 105. *see also* expenditures; leisure; leisure activities; leisure time

leisure industries, 15, 245; interaction between, 155–56, 193–99; revenue from, 158–59; and transportation, 200

leisure time: and choice of hours devoted to, 9, 37–38, 48, 51; and commuting, 209, 273n42; as cultural factor, 255n12; distribution of, 58–59, 86–87, 221; increases in, xvi, 1, 21, 44, 45, 49, 51, 52–53, 55, 59–61, 62–63, 105, 244, 246–47, 255n3; measurement of, 6, 8–11, 12, 13–14, 16, 44, 53–54, 55–56, 58, 59, 60, 67–69, 72–73, 250n25; opportunity cost of, 37, 38, 39, 51, 254n18; predictions about future, 52, 55; residual measurement of, 6, 8–9, 10, 11, 16, 44; of women, 6–7, 51–52, 54, 57–58, 59, 130, 135–38, 149, 152, 153, 154; and youth culture, 92–97. *see also* leisure; leisure activities; leisure expenditures; work hours

life expectancy. *see* longevity

Lippincott, Jesse, 165

Litman, Barry, 237, 239, 240

longevity, 34, 60, 255n34; and causes of death, 108–11, 114, 115; and class, 109, 111–12; in colonial America, 112–13; and education, 40–41, 116; and food, 35–36; and health care, 108, 112; increases in, 6, 36, 40–41, 53, 108, 109, 111–12, 115–16, 254n28; and race, 112; and working conditions, 36

Lundberg, George, 13, 24, 78–79, 119, 138

Luther, Martin, x, 17–18

Lynd, Robert S., 72, 75, 77, 80, 205–6, 222

MacDonald, Thomas, 206

magazines, 76, 140, 191, 258n43, 259n75; and bachelor culture, 105. *see also* mass media

Major League Baseball (MLB). *see* baseball

Marshall, Alfred, ix, xvi

Marx, Karl, 20–21, 28

Maslow, Abraham, 31, 39

mass media, 71, 183, 199; cost of, 156; magazines, 76, 105, 140, 191, 258n43, 259n75;

newspapers, 98, 180, 259n75, 276n72; reinforcement of, among types, 180, 195; and youth culture, 94, 96, 97, 100–101. *see also* motion pictures; radio; television

"material feminism," 151

May, Elaine Tyler, 183

Mazzarella, Sharon, 94, 96–97

Meany, George, 219

medical expenditures. *see* health care

Michelon, L. C., 89

middle class, 140, 207, 215; and advertising, 187–88; and consumption, 74, 80, 106, 150; and installment buying, 80, 258n16; and leisure activities, 23, 25, 61, 76, 79, 158, 171–73, 228, 268n6; and working women, 135. *see also* class

Mincer, Jacob, 131

Mokyr, Joel, 140–41, 146–47, 253n11

morality, ix–x, xi–xii, 18, 94, 204; and cleanliness, 140–41, 142; and the comic book industry, 98, 261n59; and dancing, 136, 264n25; and electricity, 202; and leisure, 6, 19–20, 21–23, 49, 73, 92, 106, 160, 161, 245; and motion pictures, 100–101, 137, 181, 233, 276n49; and music, 92, 225; and race, 106; and television, 161; and working women, 133, 137–38, 153, 264n13. *see also* dissipation; juvenile delinquency; religion

mortality rates, 36, 253n11. *see also* infant mortality rates; longevity

motels, 205, 208, 273n38. *see also* travel

motion pictures, 22–23, 50, 75, 78, 137, 157, 180, 244; and air conditioning, 178, 213; and antitrust issues, 183, 227–32, 233–37, 275n37, 275n42, 276n51; and attendance, 176, 177, 179–81, 182–83, 197, 198, 269n39; and "Bank Night," 181; and "block booking," 230–31, 236, 275n37; and class, 176, 177, 228, 268n6; and closed-circuit television, 183, 269n46; color, 179; and concessions, 180–81, 198–99; and consumer expenditures, 81, 82, 83, 85; and copyright, 228, 229, 231; distribution of, 227–32, 233–36, 275n42; and drive-in theaters, 182–83, 198, 201; and excise taxes, 73; and film boards of trade, 231, 235, 276n51; and innovations, 179, 183–84, 227, 232, 236; and morality, 100–101, 137, 181, 233, 276n49; and music, 163, 167, 194–95; nickelodeons, 22, 137, 156, 165, 172–73, 176–78, 193–94, 244, 268n6; and payola, 275n15; and radio, 188; revenue from, 179, 180, 182, 198–99, 230, 269n37; sound, 179; and star system, 178, 232, 233; and technology, 179, 183–84; and television, 182, 183, 197–98, 236–37, 269n39; and ticket prices, 66, 177, 178, 180, 181, 184, 230, 231, 234, 236; and VCR recordings, 192–93. *see also* leisure activities; mass media

motorboats, 76, 83
movies. *see* motion pictures
Muscular Christianity, 92, 111, 216
music, 28, 29, 72; and advertising, 162–63,
    164–65; and antitrust issues, 224–27; and
    copyright protection, 164, 224; and
    jukeboxes, 168, 268n53; and labor
    productivity, 125–26; and morality, 92; and
    motion pictures, 163, 167, 194–95; and
    pianos, 162–63, 164–65, 267n26; recorded,
    155–56, 161–62, 165–68, 169, 184, 194,
    224; rock 'n' roll, 92, 94–95, 168–69,
    224–25, 227; and videos, 169. *see also* leisure
    activities; mass media; radio

Nash, Jay B., 24
National Broadcasting Company (NBC), 189,
    190–91, 192, 238, 270n83; on radio, 185,
    186–87, 195
National Football League (NFL). *see* football
National Recreation Association, 50
"neat capitalism," 30. *see also* capitalism
newspapers, 98, 180, 259n75, 276n72. *see also*
    mass media
nickelodeons, 22, 137, 156, 165, 176–78, 244; and
    class, 172–73, 177, 193–94, 268n6. *see also*
    leisure activities; motion pictures
Nyberg, Amy, 100, 102, 103

Oldenberg, Karl, 27
Olney, Martha, 79, 80
organized labor. *see* labor unions
Osgerby, Bill, 104, 105–6
outdoor activities, 19, 50, 54, 57, 76, 84, 246.
    *see also* leisure activities
Owen, John, 15–16, 38, 250n3, 254n17, 257n8;
    on commuting, 209, 273n41; on leisure
    expenditures, 84; on vacation, 60; on
    women's leisure time, 149; on work hours,
    52, 117–18, 255n2

Paley, William S., 186, 187, 191, 193, 270n81
Paramount Pictures Corporation, 178, 186, 228,
    229, 234–35, 238. *see also* motion pictures
parks, national, 67–68, 69, 85, 202, 219, 245.
    *see also* recreational sites
payola, 224–27, 275n15, 275n17. *see also* antitrust
    issues; radio
Peck, Gustav, 109
Peixotto, Jessica B., 75
personal hygiene, 11, 141–43. *see also* household
    production
phonograph, 162, 165–68, 169, 194, 195, 224.
    *see also* music
pianos, 162–63, 164–65, 267n26. *see also* music
Pieper, Joseph, 13, 14
play, 12–13, 18–19, 22, 24. *see also* leisure time

playgrounds, 92, 93–94, 221, 222, 260n30. *see also*
    recreational sites
playthings. *see* toys and playthings
"pleasure neurotics," 27. *see also* dissipation
Poggi, Jack, 171
population growth, 33–34, 35–36, 113
pornography, 15, 57, 157
Potter, David M., 81–83
Powers, Mary, 143
productivity, agricultural. *see* agriculture
productivity, labor. *see* labor productivity
prostitution, 30, 57, 68, 136
Protestant groups, 17–18, 23, 28, 254n15; and
    asceticism, x–xi; and consumption, 64, 72,
    73; Puritans, x, xi–xii, 11, 18–20, 22, 72, 75;
    values of, 74, 204, 254n15, 255n41. *see also*
    religion
Protestant Reformation, x, xii
public health, 35–36, 109, 111, 113–14, 140–41.
    *see also* health
Puritan groups, x, xi–xii, 11, 18–20, 22, 72, 75.
    *see also* Protestant groups
Putnam, Robert, 199

race, 5, 134, 142, 265n42; and education, 91; and
    leisure activity participation, 54, 106, 180;
    and longevity, 112; and vacations, 62
radio, 5, 50, 77, 78, 83, 172, 180, 195–96; and
    advertising, 164, 185, 186, 187–88, 192,
    195; and antitrust issues, 187, 224–27,
    275n15; cost of receiver, 185, 188; credit
    and installment buying of sets, 75, 80;
    development of, 184–85; diffusion of, 185,
    188, 197; and government oversight, 95,
    185–86, 187, 195; and motion pictures, 188;
    networks, 185, 186–87, 188, 238; and
    recorded music, 168–69, 224; as
    simultaneous leisure-time activity, 184; and
    sports, 175, 186–87; and theater, 194.
    *see also* leisure activities; music; television
Radio Corporation of America (RCA), 184, 185,
    186, 190, 194, 270n83, 276n45. *see also*
    radio
railroads, 78, 79, 200, 203, 205, 210; and working
    conditions, 121–22. *see also* transportation
Ramey, Valerie, 60, 138–39, 150, 154
reading, 50, 76, 98–100, 258n43. *see also* leisure
    activities
recreational sites, 7, 50, 106, 216–17, 221–22;
    amusement parks, 103, 137, 157–59, 200,
    265n27; and national parks, 67–68, 69, 85,
    202, 219, 245; playgrounds, 92, 93–94, 221,
    222, 260n30. *see also* leisure activities
recreation leaders, 26, 49, 222
religion, ix–xii, xiv, 18, 21–22, 23, 72, 246; and
    holidays, 42; and Sunday "Blue Laws," 23,
    48, 137, 221; and work, 17–19; and work

hour decreases, 48. *see also* morality; Protestant groups

resorts, 20, 61–62

retirement, 45, 46, 53, 106–7, 116, 244; adjusting to, 89–90; age at, 47, 87–88; early, 27, 86; and health, 88, 89–90, 108, 247; involuntary, 8, 14, 86, 88; and re-entry rate, 88; and Social Security, 46, 87, 88–89, 107. *see also* leisure time

Reuther, Walter, 219

Rickards, William, 91

Riesman, David, 26, 94–95

Rifkin, Jeremy, 58–59

Roberts, Ken, 27–28, 29, 216–17; on leisure industries, 15, 84–85, 159–60

Robinson, John P., 55–58, 139

Robinson, Joseph, 49

Rojek, Chris, 29, 118–19, 216, 251n30; on "dark leisure," 30–31; on "freedom" and leisure, 15, 29–30; on status, 252n58

Roosevelt, Franklin, 49, 218, 221–22

Rosalsky, Otto A., 170

Rosen, Sherwin, 197

Rotella, Elyce, 131

rural Americans, 72, 93, 148, 149, 208; and farmers, 119, 186, 202, 205, 206. *see also* agriculture; urbanization

saloons and taverns, 19, 73, 74, 159–60, 172; and television, 161, 267nn22–23. *see also* alcohol consumption

Sarnoff, David, 184, 186, 192, 194, 195, 270n81; and television, 187, 189, 190–91, 198, 270n83

savings, 74, 79, 86, 245

scarcity, 252n58; of time, 33, 42, 56–57, 255n34

schooling. *see* education

Schor, Juliet, 54–55, 58, 256n56

Schumpeter, Joseph, 238

Scott, Walter Dill, 80

Seldes, Gilbert, 96, 160

sermons, 19, 251n17

Sherman Antitrust Act, 223, 228, 235, 240. *see also* antitrust issues

sick days, 45, 53, 54, 62, 63, 126. *see also* work hours, shorter

Simon, Julian, 33–34

single men. *see* bachelorhood

slavery, xiii, 10, 250n1

sleeping, 42, 255n41

Smith, Francis ("Borax"), 209–10

smoking, 30–31, 66, 67, 253n77

social economy, 58–59

Social Security, 46, 87, 88–89, 107. *see also* retirement

Sowell, Thomas, 28

Spalding, Albert, 176

"Special Event Management" initiatives, 30. *see also* "neat capitalism"

"spectatoritis," 24. *see also* leisure

spillover leisure, 14. *see also* leisure

sporting goods, 175–76

sports, 19, 20, 72, 73, 174, 183, 200, 273n57; and antitrust issues, 240–43; and attendance, 161, 176, 219; criticisms of, 268n1; and electricity, 201; and leisure expenditures, 81, 82, 83, 85; and radio, 186–87; and Sunday blue laws, 23; and television, 161, 175, 189, 196–97, 242, 243; and ticket prices, 241. *see also* leisure activities

Stafford, Frank, 139

standards of living, 2, 5, 21, 42–43, 66, 250n6; and food, 113; and working conditions, 118

Stanton, Frank, 187

status, xiv–xvi; and consumption, 27, 54, 70, 104, 105, 252n58, 266n1; and emulation, xiii–xiv, xv; and health, 112. *see also* class

Stein, Rebecca, 140–41, 253n11

Steiner, Jesse, 68–69, 76

Stuart, Fredric, 182

suburbanization, 138, 178, 191, 209–13; and commuting, 53, 209, 273nn41–42; and private leisure, 182, 198, 201, 211. *see also* urbanization

Sunday "Blue Laws," 23, 48, 137, 221. *see also* religion

surveys, consumer expenditure, 72–74. *see also* expenditures

surveys, time-use. *see* time-diary studies

Tandy, W. Lou, 221

taverns. *see* saloons and taverns

taxes, 73, 204–5, 216, 220, 236, 272n24; amusement, 161, 180, 219. *see also* government

taxi-dance halls, 160. *see also* dance halls

Taylor, Frederick Winslow, 125

technology, 65, 69, 85, 245; and electricity, 7, 69, 75, 77, 85, 140, 144, 145–47, 148, 167, 201–2, 209–10, 273n43; and household production, 78, 80, 82, 135, 144–47, 148–49, 150, 152, 266n65; and motion pictures, 179, 183–84, 227, 232, 236; and music, 95, 162–63, 165–68, 224, 268n54, 268n59; and productivity, 33, 34, 253n3; and television, 190, 191, 193, 238, 270n83, 271n94; and trolley cars, 209; and working conditions, 118, 125, 127, 128–29. *see also* innovation

technophysio theory, 35, 38

television, 5, 72, 81, 103, 172, 188, 195; and advertising, 189, 190–92, 193, 238, 239–40, 277n75, 277n83; and antitrust issues, 237–40, 276n72, 277n77; cable, 192–93,

television (*continued*)
199, 239, 240, 243; and children, 94, 97, 104; color, 191, 193, 270n83; cost of sets, 189–90, 267n22; diffusion of, 5, 189–90, 192, 196, 197; dominance of, 192, 199; and government intervention, 95; and motion pictures, 182, 183, 197–98, 236–37, 269n39; and music videos, 169; networks, 189, 190–91, 192, 237–40, 270n83, 276n72; pay, 183, 240, 243, 271n113; and programming, 190, 191, 198, 199, 238–40, 243, 270n74, 277n75; and sports, 161, 175, 189, 196–97, 242, 243; in taverns, 161, 267nn22–23; and technology, 190, 191, 193, 270n83, 271n94, 283; and VCRs, 192–93. *see also* leisure activities; mass media
"Ten-Hour Circular," 44–45
theater, 169–71, 172, 177, 189, 194, 268n61. *see also* leisure activities; vaudeville
theme parks. *see* amusement parks
Thoreau, Henry David, 26, 37, 254n15
time costs, 39, 56, 64
"time deepening," 56–57
Time-diary studies, 55–56, 58, 138, 139, 149, 154. *see also* leisure time; work hours
Time-labor discipline, 117, 120, 125, 127, 128. *see also* work
"time wasting," x–xi, xii, xiii, 25–26. *see also* leisure time
tobacco. *see* smoking
tourism. *see* travel
toys and playthings, 24, 83, 103–4
transportation, 122, 200–201, 214; and commuting, 53, 196, 209, 210–11, 273nn41–42; and domestic work, 144, 147–48, 149; and gas tax, 204, 205, 272n24; and legislation, 204–5, 206; and railroads, 78, 79, 121–22, 200, 203, 205, 210; and road conditions, 202–3, 204–5, 209, 210–11, 272n29; and trolley cars, 200, 209–10, 273n43, 273n45, 273n47. *see also* automobiles; travel
travel, 15, 57, 62, 67, 72, 75, 77, 84–85, 88, 245; automobile, 7, 15, 67–68, 70, 77, 78, 200, 202, 205–9; and hotels and motels, 205, 208–9, 273n38; in retirement, 90. *see also* leisure activities
trolley cars, 200, 209–10, 273n43, 273n45, 273n47. *see also* transportation
Turner, Victor, 216

underconsumption, 51. *see also* consumption
unemployment, 8, 11, 12, 14, 24, 42, 86, 255n39; and work hour decreases, 48, 49, 51. *see also* work hours, shorter
unions. *see* labor unions
United States Time Use Survey, 149

upper class, 140, 160, 171, 176; and leisure expenditures, 64, 156; and vacation, 61. *see also* class
urbanization, 34, 72, 215; and cleanliness, 140, 265n42; and leisure patterns, 22, 157; and public health, 35–36, 109, 113–14; and women's household hours, 149. *see also* suburbanization

vacation, 27, 45, 46, 53, 54, 60–62, 63, 126, 244; after World War I, 74–75; and leisure time distribution, 86. *see also* work hours, shorter
Van Buren, Martin, 218
Vanek, Joann, 149–50
vaudeville, 137, 162, 169–70, 172, 177, 185, 200. *see also* leisure activities; theater
Veblen, Thorstein, 1, 25, 81, 84; on "conspicuous leisure," xiv–xv; on underconsumption, 51; on wealth and status, xiii–xiv, xv–xvi, 70–71, 212

wage increases. *see* income increases
Walker, Louis, 221
Warner Brothers, 168, 176, 178, 179, 194–95, 229–30, 232
Wartella, Ellen, 94, 96–97
Wasserman, Lew, 187, 191, 270n81
wealthy. *see* upper class
Weber, Max, ix–x, xi, xii, 104
Weinberger, Julius, 77–78
welfare capitalism, 125, 128
Wertham, Fredric, 100, 101–2, 262n79
Wesley, John, xii, xiii
Wilensky, Harold, 14
Wilson, Sloan, 26, 105
Wilson, Woodrow, 184
Wolman, Leo, 109
women, 89, 203, 211; as breadwinners, 131; and childbearing, 36, 132, 135, 153; and cleanliness standards, 139–43, 145–46; and commercialization of household tasks, 150–52; and discrimination, 133–34; and driving chores, 144, 147–48, 149, 154, 206; and education, 60, 152; and fertility rates, 132, 135; and household production, 3, 11, 53, 59, 60, 131–32, 138–53, 154, 206, 265n36; and income increases, 131, 138, 152–53; and labor history, 131–35; and labor legislation, 133; leisure time of, 6–7, 51–52, 54, 57–58, 59, 130, 135–38, 149, 152, 153, 154; and marriage/work choices, 131, 133–34, 135, 152, 218; and occupation choices, 132, 133, 135, 136; percentage of, in the work force, 133, 134–35, 139; and physical work, 143–44, 146; and radio, 184, 185; spending patterns of, 153–54; and work

hours, 51–52, 55, 56, 57, 59, 130, 138, 139, 152, 154, 256n56

work, x, xi, 20; definitions of, 11, 12; desirability of, 17–18, 20–21, 22, 251n23, 252n35; and employment by industry, 123–25, 263n20; marginal utility of, 37, 39, 254n14; merging of, with leisure, 118–19, 126–27, 128–29; and status, xiii–xv; and time-labor discipline, 117, 120, 125, 127, 128. *see also* work hours; work hours, shorter; working conditions

work ethic, xiv, 31, 74, 127, 204

work hours: and consumption, 37, 38, 41–42, 51, 52, 58, 71, 253n13, 255n34; and education, 58, 60, 256n56; and health, 48; and household production, 138–39, 145–46, 147–50, 151, 154, 265n36; and income increases, 18, 37, 38, 41, 43, 45, 49–50, 51, 52, 130, 255n2; increases in, 51–52, 54–55, 58, 256n56, 265n36; and labor productivity, 58; measurement of, 53–54, 55, 56, 59; overestimation of, 56; and pace of work, 54, 118, 120, 125, 126–27; stabilization of, 40, 52, 60, 136, 254n27; trade of, for leisure, 37–42, 43, 45, 49, 117, 254n33; and working conditions, 38, 117–18, 254n17. *see also* leisure time; work hours, shorter

work hours, shorter, 4–5, 6, 59, 62–63, 71, 127, 218–19, 222, 244, 255n2; änd legislation, 49; and income increases, 18, 37, 38, 41, 45, 47, 49–50, 51, 130, 255n2; and labor productivity, 12, 53; and labor unions, 21, 46–48, 51; measurement of, 53–56; in the

nineteenth century, 44–45; and sick days, 45, 53, 54, 62, 63, 126; and vacation and holidays, 27, 42, 45, 46, 53, 54, 60–62, 86, 126, 257n83; and World War II, 25, 45. *see also* leisure time; work hours

working class, 1, 21, 46, 72, 73–74, 150, 244; and children, 91–92; criticisms of leisure activities of the, 23, 73, 157, 171, 172–73, 215; and food, 113; and motion pictures, 176, 177; and women's leisure activities, 136–37. *see also* class; work hours, shorter

working conditions, 5, 41, 48, 126, 127–28; and death rates on the job, 121–23; and fatigue, 38; and hours worked, 38, 117–18, 254n17; improvements in, 6, 118–19, 126, 129, 245; and labor productivity, 125–26; and longevity, 36; and pace of work, 54, 118, 120, 125, 126–27; and rules, 119–20; and safety, 18, 119, 120–23, 129; and technology, 118, 125, 127, 128. *see also* work hours

World War II, 25, 52, 81, 91, 106, 122, 134–35, 189, 216; and juvenile delinquency, 92, 94; and motion pictures, 180, 233

Wright, Harry, 175

Yaeger, Charles, 181

Young Men's Christian Association (YMCA), 92

youth culture, 92–104, 107, 168, 198

"Zoot suits," 106

Zorbaugh, Harvey, 100

Zukor, Adolph, 227, 228, 229, 230